The Impact of Large Firms on
the U.S. Economy

The Impact of Large Firms on the U.S. Economy

Edited by
J. Fred Weston
Stanley I. Ornstein

Lexington Books
D.C. Heath and Company
Lexington, Massachusetts
Toronto   London

Library of Congress Cataloging in Publication Data
Main entry under title:

The impact of large firms on the U.S. economy.

Revisions of papers originally presented at the Conference on Industrial
Economics, Nov. 21-23, 1971, Crotonville, Ossining, N.Y.
1. Big business—United States—Congresses. I. Weston, John Frederick,
ed. II. Ornstein, Stanley I., ed. III. Conference on Industrial Economics,
Ossining, N.Y., 1971.
HD2783.A3   1971   330.9'73'092   72-7011
ISBN 0-669-84889-1

Published simultaneously in Canada.

Printed in the United States of America.

International Standard Book Number: 0-669-84889-1

Library of Congress Catalog Card Number: 72-7011

Contents

v

List of Figures

List of Tables

Foreword

In November, 1971, at Crotonville, New York, the General Electric Foundation sponsored a conference on "The Impact of Large Firms on the U.S. Economy". The conference arrangements were made by General Electric and were carried out, as one would expect, with great efficiency, but the program of the conference, the choice of speakers and topics, was the responsibility of Professor Jesse Markham of Harvard, Professor J. Fred Weston of UCLA and myself. After discussing various possibilities, we finally decided that we would choose speakers who would present some of the results of current research on the subject of the conference carried out at Harvard, UCLA and Chicago. In making our decisions about subjects and speakers we were left completely free by General Electric. However, in addition to the views of academics, papers were also presented by executives of General Electric on various aspects of their vast business. A large number of scholars in the field of industrial organization from Universities and similar institutions were invited to participate in the conference and it was gratifying that about half of those invited were able to attend. Some of the speakers felt that their contributions were not in a form which was appropriate for publication but most felt able to authorize publication. The burden of editing the papers for inclusion in this volume was assumed by Professors J. Fred Weston and Stanely I. Ornstein of UCLA.

As was to be expected, the speakers espoused many different viewpoints. And, in the discussion period which followed the reading of each paper, doubts and disagreements concerning the views of the speakers were freely expressed by those attending the conference. The proceedings were indeed very lively as well as instructive.

That it was an interesting conference will be apparent to all readers of this book. But our failure to reach greater agreement is a challenge that all who attended the conference will want to meet. It is to be hoped that the publication of this book will not only enable others to read the papers given at the conference but will add to those who by their work will meet the challenge that this conference presented.

R.H. **Coase**
University of Chicago

Preface

The role of the large firm has been a perennial issue since the Agrarian movement in the United States in the 1880s. More recently, in periods such as the recession of the 1930s or the persistent inflation since 1966, legislation against large firms gathers broad support as a remedy to problems difficult of analysis and solution. Indicative of the repetition of such historical cycles is the introduction of bills in the last two sessions of Congress, aimed toward "dismantling the large corporations."

Earlier studies of the large corporation have been sporadic and within the confines of a relatively narrow theoretical framework. Recent criticisms of the large corporation have been among the strongest expressions of dissatisfaction with the "Establishment." The irony is that these heightened attacks may be directed at the primary source of administrative technology and managerial experience for solving the increasingly important social problems of an urbanized, overpopulated world and at a major source of efficiency and productivity in an economy that has become so productive that it is able to support increased social welfare programs.

The issues are of major public and private importance. For this reason government sources as well as foundations have been supporting research on the effects of market structure. This volume is the product of research financed by a variety of sources, including university research funds, foundations and support programs established by business firms. The research reported in this volume has been conducted at Harvard University, the University of Chicago, and the University of California at Los Angeles. Both in 1967 and in 1971, the General Electric Company, whose educational foundation is one of the contributors to the research programs described, has sponsored a conference to report research findings on industrial economics to a broader group of interested economists. The purpose has been to stimulate critical discussions and to facilitate increased communication between researchers throughout the country. This type of conference performs a unique function. Compared with the usual scholarly association meetings, more time is available for broader interactive discussions among scholars in an area of research activity. As compared with government committee hearings, it seeks participation of the broadest range of views and is not adversary in spirit.

The conference in 1971 was conducted at the General Electric Company's management training facility at Crotonville, New York on November 21-23. It was attended by the participants listed in Appendix A. More than twice the number of academic participants were invited, seeking to obtain all points of view and inputs from a broad range of research activites. The proceedings of the conference were recorded and transcribed. Although they are not reproduced in this volume, the revision of the papers by the authors benefited from reading the transcripts and the editors have reflected some of the discussions in the introduction to each of the five parts of the book.

Most of the papers in this volume will be published as journal articles or subjected to other critical editorial publication reviews. This book seeks to bring the individual contributions together into an integrated whole. We are most grateful to the authors for their cooperation. We also express our appreciation to Professor Ronald H. Coase of the University of Chicago Law School and to Professor Jesse W. Markham of the Harvard Graduate School of Business Administration who performed major roles in planning and conducting the conference, thereby leading to the creation of the papers in this volume. We cheerfully acknowledge them as intellectual and spiritual co-editors. We also express our appreciation to the General Electric Foundation for responding to our proposals to support the conference and for their cooperation in providing presentation of in-depth case studies of General Electric's management processes and corporate experiences. We are also grateful to a number of General Electric executives, particularly to Robert M. Estes, Senior Vice President, L. Earle Birdzell, Counsel, Special Legal Assignments, and Donald J. Watson, Manager, Educational Relations and Support, for their help and for establishing independence for Professors Coase, Markham and Weston in the formulation and conduct of the conference.

New research findings are bringing about a revision of older views and a reexamination of empirical studies in the industrial economics field. In many respects the field is in more turmoil than in earlier years. The importance of the issues makes this a challenging area for continued research, especially since the basis for easy generalization and popular slogans no longer seems to exist. We were gratified that the intellectual quality of the discussions at Crotonville helped to bring to light current research activity throughout the country. Of course, not all issues were resolved, but the extended discussions were useful in clarifying the different views, narrowing the range of disagreement, and pointing up areas for additional research. Professor Coase expressed the point effectively in his closing remarks to the conference.

"Looking back on the 1967 conference and comparing it with this one it seems to me very interesting to see the difference in General Electric's position. In 1967, it appeared they hadn't found their way. We also reported on academic studies, we hadn't found our way either. Now, we've had another meeting and General Electric seems to have found their way. We have reported again, we haven't yet found ours. But, if there's another meeting of this sort (and I hope there will be because it has certainly been very stimulating and constructive), I suppose General Electric will report that they've achieved success. But what I wonder is whether we will report that we found our way."

We are most indebted to a staff who typed, modified and corrected repeatedly in the effort to conform the 16 essays into a coordinated presentation. These include: Lynn Hickman, Marilyn McElroy, Reba Kravitz, Sol Jones,

Eddie Harris, Thelma Salinas and Ken Weston. We alone are responsible for the points of view expressed in the introductions to each of the five sections and for any errors.

J. Fred Weston

Stanley I. Ornstein

Los Angeles, California
September 1, 1972

The Impact of Large Firms on
the U.S. Economy

Part I:
Studies on Concentration

It has become increasingly popular to disparage large corporations in America. Such recent publications as Galbraith's, The New Industrial State, Mintz and Cohen's, America, Inc., and Green's, The Closed Enterprise System, have castigated American business enterprise for past, current, and predicted social, political, and economic ills. Corporations have been closely linked to and identified as the chief culprits in some instances for such phenomena as pollution, income inequality, unemployment, inflation, and concentration of political and economic power. These popular books have drawn on research by economists. However, they have drawn on academic and government work selectively to support the positions taken. The aim of this book is to provide a more balanced treatment of the subject.

Industrial concentration has become a focal point of claims about the alleged abusive power of corporations. Although number and size distribution of buyers and sellers, entry and exit conditions, market demand elasticity, level and structure of costs, and degree of product homogeneity, affect the behavior of business firms; these have all been collapsed for empirical work into the concentration ratio. While clearly a gross oversimplification, the use of the concentration ratio as a proxy for many other economic variables represents the (implicit) assumption of much empirical work on market structure and performance.

Our joint survey in the first paper shows that economists are in anything but agreement over many of the economic issues raised by concentration as it centers on the power of big corporate enterprise to control markets and consumers. Our review of studies of trends in aggregate concentration shows they are subject to many statistical biases. Correcting for these biases, we find practically no change in aggregate concentration between 1954-58 and 1963-67. Concentration in individual markets is examined and shown to be subject to no clear trend. Finally, the causes of industrial concentration are examined including economies of scale, economies of multi-department and vertical integration, and the role of mergers. We show that the role of technological and managerial factors have been given too little weight in earlier works on the causes of concentration. The data also demonstrate that the role of mergers in concentration has generally been exaggerated.

The joint paper of Chapter 2 by Intriligator, et. al., attempts to develop a new approach to the study of industrial organization. It is a summary of a large scale econometric model under construction by the Research Program in Competition and Business Policy at UCLA that treats structure, conduct, and performance factors in industrial organization. In terms of application, it focuses on one subcomponent of the overall model, explaining differential *concentration across industries, reviewing previous literature and offering new approaches to the problem. More importantly, by outlining the econometric model under construction it shows how many-faceted and complex the causal relationships between structure, conduct, and performance are, and how vitally important it is to incorporate the feedback effects of conduct and performance on structure. The structural position and single equation regression models to date have been overly simplistic.*

1

Trends and Causes of Concentration—A Survey

J. Fred Weston
Stanley I. Ornstein*

At least three different views may be found on the nature and extent of business power over markets and consumers. One view holds that substantial departures from the ideal of atomistic markets have resulted in higher prices, poor product quality, excessive wastes, and misallocation of resources in the U.S. economy.[1] A second view sees the U.S. economy as vigorously competitive, efficient, progressive, with a long-term record of relative price stability except for periods of war and unsound governmental fiscal and monetary policies.[2] A third position is that the evidence is not sufficiently complete or clear to provide definitive answers on a number of important issues with a need for additional fundamental research.[3,4]

The most succinct statement of the first view which has dominated government and supreme court policies in recent years is found in Study Paper Number Two of the *Studies by the Staff of the Cabinet Committee on Price Stability* [Mueller, 170]. Accordingly, with that presentation as the central core, the position that business has substantial power over markets and consumers is first set forth. This view has also been described as the "structural theory" which states that industrial conduct and performance can be predicted from industrial structure, i.e., the *degree of concentration*.[5]

The position that firms have excessive power over markets and consumers has been summarized into five points. One, aggregate concentration has been increasing mostly due to mergers. Two, concentration in individual markets is high with advertising a major factor in high and increasing concentration. Three, economies of plant scale of operations do not require the existing high levels of concentration; mergers, more than any single factor, explain existing concentration. Four, concentration in industries leads to discretionary business market power. Five, discretionary market power results in high prices, excessive profits, inefficiencies resulting from the lack of discipline of the market, misallocation of resources, and lower income and economic growth. Each of these five points will be examined in the light of available evidence and related analysis.

Aggregate Concentration and Trends

Citing as evidence "of increasing control of manufacturing by the two hundred largest firms," the Staff Report emphasized that between 1948 and 1967 the

3

share of total manufacturing assets controlled by the two hundred largest manufacturing firms rose from 48.1 percent to 58.7 percent [170, p. 45]. The data on aggregate concentration in the Staff Report were presented for the manufacturing sector of the economy. Table 1-1 presents a distribution of U.S. gross national product by sector of origin for 1970. Manufacturing accounts for less than 30 percent of the economy. Thus the 58.7 percent of total manufacturing assets accounted for by the top two hundred manufacturing firms must be scaled down to 16.4 percent as a measure of their share of the aggregate economy.

With regard to trends in the share of the top two hundred industrial firms, some important measurement issues are involved. One is the choice of base periods which Dr. Betty Bock has referred to as "playing statistical games." The initial year game is to follow the progress of the two hundred that were largest in 1954. Table 1-2 shows that their share increased by 0.4 of one percentage point between 1954 and 1968. Playing the terminal year game shows a 13.7 percentage point increase; the mixed game shows a 11.5 percentage point increase.

But more statistical problems are involved. Dr. Bock found in her studies that the largest corporations increasingly included their foreign subsidiaries into their reported total assets and also diversified out of manufacturing during the 1954-68 period. This exaggerates the total assets of the top two hundred in relation to all manufacturing assets to an increasing degree since the early fifties.

Table 1-1
National Income by Industry Division, 1970

	Billions of Dollars	Percent of Total
All Industries, Total	800.1	100.0
Agriculture, forestry and fisheries	24.6	3.1
Mining and construction	49.6	6.2
Manufacturing	220.4	27.5
Transportation	30.3	3.9
Communications	16.3	2.0
Electric, gas, and sanitary services	14.7	1.8
Wholesale and retail trade	121.7	15.2
Finance, insurance and real estate	88.3	11.0
Services	104.4	13.0
Government and government enterprises	125.2	15.6
Rest of World	4.6	.6

Source: "Survey of Current Business," U.S. Department of Commerce, Office of Business Economics, Vol. 51, May, 1971. P. 12, Table 7.

To avoid some of the biases in the use of total assets, the share of value added by manufacture (an approximation to gross national product generated) by the largest manufacturing companies is set forth in Table 1-3. The table shows the largest percentage point changes in value added by manufacture accounted for by the largest firms occurred between 1947 and 1954. But any of the years during 1946-49 while the pipelines of postwar demands were being filled exaggerated the normal long-term share of smaller and newer firms. There was virtually no change in the share of the largest firms during the intercensus years 1954-58 nor during 1963-67. These results are further confirmation of the biases involved in the use of the total asset data. The use of total assets involved another overstatement in that these largest firms are capital intensive, so that their total assets are large relative to their sales. While the total assets of the two hundred largest industrials were 58.7 percent of total manufacturing assets in 1968, their share of value added by manufacture (a year earlier) was only 42 percent.

But we need to consider the fundamental causes of aggregate concentration. Table 1-4 shows that 6 of the some 150 Census three-digit industries account for over 40 percent of total manufacturing assets.

The share of these industries in the total economy is determined by fundamental technological and economic forces, with capital intensity a major explanatory factor.

Table 1-5 provides a tabulation of the number of firms in the largest 100 firms represented in these six industries. Fifty-three percent or more than half of the largest one hundred firms in manufacturing are found in these six industries. Thus, the basic source of the large share of the top one hundred and hence the top two hundred firms is the large share of total manufacturing represented by the highly capital intensive industries.

Table 1-2
Trends in Share of the 200 Largest Industrial Corporations, 1954-68

	Total Assets in Billions				
	1954		1968		Change 1954-1968 Percentage Points
	Amt.	Percent	Amt.	Percent	
1. 200 largest in 1954	91	50.8	249	51.2	.4
2. 200 largest in 1968	87	48.6	303	62.3	13.7
3. 200 largest in 1954 and in 1968	91	50.8	303	62.3	11.5
4. All Manufacturing Corporations	179	100.0	486	100.0	

Source: Betty Bock, *Statistical Games and the "200 Largest" Industrials: 1954 and 1968,* The National Industrial Conference Board, Inc., New York, 1970, Table 1, p. 10.

Table 1-6 provides data on value added by manufacture per establishment for these six industries compared with an average for all industry groups. The value added by manufacture is a measure of the manufacturing processing activity carried on in the enterprise itself. The average value added by manufacture per establishment or plant is some indication of the average size of plants in these industries and thus provides inferential evidence on economies of scale. Table 1-6 shows that the average value added by manufacture in the six industries that account for over 40 percent of manufacturing value added was 8.4 million dollars per plant as compared with 0.8 million dollars per plant as the average for all industry groups. Thus the average size of plant measured by value added was

Table 1-3
Share of Value Added by Manufacture[1]
Accounted for by the 200, 100, and 50 Largest Manufacturing Companies,[2]
1947-1967

Year	Value added by Manufacture by all Manufacturing Companies (dollars in millions)	Percent of Value Added by Manufacture Accounted for by 200 Largest	100 Largest (in each year)	50 Largest	Percentage Point Change in Value Added by Manufacture Accounted for by 200 Largest	100 Largest (during each period)	50 Largest
	(1)	(2)	(3)	(4)	(5)	(6)	(7)
1947	$74,290	30	23	17			
					7	7	6
1954	117,032	37	30	23			
					1	0	0
1958	141,541	38	30	23			
					3	3	2
1963	192,103	41	33	25			
					1	0	0
1967	262,131	42	33	25			

[1]Value added by manufacture is calculated for each manufacturing establishment or plant reporting to the Bureau of the Census. The method of calculation was changed in 1958 and, therefore, the method used for 1947 and 1954 differs from that for 1958, 1963, and 1967.

For 1947 and 1954, value added by an establishment was calculated by subtracting the cost of materials, supplies, containers, fuels, purchased electric energy, and contract work from the value of shipments for products manufactured plus miscellaneous receipts for services rendered. Beginning in 1958, the measure of value added was adjusted for each establishment in two ways so that, for 1958 and later years, it includes value added by merchandising plus an adjustment for net change in finished goods and work in process inventories between the beginning and end of the year.

[2]Rankings for companies are arrived at by the Bureau of the Census by aggregating value added for all manufacturing establishments of a given company irrespective of the industry classification of the establishment. Companies are then arrayed by magnitude of value added in each year and totals computed for the 50, 100, and 200 largest companies.

Source: *Census of Manufacturers*, "Concentration Ratios in Manufacturing," Special Report Series, Part 1, MC67(S)2.1, U.S. Bureau of the Census, U.S. Government Printing Office, Washington, D.C., 1970, Table 1; *Census of Manufactures*, Volume 1 Primary and Subject Statistics in 1947, 1954, 1958, 1963 and 1967 (preliminary), U.S. Bureau of the Census, U.S. Government Printing Office, Washington, D.C. This material was compiled by Dr. Betty Bock, *The Conference Board*.

over ten times larger in the six industries than among manufacturing plants generally.

In summary with regard to aggregate concentration, the use of total asset data involves many statistical biases. More meaningful comparisons utilizing value added show that aggregate concentration is 16.7 percentage points lower. Between 1954-58 and 1963-67, there was virtually no change in the share of largest fifty, one hundred, two hundred firms. The data further show that the main cause of aggregate concentration is concentration resulting from the large share of individual industries rather than associated with individual firms. Further, the data showed that half of the largest one hundred firms in all manufacturing are in six industries. Finally, these six industries have an average plant size which is ten times that of the average for all industry groups. We next examine concentration among individual markets.

Market Concentration

The *Staff Report* data on the distribution of individual industries by concentration ratios is presented in Table 1-7. Less than ten percent of the Table 1-7

Table 1-4
Relative Importance of Three-Digit Industries in Manufacturing Concentration, Selected Years 1947-69

SIC	Industry	Total Assets (Billions of Dollars)					
		1947	1954	1958	1963	1967	1968
291	Petroleum Refining	13.0+	25.4	34.6	47.0	67.6	75.3
371	Motor Vehicles & Equipment	6.1	12.9	15.4	24.5	32.9	35.9
331	Primary Iron & Steel	7.8	13.5	17.8	20.3	25.2	26.8
281	Basic Chemicals	8.7*	15.6*	12.8	17.0	26.1	26.7
333	Nonferrous Metals	3.6	6.7	9.1	11.3	16.8	21.1
372	Aircraft & Parts	–	–	6.5	8.3	16.6	19.3
	Total Assets of the Six Industries	39.2	74.1	96.2	128.4	185.2	205.1
	Total Assets all Manufacturing	97.6	175.1	226.0	302.6	437.2	485.9
	Six Industries Total All Manf.	40.2%	42.3%	42.6%	42.4%	42.4%	42.2%

*Chemicals and allied products
+Products of petroleum and coal

Source: SIC numbers: U.S. Bureau of the Budget, *Standard Industrial Classification Manual 1967.*

Asset Figures: Federal Trade Commission-Securities and Exchange Commission, *Quarterly Financial Report for Manufacturing Corporations, 1947-70.*

Table 1-5

Relative Importance of Three-Digit Industries in Manufacturing Concentration, 1968

1	2	3	4	5
SIC	Industry	(Billions of Dollars) Total Assets	Number of Firms in Largest 100	(Billions of Dollars) Total Assets
291	Petroleum Refining	75.3	17	75.6
371	Motor Vehicles & Equipment	35.9	4	28.6
331	Primary Iron & Steel	26.8	7	16.3
281	Basic Chemicals	26.7	10	18.5
333	Nonferrous Metals	21.1	6	10.5
372	Aircraft & Parts	19.3	9	11.6
	Total Six Industries	205.1	53	161.1
	Total all manufacturing	485.9	Percent 53 Firms total of six industries	
	Percent six industries/all manf.	42.2%		78.5%

Sources: SIC numbers: U.S. Bureau of the Budget, *Standard Industrial Classification Manual 1967*.

Asset Figures: Federal Trade Commission—Securities and Exchange Commission, *Quarterly Financial Report for Manufacturing Corporations, 1969*.

Company Data: *Fortune Directory*, May 15, 1969.

Table 1-6

Comparisons of Value Added by Manufacture per Establishment in Six Capital Intensive Industries, All Manufacturing Industry Groups, 1967 (Dollars in Millions)

SIC Code	Industry Group	Value Added by Manufacture per Establishment, 1967
291	Petroleum Refining	$10.8
371	Motor Vehicles and Equipment	5.2
331	Blast Furnaces and Basic Steel Products	11.9
281	Industrial Chemicals	3.8
333	Primary Nonferrous Metals	10.0
372	Aircraft and Parts	8.8
	Average—six groups	$ 8.4
	Average—all industry groups	$ .8

Source: *1967 Census of Manufactures*, Summary Series, Preliminary Report (Series MC 67 (p)—3).

industries were in the highest concentration quartile, yet Table 1-4 demonstrated that six large industries accounted for 42 percent of manufacturing assets. Only one of the six is represented in the thirty-three industries of concentration over 75 percent, indicating that while the largest industries account for a major portion of aggregate concentration, they are not characterized by the highest degree of individual market concentration.

"The average level of four-firm concentration for all industries was 41.2 percent in 1947 and 41.8 percent in 1966." [170, p. 59]. Within this broad overall stability, the *Staff Report* states that "the average decline in concentration in producer goods industries was offset by a substantial upper movement in consumer goods industries" [170, p. 60]. Consumer goods industries were divided into three categories on the basis of the percentage of advertising expenditures to sales. The industry was called undifferentiated if the ratio of advertising expenditures to sales was less than 1 percent. For highly differentiated industries, the ratio was "often in excess of 10 percent of sales." Between 1947 and 1966, the undifferentiated consumer goods industries showed an increase in average concentration of less than 1 percentage point, the moderately differentiated showed an increase of 4.5 percentage points and highly differentiated an increase of 12 percentage points.

However, for the highly differentiated consumer goods industries some statistical infirmities are observed in the procedures [215, p. 91]. When the criteria employed by the *Staff Report* are strictly followed and a weighted rather than an unweighted average is used, the average concentration ratio for the highly differentiated consumers industries remained unchanged at 48 percent for both 1947 and 1963 [215, p. 91]. Thus the conclusions are greatly influenced by the consistency and validity of measurement procedures.

Furthermore, the analyses in the *Staff Report* on trends in concentration by individual markets are based on only those 213 of 450 industries that the Bureau of Census had designated as comparable between the census years. But the 237

Table 1-7
Distribution of Manufacturing Industries by 4-Firm Concentration Ratio Quartiles, 1966

Concentration Ratios	Value of Shipments		Number of Industries	
	Dollar Amounts (Billions of Dollars)	Percentage of Total	Number	Percentage of Total
Over 75%	$ 66	14%	33	9%
50-74%	89	19%	90	24%
25-49%	189	40%	154	40%
Less than 25%	124	27%	105	27%
	$468	100%	382	100%

Source: Staff Report, op. cit., p. 57.

industries in which change has been so considerable that they could not be made comparable represent the highly dynamic segment of the economy. Therefore, it is not appropriate to place too great a weight on trends in the 213 industries representing the static segment of the economy.

Another measurement consideration relates to the geographic dimensions of the market. Data representing national concentration figures understate the degree of concentration for those industries that are primarily local or regional in their characteristics. This would be the case with products for which transportation costs are high relative to the value of the products.

These are not static relationships. The beer industry which used to be primarily local or regional in market scope is now international. We have all become aware of competition between western beer and eastern beer and the impact in the United States of some well-known foreign brands of beer names. Continued improvement in the technology of containerization, refrigeration, food preservation and transportation are increasingly transforming a wider number of products from local or regional markets into national or international markets.

For the markets that have become international, and this is increasingly true of the most highly concentrated industries in the United States, the concentration measures that are relevant from an economic standpoint are not for national markets. An example of this is the automobile industry. Since the market outside the United States is about equal in total to that of the United States, the concentration figures for individual company market share for the United States would have to be divided by approximately two in order to obtain economically meaningful measures of concentration.

Trends in Concentration

Other studies over the first half of this century and in the post-war period have found little or no change in intra-industry concentration [Adelman, 1; Shepherd, 206]. In a recent study Bain found a moderate increasing trend in concentration from 1954 to 1963 and an acceleration of the trend from 1963 to 1966 [20]. Inherent in any analysis of trends over three or four census periods is a bias toward increasing concentration since the sample is restricted to comparable industries which are the slowest growing, least dynamic, and most subject to increases in concentration. We focus on the 1963 to 1967 period which is quite short but allows for a much larger sample to avoid this problem.

Test Results

The frequency of change in concentration by concentration interval is given in Table 1-8. Two samples are analyzed, four hundred out of 420 possible

Table 1-8
Frequency of Concentration Change

		1963-1967		
Percent Change	N=400 Frequency	Percent	N=351 Frequency	Percent
$\geqslant 10$	16	4.00	10	2.85
$\geqslant 5 \leqslant 9$	45	11.25	39	11.10
$\geqslant 3 \leqslant 4$	48	12.00	41	11.68
$\geqslant 2 \leqslant 3$	37	9.25	33	9.40
$\geqslant -1 \leqslant +1$	138	34.50	126	35.90
$\leqslant -2 \geqslant -3$	24	6.00	21	6.00
$\leqslant -3 \geqslant -4$	43	10.75	39	11.10
$\leqslant -5 \geqslant -9$	37	9.25	32	9.12
$\leqslant -10$	12	3.00	10	2.85
	400		351	

Mean Difference = +0.577   + .475
Standard Deviation = 5.26   4.53

Source: U.S. Bureau of the Census, Census of Manufacturers, 1967 *Special Report Series: Concentration Ratios in Manufacturing, MC67(s)–2.1*. U.S. Government Printing Office, Washington, D.C. 1970.

comparable industries from 1963 to 1967 and a sample of 351 industries excluding the census group of industries, "not elsewhere classified." The data in Table 1-8 are used to test the hypothesis that the pair-wise mean differences or the average individual industry change in concentration is significantly greater than zero. For 1963 to 1967, across four hundred industries, the test yields a t-statistic of 2.19, significant at the 0.05 level, and for the sample of 351, t equals 1.75, significant at the 0.10 level. The mean differences are slight in both cases, +0.577 and +0.425 respectively. However, the standard errors are small due to the large sample size and small standard deviation of mean differences. The latter results from a high covariance term due to the high correlation between concentration in 1963 and 1967, or for that matter, between any two adjacent Census years. Thus, it would not be appropriate to accept the hypothesis that there is a trend toward increasing concentration since between any two Census years the mean difference is likely to be significantly different from zero.

This is seen in Table 1-9 which shows the distribution of employment by concentration deciles from 1947 to 1967 and average concentration levels.[6] Although a mean difference test cannot be applied between any two years due to changes in SIC definitions, the difference in average concentration ratios suggests that if one could make such a test the results would likely be: a significant increase in concentration from 1947 to 1954, a decrease from 1954 to 1958, no change from 1958 to 1963, an increase from 1963 to 1967 and no

Table 1-9

Distribution of Employment by Four-Firm Value of Shipments Concentration Ratios for Manufacturing Industries

Concentration Deciles	1947	1954	1958	1963	1967
90-100	1.9	1.4	1.4	1.6	1.2
80-89	1.1	2.5	1.3	1.0	1.6
70-79	4.3	7.4	7.1	6.2	6.4
60-69	4.2	4.9	3.2	3.1	7.1
50-59	14.5	10.3	11.9	9.6	4.0
40-49	8.4	6.0	6.9	10.9	13.5
30-39	11.5	13.5	11.7	13.5	12.1
20-29	22.7	21.1	24.5	24.4	28.4
10-19	21.0	23.5	22.3	21.6	18.2
0-9	10.4	9.4	9.7	8.1	7.5
Total	100.0	100.0	100.0	100.0	100.0
70 and higher	7.3	11.3	9.8	8.8	9.2
50 and higher	26.0	26.5	24.9	21.5	20.3
Avg. Concentration Ratio	33.8	34.5	33.5	33.5	34.2

Source: U.S. Bureau of the Census, Census of Manufacturers, *1967 Special Report Series: Concentration Ratios in Manufacturing,* MC67(S)–2.1 U.S. Government Printing Office, Washington, D.C. 1970.
_____ , Census of Manufacturers, 1947, 1954, 1958. U.S. Government Printing Office, Washington, D.C.

change or possibly a decrease from 1954 to 1967. In addition, there is a noticeable decline in the share of employment in the greater than 50 percent concentration industries from 1954 to 1967. This decline may reflect (1) changes in the capital/labor ratio relative to concentration over time, (2) a decline in intra-industry concentration, or (3) simply SIC definition changes in 1958.

While the mean difference in concentration is positive from 1963 to 1967, the changes are positive, negative, and zero for other time segments within the twenty year span of 1947 to 1967. Hence there is little basis for concluding concentration has increased. Average concentration ratios show remarkable stability and there has been little or no change in intra-industry concentration from 1947 to 1967.

Bain's findings are due to the sample he selected and time period covered. Over the period of his finding of an accelerating trend in concentration, 1963 to 1966, there is little evidence of acceleration, when a less biased larger sample is examined and the terminal year is changed to 1967. This calls for an examination of his arguments that the trend he found is due to (1) enough large horizontal and market extension mergers from 1951 to 1966 to increase intra-industry concentration and (2) an increase in aggregate manufacturing concentration from 1947 to 1963.

Using FTC data on total new assets (expenditures for new plant and equipment plus mergers) for all mining and manufacturing from 1948 to 1967, it was found that (1) total mergers represented 14.4 percent of total new assets, and (2) for "large" mergers only (acquired firm had assets of ten million dollars or more), horizontal and market extension mergers accounted for 2.6 percent of total new assets. To allow for small firm mergers it was assumed the percentage of horizontal and market extension mergers for total small mergers was the same as for large mergers. Under this assumption horizontal and market extension mergers accounted for 3.5 percent of total new assets.[7] Hence the share of new asset growth by potentially concentration-increasing mergers from 1948 to 1967 was approximately 3.5 percent; a figure so low as to cast doubt on Bain's argument of sufficient mergers to raise concentration. In addition, those mergers that were consummated, that is, not successfully challenged by the government, can by no means be automatically assumed to have led to an increase in four-firm concentration.

Furthermore, if mergers did account for Bain's increase in concentration, it is likely that merger activity and increases in concentration would be related across industry categories. In fact, for Bain's sample of 195 industries from 1954 to 1967 the rank correlation between positive changes in concentration by two-digit industries and number of large mergers is +0.197 and +0.141 for value of assets acquired by merger, neither of which is significant at the 0.10 level.[8] This comparison indicates those two-digit industries experiencing the greatest number of increases in concentration were not, in general, those with the greatest amount of merger activity.

Bain's second argument attributed intra-industry concentration to rises in aggregate concentration, that is, the largest fifty, one-hundred, or two-hundred manufacturing firms. Rises in aggregate concentration may arise from (1) the largest firms increasing their share of own industry output, (2) the largest firms are in industries growing at a faster rate than all other industries, or (3) the largest firms engage in diversification across industry lines. Only the first would lead to intra-industry concentration increases. For the period in question, there is no strong *a priori* reason to expect the first to dominate. To the extent that the largest firms are in the industries of highest concentration, our empirical results show that there were appreciably more concentration decreases than increases in the high concentration range, sixty to one-hundred percent, which contradicts Bain's reasoning. In addition, most studies attribute possible increases in aggregate concentration since 1947 to diversification characterized by conglomerate merger across industry lines.[9] The invalidity of Bain's explanation for an accelerating trend in concentration after 1963 is to be expected since there was no such trend to explain.

In summary, concentration has undergone little change over all industries from 1947 to 1967 but specific industries have experienced substantial changes. The answer to what accounts for this stability must be sought in what explains concentration differentials across industries.

Causes of Industrial Concentration

Economies of Scale

The first issue in connection with an analysis of the sources of industrial concentration in the United States is the role of the economies of plant scale. The most widely quoted study on this subject contains data gathered in the early 1950s [18]. The conclusion of that study was that for most industries no more than about 5 percent of total industry capacity was required to achieve the major portion of potential economies of plant scale. This 5 percent figure is, of course, well below the share of their markets of the leading firms in the highly concentrated industries.

But the methodology of the study involved a considerable amount of judgment on the part of the respondent to the questionnaire employed. In addition, the questionnaire was directed to engineering staffs who would be expected to focus on technological aspects rather than a broader range of managerial considerations. Furthermore, subjective judgment was exercised by the researcher himself in order to arrive at quantitative estimates in his conclusions.

The evidence already presented in Table 1-6 indicates that there are indeed wide differentials between the average size of plant of firms in the most highly concentrated industries and the average size of plant in industry generally. The ratio is more than ten to one.

On one of the six industries on which we have developed data from close contact over a period of years, the importance of scale of operations is high. High concentration in the aerospace industry is caused by the huge investments required for product program. Not only are the investments huge, but so are the risks as the recent experience of the industry amply demonstrates. For new major airplane programs, the orders of magnitude of the numbers involved are the following:

1. Approximate number of planes to be sold is 2,000 over a five-year period in a price range of three and one-half million dollars per unit.
2. Special tooling and development costs for the new plane—two-hundred million dollars (five year life).
3. Other more general investment requirements in plant and equipment for production—six-hundred million dollars (ten year life).
4. Variable costs per unit of production—70 percent of selling price.

Amortizing the special tooling and development costs over five years represents a cost of forty million dollars per year and amortizing the more general investment requirements in plant and equipment over ten years represents a cost of sixty million dollars per year or a total fixed cost of $100 million during each of the five-year expected life of active sales of this family of airplanes. With the variable costs per airplane of 2.5 million dollars, the volume required for a manufacturer to break even on an annual basis would be:

$$\$100,000,000 + \$2,500,000X = \$3,500,000X$$

$$X = 100 \text{ planes}$$

Thus, a firm would have to sell at least a hundred planes a year for each of the five years for a total of five-hundred planes in order to break even over the five-year period. To make any profit, more than one-hundred planes would have to be sold. Since the total planes that would be sold each year is estimated to be four-hundred, profitable operations would permit only three firms in the industry. While these numbers do not presume to represent precise facts, the general pattern is realistic. The data demonstrates how the requirements of large minimum investments limit the number of firms that may economically exist in industry. Thus, concentration in such an industry is unavoidable and is an illustration of the concept of capital intensity.

To achieve atomistic conditions of the kind required to meet the assumption of the atomistic competition model which dominates antitrust policy discussion is simply not feasible in this kind of industry nor in an increasing number of industries in the world economy. This is readily seen, but is frequently forgotten in discussions of comparisons of ideal output and pricing behavior between concentrated and atomistic industries. The point may be illustrated by consideration of the possibility of twenty firms in the industry just described. This would still be far short of atomistic conditions of perfect competition theory.

With twenty firms and a total industry volume of four-hundred units sold each year, the average number of units that could be sold by one firm would be twenty per year. With a smaller planned-for volume of operations, fixed costs could conceivably be reduced to one-half the fixed costs involved in producing a larger volume. This is highly doubtful, however, since the special tooling and development costs involved for a new plane are unavoidable. Hence, the fifty million dollars probably represents an understatement of what the fixed costs per year would be for a smaller volume producer. Variable costs must inherently increase since a much smaller than optimal plant size is being utilized and the learning curve experience factor characteristic of the aerospace industry will be truncated. A minimal estimate is that variable costs would increase by one-fifth on each plane. The new break-even equation for price would therefore become:

$$\$50,000,000 + \$3,000,000(20) = 20P$$

$$P = \$5,500,000$$

The required break-even price becomes 5.5 million dollars per plane. In order to achieve more "competitive" conditions in the industry, the selling price per plane would have to increase from 3.5 to 5.5 million dollars per unit for break-even operations for the individual firms.

We emphasize that we do not argue that these numbers have precision, but that they are realistic for the aerospace industry. In fact, widely available data suggests that for each new generation of modern airplanes being produced today, it is doubtful whether the entire world economy can support the profitable operations of more than one and certainly not more than two producers of a given family of airborne transportation systems.

This example suggests that economies of plant scale may be much more substantial than those suggested by the one previous study in the early 1950s of twenty industries. There are other pieces of evidence corroborative of the example. We observe substantial differences in the degree of concentration and in the relative size of firms between industries. The dominant view summarized holds that a major motive for size and concentration is the desire to be in charge of large firms and to achieve market control positions. But such motives and incentives would apply to all industries in equal degrees. If the aggrandizement theory were valid, entrepreneurs would move into industries that had not yet been restructured into a small number of large units and bring this about. But this has not happened and the data show that there is no trend toward wiping out these wide disparities in concentration among industries in the United States. The data therefore are consistent with the conclusion that it is technological and economic factors that determine that there will be large scale operations and high concentration in some industries and smaller scale operations and unconcentrated operations in other industries.

The second piece of evidence on the existence of plant economies of scale are recent developments taking place abroad. The creation of the larger Common Market of the European Economic Community has stimulated a wave of horizontal mergers in a large number of industries among European firms. Furthermore, such horizontal mergers have actually been encouraged by the governments involved. This is additional evidence of economies of large scale operations. A related piece of evidence is that in the Soviet Union, the average size of firms is much larger than in any other country of the world including the United States. If there are no plant economies of size, there would have been no basis for large scale operations in the Soviet Union. Furthermore, the recent changes for decentralization in the Soviet Union have not been to reduce the size of plants, but to regionalize planning and control operations.

Economies of Multi-department Operations

But in addition to plant scale economies, there are two other types of potential economies for large firms. One is the economy of multi-plant or multi-divisional operations and the other is economies of multi-plant or multi-divisional operations related to vertical integration. Space does not permit more than listing potential multi-division economies. These are set forth in detail by Williamson. [260]

Illustrative Multi-Divisional (*M-D*) Economies:

1. *M-D* results in increased coordination among the divisions. Transactions and communication costs are lower than those prevailing in the market.
2. Internally, *M-D* results in savings due to a reduction in the need for information transmittal—up from lower levels and down from higher levels. *M-D* reduces the amount of information with which any one individual must deal.
3. *M-D* results in superior control of the division. Divisions can be assessed by persons not attached to them—and having no self interest in the result of the assessment other than that it is objective. *M-D* results in economies since resource allocation can be used to control divisions.
4. *M-D* results in economies since inefficient behavior is more easily audited and pinpointed. *M-D* results in economies since it has greater depth of information with which to guide the allocation of scarce resources internally.
5. *M-D* results in social efficiencies since it can react faster to changes in the economy than can the capital market.
6. *M-D* results in economies since this type of firm implies a displacement threat to inefficient firms.
   A. Large *M-D* are more knowledgeable in discerning good opportunities—in assessing the efficiency of small firms.
   B. They have a staff whose job it is to seek out such opportunities.
7. *M-D* frees top people from routine operations and allows them to concentrate on investment and expansion—long-range planning.

Economies of Vertical Integration

The list of potential gains from vertical integration is also extensive. The nature of these economies will only be summarized here. [261]

Potential economies from vertical integration (VI):

1. VI achieves economies through savings of time and transportation costs when production involves successive processes that could follow immediately in time and place.
2. VI achieves economies through technical complementarity. This is probably more important in flow processes, like chemicals. In iron and steel, thermal economies are available through integration.
3. VI allows a firm to plan with greater certainty.
4. VI reduces costs involved in coordinating responses to changes in the environment.
5. VI allows the firm to exert greater control over an activity than it could if its relationship to that activity was as a buyer.

6. VI makes the firm better able to make *ex post* evaluations since it has more complete data.
7. If market transactions costs are greater than the cost of performing the same transaction within the firm, vertical integration achieves economies.
8. VI reduces the cost of information gathering implicit in an unintegrated operation. VI also helps to insure the veracity of information.
9. Both long- and short-term contracts provide difficulties to the firm whose product is subject to frequent redesigning. Bargaining and haggling become inevitable. VI reduces these difficulties.

Thus, large scale and concentrated activity may result from economies of plant scale, multi-plant economies, multi-divisional operations and vertical integration. But the alternative view holds that the major single explanation for concentration lies in mergers between firms. It is frequently argued that the major merger movements at the turn of the century gave American industry its characteristic pattern of concentration. However, the merger movement of the turn of the century cannot explain concentration in industries that came into existence, for example, after World War I.

The Role of Mergers as a Cause of Large Firms

From a broad historical standpoint, more analysis is required to distinguish the role of mergers. In recent years we have seen that the alternative to mergers has been bankruptcy. In a number of industries in the United States at about the turn of the century, there were hundreds of firms in an industry and sometimes even more than a thousand. For example, we can find no evidence of more than ten mergers in an industry such as the typewriter industry and certainly the number of mergers in the automobile industry has been a small fraction of the thousands of firms that existed at various times during the life cycle of the automobile industry. From the standpoint of the selling firm, mergers represent a preferred alternative to bankruptcy. When the selling firm has something of value such as a good product image, elements of a marketing organization, a skilled research or production organization, or other elements of management skills, the firm may be able to be acquired, thus selling and preserving some organization values instead of going into bankruptcy.

But short of bankruptcy, mergers also perform an important role in the market for capital assets. There are frequently industry trends that may be unfavorable for a firm or the outlook for a firm may be taking a turn for the worse in relation to new industry developments. An example would be a firm that has developed a relatively unique product which will shortly be imitated by other firms.

The firm which has developed the differentiated product will seek to sell out while its outlook appears relatively good—thus obtaining a higher price. So there are strong business motives for selling out apart from the antitrust doctrines of the failing firm or even the floundering firm.

This analysis suggests another point with regard to the role of mergers. The total number of mergers recorded in recent years has risen to large numbers; in the peak year in 1968 the acquisitions recorded exceeded 4,000. But these numbers must be placed in perspective. Table 1-10 presents the data. Acquisitions as a percent of the total business population were little over 1/100 of 1 percent in 1960. At the merger peak this number had risen to only slightly over 3/100 of 1 percent.

Table 1-11 suggests another concept. Table 1-9 relates acquisitions recorded to new incorporations (which represents only a fraction of the new firms formed). Nevertheless, in 1960 acquisitions were less than 1 percent of new incorporations. At the peak of the merger movement in 1968, acquisitions were still less than 2 percent of new incorporations. But this suggests a further important point. There is strong economic logic to suggest that the opportunity for starting a new firm and then selling out on a capital gains basis to another corporation may represent an important stimulus to entrepreneurial activity and the formation of new firms with new product concepts in the United States

Table 1-10
Acquisitions as a Percent of Total Business Population, 1960-68

Year	Acquisitions Recorded[1]	Total Business Population	Acquisitions as a Percent of Total Business Population
		$(x10^3)$	
1960	1345	11,172	0.012
1961	1724	11,371	0.015
1962	1667	11,383	0.014
1963	1479	11,383	0.013
1964	1797	11,489	0.015
1965	1893	11,416	0.017
1966	1746	11,516[2]	0.015
1967	2384	11,616[2]	0.020
1968	4003	12,630[2]	0.032

[1] Includes partial acquisitions (less than 50 percent).
[2] Estimates.

Sources: Federal Trade Commission, *Current Trends in Merger Activity, 1968*, March 1969, p. 8.

Statistics of Income, Internal Revenue Service, Department of the Treasury, Annual 1960-65.

Table 1-11
Total Acquisitions as a Percent of New Incorporations, 1960-1968

Year	Acquisitions Recorded[1]	New Incorporations	Acquisitions as a Percent of New Incorporations
		$(x10^3)$	
1960	1345	182.7	0.74
1961	1724	181.5	0.95
1962	1667	182.1	0.92
1963	1479	186.4	0.79
1964	1797	197.7	0.91
1965	1893	203.8	0.93
1966	1746	200.0	0.87
1967	2384	206.6	1.15
1968	4003	210.0[2]	1.91

[1]Includes incorporated and non-incorporated firms and partial acquisitions (less than 50 percent).
[2]Estimated.
Sources: *Current Trends in Merger Activity*, Federal Trade Commission, March 1969, p. 8.
Economic Report of the President, January 1969, p. 316.

economy. Thus in appraising the effect of mergers on the number of firms and on concentration we have to take into account these indirect effects as well as the obvious initial impact. The stimulus of mergers to the market for capital assets may well result in a larger business population and less concentration than otherwise would exist.

The *Staff Report* stated that acquired companies frequently held leading positions in one or more industries and were profitable companies. Analysis of the relevant data indicates that no more than one-seventh of the mergers since 1950 involved product classes in which the acquired company had a position among the largest four-firms in a concentrated market [Backman, 16].

With regard to profitability, the average return for acquired companies was 9.9 percent which was 1.3 percentage points lower than the average for manufacturing companies between 1950 and 1968 reported by the FTC-SEC Series. Related to the profits data compiled by the First National City Bank for leading corporations for the same period, their weighted return of 12.5 percent was 2.6 percentage points higher than the average for the acquired companies. [16]

Thus, the acquired companies did not have spectacular profitability on the average, and, furthermore, the profitability of acquired companies is typically overstated. In contemplation of being acquired and within the broad boundaries permitted by acceptable accounting practices, companies contemplating selling out often engage in window dressing of profits. This does not necessarily fool the acquiring company whose emphasis may be on synergistic potentials that may be realized from the merger. Analyses of prospectuses related to mergers indicate that the acquiring company will frequently take a write off of the overstated profits and assets of the acquired company at the time of merger and that its more conservative accounting practices following the merger will result in an apparent initial decrease in profitability. It is important to keep these considerations in mind because the uncritical use of pre-merger and post-merger profitability data has lead to unwarranted conclusions by some.

The discussion of the role of firms in the ten to twenty-five million size class in the *Staff Report* is particularly misleading. The argument is made that mergers took a heavy toll of medium-size companies which have the greatest capacity to compete with the top two-hundred. Medium size is defined as over twenty-five million dollars in assets. The argument is made that had the number of these companies grown from 1959 to 1968 at the same rate relative to total manufacturing asset growth as they did from 1941 to 1959, there would have been 1,970 of them at the end of 1968 instead of 1,320.

However, during the 1941 to 1959 period, the number of firms with over twenty-five million dollars in assets grew at a rate almost 30 percent faster than the rate of all manufacturing assets. It is clear therefore that the comparison period employed was one in which the number of firms reaching over twenty-five million dollars in assets was abnormally high. Part of this, of course, was undoubtedly due to inflation during the period, particularly the inflation taking place over the war period and the immediate post-war period. On a percentage basis, this would more than have doubled the size of assets of firms of ten to fifteen million dollars in assets without any real growth at all.

Thus the trends reported in the *Staff Report* and the use of the data are seriously misleading. But more important are the consequences of concentration in the U.S. economy regardless of its degree. These matters will be treated after analysis of important aspects of the theory in the final chapter of this book.

2

Conceptual Framework of an Econometric Model of Industrial Organization

M.D. Intriligator, S.I. Ornstein,
R.E. Shrieves and J.F. Weston*

Previous Approaches to Industrial Organization[1]

The field of industrial organization has traditionally been nonquantitative or semiquantitative. Initial efforts included either case studies[2] or applications of the basic paradigms of price theory.[3] Subsequent efforts compared certain data or derived statistics, such as concentration ratios, without any formal analytic structure.[4]

Over the last decade there has emerged a quantitative school of industrial organization, relying heavily upon regression analysis to relate some of the factors included in the traditional approaches. Most of these studies involve measures of concentration, typically concentration ratios. One group of studies seeks to explain differences in concentration among various industries.[5] Another group seeks to explain changes in concentration over time.[6] Others relate concentration to other factors, such as profits,[7] prices,[8] wages,[9] advertising,[10] research and development,[11] and productivity.[12] These studies typically relate several variables in an estimated regression equation either without a formal model at all or with only the bare outlines of such a model.

Since concentration is widely used as a predictor of conduct and performance, studies "explaining" concentration are first analyzed to illustrate the foregoing generalizations. Two aspects are involved. One is differential concentration among industries. The other is changes in concentration among industries over time. The two are related by economic logic. If a set of variables successfully explains a high percentage of variations in differential concentration among individual industries, the time rate of change in these variables should also explain changes in concentration over time. Conversely, variables whose time rates of change are appropriate for explaining changes in concentration patterns over time should, in cross-section studies, explain differential concentration among industries. Previous studies have not taken account of these relationships.

Changes in Concentration

We begin with the latter group of studies summarized in Tables 2-1 and 2-2. Three explanatory variables were related to changes in concentration.[13] These

23

Table 2-1
Studies of Changes in Concentration Over Time*

Source	Time Period	Conc. Measure	Constant Term	ΔValue Added	ΔEmployment	ΔValue of Shipments	ΔNo. of Firms	ΔMES	R^2
Nelson, Book 1963	1935-54	CR_4	8.18	-1.45	-2.085				0.15
	1947-54	CR_4	2.247						0.04
Weiss, RES, Feb. 1963	1947-58	CR_4	70.19			-0.22ns		0.295 (3.1)	0.26
Shepherd, RES, May 1964	1947-58	CR_4			-.038 (5.7)	-0.010 (4.11)			0.07
	1947-58	CR_4							0.04
	1947-58	CR_4			-.013 (1.7)		-.0040 (6.1)		0.15
	1947-58	CR_4				-.003 (1.1)	-.043 (7.2)		0.14
Kamerchen, JASA, March 1968	1947-63	CR_4				-.009 (1.2)	-.081 (3.9)		0.11
	1954-63	CR_4				+.027 (2.3)	+.121 (5.2)		0.12
	1958-63	CR_4				+.004 (0.94)	+.018 (1.95)		0.02

*Numbers in parentheses are "t" values in Table 2-1 and 2-3.

Glossary of Symbols and Abbreviations Used in Tables 2-1 and 2-2

AA	*Advertising Age Magazine*	NAI	*National Advertising Investments*
AFS	Average Firm Size	NPL	Number of plants of the large firms accounting for 50 percent of industry VS
A/S	Advertising to Sales Ratio in Percent		
CL	Critical Level of Concentration, approximately 40 percent in Greer Study	ns	Not significant at the 5 percent level
		PI	*Printer's Ink Magazine*
CR_4	Four Firm Concentration Ratio	S	Sales of the firm or industry
L	Lorenz coefficient	TA	Total assets of the firm or industry
MES	Minimum efficient firm size	VA	Value added
n or N	Number of firms in the industry	VS	Value of Shipments

Table 2-2
Measurements of Variables in Studies of Changes in Concentration Over Time

	Nelson 1963, pp. 53	Shepherd, RES May 1964	Weiss, RES Feb. 1963	Kamerschen, JASA May 1968
1. Sample	101 industries, 4 digit	426 industries 4 digit	87 large 4 digit	4 digit, approx. 200
2. Concentration Change	X_1 change in CR_4, 1935-54	$\triangle C$, change in CR_4, 1947-58	$\triangle C$, change in CR_4, 1947-54	$\triangle C$, change in CR_4, 1947-63, 1954-63, 1958-63
3. Change in industry size	X_2 ratio of industry value added, 1954-35	$\triangle E$ percentage change in employment	$\triangle VS$, change in deflated value of shipments	
		$\triangle VS$ percentage change in value of shipments		Same as Shepherd
		$\triangle NF$ percentage change in total number of firms		Same as Shepherd
4. MES			$P =$ 1954 mid-pt. plant size 1954 industry size 1947 mid-pt. plant size 1947 industry size	

were: change in size of industry, change in number of firms, and change in optimal size of plant. Change in size of industry was measured by change in value added, employment, and/or value of shipments. Change in size of industry was generally not significant when measured by value added or value of shipments, but significant when measured by change in employment.

The regression coefficient measuring the relation between changes in concentration and changes in the number of firms was almost always negative and significant. This is to be expected since concentration measures can be shown to have a numbers equivalent.[14]

Only one of the studies summarized included a measure of changes in optimal plant size. Conceptually, this is a desirable measure to employ since it seeks to reflect economies of scale. The larger the optimal size plant or firm, the greater is concentration likely to be. Measurement was made by utilizing a cumulative sum of value added by employment plant size and selecting the class interval associated with the mid-point of the array. This measure of optimal plant size or "most efficient size of plant" (MES), in common with other measures used in studies of differential concentration, is highly correlated with size of industry divided by the number of firms. Since the number of firms is contained in this compound measure, the variable will be significantly related to concentration.

Predictably, therefore, the change in this measure of "optimal plant size" is significantly related to changes in concentration. However, only about one-fourth of the variation in concentration changes is explained in the Weiss [80] study. This also indicates that this construct only partially captures the sought-for measure of optimal plant scale. Nevertheless, this attempt to measure optimal plant size achieves a higher R^2 than any other two variables combined. But the generally low levels of R^2 indicate that the studies of changes in concentration over time summarized did not achieve explanations of changes in concentration over time.

Differential Concentration among Industries

Since the time rate of change in three variables were employed in studies of changes in concentration, theory would suggest that the absolute levels of the same three variables would be employed in cross section studies of differential concentration. But studies of differential concentration have employed a much larger number of variables as indicated by the ten variables listed in Table 2-3.

Industry size is significantly inversely related to concentration except in Greer's [93] study in which forty-one consumer goods industries are broken into Class I—convenience goods, Class II—specialty goods or shopping goods, Class III—characteristics intermediate between I and II. A variant of industry size in some sense is the grouping of industries into national and regional markets. Concentration is negatively correlated with industries characterized by regional markets for obvious economic reasons.

Whenever concentration is related to the number of firms, the regression coefficient is highly significant and the R^2 relatively large for the reasons already set forth. Pashigian [182] introduces the concept of relative industry size defined as the absolute size of the market divided by size of the optimal size firm. He measures relative industry size by the reciprocal of the number of firms. Predictably, this measure has the same explanatory power as N, the number of firms, but with the opposite sign as expected.

MES and its variants are also generally significant with the expected positive sign. Pashigian employs five measures of MES. Three are measures of central tendency—unweighted mean, weighted mean, and modal size. Two reflect the survivor method. The weighted average size yielded the highest multiples and values of R^2 as would be expected since weighting would push the average in the direction of the larger size plants or firms as did the measure of central tendency employed by Weiss.

Inequality of firm size as measured is another variant of MES and behaves accordingly. The MES measure of Comanor and Wilson [53] described in Table 2-3a, is the reciprocal of twice the number of plants required to produce 50 percent of an industry's value of shipments. Like other measures of MES or inequality of firm size, this measure would reflect the explanatory power of the number of firms, the numbers equivalent of concentration measures.

The capital requirements measure of Comanor and Wilson is obtained by multiplying their measure of MES by the asset to sales ratio. For statistical reasons it would seem preferable that the asset to sales measure of capital intensity should not be combined with the MES measure already in the regression equation. Particularly, if the capital intensity measure had not been combined with the MES measure, the variable would have remained free of confounding it with N, the number of plants. Rosenbluth has a measure of capital intensity that is the best employed and difficult to replicate—horsepower per worker or kilowatt hours per worker. The closest approximation to these purely technological measures is capital per worker or per labor hour.

The influence of advertising and changes in advertising are also related to concentration and changes in concentration in simple and multiple regression studies. The evidence to date is conflicting. Advertising is not a general explanatory variable since all these studies agreed in limiting their scope to forty-two or less consumer goods industries.

The analysis of the studies summarized in Tables 2-1 and 2-3 suggests some prescriptions for follow-on work: (1) Avoid employing measures which include n, the number of firms or plants because of the numbers equivalent characteristic of concentration measures. (2) Seek to measure economies of scale as directly as possible to explain both the absolute and relative size of plants and firms. (3) Seek to explain statistically economies of scale to get at the fundamental economic causes of concentration. (4) Because of the limited explanatory power of available measures of capital intensity, seek to measure other aspects of economies of scale, including the influences of changing managerial technologies.[15] (5) Seek to investigate more fully the role of advertising expenditures: (a) are there economies of scale in the purchase of advertising? (b) are there economies of scale in promotional efforts employed? (c) are there important cumulative persistence effects of promotional efforts creating large capital requirement barriers to entry? (c) to what extent therefore should promotional efforts be capitalized, in which case they would increase the investment base upon which profit rates are calculated?

The previous work in industrial organization form a trend not uncommon in other areas of economics or even in other social sciences or natural sciences: studies of highly particular cases led to simple theories. Additional considerations on both theoretical and empirical levels suggest more complex formulations. The logical next step might be a multi-equation econometric model of industrial organization.

The Econometric Approach to Industrial Organization

Econometrics combines theories, data and statistical concepts in order to measure and test economic relationships.[16] The econometric approach has been refined over the past several years and has been widely used in studies of the

Table 2-3
Studies of Differential Concentration Among Industries

Study	Concentration	Industry Size	Inequality in Firm Size	Number of Firms	Regional Effects	Advertising	MES or Average Firm Size	Capital Intensity or Requirements	Constant Term	R^2
Rosenbluth [195] (90 Canadian Industries, 1948)	$\log c' = \dfrac{1}{CR}$	0.32 log i (3.7)			+1.08t (7.2)			−0.70 log m (6.4)	2.393	.62
Pashigian [182] (90 U.S. Industries, 1947, 1954)	1947 log C	−0.32 log S (7.1)	−0.15 log P (1.5)		−0.35 Log L (2.3)		+0.40 log M (10.7)		3.60	.72
	1947 log C		−0.23 log P (2.4)		−0.42 log L (2.8)		−0.38 log (S/M) (10.1)		4.55	.70
	1954 log C	−0.28 log S (7.2)	−0.20 log P (3.4)		−0.60 log L (4.9)		+0.35 log M (10.4)		3.44	.81
	1954 log C		−0.25 log P (4.2)		−0.66 Log L (5.2)		−3.34 log (S/M) (9.5)		4.40	.79
Pashigian [181] (446 U.S., 1954)	US 1954 CR 4			.1005 (2.7) 9.851x (5.2)					−6.33	.64
(216 U.K., 1951)	UK 1951 CR 3	.153 (2.5) 10.13x (6.2)							−5.40	.74

Comanor and Wilson [53]								
Natural units	1954C		−11.2 (1.2)		6.91 (2.6)	7.08 (3.9)	49.9	.68
41 Cons. Ind., 1954-57 Logs	1954C		−0.294 (1.2)		.238 (3.4)	.244 (5.1)	3.85	.79
Telser [228]								
42 Cons. Ind. 1947-58	1958C			1.1 5r (1.09)			34.32	.17
	1947-58ΔC			1.05Δr (0.93)			1.24	.15
Mann, et al. [145]								
42 Firms Assigned To	1963C			9.64 X (3.04)			35.87	.46
14 Four-Digit Ind. 1954-65				3.12X (1.53)			38.03	.29
Guth [97]								
35 IRS Industries	1963 log CR 4			0.018 (0.27)	0.33 (4.27)	0.12 (2.10)	2.16	.71
	1963 Natural			0.70 (0.9 2)	4.14 (5.12)	0.00 (1.56)	18.67	.55
Greer [93]								
41 Cons. Ind. 1947-57	1957 CR 4 I	+19.4 S (0.9)		7.16 A (4.3)	1.14 M (5.7)	.56 log K (2.1)	−14.3	.91
	2SLS II	−2.0 S (0.1)		48.0 A (2.7)	−15.3 M (2.6)	.21 log K (0.3)	−75.3	.85

Table 2-3a

Measurement of Variables in Differential Concentration Studies

Variable	Rosenbluth [195]	Pashigian [182]	Pashigian [181]	Comanor & Wilson [53]	Telser [228]	Mann, et al. [165]	Guth [97]	Greer [93]
Concentration	c = log of no. of firms for 80% employment = 1/CR	CR_4 for 3 digit SIC, calculated by weighting 4 digit CR_4 by value-added or value of shipments	CR_4 US CR_3 UK $$Y = \ln\left(\frac{C_4}{1-C_4}\right)$$	CR_4^{Δ}	CR_4	CR_4	CR_4 Lorenz Index	CR_4
Industry Size	i = log of total employment	S = total corporate assets, no attempt to add noncorporate sector	X = relative size of market $$= \frac{1}{N-4}$$					S is undeflated growth in sales.
Inequality in Firm Size	E = Proportion of firms accounting for 80% employment	Proportion of output produced inefficiently—output produced by firms of size less than M; combined share or total assets						
Number of Firms	N		n = number of firms in the industry = N					
Regional Effects	1 for industries with separate regional mkts; 0 for others	1 for nat'l industries; 2 for regional markets		Kaysen & Turner Dummy Variables				

Advertising	Advertising to Sales ratios, r $\triangle$ r is for 1947-58		Same as Telser	Same as Telser	Same as Telser Also Adv. & Conc. interaction term
MES or Average Firm Size	Minimum efficient size M_1 survivor method, ave. of size of firms whose shares increasing M_2 weighted average size (highest R^2 and t values) M_3 unweighted average size M_4 asset class with largest share of indus. assets M_5 smallest asset size whose share increased 1948-54	VS of plants accounting for 50% of industry VS no. of plants of those firms = NPL/ (Total VS) = 1/2NPL		Same as Comanor & Wilson	Same as Comanor & Wilson
Capital intensity or requirements	m = log of horsepower worker or KW hours worker	$\text{MES}(TA/S) = \dfrac{TA}{2(NPL)S}$		Same as Comanor & Wilson	Same as Comanor & Wilson

national economy, where it has reached a level of maturity and acceptance. The econometric approach is outlined in Figure 2-1.

Theories and observations are refined into an econometric model, explaining one set of variables, the endogenous variables, in terms of another set of variables, the predetermined variables. The predetermined variables influence the system, but are not in turn influenced by it. They include lagged endogenous variables, determined by the model at an earlier point in time, and exogenous variables, determined at the same point in time, but by a mechanism not explained within the model. Data, available from different sources, must be combined, edited, and "massaged" in various ways to make them usable within the econometric approach. Statistical techniques, primarily those of multiple regression analysis, are refined into econometric models, typically simultaneous equation systems. The estimated model, a quantitative inference about economic phenomena, can then be used for the purposes shown in Figure 2-1.

Structural analysis is the quantitative measurement of economic relationships. Forecasting is the quantitative prediction of values of certain economic variables. Policy evaluation can be based upon alternative forecasts each being a conditional forecast, dependent on a particular policy. The range of policy options would yield a range of values taken by relevant variables in the econometric model, based upon the estimated model.

In combining economic theory with economic facts, econometrics avoids the extreme approaches of "theory without facts," on the one hand, which treats economics as a purely deductive science, and "facts without theory" on the other hand, which treats economics as a purely observational science. Econometrics utilizes the theories of the former and the data of the latter, combining

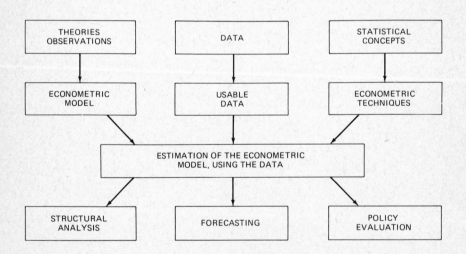

Figure 2-1. The Econometric Approach.

them, using refinement of statistical techniques, to give empirical content to *a priori* economic reasoning.

The econometric approach is a technique of analysis that can be applied to a wide variety of problem areas in economics and other social sciences. To date it has been applied largely to studies of macroeconomic phenomena, and various econometric models have been formulated and estimated for the U.S. and other economies.[17] The fact that this approach has been successfully applied in the macroeconomic area should indicate its potential application to other areas, specifically to industrial organization.

An econometric approach can be envisaged for industrial organization, whereby an econometric model of industrial organization, structure, and performance is formulated and estimated using data on industries and firms. The recent quantitative approaches discussed above could then be interpreted as individual components, typically single equations, of the overall model. Indeed a major goal is the testing of previous empirical studies in the broader framework of the complete model.

In econometric models of complex phenomena it is often useful to break the model into submodels. These submodels, referred to as *modules*, form the building blocks of the overall model, which can be estimated by first estimating the modules and then reestimating to obtain consistent estimators.[18] One approach to an econometric model of industrial organization would divide the model into five interacting modules of a block recursive system as shown in Figure 2-2.[19]

Module 1: Underlying Considerations includes production functions, cost functions, and demand functions. The production functions summarize technological capabilities in various industries, including such considerations as capital intensity and factor proportions in general, returns to scale, productivity, and technological change. There has been a considerable literature on production functions,[20] cost functions,[21] and demand functions,[22] but none of these has set the estimation of these functions in the overall framework of an econometric model of industrial organization.

Module 2: Industry Structure includes the size of industries, the number of firms, their size distribution, and the conditions of entry and exit. These elements have been treated in many single equation studies. As Figure 2-2 portrays, industry structure is influenced by the underlying considerations and by feedback effects from all of the other blocks. The need for a structural explanation of industry structure is indicated.

Module 3: Decisions at the Firm Level includes output, employment, prices, advertising and research and development decisions. There have been studies of each or some of these decisions, but none of these studies has treated all these decisions within the framework of an overall model.[23] Most of the considerations treated here fall under the area of conduct or behavior.

Module 4: Social Performance Measures includes resource allocation conse-

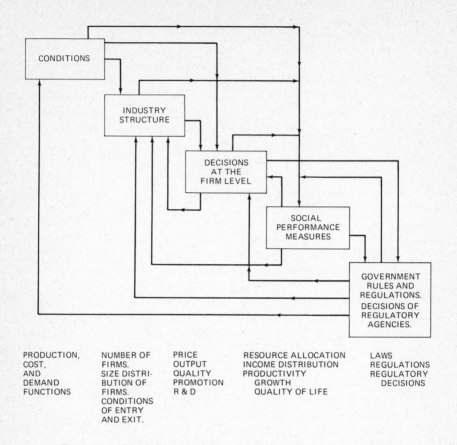

Figure 2-2. Block Recursive Structure of the Econometric Model.

quences, income distribution, productivity and its rate of improvement, the rate of real economic growth, and measures of the quality of life. Profits are usually included in performance measures. However, we argue that risk and return relations are reflected in the goal and constraint functions utilized in formulating the decisions of the firm.

Module 5: Decisions of the Regulatory Agencies includes decisions to initiate action, regulatory decisions, and court decisions. Despite their obviously important feedback effects, these considerations have typically not been treated explicitly in previous studies of industrial organization.

The modules are presented in this order because it represents a natural flow of causation: decisions at the firm level being based on underlying considerations, outcomes for the industry resulting from firm decisions, and regulatory decisions based upon outcomes for the industry. The overall model *does,* however, also include "jumps" between modules, e.g., effects of decisions at the firm level on decisions of regulatory agencies. It also *does* allow for "feedback" effects, e.g., effects of outcomes for the industry on decisions at the firm level and effects of regulatory decisions on all the previous blocks. The feedback effects, some of which may be lagged, can be of critical importance in the workings of the complete model.

This general description of an econometric approach represents a statement of our research design. We shall next provide a summary of our efforts to date, beginning with a description of the building of a data bank for utilization in developing econometric industrial organization models.

The Development of a Data Bank

Many previous studies in the area of industrial organization have relied heavily on Department of Commerce (*Census of Manufactures* and *Annual Survey of Manufactures*), and Internal Revenue Service (*Statistics of Income* and *Source Book of Statistics of Income*) sources of data. These sources provide data at the two-, three-, and four-digit levels of industry aggregation, in terms of the census classification scheme. Other studies have relied on sampling methods to collect data at the firm level for both intra- and interindustry studies. Sources for such data include *Moody's, Standard & Poor's*, the *Fortune 500 Directory*, annual reports and questionnaire surveys.

Obviously, there are advantages and disadvantages of each source of data. Census sources include data on employment, wages, value added, and concentration ratios not published by the Internal Revenue Service. The list of variables that may be developed from census data is set out in Table 2-4. On the other hand, IRS statistics include data on total assets, advertising, net income, interest paid, and stockholders' equity, not available on the Census industry basis. The items on which data are available from the IRS sources are set forth in Table 2-5. Thus, whichever source has been chosen by researchers in industrial organization, they were likely to suffer from inadequacies in data for which they were forced to improvise substitutes with varying degrees of success.

Recognizing from the outset the implications for data problems of the scope of our econometric approach, we have devoted much effort to the assembly of a complete and "clean" data bank. The Department of Commerce *Link of Census Establishment and IRS Corporation Data* provides a substantive beginning toward the development of such a data bank. The *Link* was first available for the 1958 *Census of Manufactures* and IRS *Source Book*.

As the primary need is for cross-section data, we have collected *1963 Census of Manufactures* data at the four-digit SIC level of aggregation, and separately, data from the IRS *Source Book of Statistics of Income, 1963* at approximately the three-digit level of aggregation. But in order to estimate measures of growth,

Table 2-4
List of Variables for Augmented Census Data Set

1. Number of companies	45. CR 50, Value added
2. Number of establishments	46. CR 50, Capital expenditures
3. Value of shipments	47. Gross Book Value of Assets, 1964
4. Number of employees	48. Gross Book Value of Assets, 1963
5. Payroll	49. Gross Book Value of Assets, 1962
6. Number of production workers	50. Gross Book Value of Assets, 1957
7. Man-hours	51. Establishments/Companies
8. Wages	52. Number of employees/Establishments
9. Value added	53. Value added/Establishments
10. Capital expenditures	54. Value added/Number of Employees
11. CR 4, Establishments	55. (Value Added–Wages)/Value of
12. CR 4, Shipments	Shipments
13. CR 4, Employees	56. Value of Shipments/Man-hours
14. CR 4, Payroll	57. (Value of Shipments–Value Added)/
15. CR 4, Production workers	Value of Shipments
16. CR 4, Man-hours	58. Capital Expenditures/Value of
17. CR 4, Wages	Shipments
18. CR 4, Value added	59. Wages/Value of Shipments
19. CR 4, Capital expenditures	60. Wages/Man-hours
20. CR 8, Establishments	61. Man hours/Production workers
21. CR 8, Shipments	62. Production workers/Number of
22. CR 8, Employees	Employees
23. CR 8, Payroll	63. Payroll/Number of Employees
24. CR 8, Production workers	64. Payroll/Value added
25. CR 8, Man-hours	65. Value of Shipments/GBVA, 1963
26. CR 8, Wages	66. GBVA, 1963/Number of Production
27. CR 8, Value Added	Workers
28. CR 8, Capital expenditures	67. Value Added/GBVA, 1963
29. CR 20, Establishments	68. Shipments/Establishments
30. CR 20, Shipments	69. Value added/Companies
31. CR 20, Employees	70. Shipments/Companies
32. CR 20, Payroll	71. GBVA/Establishments
33. CR 20, Production workers	72. GBVA/Companies
34. CR 20, Man-hours	73. Consumption goods/Total output
35. CR 20, Wages	74. Investment goods/Total output
36. CR 20, Value Added	75. Gov't. Purchases/Total output
37. CR 20, Capital Expenditures	76. Fed. Gov't. purchases/Total output
38. CR 50, Establishments	77. Intermediate goods/Total output
39. CR 50, Shipments	78. Growth rate in value added, 1958-68
40. CR 50, Employees	79. Variability of value added about
41. CR 50, Payroll	its time trend
42. CR 50, Production workers	80. Cost of materials
43. CR 50, Man-hours	81. Specialization ratio
44. CR 50, Wages	82. Coverage ratio

stability, and parameters of production and demand, it is necessary to have time series data. The best available source for such data at the comparable four-digit SIC level appears to be the *Industry Profiles, 1958-1968* publication of the Department of Commerce. The *Profiles* data include employment, output,

Table 2-5
List of Variables for Augmented IRS Data Set

1. IRS industry code
2. Number of returns
3. Total Assets
4. Inventories
5. Depreciable assets
6. Accumulated depreciation
7. Capital stock
8. Paid-in or capital surplus
9. Surplus reserves
10. Earned surplus and undivided profits
11. Business receipts
12. Interest on state and local obligations
13. Cost of sales and operations
14. Compensation of officers
15. Rent paid
16. Taxes paid
17. Interest paid
18. Depreciation
19. Depletion
20. Advertising
21. Pensions, etc.
22. Other employee benefits
23. Net income or deficit
24. Net income after taxes
25. Number of companies
26. Number of establishments
27. Number of employee.
28. Total payroll
29. Sales and Receipts
30. Value added
31. New capital expenditures
32. CR_4
33. Consumption ratio
34. Investment ratio
35. Total government ratio
36. Federal government ratio
37. Intermediate goods ratio
38. Growth in value added
39. Variability in output
40. Cost of materials
41. Value added/establishment
42. Value added/returns
43. Value added/employees
44. Value added/depreciable assets
45. Value added/total assets
46. Depreciable assets/returns
47. Total assets/returns
48. Depreciable assets/employees
49. Total assets/employees
50. Business receipts/depreciable assets
51. Business receipts/total assets
52. Advertising/business receipts
53. (Net income + interest paid)/total assets
54. Equity
55. Net income/equity
56. Rent paid/business receipts
57. Pensions, etc./employees
58. (Payroll + pensions)/employees

Table 2-6
List of Industry Profiles Variables

1. number of employees
2. payroll
3. number of production workers
4. production worker man-hours
5. wages
6. value added
7. cost of materials
8. value of shipments
9. capital expenditures
10. end-of-year inventories

capital expenditures and inventory information for the years indicated. Information available on an annual basis is shown in Table 2-6. To date, we have utilized these time series data for computing the growth rate and the percentage variation of output from its time trend for each industry.

Another set of variables considered useful for our econometric approach are those relating to the input-output structure of the economy. The source for these data is the *Input-Output Structure of the U.S. Economy: 1963*, published by the Office of Business Economics. Though the OBE industry classification scheme is slightly more aggregative than that of the census (284 OBE manufacturing industries vs. 417 census manufacturing industries), a "link" is constructed by assigning to each census industry the input-output ratios computed for the OBE industry to which the Census industry is matched. The matching is according to a table provided for such a purpose by the OBE in the publication itself. Input-output ratios computed for each industry are the ratios of each of the following variables to total industry output:

(1) consumption goods sales
(2) investment goods sales
(3) government purchases
(4) Federal government purchases
(5) intermediate goods sales.

Thus, we have augmented the 1963 Census data using the *Profiles* and input-output data as described above. The *Link of Census Establishment and IRS Corporation Data* was used to augment the IRS *Source Book* data by adding the following variables from the augmented census data:

(1) concentration ratio
(2) value added
(3) employment data
(4) input-output ratios
(5) growth and stability measures.

Table 3, Part C of the *Link* provides the number of employees in each four-digit census industry in which matched IRS corporations had one or more establishments in 1963. The essence of the *Link* as we have used it is the construction of a set of weights based on the employment statistics of Table 3, Part C. These weights have been used to transform census four-digit industry measures into IRS three-digit industry measures for each IRS industry, for each of the variables linked.

Part B of Table 3 provides a means of adjusting the linked values, where appropriate, to compensate for errors in the matching procedure. The adjustment factor is the ratio of total IRS industry business receipts, as given by the *Source Book*, to total sales and receipts for census matched corporations, as given by Part B of Table 3 of the *Link*. Thus, any aggregate data such as payroll, employees, or value-added may be adjusted by this ratio to compensate for over- or undermatching. Figure 2-3 is a schematic diagram of the construction of the augmented census and IRS data banks as discussed above.

Another valuable source of information based on IRS industry classifications is the size distribution data included in the IRS *Source Book*. The corporations in each IRS industry are classified by size of total assets into twelve size classes, with balance sheet and income statement items presented for each size class. This partition of the IRS data by size classes makes possible the statistical separation and identification of "size effects" from "industry effects." However, partitioning of the variables linked from the census data is not possible.

For data at the firm level, Standard and Poor's *Compustat Tapes* provide a relatively complete and convenient source. Covering some 1700 U.S. corporations, these magnetic computer tapes contain sixty items of balance sheet, income statement, and stock market information for twenty years as set forth in Table 2-7. Furthermore, the corporations on the tape are classified into the four-digit census industry into which most of their sales fall. Thus, with due caution, sampling studies may be designed to utilize company data in intra- as well as interindustry analyses.

Some Preliminary Statistical Analysis

Introduction

Since structure is generally considered to have an important influence on performance and there are likely to be important feedback effects on structure, it seemed useful to attempt an explanation of structural parameters. We aimed, particularly, to attempt to distinguish between the relative influence of predetermined conditions as compared with the feedback effects on determinants of industry structure depicted in Figure 2-2.

The purpose of explaining concentration is to identify the underlying determinants of market structure characteristics. We begin with a focus on concentration, not because of any inherent information it conveys about competition or rivalry, but rather for its convenient summarization of some aspects of industry structure, i.e., whether there are few or many firms in an industry. For this purpose, however, we could have justifiably used the number of firms in an industry.

Alternative Theoretical Approaches

Under a perfectly competitive market in long-run equilibrium, the number of firms and concentration are determined by the unique optimum firm size

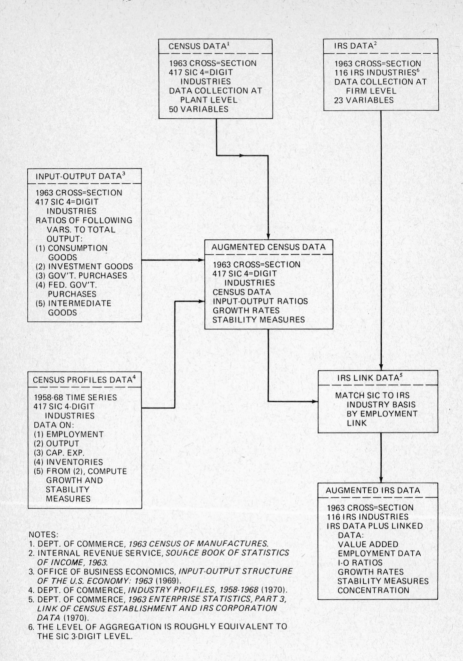

Figure 2-3. Sources of Augmented Census and IRS Data Banks.

Table 2-7
List of COMPUSTAT Variables

1 Cash and Equivalent	35 Deferred Taxes and Investment
2 Receivables	Credit
3 Inventories	36 Number of Common Shares Purchased/Sold–
4 Current Assets	Net
5 Current Liabilities	37 Total Invested Capital
6 Assets and/or Liabilities	38 Minority Interest and Subsidiary
7 Gross Plant	Preferred Stock
8 Net Plant	39 Amount of Convertible Debt
9 Long Term Debt	and Preferred Stock
10 Preferred Stock	40 Number of Shares Reserved for Conversion
11 Common Equity	41 Cost of Goods Sold
12 Net Sales	42 Labor and Related Expense
13 Operating Income	43 Pension and Retirement Expense
14 Depreciation and Amortization	44 Incentive Compensation Expense
15 Fixed Charges	45 Selling and Advertising Expense
16 Income Taxes	46 Research and Development Expense
17 Non-Recurring Income/Expense	47 Rental Expense
(Not net of taxes)	48 Non-Recurring Income/Expense
18 Net Income (Before Netted Non-Recurring)	(Net of Taxes)
19 Preferred Dividends	49 Minority Interest
20 Available for Common	50 Deferred Taxes
21 Common Dividends	51 Investment Credit
22 Stock Price–High	52 Carry Forward Tax Loss
23 Stock Price–Low	53 Unconsolidated Subsidiaries–
24 Stock Price–Close	Excess Equity
25 Number of Shares Outstanding	54 Unconsolidated Subsidiaries–
26 Dividends Per Share	Unremitted Earnings
27 Adjustment Factor	55 Unconsolidated Subsidiaries–
28 Number of Shares Traded	Remitted Earnings
29 Number of Employees	56 Preferred Stock at Redemption Value
30 Capital Expenditures	57 Market Value of Stk. Rights and
31 Investment and Advances to Subsidiaries	Spin-Offs (Per Share)
32 Investment and Advances–Other	58 Earnings Per Share As Reported
33 Intangibles	59 Inventory Valuation
34 Debt in Current Liabilities	60 Inventory Cost

relative to total market size.[24] Concentration is inversely related to total market size and directly related to optimum firm size, while the number of firms is directly related to total market size and inversely related to optimum size. Concentration and number of firms are thus interchangeable measures of market structure. Changes in market size through upward shifts in demand will reduce concentration due to new firm entry, assuming no offsetting changes in optimum firm size. With changes in both market size and optimum firm size, concentration will either increase, decrease, or remain constant depending on their respective relative change.

In non-perfectly competitive markets with no unique optimum firm size, four-firm concentration probably is largely a function of economies of scale in the largest size firms relative to total market size. The number of firms is influenced by the shape of the long run average cost curve and may depend on the minimum efficient firm size relative to total market size. Concentration and number of firms are most likely highly inversely correlated but not perfectly so, due to the unequal size distribution of firms. Shifts in concentration and in the number of firms are a function of relative changes in total market size and economies of scale. Concentration may also depend on the relative growth rates of firms, with the greater the variability, the greater the concentration. The number of firms and concentration may also depend on the conditions of entry, i.e., prospective costs and risks relative to expected returns.

Building on the foregoing relationships, a number of theories have been formulated to explain differential concentration. These alternative theories are briefly summarized.

Concentration is a function of scale economies. There are few firms where there are large economies of scale relative to market size and many firms where there are small economies of scale relative to market size. One measure is the relative market size defined as the total market divided by optimal firm size. Relative market size has been measured by the reciprocal of N, the number of firms in an industry. Alternative measures are some measure of optimal firm size, such as average firm size, the capital-labor ratio reflecting indivisibilities in production, and measures of the extent of specific economies. The size of market must be held constant when using the latter group of measures of scale economies. See, e.g., Rosenbluth [195], Pashigian [182].

Concentration is explained by barriers to entry. Entry barriers are traditionally defined by economies of scale, the size of capital requirements, product differentiation, and the comparative levels of cost functions. High barriers lead to high concentration and vice versa. Economies of scale have been measured by total market size relative to the optimal size of firm, i.e., the number of firms. Capital requirements have been measured by average firm size or the capital-labor ratio. Product differentiation has been approached by use of measures of advertising intensity. Relative levels of cost functions have not been investigated, but analysis of intra-industry profit distributions could provide some evidence. See, e.g., Comanor and Wilson [53], Guth [97].

Concentration is caused by cumulative stochastic processes. The law of proportionate effect attributes differences in concentration to the underlying probability of equal percentages of growth by firms of all sizes, disturbed by random influences. In addition to demonstrations of the influence of random shocks by simulation studies this theory has stimulated studies of differential growth rates and variability of growth rates among firms. Analogously, interindustry concentration differences are a function of the variability of industry growth rates. See, e.g., Hart and Prais [103], Simon and Bonini [211], Hymer and Pashigian [111].

Concentration has spread due to countervailing power. The theory of countervailing power states that concentration on one side of the market stimulates concentration on the other side. One test of the proposition is to examine the influence of buyer concentration represented by sales to the government. See, e.g., Galbraith, [84].

Mergers are a major source of concentration. The merger movements have been widely held to be a major cause of concentration in the United States. Much attention has been given to mergers and government policy toward mergers and size as important influences on concentration levels. These factors have not been investigated in our preliminary analysis to date. See, e.g., Markham [150], Mueller [169].

*Construction of Some Preliminary Single
Equation Regression Models*

In our preliminary investigations we sought to gain some insights on the alternative theoretical formulations. We tried to do this by replicating selective previous studies with the objectives of comparing results using data from the 1960s with results using earlier data; testing alternative groupings of variables consistent with theory; obtaining a better "feel" for the nature of the data; increasing our understanding of alternative theoretical formulations; and hopefully obtaining some usable single equations or small groupings of equations leading to a more general econometric model of industrial organization.

Previous studies suggested the following four alternative single equation regression models. (The symbols are identified in Tables 2-10 and 2-11.)

THEORY I (a): $CR = f(N)$

I (b): $CR = f(S/N \text{ or } K/L, A/S \text{ or } C/TO, S)$

THEORY II (a): $CR = f[(S)/(S/N)]$

II (b): $CR = f(S/N \text{ or } K/L, C/TO \text{ or } A/S)$

THEORY III: $CR = f(GR, VGR)$

THEORY IV: $CR = f(G/TO)$

The problem in distinguishing between Theory I (a) and Theory II (a) is obvious. What may not be obvious is the problem in distinguishing between I (a) and I (b).

Table 2-8
Correlation Coefficients Among Census Variables, 1963

	$\ln(N)$	$\ln(S_1)$	$\ln(CR)$	$\ln(S_1/P)$	$\ln(K/L)$	$\ln(S_1/N)$	$\ln(S_2/N)$
$\ln(N)$	1.00000	0.41737	−0.75094	−0.64957	−0.34149	−0.67621	−0.66473
$\ln(S_1)$	0.41737	1.00000	−0.10576	0.40723	0.24960	0.38725	0.33451
$\ln(CR)$	−0.75094	−0.10576	1.00000	0.67399	0.44383	0.67614	0.65501
$\ln(S_1/P)$	−0.64957	0.40723	0.67399	1.00000	0.51143	0.98917	0.91734
$\ln(K/L)$	−0.34149	0.24960	0.44383	0.51143	1.00000	0.54881	0.74021
$\ln(S_1/N)$	−0.67621	0.38725	0.67614	0.98917	0.54881	1.00000	0.94560
$\ln(S_2/N)$	−0.66473	0.33451	0.65501	0.91734	0.74021	0.94560	1.00000
C/TO	0.08288	−0.07295	−0.07369	−0.12687	−0.41264	−0.14323	−0.28545
G/TO	0.00557	0.21774	0.13157	0.19608	−0.01771	0.17087	0.09295
GR	0.13582	0.17912	−0.02487	0.03440	0.02199	0.00742	−0.02980
VGR	−0.23040	−0.38205	0.16538	−0.07317	0.01896	−0.07597	−0.02666

	C/TO	G/TO	GR	VGR
$\ln(N)$	0.08288	0.00557	0.13582	−0.23040
$\ln(S_1)$	−0.07295	0.21774	0.17912	−0.38205
$\ln(CR)$	−0.07369	0.13157	−0.02487	0.16538
$\ln(S_1/P)$	−0.12687	0.19608	0.03440	−0.07317
$\ln(K/L)$	−0.41264	−0.01771	0.02199	0.01896
$\ln(S_1/N)$	−0.14323	0.17087	0.00742	−0.07597
$\ln(S/N)$	−0.28545	0.09295	−0.02980	−0.02666
C/TO	1.00000	−0.13180	−0.10494	−0.12262
G/TO	−0.13180	1.00000	0.08025	0.11768
GR	−0.10494	0.08025	1.00000	0.10304
VGR	−0.12262	0.11768	0.10304	1.00000

$|r| \geqslant 0.075$ is significant at the 0.05 level.
$|r| \geqslant 0.104$ is significant at the 0.01 level.

In all of our regressions, logarithms of all variables except the ratios A/S, C/TO, G/TO, GR, and VGR were used. For the census sample of 409 industries the log (N) explained 57 percent of the variation in log $(CR4)$; for the IRS sample of 113 industries, about 34 percent. Both of these percentages indicate highly significant relationships. See Tables 2-8 and 2-9 for partial correlations among the variables used in our regressions. Similar results hold for other census years; the explained variation for census industries was 61 percent in both 1954 and 1967.

These percentages are indicative of the tautological nature of the relationship between C and N, as discussed previously. This conclusion forces us to the use of theories I (b) or II (b) in order to avoid the tautology. But we must proceed with caution, for the fact that I (a) and I (b) are two representations of the same

Table 2-9
Correlation Coefficients Among IRS Variables, 1963

	$\ln(CR)$	$\ln(N)$	$\ln(K/L)$	$\ln(S_3/N)$	$\ln(S_4/N)$	$\ln(S_3)$
$\ln(CR)$	1.00000	−0.57908	0.52895	0.62134	0.62806	0.07940
$\ln(N)$	−0.57908	1.00000	−0.38207	−0.73263	−0.75139	0.33419
$\ln(K/L)$	0.52895	−0.38207	1.00000	0.55806	0.61230	0.25748
$\ln(S_3/N)$	0.62134	−0.73263	0.55806	1.00000	0.98128	0.39666
$\ln(S_4/N)$	0.62806	−0.75139	0.61230	0.98128	1.00000	0.34542
$\ln(S_3)$	0.07940	0.33419	0.25748	0.39666	0.34542	1.00000
$\ln(A/S_3)$	0.26703	−0.01748	0.11419	−0.01078	−0.03490	−0.03850
G/TO	0.24539	−0.09054	−0.10275	0.19280	0.19741	0.14487
GR	0.02590	0.05624	0.01739	−0.05603	−0.02815	−0.00173
VGR	0.20825	−0.20852	0.01939	0.12198	0.13443	−0.11231
C/TO	−0.03775	0.04352	−0.08952	−0.02266	−0.11225	0.02731

	$\ln(A/S_3)$	G/TO	GR	VGR	C/TO
$\ln(CR)$	0.26703	0.24539	0.02590	0.20825	−0.03775
$\ln(N)$	−0.01748	−0.09054	0.05624	−0.20852	0.04352
$\ln(K/L)$	0.11419	−0.10275	0.01739	0.01939	−0.08952
$\ln(S_3/N)$	−0.01078	0.19280	−0.05603	0.12198	−0.02266
$\ln(S_4/N)$	−0.03490	0.19741	−0.02815	0.13443	−0.11225
$\ln(S_3)$	−0.03850	0.14487	−0.00173	−0.11231	0.02731
$\ln(A/S_3)$	1.00000	−0.13436	0.07765	−0.32707	0.56149
G/TO	−0.13436	1.00000	0.23000	0.35279	−0.22308
GR	0.07765	0.23000	1.00000	0.41287	−0.21439
VGR	−0.32707	0.35279	0.41287	1.00000	−0.38941
C/TO	0.56149	−0.22308	−0.21439	−0.38941	1.00000

$|r| \geqslant 0.16$ is significant at the 0.05 level.
$|r| \geqslant 0.23$ is significant at the 0.01 level.

theory should lead us to expect a logical equivalence between them. We saw with the results of earlier investigations, inclusion of terms representing optimal firm size and industry size together is tantamount to the use of N. To illustrate, consider the case in which optimal firm size is measured by average firm size, S/N. Then our regression may be written as:

(1) $\ln(CR) = k + a \ln(S/N) + b \ln(S) + c \ln(X) + e$ where X represents all other variables in the equation and e is a random error term. Alternatively, we may write:

(2) $CR = e^k (S/N)^a S^b X^c e^e$ This is equivalent to:

(3) $CR = e^k S^{a+b} N^{-a} X^c e^e$

If it turns out empirically that (a) approximates the absolute value of ($-b$), then (3) reduces to:

(4) $CR = e^k \, N^{-a} \, X^c \, e^e$

Thus concentration under these assumptions is demonstrated to be the inverse of the number of firms in the industry.

We may attempt to avoid this outcome, should it occur, by choosing alternative measures of optimum firm size and industry size. However, this is quite difficult in view of the high correlation between the alternatives available. Equations (3) and (4) also show the possible error of interpreting the coefficients directly as elasticities; e.g., Pashigian [182] concluded that proportional and offsetting changes in S and S/N account for the relative stability observed in concentration without, apparently, recognizing this confounding problem. Our own results indicate that using the capital labor ratio (K/L) to measure scale effects is one way of approaching the problem. In this respect, our conclusions are similar to those of Rosenbluth [195].

All of these foregoing variables have been offered both theoretically and empirically as measures of differences in industry concentration. The significance which can be attached to specific variables is not always clear since multiple interpretation of the same variable serves to obscure rather than illuminate underlying forces. For example, variables that have been used to measure scale economies and barriers to entry are often identical. This indicates the artificiality of calling scale economies a barrier to entry, and emphasizes the need to develop truly independent measures of scale economies and barriers to entry, as well as the need to provide further clarification of the highly ambiguous concept of barriers to entry.

To further complicate matters, the capital-labor ratio can be conceived of as a measure of operating risk due to cyclical fluctuations and may pick up some of the effects due to variability of growth. A measure of advertising intensity may also be thought of as an index of risk to the extent that advertising is a risky investment. Measures of growth are also a reflection of entry opportunities.

These difficulties have tended to obscure the results of previous studies. They have suffered from confounding of regression coefficients, and regressing CR on itself, i.e., on N in one form or another. In addition, there are the usual econometric problems of multicollinearity, autocorrelation, heteroskedasticity, and underidentification. The regression equations presented below also suffer from some of these difficulties. However, the purpose of the regression exercise is to provide further understanding of these problems in future research and to mitigate them to some degree.

Some Preliminary Regression Results

To explore the effects of the relations described in the previous section, we utilized a regression equation of the following expanded form. Various combinations of the variables were tested to clarify their respective influences.

$$\ln CR = a + b \ \ln N + c \ \ln S + d \ \ln(S/N) + e \ \ln(K/L) + f(A/S)$$
$$+ g(G/TO) + h(GR) + i(VGR) + u$$

The variables in the above equation are identified in Table 2-10 below.

Table 2-10
List of Variables Used

CR	= concentration measure
N	= number of firms
P	= number of plants
S	= total market size
S/N	= average firm size
K/L	= capital–labor ratio
A	= advertising
A/S	= advertising–sales ratio
G/TO	= government expenditures to total output
GR	= compound market growth rate
VGR	= variability of growth rate
u	= stochastic error term

As outlined in The Development of a Data Bank, we have developed two basic samples to date: the Census four-digit industries for 1963 and the IRS industries for 1963 at approximately the three-digit level. The Census sample covers 409 out of 417 possible industries and the IRS sample is based on 113 out of 116 possible industries. The reductions are due to data deficiencies in certain industries, e.g., no concentration ratio given. The Census sample is further reduced from 409 to 374 when growth rates are included in the regressions since the requisite data were not available for thirty-five industries. The measurement of variables used was influenced by whether the source was the Census or IRS. An explanation of the measurement of variables used is set forth in Table 2-11.

With regard to the measurement of variables, two points regarding differences in the IRS and Census samples should be made. First, the level of aggregation for the IRS industries is greater than for the Census industries, and the sample size is correspondingly smaller (113 vs. 409). The manner in which the *Link* was used in transforming Census measures to an IRS industry basis was essentially an averaging process. Hence our transformed concentration ratios do not bear precisely the same interpretation as they did with the Census industry sample. They no longer correspond to the share of the largest four firms in industry value added, but to an average of several such ratios, and as the law of large numbers predicts, the variability in this "average" is reduced due to the averaging process. The second point is that we now have a more direct measure of the importance of advertising, since the IRS data include aggregate industry

Table 2-11
Measurement of Variables Used

CR	= The Census four-firm unadjusted value added concentration ratio is used. The link is used to calculate IRS industry concentration ratios using employment figures as weights.
N	= The Census figures for number of companies is used and the number of returns for IRS industries.
S_1	= Census total value added
S_2	= Census gross book, value of assets
S_3	= IRS total business receipts
S_4	= IRS total assets
K/L	= The capital-labor ratio is measured by the gross book value of assets per production worker for the Census and total assets per employee in IRS. Employees are linked from Census to IRS.
A/S_3	= The ratio of advertising expenditures to business receipts from IRS.
C/TO	= The ratio of consumption expenditures to total output taken from the OBE input-output table for 1963. It is used as a proxy for advertising to sales for the Census industries.
G/TO	= Government expenditures to total output is taken from 1963 input-output tables for the Census and linked to IRS industries.
GR	= Growth rate is the compound growth rate of Census industry value added from 1958 to 1968. The growth rate is linked to IRS industries.
VGR	= Variability of growth rate is the percent variation of value added about its time trend. It is also linked to IRS industries.

advertising expenditures. The variable used as a proxy for advertising for the Census sample was the ratio of consumption goods sales to total industry output.

The regression results are presented in Table 2-12 (Census) and Table 2-13 (IRS). In both regression tables the number of firms is highly significant in all cases, as expected, and accounts for most of the explained variation in *CR4*. Naturally, this results whether N appears individually or in S/N or some variation thereof. When N is removed, as in Equation 7 in Table 2-11, R^2 is halved. The tautology is not avoided when average plant size is substituted for average firm size, as in Equation 9, reflecting the high collinearity between average firm and average plant size.

The results in both the Census and IRS samples show that the inclusion of an average firm size variable into an equation containing S and K/L, Equations 8 and $8'$, acts to change the absolute coefficient of S in the direction of the coefficient of S/N in the resulting equations, supporting the algebraic relationship implied by the transition from Equations (3) and (4) discussed above.

The results indicate that one way of avoiding the tautology and confounding problems is to use the K/L ratio to measure scale effects. The K/L ratio is significant in all cases under both samples reflecting the importance of capital

Table 2-12
Subject: Census Differential Concentration, 1963

Dependent Variable: LOG (CR)   Figures in Parentheses are t-Statistics

Equ. #	Variable	Constant	Log N	Log S_1	Log K/L	Log S_1/N	Log S_2/N	C/TO	G/TO	GR	VGR	Log S_1/P	Std. Error	R^2	F
1		2.587	-0.334 (-20.6)		0.175 (7.8)								0.436	0.613	321.9
2		2.385	-0.336 (-19.4)		0.193 (7.1)			0.002 (3.3)	0.014 (4.7)	0.012 (.9)	-0.001 (0.0)		0.416	0.637	107.2
3		2.835	-0.270 (13.4)		0.107 (3.9)	0.120 (4.2)							0.423	0.637	237.1
4		2.567	-0.276 (-11.6)		0.141 (4.6)	0.094 (3.5)		0.002 (2.9)	0.010 (3.3)	0.008 (1.3)	0.006 (1.2)		0.410	0.648	96.4
5		3.119	-0.275 (-13.6)				0.120 (7.3)						0.434	0.616	326.0
6		2.942	-0.273 (-11.8)				0.119 (6.3)	0.002 (2.4)	0.010 (3.3)	0.011 (1.7)	0.005 (1.0)		0.421	0.629	103.5
7		2.011		-0.166 (-5.1)	0.439 (11.9)			0.004 (3.8)	0.020 (4.8)	0.002 (0.0)	0.006 (1.0)		0.572	0.314	28.0
8		2.996		-0.250 (-9.9)	0.004 (0.0)		0.325 (16.0)	0.004 (4.4)	0.014 (4.4)	0.014 (2.1)	0.003 (0.3)		0.440	0.595	77.0
9		3.009			0.120 (3.4)			0.002 (2.3)	0.000 (0.0)	-0.012 (-1.7)	0.030 (6.1)	0.342 (14.1)	0.447	0.523	67.0

Sample size is 374 for equations with GR, VGR
Sample size is 409 for other equations

	2.33
	.01
$|t_{500}| \geq 1.65$ is significant at the .05 level.	
1.28	.10

Table 2-13
Subject: IRS Differential Concentration, 1963

Dependent Variable: LOG (CR)   Figures in Parentheses are t-Statistics

Equ. # / Variable	Constant	Log N	Log S$_3$	Log K/L	Log S$_3$/N	Log S$_4$/N	C/TO	G/TO	GR	VGR	Log A	Log A/S$_3$	Std. Error	R^2	F
1′	2.697	-.163 (-5.8)		.255 (4.7)									.353	.446	44.3
2′	2.353	-.141 (-5.0)		.295 (5.6)			.002 (1.3)	.013 (3.4)	-.007 (-.5)	.016 (1.0)			.336	.517	18.9
3′	2.743	-.104 (-2.8)		.195 (3.3)	.093 (2.3)								.347	.471	32.4
4′	2.413	-.108 (-2.9)		.256 (4.2)	.054 (1.3)		.001 (1.2)	.011 (2.8)	-.005 (-.3)	.017 (1.0)			.335	.524	16.5
5′	3.323	-.091 (-2.2)				.148 (4.2)							.361	.421	40.0
6′	3.126	-.086 (2.5)				.142 (3.8)	.001 (1.0)	.007 (1.6)	.001 (0.0)	.017 (1.0)			.359	.449	14.4
7′	1.977		-.053 (-1.3)	.424 (7.6)			.002 (1.6)	.016 (3.8)	-.023 (-1.2)	.031 (1.8)			.371	.413	12.4
8′	2.471		-.091 (-2.4)	.241 (3.7)		.147 (4.6)	.002 (1.8)	.011 (2.8)	-.008 (-.4)	.021 (1.3)			.340	.512	15.7
10	0.493		-.205 (-4.1)	.377 (7.2)				.016 (3.9)	-.046 (-2.5)	.054 (3.2)	.177 (4.6)		.343	.498	17.6
11	2.233		-.023 (-0.6)	.365 (6.8)			-.002 (-1.0)	.015 (3.8)	-.050 (-2.7)	.052 (3.1)		.203 (4.4)	.343	.503	15.2

Sample size is 113

2.37   .01
$|t_{100}| \geq 1.66$ is significant at the .05 level.
1.28   .10

intensity in highly concentrated industries. The results in Equations 7 and 7′ show S highly significant and the level of significance of K/L rises once S is taken into account. The insignificance of K/L in Equation 8 and the reduction of its insignificance in 8′ is due to the collinearity between K/L and average firm size in assets, (S_2/N).

The proxy for advertising intensity, C/TO, in the Census regression is of the expected sign and significant in all cases. The simple correlation between C/TO and advertising to sales for IRS industries is 0.56, indicating that the Census regressions are picking up some of the effects due to advertising. However, the implications of this variable are not clear, other than that concentration tends to be higher in consumer goods or high advertising industries. On the other hand, it could be argued that to the extent that C/TO is a measure of countervailing power, consumer goods industries should be less concentrated due to the dispersion of power among a large number of consumers as opposed to a relatively few purchasers in producer good industries.

Our *a priori* notion was that the relation between consumption goods and advertising requirements was stronger than the relation between consumption goods and the theory of countervailing power, and the resulting regressions bore out this notion. With the IRS data, we can directly test the dual nature of the consumption goods to total output ratio by including the advertising measure in the regressions, and noting the resulting impact on the consumption goods ratio. The impact is to reverse the sign of the coefficient from positive to negative, although the latter was not significant, even at the 10 percent level.

This effect can be observed in Equations 8′ and 11 of Table 2-13. Thus, once we account for advertising, the consumption goods ratio does lend some support to a variant of the countervailing power thesis.

The ratio of government purchases to total output is generally significant and positive for both Census and IRS, supporting another variant of the theory of countervailing power, although it contributes little to the explained variation in concentration.

With the introduction of the advertising measure the coefficients of GR and VGR become significant above the 1 percent level. These results (Equations 10 and 11) are consistent with the hypotheses relating those variables to concentration. GR, the growth rate in industry value added, is a proxy for ease of entry due to expansion of industry output. This is admittedly a rough measure, since it does not permit us to distinguish between growth resulting from shifts in demand, and growth resulting from technological change (shift in supply curve). Both sources of growth may facilitate entry, though scale effects of a change in technology should also be taken into consideration for a properly specified model. Our results indicate that concentration is inversely related to this proxy for ease of entry, once economies resulting from advertising are accounted for in the regressions.

The variability of growth measure is generally positive for both Census and

IRS, supporting the theory based on the law of proportionate effect. However, it is generally not significant. It contributes almost nothing to the explained variation in concentration.

Concentration and the Size Distribution of Firms

Much of the criticisms of four-firm concentration is that it ignores the size distribution of firms and thus hides useful information. The consequences of this can be seen in concentration-profit studies. Relating the top four firms to industry accounting rates of return is biased since concentration is a proxy for the weight given the largest firms in average industry returns. Consequently, concentration may simply be accounting for the relative size effects of firms.

An initial attempt was made to separate the effects of size and concentration by correlating concentration with four variables, advertising to sales, total assets to sales, depreciable assets to sales, and net income plus interest to total assets, within IRS firm size classifications. The sample was constructed such that all industries are represented in each size class. (Table 2-14.)

Advertising to sales is significantly correlated with concentration at the 0.05 level for the smallest size class only. Given that both producer and consumer good industries are covered, the insignificant correlations may not be unexpected. However, the mean ratio does rise over size classes. The significant correlation in this smallest size class indicates that small firms in highly

Table 2-14
IRS Concentration Correlation Coefficients and Mean Values (Percent) by Grouped Asset Size Class, 1963

N = 98 Variables		0 to 500	500 to 5,000	5,000 to 50,000	50,000 Above
		Asset Size Class (000)			
Advertising	Corr. W/CR$_4$	0.21	0.05	0.07	0.12
Business Receipts	Mean	1.2%	1.2%	1.9%	2.4%
Total Assets	Corr. W/CR$_4$	0.16	0.05	−0.02	−0.19
Business Receipts	Mean	55.2%	56.7%	75.7%	94.3%
Depreciable Assets	Corr. W/CR$_4$	0.07	−0.08	−0.05	0.13
Business Receipts	Mean	26.5%	28.0%	38.7%	49.2%
Net Income + Interest	Corr. W/CR$_4$	−0.20	0.03	0.12	0.28
Total Assets	Mean	4.8%	9.0%	10.2%	10.5%

$|r| \geqslant 0.16$ is significant at the 0.05 level.
$|r| \geqslant 0.23$ is significant at the 0.01 level.

concentrated industries spend a larger proportion of sales on advertising than small firms in less concentrated industries. This may reflect the fact that advertising is a prime vehicle for entry in highly concentrated industries.

The next two variables are capital-output ratios. Using depreciable assets none of the correlations are significant. However, depreciable assets are subject to wide discretionary treatment by accountants and may be an inaccurate estimate of capital stock. The total assets to output ratio is significant at the 0.05 level in both the smallest and largest size categories, but with opposite sign. The ratio rises monotonically over class size approaching unity for the large size class. The correlations provide evidence that concentration is, at least in part technologically induced. Small firms in highly concentrated industries are striving to achieve minimum efficient scale, resulting in a higher capital-output ratio than small firms in less concentrated industries. The significant inverse correlation for the largest size class suggests that managerial economies may account for large firm success in highly concentrated industries.

The rate of return measure is significantly inversely correlated with concentration for the smallest size class and significantly positively correlated for the largest size class. The numerous studies on concentration and return appear to have been picking up this size effect [179]. Our evidence contradicts the conventional hypothesis that collusion accounts for high return in highly concentrated industries since small firms in highly concentrated industries earn lower returns than small firms in less concentrated industries. If collusion were taking place, small firms would be under the collusive price umbrella or engage in cheating. Under either alternative their profit rates would be enhanced.

The foregoing empirical efforts have provided some progress toward developing useful equations for explaining industry structure. Measures related to economies of scale such as the capital labor ratio have theoretical merit and some empirical strength. The size of industry may also be included. Our measures developed from the input-output tables were statistically significant, but did not add appreciably to the percentage of variation explained. We shall need to do more work with the advertising variables to determine their appropriate use.

We shall attempt to recombine existing data to develop new combinations of variables and shall seek additional kinds of data to develop new variables as close as possible to the underlying theory. Our preliminary work with analysis of the size distributions encourages us to broaden the range of variables so analyzed.

Plans for the Future

Plans for the future involve a systematic approach to the estimation of the complete model. While the estimated complete model is the long-range goal, there are several specific short-range goals which, in addition to providing logical steps toward the long-range goal, are of value in themselves.

The first step is (a) augmenting the data, (b) obtaining new variables or combinations of variables closer to the underlying economic phenomena involved and (c) integrating the various data sources to develop the most comprehensive and useful data bank for use in the area of industrial organization.

The second step is that of further iterating previous quantitative studies of industrial organization. Many of the previous studies utilized data from the 1950s. Using the data bank, they will be repeated for data from the 1960s and 1970s. As already noted, the results of these iterations of previous studies can be interpreted as potential candidates for becoming single equations for the overall econometric model.

The third step is that of performing various statistical tests on the data bank. These statistical tests will include correlation, regression, factor and discriminant analyses. Some of the preliminary results using correlation and regression analyses have already been presented and discussed above in the section on preliminary statistical analysis. The factor and discriminant analyses will lead to certain statistical groupings of variables which, among other things, will enable us to judge whether the term "concentration" is in fact a meaningful concept. If it is meaningful there should be a well-defined set of variables associated with concentration, which should become evident in the statistical analysis. If they are not evident, then the whole concept of concentration, which has played such a central role in previous studies of industrial organizations, may have to be eliminated altogether and replaced by a set of considerations, such as those appearing in *Module 1*. The results of all of the statistical analyses and the iterations of previous studies will give us a "feel" for the data, facilitating the next step.

The fourth step is that of working within the individual modules, developing analyses and estimating single equations and small groupings of equations. Thus in *Module 1* we will be estimating demand functions and production and cost functions. The empirical efforts reported in the last section of this paper relate to *Module 2*. In *Module 3* we will be estimating models dealing with individual firm variables. In *Module 4* we intend to measure performance measures by other than the traditional profit variables. Finally, in *Module 5*, we will be estimating models of decisions to initiate regulatory action.

The fifth step is that of studying the interrelationships among the modules. Under *Modules 1* and *2* we would be estimating the effect of the estimated production functions on concentration and size distribution of firms, specifically the effects of such considerations as scale economies and factor proportions.

Under *Modules 1* and *3* we would be estimating the effects of product demand on factor demand and on pricing. Under *Modules 2* and *3* we would be estimating the effects of pricing and advertising on concentration and size distribution of firms. Under *Modules 3* and *5* we would be estimating the effects of pricing on regulatory action. Under *Modules 4* and *5* we would be relating performance results to regulatory action. Many of the results in this part of the overall analysis can be interpreted as extensions and generalizations of previous quantitative analyses, as outlined in the section on the econometric approach to industrial organization.

The sixth step is that of studying the feedback effects from higher numbered to lower numbered modules. In particular, we are interested in studying the effects of regulatory actions in *Module 5* on pricing decisions in *Module 3* and on concentration and the size distribution of firms in *Module 2*. We are also interested in studying the effects of performance in *Module 4* on research and development activities in *Module 3* and the effects of such activities on technological change in *Module 1*.

The seventh step is that of estimating the entire model. This step may entail reestimation of the individual modules to insure consistent estimation. The resulting estimates could be used for the various purposes outlined for the econometric approach in Figure 2-1: structural analysis, forecasting, and policy evaluation.

Structural analysis would involve studying in a quantitative way the underlying structure of the system. In particular, it would include studying the implications of various hypotheses of industrial economics for their related policy actions and the important feedback effects from the regulatory module.

Forecasting and policy evaluation using the estimated complete model would be based upon unconditional and conditional predictions respectively, using the model. The estimated model could play a useful role in formulating public policy, guiding actions of regulatory agencies.

Part II:
Industry Structure and Profits

There have been close to forty studies testing for the existence of monopoly power by relating industry concentration to industry or firm profit rates since Professor Joe Bain's seminal work in 1951. Under the hypothesis tested, profit rates are taken to be a reflection of how efficiently resources are allocated in the long run and concentration is assumed to be a proxy for the likelihood of collusion and joint profit maximization. Most earlier studies appeared to support the conventional hypothesis in finding a significant positive association between concentration and profits but there is usually a large percentage of unexplained variation in inter-industry profit rates. Investigators usually attributed this unexplained variation to such factors as poor data on concentration and profits, differences in risk, different elasticities of market demand, disequilibrium conditions, and barriers to entry.

Except for a minority of economists and lawyers, the traditional view has rarely been challenged. This minority remained skeptical because the empirical studies were plagued by a multitude of problems, including the lack of a clear theoretical content, the use of accounting profit rates that seemed to have little relation to economic profits, the failure to investigate alternative hypotheses that could account for the empirical relationships and the failure to look at profits over time. In recent years new studies have provided important evidence contradicting previous findings. These new studies provide a basis for a reversal of the conventional position.

The studies in this section by Brozen, Demsetz, and Ornstein illustrate the challenges to earlier findings. Preston's paper questions the internal logic of the new research on profit and supports the conventional hypothesis. His statement exemplifies the position of such economists as Weiss, Mueller, Shepherd and Blair. Their basic position is that due to the large number of studies showing a positive relationship between concentration and profit there must be something to the traditional hypothesis.

Brozen examined the possibility that Bain and others used samples that were not in long run equilibrium and that Bain's sample of industries and firms was not representative. He found that the correlation of rates of return and concentration declined over time supporting his a priori hypothesis of disequilibrium. Rates of return are not persistently high in high concentration industries. By using a sample double the size of Bain's he found no correlation between concentration and profits. He concludes that industries are concentrated or unconcentrated because that is the most efficient way to organize them.

Demsetz's paper clears away much of the confusion in interpreting structural differences between perfect competition and monopoly that has plagued all previous studies on concentration and profits and neo-classical theory in general. High profits are attributed to superior efficiency, that is, lower costs of production. Postulating rivalry and the absence of effective barriers to entry, leads to concentration based on superior firm operation. Since rivalry stems from both existing and potential producers, one cannot conclude that an industry of few firms faces less rivalry than one of many firms. His evidence of rates of return by asset size and concentration shows that the positive association is due to more efficient performance of large firms (or lower costs of operation) not to collusive practices. An implication of his findings is that a comprehensive deconcentration policy could do great harm by decreasing efficient performance and removing part of the incentive toward improving performance in a behaviorally competitive industry.

Preston sets forth the reasons why he judges that much work to date is incomplete due to severe data limitations and misspecification of the estimated equations. Nevertheless, it is his position that there is simply no other systematic way to measure monopoly power other than by market share and profitability. More importantly, he urges there is ample evidence to show that high market share industries earn higher profits regardless of whether the cause is collusion, efficiency or other factors. Therefore, he concludes that the vast body of earlier work showing a positive relationship must be considered as evidence of some misallocation of resources.

Ornstein's paper uses a multiple regression analysis in contrast to many previous studies which look solely at concentration and profits. When he includes such factors as measures of barriers to entry, firm size, and industry and firm growth in the analysis, he finds no relation between concentration and firm profits. For the sample of 131 firms selected, profit rates are significantly related to economies of scale in production and industry and firm growth but not to concentration, firm size, entry capital requirements, capital intensity, change in labor cost, or whether a firm is in a consumer or producer good industry. He concludes that evidence on concentration and profits is far from clear and that much further work is required before the issue is settled.

3

Concentration and Profits: Does Concentration Matter?

Yale Brozen

Early Views on Concentration and Competition

In the post-World War II period, the economics profession made a 180 degree turn from its pre-Great Depression position in its view of concentration. In the late nineteenth and early twentieth century, the prevailing view seems to have been that even with only a few firms in an industry, price competition would be persistent and collusion difficult. There was little concern with any probability of successful collusion (shared monopoly or oligopoly) in industries where four firms had, say, 70 percent or more of an industry's capacity or sales. Three or four firms were felt to be sufficient for competitive behavior.[1] What concern was expressed was in terms of "trusts" combining most of an industry's capacity under a single management.

Even where more than 70 percent of an industry's capacity had been combined to form a *single* firm, no fear was felt by many economists that a monopoly result would ensue.[2] (Some expressed approval of such combinations in terms of the economies that would be realized.)[3] J.B. Clark, for example, pointed to the power of potential competition to produce the same competitive result as a larger number of firms or non-colluding behavior of a few saying

Let any combination of producers raise the prices beyond a certain limit, and it will encounter this difficulty. The new mills that will spring into existence will break down prices; and the fear of these new mills, without their actual coming, is often enough to keep prices from rising to an extortionate height. The mill that has never been built is already a power in the market: for it will surely be built under certain conditions, the effect of this certainty is to keep prices down.[4]

Even Professor Jones, who believed in the necessity of active government intervention to break up trusts because they would seek to maintain unfairly high prices, provides evidence of the failure of the trusts to accomplish their objective. He lists a number which failed financially and were voluntarily dissolved. In addition, he mentions others which were unable to keep the dominant position required to maintain prices above the competitive level when they attempted to do so.[5]

Professor A.S. Dewing undertook an empirical analysis to determine whether or not any advantages accrued to "large scale enterprises brought about through combination—the so-called 'trusts' " [63, p. 84]. Choosing "a random selection of thirty-five industrial combinations" where "at least five separate, independent and competing plants" were merged, he examined profits of the independent companies in the year preceding consolidation. He also compared them with the profits in the year following consolidation, in the tenth year following consolidation, and average profits in the ten years following. He found no evidence showing, on the average, that cominations of 40 to 95 percent of an industry's capacity produced any enhancement of profits either through economies of scale or combination or through monopoly [63].

Roughly, the promoters of the consolidations believed that the mere act of combination would increase the earnings by about a half. But in actual results the earnings before the consolidation were nearly a fifth *greater* (18%) than the earnings of the first year after consolidation. The promoters expected the earnings to be a half greater than the aggregate of the competing plants; instead they were about a sixth less. Nor were the sustained earnings an improvement, for the earnings before the consolidation were between a fifth and a sixth greater than the average for the ten years following the consolidation. In brief, the earnings of the separate plants before consolidation were greater than the earnings of the same plants after consolidation.[6]

As late as the 1930s, after the discussion of administered (rigid) prices in concentrated industries had begun, Professor Henry Simons [213] said

I am, indeed, not much distressed about private monopoly power ... Serious exploitation could be prevented by suppression of lawless violence ... The ways of competition are devious, and its vengeance—government intervention apart—will generally be adequate and admirable.[7]

In the post World War II era, in contrast to this earlier view, "most practitioners assumed that successful (tacit or explicit) collusion [among oligopolists] would approach joint maximization and that the ability to collude increases with concentration" [Weiss, 248]. A major exception to this post World War II view appeared in a book by Paul MacAvoy, describing competition among the few in transportation "between the Mississippi River Valley and the East Coast" [142].

Discussing the observed behavior of these few firms, MacAvoy found that collusion was not effective despite being *explicitly* agreed upon among them. He observes that ". . . there seems to have been persistent 'cheating' on the rates set in conference, so that the level of rates declined markedly as one agreement after another broke down" [142]. He goes on to point out that collusively determined rates became the actual rates only after governmental support was provided in 1887 under the Act to Regulate Interstate Commerce. As he says, "The effect of regulation seems to have been to establish the cartel rates as the actual rates" [142].

Early Studies on Concentration and Profits

The question, "Why did economists' views shift from the earlier outlook to the opposite view characteristic of the post war period?", may well be raised. The answer appears to be that the data relating concentration and profits first provided by Bain and later by other students in industrial organization convinced economists that they had been wrong. The groundwork for acceptance had been laid by various discussions of administered pricing beginning in the thirties [112].

This view that successful tacit or explicit collusion was probable in concentrated industries reached a culmination in the recommendation of the White House Antitrust Force that a deconcentration act be added to the antitrust arsenal [257]. The Task Force stated that there was some evidence for the view that underlay the recommendation, although it cited none. When the Staff Director of the Antitrust Task Force was asked for the evidence used, he referred to the articles by Bain, Mann, Stigler and others showing correlations between concentration and profitability and to the price selected cost margin studies of Collins and Preston [17, 51, 145, 222].

The Task Force had stated that the evidence showed "a close association between high levels of concentration and persistently high rates of return" [257]. None of the studies cited by the Staff Director, however, had examined the *persistence* of high rates of return in concentrated industries. Each had provided a spot correlation showing a weak relationship between concentration and accounting rates of return at a given time. None had looked at the profitability of the same industries at a later time to determine whether the above average rates of return in concentrated industries had persisted.

**The Evidence on the Persistence of
High Rates of Return**

Since there was no evidence on persistence (or lack of persistence) of above average ("high") rates of return in concentrated industries, I compiled data on accounting rates of return at a later time in the industries used in the studies cited by the Task Force staff. For each of the samples of industries used by Bain, Mann, and Stigler, rates of return in concentrated industries at a later time all turned out to be insignificantly different from those in less concentrated industries [38, p. 279].

The correlations between concentration and accounting profits, which were weak in the original studies, deteriorated to insignificance with the passage of time. In the seventeen Bain industries which were more than 60 percent concentrated (four-firm), the coefficient of determination dropped from 40 percent for 1936-40 profitability on 1935 concentration ratios to a non-significant 16 percent for 1953-57 profitability on 1954 concentration. It continued non-significant at 9 percent for 1962-66 profitability on 1963 concentration. Similarly, Stigler's seventeen industries (eleven of which were in the Bain seventeen) showed a decline in the coefficient of determination from 34 percent for 1953-57 profitability on 1954 concentration to a non-significant seventeen percent for 1963 concentration on 1962-66 profitability [38, pp. 287, 289].

The Task Force economists replied saying that the wrong industries had been selected [143]. They thoughtfully provided a list of the appropriate industries where concentration had been persistently high and said persistently high returns would be found in those industries. Examining rates of return for the industries they specified, it was found that rates of return were not even high (significantly above average), much less persistently high [40].

Effects of Sample Size on
Concentration-Profit Relation

There was still the puzzling fact that any correlation had been found between concentration and rates of return at any given time in some studies. Since there had been convergence on mean rates of return, it seemed that what had been found was a disequilibrium phenomenon. That is, concentrated industries happened to be earning above equilibrium rates of return which disappeared with the passage of time, as would occur under competitive circumstances. But why had a disproportionate number of concentrated industries been earning above equilibrium rates of return while a disproprotionate number of less concentrated industries had been earning below equilibrium returns?

Since Bain had used only forty-two industries out of 340 industries in the 1935 Census of Manufacturers to test for differences in rates of return between more and less concentrated industries, it was possible that his result was the consequence of the non-representativeness of his sample. Also, each of his industries was represented by only a few firms (three or more). Those he chose might have been non-representative of their industries.

In order to test whether Bain's forty-two industries are representative, an enlarged sample of ninety-eight industries (including Bain's forty-two) has been assembled (Tables 3-1 and 3-2). Industries for which less than three firms could be found were omitted (Tables 3-1a and 3-2a). In a few instances, rates of return computed by Bain have been recomputed using a larger number of firms (Table 3-3).

The results are strikingly opposed to those found in Bain's smaller sample. Where he found that the accounting profitability of concentrated industries was 4.4 percentage points *greater* than that of the less concentrated industries, the ninety-eight industry sample shows profitability to be *less* (insignificantly) in the concentrated industries (Table 3-4).

Bain's sample contained fourteen concentrated industries (out of twenty-one) showing an accounting return greater than the sample average. The majority (67 percent) of his concentrated industries were earning above equilibrium (sample average) rates of return (if we can assume that accounting biases did not differentially affect rates of return). The ninety-eight industry sample contains seventeen concentrated industries (out of thirty-eight) showing an accounting rate of return greater than the sample average. In contrast to Bain's 67 percent, only 45 percent of the concentrated industries in the enlarged sample earned above equilibrium (sample average) rates of return. This is in the range we can expect by chance. It is the same proportion as that found in the less concentrated portion of the ninety-eight industry sample (43 percent). In Bain's sample of less concentrated industries, only three (14 percent) earned above sample average rates of return.

In the ninety-eight industry sample, there is not a disproportionate number of concentrated industries earning more than the sample average. Neither is there a disproportionate number of less concentrated industries earning less than the sample average. There are no differences to explain. The distribution is about as might be expected under competitive circumstances, confirming the finding that the behavior of rates of return in Bain's sample of industries over time indicates competitive circumstances in both concentrated and less concentrated industries.

Bain warned that his forty-two industry sample might not be representative. He discussed thirty-four industries he had excluded from his sample because data were available for only one or two firms in the thirty-four. He pointed out that, "Averages of industry profit rates above and below the 70 percent concentration line in these thirty-four industries were 9.1 and 10.5 percent respectively,"–[17, p. 315. n. 8] the reverse of the relationship in his forty-two industry sample.

Table 3-1
Concentrated Industries

Census No.[a]	Industry	Concentration Ratio (1935)[b]		Profit Rate (Percent of Book Net Worth)[c] 1936-40
		4 Firm	8 Firm	
1406	Locomotives	D	D	1.7(3)
222	Linoleum	81.5	100.0	8.4(4,5)
1215	Sm. & ref. copper	82.1	D	6.9(6)
1652	Cigarettes	89.7	99.4	14.4(7)
1314	Typewriters	(91.2)	99.3	15.0(4)
108	Chewing gum	92.0	97.3	16.9(3)
113	Corn prods.	79.2	95.0	9.2(4)
1408	Motor vehicles	87.3	94.2	16.3(17,22)
1106	Firearms	81.9	92.4	9.0(4)
606	Carbon black	81.0	92.1	12.7(4)

Table 3-1(cont.)

Census No.[a]	Industry	Concentration Ratio (1935)[b] 4 Firm	8 Firm	Profit Rate (Percent of Book Net Worth)[c] 1936-40
<u>312</u>	Matches	70.3	91.3	4.8(4,9)
803	Rubber tires	80.9	90.4	8.0(9,11)
<u>1312</u>	Sewing mach.	78.9	90.4	7.2(3,8)
629	Rayon	74.3	90.2	9.0(8,9)
1301	Agricult. implem.	72.4	87.7	9.1(9,10)
<u>610</u>	Compressed gases	79.2	87.0	13.9(4)
1022	Gypsum prods.	76.1	86.4	10.1(3)
<u>120</u>	Shortening, cook, & salad oil	69.0	85.9	6.0(3)
1123	Tin cans	80.8	85.6	9.1(4,5)
636	Photo. app. & mat.	77.9	84.9	12.9(2,4)
1647	Tobacco, ch. & sm.	63.5	84.3	11.7(4)
1405	Cars, Railroad	71.7	84.0	2.8(5)
1201	Aluminum prods.	76.0	83.7	9.7
631	Soap	73.5	83.1	14.8(4)
1634	Pens, Fountain, etc.	70.4	82.8	12.3(3)
<u>1110</u>	Blast furnace prods.	66.0	82.8	3.7(4)
106	Cereals	68.1	82.2	14.7(4)
1218	Sm. & ref. zinc.	64.0	82.2	4.7
1315	Washing machines, driers	56.0	79.7	13.5(6)
<u>1001</u>	Asbestos	63.1	78.4	8.5(3)
<u>1407</u>	Motor veh. parts	69.4	76.8	11.9(30)
<u>1630</u>	Pianos	51.1	75.8	3.6(5)
<u>1021</u>	Abrasives	67.4	74.3	24.9(4)
1401	Aircraft & parts	53.9	72.8	20.3(18,31)
133	Liquors, dist.	51.2	71.4	14.2(8,10)
<u>1631</u>	Optical goods	62.3	70.7	10.5(3)
129	Sugar, beet	68.8	89.4[c]	8.3(6)
<u>131</u>	Sugar ref., cane	69.6	88.3[c]	3.0(5,6)

[a]Census number is underlined for those industries added to the Bain sample.

[b]Natural Resources Committee, *Structure of the American Economy*, 249-259 (1939).

[c]Joe S. Bain, "Relation of Profit Rate to Industry Concentration: American Manufacturing, 1936-1940," *Q.J. Econ.* 312 (1951); Securities and Exchange Commission, Survey of American Listed Corporations, Data on Profits and Operations, 1936-1942 (1944), Moody's Industrials, various issues. Profit rate is underlined where it differs from that shown by Professor Bain. The difference occurs where a larger number of firms is used than that used by Professor Bain except for soap and typewriters. In the latter case, a weighted average of firm rates of return is substituted for the simple average used by Professor Bain. All other profit rates are weighted averages. Professor Bain's profit rate for the soap industry included cosmetics and toiletries firms. These were excluded for this computation. Figure in parentheses is the number of firms used to compute profit rate. Number of firms is not shown where Bain's rate of return could not be replicated using his data source.

Table 3-1a
Concentrated Industries (Fewer than Three Firms)

		Concentration Ratio (1935)		Profit Rate 1936-40
		4 Firm	8 Firm	
1010	Graphite	86.4	100	13.3(1)
302	Billiard tables, b. alleys	D	D	11.4(1)
613	Explosives	82.0	93.1	10.2(2)
307	Cork products	76.9	90.2	6.1(1)
1206	Fire extinguishers	77.1	87.3	8.2(1)
1641	Soda fountains	74.0	80.4	18.9(1)
630	Salt	60.3	78.2	7.3(1,2)
1629	Organs	57.0	77.5	9.3(2)
1311	Scales and balances	54.8	72.9	10.9(1)
Average accounting profit rate on book equity				10.6

Table 3-2
Less Concentrated Industries

Census No.[a]	Industry	Concentration Ratio (1935)[b]		Profit Rate (Percent of Book Equity)[c] 1936-40
		4 Firm	8 Firm	
1638	Roofing	42.8	68.2	7.4(4)[d]
201	Carpets & rugs	51.1	68.2	4.7(3)
1213	Silverware	56.6	68.0	6.6(4)
1611	Dental equip.	51.6	67.6	7.6(3)
1410	Ship bldg.	44.8	64.7	10.8(3,6)
1112	Steel-works & roll. mills	49.2	63.8	4.9(26,30)
123	Meat packing	55.6	63.5	3.6(12,13)
1102	Cast iron pipe	42.4	63.0	8.6
111	Condensed milk	44.6	62.7	10.2(3)
1008	Glass	44.9	61.0	14.3(7,8)
618	Printing ink	49.0	60.9	11.8(3,4)
1202	Clocks, watches	37.7	59.1	13.7(5)
705	Petroleum refining	38.2	58.9	6.8(33,36)
1126	Wire drawn from pur. rods	40.2	54.0	7.5
115	Flavoring extracts	47.7	54.0	41.5(5,7)
1303	Elect. mach., apparatus	44.1	52.3	12.3(28,33)
1608	Cigars	38.5	50.7	6.9(8)

Table 3-2 (cont.)

Census No.[a]	Industry	Concentration Ratio (1935)[b]		Profit Rate (Percent of Book Equity)[c] 1936-40
		4 Firm	8 Firm	
1104	Doors & shutters, metal	33.3	49.0	18.3
1325	Printers' mach.	32.5	47.4	2.9(8)
1304	Engines, turb., w.w.	30.7	47.2	11.1(6,8)
30	Sugar, cane (excl. ref.)	33.5	47.1	8.1(11,14)
103	Cutting & edge tools	36.3	45.2	12.2(3)
1002	Cement	29.9	44.7	6.0(14)
1324	Cranes, dredging, excav. mach.	29.3	44.5	9.1(8)
626	Paints	32.3	41.8	7.9(11,15)
614	Fertilizers	25.9	41.6	3.4(7,8)
628	Perf. cosm. toil.	25.3	40.7	15.9(6,8)
609	Cleaning & polish. prep.	28.0	39.9	20.7(3)
104	Canned fish	28.6	38.7	3.6(6,7)
1319	Radio & phonograph	28.6	38.6	11.1(8,14)
116	Flour & other grain mill prd.	29.4	37.0	7.6(3)
1127	Wirework	23.1	35.3	10.3(4,5)
1309	Pumps	22.7	35.2	15.4(5,6)
410	Pulp	22.7	34.5	14.2(2,4)
907	Leather	22.5	34.3	2.1(8)
611	Drugs & medicines	23.4	33.5	21.6(12,14)
1117	Screw mach. prod.	22.2	32.9	8.2(5,8)
1322	Foundries	25.2	32.9	5.8(8,9)
212	Wool & hair mfr.	24.2	32.9	1.8(7,9)
1302	Cash reg. & other bus. mach.	21.3	31.4	14.1(4)
904	Boots & shoes	26.0	30.8	7.5(12,14)
1318	Machine tool acc.	21.8	30.7	12.8(6)
105	Canned fruits & veg., etc.	22.7	30.4	7.5(9)
802	Rubber gds. (exc. tires, shoes)	19.2	28.5	11.5(3,5)
209	Rayon mfrs.	18.5	27.1	8.4
1004	Clay prods. & nonclay refract.	19.3	26.6	3.7(12,13)
102	Bread & bak. prods.	18.2	25.6	8.2 (21,22)
1648	Toys, playground equip.	16.6	25.6	17.1(3)
408	Paper goods, n.e.c.	14.2	23.7	12.4
1307	Machine tools	13.8	23.5	23.2(9,11)
1121	Stoves & ranges & warm air f.	16.1	23.0	14.4(5,6)
402	Boxes, paper	14.1	20.7	9.1(8,9)
112	Confectionary	12.5	19.9	17.0(9)
134	Liquors, malt	11.8	17.7	15.2(31,34)

Table   3-2 (cont.)

Census No.[a]	Industry	Concentration Ratio (1935)[b]		Profit Rate (Percent of Book Equity)[c] 1936-40
		4 Firm	8 Firm	
<u>1326</u>	Machine shops	8.7	14.6	19.1(7,9)
<u>203</u>	Cotton mfrs.	8.4	14.4	3.2(45,54)
<u>101</u>	Beverages nonalc.	8.7	13.2	12.5(6,9)
<u>309</u>	Furniture	5.6	8.8	7.5(7)

[a]Census number is underlined for those industries added to the Bain sample.

[b]National Resources Committee, *Structure of the American Economy*, 249-259 (1939).

[c]Joe S. Bain, "Relation of Profit Rate to Industry Concentration: American Manufacturing, 1936-1940," *Q.J. Econ. 312* (1951); Securities and Exchange Commission, Survey of American Listed Corporations, Data on Profits and Operations, 1936-1942 (1944), Moody's Industrials, various issues. Profit rate is underlined where it differs from that shown by Professor Bain. The difference occurs where a larger number of firms is used than that used by Professor Bain except for soap and typewriters. In the latter case, a weighted average of firm rates of return is substituted for the simple average used by Professor Bain. All other profit rates are weighted averages. Professor Bain's profit rate for the soap industry included cosmetics and toiletries firms. These were excluded for this computation. Figure in parentheses is the number of firms used to compute profit rate. Number of firms is not shown where Bain's rate of return could not be replicated using his data source.

[d]The roofing industry rate of return based on three companies is 9.4 percent. The fourth company evidently included by Bain had a 2.3 percent return, reducing the industry return to 7.4 percent. The fourth company (Certain-teed), however, was also the third largest firm in the gypsum industry (but was not used in calculating gypsum's rate of return). It would seem that it should be omitted in calculating roofing as well as having been omitted in calculating gypsum (or used in both places). We have, however, accepted Bain's figures for both these industries in the tabulation.

Table 3-2a
Less Concentrated Industries (Fewer than Three Firms)

<u>122</u>	Malt	44.6	65.5	19.1(2)
<u>1128</u>	Wrought pipe	47.4	64.8	2.9(1)
<u>319</u>	Wood preserving	50.5	60.2	18.7(1)
<u>411</u>	Wallpaper	41.4	58.9	2.1(1)
<u>1310</u>	Refrigerators	46.1	58.0	27.7(2)
<u>1642</u>	Sporting & athletic goods	36.0	47.2	−4.5(1)
306	Cooperate	25.9	40.5	13.3(1)
<u>118</u>	Ice cream	32.7	37.7	6.0(1)
135	Liquors, vinous	26.8	37.6	10.7(2)
114	Feeds, prepared	23.0	34.3	14.6(2)
<u>1624</u>	Mattresses	25.8	31.2	15.7(1)
<u>1606</u>	Buttons	15.4	27.0	12.4(1)
<u>1640</u>	Signs & adv. novelties	9.2	14.7	13.2(2)
<u>314</u>	Planing mills	4.6	8.1	7.7(2)
Average accounting profit rate on book equity				11.4

Table 3-3
Changes in 1936-40 Accounting Rates of Return from Those Shown by Bain

	Bain[a]	New Rates[b]
105 Canned fruits & veg.	7.4%(8,9)	7.5%(9)
113 Corn products	9.3 (3)	9.2 (4)
115 Flavoring extracts & sirups	1.8	41.5 (5,7)
222 Linoleum	9.0 (3)	8.4 (4,5)
629 Rayon	12.1	9.0 (8,9)
631 Soap	15.2 (8,10)	14.8 (4)
803 Rubber tires	8.2	8.0 (9,11)
907 Leather	0.8 (5)	2.1 (8)
1314 Typewriters	15.8 (4)	15.0 (4)
1315 Washing mach.	14.0	13.5 (6)
1325 Printers' machinery	2.2 (6)	2.9 (8)

[a]Joe S. Bain, supra Table 3-2, note c. Number of firms used by Bain shown in parentheses where it was possible to replicate from data in Securities and Exchange Commission, *Survey of American Listed Corporations, Data on Profits and Operations*, 1936-1942 (1944).
[b]See footnote c, Table 3-2.

In assembling the ninety-eight industry sample (in which no difference was found in rates of return between more and less concentrated industries), some industries have been excluded for the same reason Bain excluded some from his sample: in twenty-three industries, data could be found for only one or two firms. In the nine more than 70 percent concentrated (eight firm) excluded industries, however, the accounting rate of return is *less* than that in the fourteen less concentrated industries (Tables 3-1a and 3-2a). The return in the concentrated group of excluded industries is 10.6 percent while that in the less concentrated industries is 11.4 percent. The findings in the excluded group do *not* contradict the findings in the sample group.

There remain the Mann and Stigler findings using post World War II data to be explained. If competition is prevalent in concentrated industries, as is indicated by the convergence of rates of return on the average, why did Professors Mann and Stigler find a correlation at any given point in time between accounting profitability and concentration? Again, the non-representativeness of their small samples apparently accounts for their findings.

Professor James Ellert has examined the post war data using larger samples of industries. He was unable to find a dichotomous relationship. Using 141 industries with 565 firms he finds no significant difference between more and less concentrated industries in any postwar period. What differences there are frequently have the wrong sign [76].

Professor Ellert also examined the high stable concentration group of industries. His findings agree with mine. That is, the rate of return in the high stable group is not high, much less persistently high.

Table 3-4

Average of Industry Average Profit Rates Within Concentration Deciles (42 and 96 Industries), 1936-1940

Concentration Range Percent of Value Product Supplied by Eight Firms (1935) a	Number of Industries b	Average of Industry Profit Rates[a] 1936-1940 c	No. of Ind. d	Profit Rates[a] 1936-40 e
90-100	8	12.7%	14	10.0%
80-89.9	10	9.8	14	9.7
70-79.9	3	16.3	10	11.9
60-69.9	5	5.8	11	8.2
50-59.9	4	5.8	6	14.8
40-49.9	3	8.6	10	9.5
30-39.9	5	6.3	16	10.4
20-29.9	2	10.4	9	12.0
10-19.9	1	17.0	5	13.4
0-9.9	1	9.1	3	7.6
0-100	42	9.6	98	10.5
70-100	21	11.8	38	10.4
0-70	21	7.5	60	10.6
Difference		4.4		−0.2

Sources: Columns a, b, and c from Joe S. Bain, "Relation of Profit Rate to Industry Concentration: American Manufacturing, 1936-40," *Quarterly Journal of Economics*, 65 (1951), p. 313, as corrected in Corrigendum, *Quarterly Journal of Economics*, 65 (1951), p. 602. Columns d and e from Tables 3-1 and 3-2.

[a]Average of net profits after income taxes as percentage of net worth.

Differential Profitability and Resource Flows

A most interesting finding that emerged from a study of Bain's data was the relationship between rates of return in the Big Four in the industries he selected for his book on *Barriers to Competition* [18] and other firms in those industries. Where the Big Four showed higher accounting rates of return than smaller firms, they tended to grow more rapidly than their industries. Such behavior is that to be expected if the Big Four behave competitively and we can take intra-industry comparisons of accounting rates of return seriously. Where the Big Four showed lower accounting rates of return than smaller firms, they tended to grow less rapidly than their industries and concentration tended to decrease. [39]

This would seem to indicate that relatively high rates of return in manufacturing are manifestations of relative efficiency, if we can generalize from the inadequate sample of industries and firms provided by Bain. Resources flow from less efficient to more efficient firms. Manufacturing industry structure moves over time toward that dictated by an efficient allocation of resources.

Persistent high concentration, where it is found, is a consequence of the economies of scale or the relative efficiency of specific managerial groups.[8] Mandatory deconcentration would cause a loss of efficiency with no gain in the competitiveness of the economy.[9]

4

Industry Structure, Market Rivalry, and Public Policy *

Harold Demsetz**

Structure vs. Rivalry

Quantitative work in industrial organization has been directed mainly to the task of searching for monopoly even though a vast number of other interesting topics have been available to the student of economic organization. The motives for this preoccupation with monopoly are numerous, but important among them are the desire to be policy-relevant and the ease with which industrial concentration data can be secured. This paper first takes a critical view of contemporary doctrine in this area and then presents data which suggest that this doctrine offers a dangerous base upon which to build a public policy toward business.

The contemporary economic doctrine in this area rests upon an asserted close relationship between an industry's structure and the intensity of competition. The more concentrated is the structure, the more monopolistic is the behavior expected from the industry. The asserted relationship between structure and performance creates difficulties in the analysis of both monopoly and competition by obscuring the importance to the competitive process of rivalrous behavior. In order to contrast the competitive role of *structure* and that of *rivalry*, it will be useful initially to consider a change in output by one firm on the assumption that there is no rivalrous response from any of the other firms, i.e., that other firms continue, *a la* Cournot, to produce the same output rates, and then to compare this with a situation where rivalrous behavior is present.

In Figure 4-1 let D_M and MR_M represent the market demand and marginal revenue and let price and output be at P and Q_M. An increase in output equal to ΔQ will cause price to fall by ΔP. The price response of a change in output by a firm that is large relative to the market, then, is $\Delta P/\Delta Q$.

Now let Q_c measure the output rate of one of many small firms at price P and consider an equal increase in output, ΔQ. Since we are abstracting from the effect of rivalry, all other firms in the industry are assumed to continue to produce $Q_M - Q_c$, the amount they produced before the increase in the output of the one firm that we are now examining. The reduction in price that results must again be ΔP because industry output again must increase from Q_M to $Q_M + \Delta Q$.

With no rivalry, the demand curve facing one of many small firms will have the same negative slope as that which faces a single large firm producing the

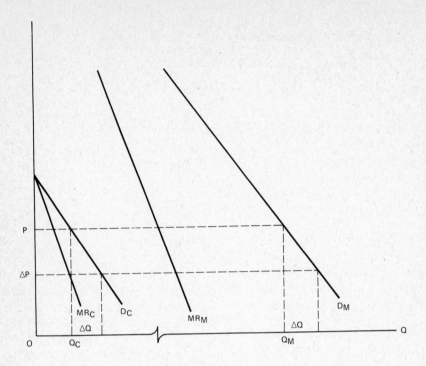

Figure 4-1. Comparative Price Responses to Output Changes.

entire industry output. No matter how large is the number of firms populating an atomistically structured industry, the price response, or demand curve slope, that faces one such firm, *in the absence of rivalry*, must be identical to that which faces the firm in a one-firm industry. *The demand curve facing a competitive firm does not become horizontal, nor does it become less steep, as the number of firms producing a given output rate is increased.* In the absence of rivalrous responses from other sellers, a relatively small firm has exactly as much influence on price as does a relatively large firm.

While the slope of the demand curve facing a firm, at any given prices, remains the same for different industry structures in the absence of rivalrous responses, the elasticity of the firm's demand does increase as the number of firms is increased. The demand slope, which remains unchanged, will be associated with smaller firm output rates as the number of firms is increased. Hence, in the absence of rivalry, for any given price and for any given marginal cost, a large firm will find an increase in output less rewarding than will a small firm.[1] The price reduction associated with output increase ΔQ in Figure 4-1 reduces the revenue obtainable from OQ_c units by ΔP per unit for the relatively small firm while, for the single large firm, this reduction in unit revenue will apply to OQ_M units, although both firms increase output at the new price by ΔQ. The increase in elasticity that is associated with dividing a given industry output among a larger number of smaller producers is mistakenly interpreted as an increase in the degree to which the firm's demand curve approximates the horizontal demand curve of a price-taker.[2] But this is a confusion between the increased elasticity that results from a leftward shift of demand and that which results from a rotation of the demand curve. Simply increasing the number of firms cannot alter the slope of the firm's demand curve nor can it yield marginal cost pricing so long as there is some small range of output over which the firm's average cost falls. The firm in an atomistically structured industry always retains an incentive to reduce output from the level that would equate price to marginal cost *in the absence of rivalrous response.*

Moreover, if all firms attempt to reduce output, each assuming that there will be no rivalrous response from others, the reduction in output for the industry as a whole will approximate the reduction that would have been brought about simply by monopolizing the industry. Each firm, after the initial decrease in output, might then need to adjust its beliefs about the demand that it faces and the analysis is quickly carried into unresolved dynamic problems. Nonetheless, the point is that even if an industry is assumed to be atomistically structured, with each firm viewing its output decision as having no repercussions on the decisions of others, that is, with the standard assumptions of the classical competitive model, it is possible to produce a monopoly rate of output (in the absence of rivalrous behavior).

What then is the main source of difference between monopoly and competition? It is not to be found in the bare arithmetic of relative size but in the reaction of rivals to output changes. The classical notion of perfect competition leads us to slight this source of difference. In the monopoly case, by definition, no expansion of output by rivals takes place, but in the competitive case, an attempt to raise price causes output to expand enough to bring price back to its equilibrium level. It is not the relative size of the firm that tends to make it a price taker but the inclination of rivals to negate any effect on price by an opposite and, in equilibrium, equal change in quantity. The rivalrous behavior of other firms imposes losses on a firm that departs from a rate of output that equates price and marginal cost. If the firm reduces output, its losses are increased by rivals whose action will tend to hold price to its equilibrium level. This distinction between monopoly and competition retains the importance of intensely rivalrous behavior at the same time that it allows the analysis to assume that the competitor is a price-taker. He acts as if he is a price-taker precisely because of the intense rivalry that quickly negates any effect on price that a change in his output would otherwise cause.

It is misleading to claim that rivalry is absent in highly atomistic market structures when what probably is meant is that competitive behavior does not require rivals to know who it is that their behavior harms or benefits. Intensive economic competition may not require such detailed knowledge but it does require rivalrous responses to price, quality, or output changes that otherwise would yield profits. The farmer behaves in a rivalrous fashion when he chooses to market his grain at one country elevator rather than another, or when he sells to the terminal market or cereal producer instead of to the country elevator. He is expanding output in that submarket in which he believes the return is highest. In the process of choosing he may or may not bargain at a personal level with the owner of the local elevator and he may or may not realize that by some quantum he is reducing the return to other sellers in the market in which he chooses to sell; these aspects of his behavior concern only the *manner* in which he carries on his rivalry or the knowledge he possesses about the consequences of his behavior. Whatever is true with regard to these matters, *his decision to sell dear and to buy cheap must be considered rivalrous behavior from the viewpoint of economics.*

Similarly, competitors may be very knowledgeable about the consequences of their behavior in oligopolistic situations, but it is not possible with present theory to deduce from the existence of this knowledge that rivalry yields a less efficient allocation of resources than that which obtains when rivals cannot fathom some of the consequences of their behavior. All that can be deduced is that knowledge of these consequences comes more cheaply in the one case than in the other.

The rivalrous behavior that *is* competition comes from both existing producers of a product and prospective producers. It is revealed by the willingness and ability of either group to undertake expansions in output when price rises. The concept of perfect competition, with its emphasis on the existence of many small producing firms has provided a cloak of theoretical respectability for the notion that a highly developed theoretical link between industrial concentration and monopoly power exists. An industry with few firms may face more effective rivalry from prospective sellers than an industry with many firms. An attempt to raise the price of chewing gum, which is produced by a highly concentrated industry, may very well fail because new suppliers can enter easily. On the other hand, successful corners of an agricultural commodity have been achieved despite the openness of exchange and the active participation of very many traders because, once harvested, it is difficult to augment the supply of a crop until the next growing season. Hence, any trader astute enough to gain control of the existing supply may be able to enjoy a monopoly return. The natural obstacle to short-term increases in supply of agricultural commodities makes withholding actions to raise prices in the short-run sufficiently probable, even in the context of an atomistic structure of trading, that the commodity exchanges have found it desirable to adopt a variety of rules and regulations to reduce the probability of successful corners.

What we call the theory of monopoly is a logical apparatus for deducing the behavior of the firm *if* the firm has monopoly power. The classical theory of monopoly is not an explanation of how monopoly power arises but how it will be exercised once obtained. Because we have no theory of the source of monopoly power, we have grasped the key structural assumption of the monopoly model—the *one* firm industry—to identify the source of real-world monopoly power. But the proper theoretical role of this assumption is to facilitate thinking about the exercise of existing monopoly power and it should not be confused with the empirical description of a monopoly; it is merely a short hand way of assuming the *absence of rivalry*. Monopoly theory offers no reason to suppose that an actual one firm industry has monopoly power if there are no detectable effective entry barriers. It may be that this firm merely does a superior job of producing and marketing its product. Indeed, this is precisely the conclusion (to be discussed in more detail below) to which a theory of industrial structure based on rivalry would point in the absence of entry restrictions. The single firm assumption of monopoly theory merely says that rivalry can be ignored in predicting behavior, and the theory is abused when the one firm assumption is interpreted literally as the structural precondition of monopoly.[3]

Concentration Through Competition

Under the pressure of competitive rivalry, and in the apparent absence of effective barriers to entry, it would seem that the concentration of an industry's output in a few firms could only derive from their superiority in producing and marketing products or in the superiority of a structure of industry in which there are only a few firms. In a world in which information and resource mobility can be secured only at a cost, an industry becomes more concentrated under competitive conditions only if a differential advantage in expanding output develops in some firms. Such expansion will increase the degree of concentration at the same time that it increases the rate of return that these firms earn. The cost advantage that gives rise to increased concentration may be reflected in scale economies or in downward shifts in positively sloped marginal cost curves, or it may be reflected in better products which satisfy demand at a lower cost. New efficiencies can, of course, arise in other ways. Some firms might discover ways of lowering cost that require that firms become smaller, so that spinoffs might be in order. In such cases, smaller firms will tend to earn relatively high rates of return. Which type of new efficiency arises most frequently is a question of fact.

Such profits need not be eliminated soon by competition. It may well be that superior competitive performance is unique to the firm, viewed as a team, and unobtainable to others except by purchasing the firm itself. In this case the return to superior performance is in the nature of a gain that is completely captured by the owner of the firm itself, not by its inputs.[4] Here, although the industry structure may change because as the superior firm grows, the resulting increase in profit cannot easily serve to guide competitors to similar success. The firm may have established a reputation or goodwill that is difficult to separate from the firm itself and which should be carried at higher value on its books. Or it may be that the members of the employee team derive their higher productivity from the knowledge they possess about each other in the environment of the particular firm in which they work, a source of productivity that may be difficult to transfer piecemeal. It should be remembered that we are discussing complex, large enterprises, many larger (and more productive) than entire nations. One such enterprise happens to "click" for some time and while others do not. It may be very difficult for these firms to understand the reasons for this difference in performance or to know which inputs are responsible for the performance of the successful firm. It is not easy to ascertain just why G.M. and I.B.M. perform better than their competitors. The complexity of these organizations defies easy analysis, so that the inputs responsible for success may be undervalued by the market for some time. By the same token, inputs owned by complex, unsuccessful firms may be overvalued for some time. The success of firms will be reflected in higher returns and stock prices, not higher input prices, and lack of success will be recorded in lower returns and stock prices, not lower input prices.

Moreover, inputs are acquired at historic cost, but the use made of these inputs, including the managerial inputs, yields only uncertain outcomes. Because the outcomes of managerial decisions are surrounded by uncertainty and are specific to a particular firm at a particular point in its history, the acquisition cost of inputs may fail to reflect their value to the firm at some subsequent time. By the time their value to the firm is recognized, they are beyond acquisition by other firms at the same historic cost, and, in the interim, shareholders of the successful or lucky firm will have enjoyed higher profit rates. When nature cooperates to make such decisions correct, they can give rise to high accounting returns for several years or to a once and for all capital gain, if accountants could value *a priori* decisions that turn out to be correct *ex post*. During the period when such decisions determine the course of events, output will tend to be concentrated in those firms fortunate enough to have made the correct decisions.

None of this is necessarily monopolistic (although monopoly may play some role). Profit does not arise because the firm creates "artificial scarcity" through a reduction in its output. Nor does it arise because of collusion. Superior performance can be attributed to the combination of great uncertainty plus luck or atypical insight by the management of a firm. It is not until the experiments are actually tried that we learn which succeed and which fail. By the time the results are in, it is the shareholder that has captured (some of) the value, positive or negative, of past decisions. Even though the profits that arise from a firm's activities may be eroded by competitive imitation, since information is costly to obtain and techniques are difficult to duplicate, the firm may enjoy growth and a superior rate of return for some time.

Superior ability also may be interpreted as a competitive basis for acquiring a measure of monopoly power. In a world in which information is costly and the future is uncertain, a firm that seizes an opportunity to better serve customers does so because it expects to enjoy some protection from rivals because of their ignorance of this opportunity or because of their inability to imitate quickly. One possible source of some monopoly power is superior entrepreneurship. Our patent, copyright, and trademark laws explicitly provide as a reward for uncovering new methods (and for revealing these methods) legal protection against free imitation. It may be true in some cases that an astute rival acquires the exclusive rights to some resource that *later* becomes valuable. There is no reason to suppose that competitive behavior never yields monopoly power, although in many cases such power may be exercised not by creating entry barriers, but through the natural frictions and ignorance that characterize any real economy. If rivals seek better ways to satisfy buyers or to produce a product, and if one or a few succeed in such endeavors, then the reward for their entrepreneurial efforts is likely to be some (short term) monopoly power and this may be associated with increased industrial concentration. To destroy such power when it arises may very well remove the incentive for progress. This is to be contrasted with a situation in which a high rate of return is obtained through a successful *collusion* to restrict output; here there is less danger to progress if the collusive agreement is penalized. Evidence presented below suggests that there are definite dangers of decreasing efficiency through the use of deconcentration or anti-merger policies.

Inefficiency Through Anti-Concentration Public Policy

The discussion in the second section noted that concentration may be brought about because a workable system of incentives implies that firms better serving buyers will tend to grow relative to other firms. One way in which a firm could better serve buyers is by seizing opportunities to exploit scale economics, although if scale economics are the main course of concentration, it is difficult to understand why there is no significant trend toward one-firm industries; the lack of such a trend seems to suggest that superiority results in lower but *positively* sloped cost curves in the relevant range of large firm operations. This would set limits to the size of even the successful firms. Successful firms thus would seem to be more closely related to the "superior land" of classical economic rent analysis than they do to the single firm of natural monopoly theory. Whether or not superiority is reflected in scale economics, deconcentration may have the total effect of promoting inefficiency even though it also may reduce some monopoly-caused inefficiencies.[5]

The classic portrayal of the inefficiency produced by concentration through the exercise of monopoly power is that of a group of firms cooperating to somehow restrict entry and prevent rivalrous price behavior. Successfully pursued, this policy results in a product price and rate of return in excess of that which would have prevailed in the absence of collusion. However, if all firms are able to produce at the same cost, then the rate of return to successfully colluding firms should be independent of the particular sizes adopted by these firms to achieve low cost production. One firm may require a small scale, and hence have a smaller investment, while another may require a large scale and corresponding large investment. At any given collusive price, the absolute amounts of monopoly profits will be proportional to output, but capital investment also will be proportionate to output, so we can expect the rate of return to be invariant with respect to size of firm.

If one size of firm earns a higher rate of return than another size, given any collusive price, then there must exist differences in the cost of production which favor the firm that earns the higher rate of return. Alternatively, if there is no single price upon which the industry agrees, but, rather a range of prices, then one firm can earn a higher rate of return if it produces a superior product and sells it at a higher price without thereby incurring proportionately higher costs; here, also, the firm that earns the higher rate of return can be judged to be more efficient because it delivers more value per dollar of cost incurred.

A deconcentration or antimerger policy is more likely to have benign results if small firms in concentrated industries earn the same or higher rates of return than large firms, for, then, deconcentration may reduce collusion,[6] if it is present, while simultaneously allocating larger shares of industry output to smaller firms which are no less efficient than larger firms. But if increased concentration has come about because of the superior efficiency of those firms that have become large, then a deconcentration policy, while it may reduce the ease of colluding, courts the danger of reducing efficiency either by the penalties that it places on innovative success or by the shift in output to the higher cost, smaller firms that it brings about. This would seem to be a distinct possibility if large firms in concentrated industries earn higher rates of return than small firms.

The problem posed is how to organize data to shed light on the probability that deconcentration will promote inefficiency. Correlating industry rate of return with concentration will not be enlightening for this problem, for even if concentrated industries exhibit higher rates of return, it is difficult to determine whether it is efficiency or monopoly power that is at work. Similarly, large firms would tend to earn high profit rates in concentrated industries either because they are efficient or because they are colluding. However, partitioning industry data by size of firm does suggest that there exists a real danger from a deconcentration or anti-merger public policy, for the rates of return earned by small firms give no support to the doctrine relating collusion to concentration. A successful collusion is very likely to benefit the smaller firms, and this suggests that there should be a positive correlation between the rate of return earned by small firms and the degree to which the industry is concentrated. By the same token, if efficiency is associated with concentration, there should be a positive correlation between concentration and the difference between the rate of return earned by large firms and that earned by small firms, i.e., large firms have become large because they are more efficient than other firms and are able to earn a higher rate of return than other firms.

Tables 4-1 and 4-2 show 1963 rates of return based on internal revenue data partitioned by size of firm and industry concentration for ninety-five three-digit industries. In these tables, C_{63} designates the four-firm concentration ratio measured on industry sales, R_1, R_2, R_3, and R_4, respectively, measure accounting rates of return, (profit plus interest)/total assets, for firms with asset value less than \$500,000, \$500,000 to \$5,000,000, \$5,000,000 to \$50,000,000, and over \$50,000,000. Table 4-1 is calculated by assigning equal weight to all industries. It is based, therefore, on the assumption that each industry, regardless of size, offers an equally good observational unit for comparing the efficiency and monopolistic aspects of industry structure. Table 4-2 presents the same basic data with accounting rates of return weighted by asset value. Hence, an industry

Table 4-1
Rates of Return by Size and Concentration (Unweighted)

C_{63}	No. of Industries	R_1	R_2	R_3	R_4	$\bar{R}$
10-20%	14	6.7%	9.0%	10.8%	10.3%	9.2%
20-30	22	4.5	9.1	9.7	10.4	8.4
30-40	24	5.2	8.7	9.9	11.0	8.7
40-50	21	5.8	9.0	9.5	9.0	8.3
50-60	11	6.7	9.8	10.5	13.4	10.1
Over 60	3	5.3	10.1	11.5	23.1	12.5

Table 4-2
Rates of Return by Size and Concentration (Weighted by Assets)

C_{63}	No. of Industries	R_1	R_2	R_3	R_4	$\bar{R}$
10-20%	14	7.3%	9.5%	10.6%	8.0%	8.8%
20-30	22	4.4	8.6	9.9	10.6	8.4
30-40	24	5.1	9.0	9.4	11.7	8.8
40-50	21	4.8	9.5	11.2	9.4	8.7
50-60	11	0.9	9.6	10.8	12.2	8.4
Over 60	3	5.0	8.6	10.3	21.6	11.3

with many assets owned by small firms receives a larger weight in calculating the small firm rate of return for a given interval of concentration ratios.

Both tables fail to reveal the beneficial effects to small firms that we would expect from an association of collusion and industry concentration. The rate of return earned by firms in the smallest asset size does not increase with concentration. This seems to be true for the next two larger asset size classifications also, although in Table 4-1 the 11.5 percent earned by R_3 firms in industries with concentration ratios higher than 60 percent offers some indication of a larger rate of return than in less concentrated industries.[7] The data do not seem to support the notion that concentration and collusion are closely related, and, therefore, it is difficult to remain optimistic about the beneficial efficiency effects of a deconcentration or anti-merger public policy. On the contrary, the data suggest that such policies will reduce efficiency by impairing the survival of large firms in concentrated industries, for these firms do seem better able to produce at lower cost than their competitors.[8] Both tables indicate that R_4 size firms in industries with concentration ratios greater than 50 percent produce at lower average cost.

Since a larger fraction of industry output is produced by larger firms in the more concentrated industries, these industries should exhibit higher rates of return than other industries. That this is so can be seen from the unweighted row averages given by column $\bar{R}$. Industries with $C_{63} > 50$ percent seem to have earned higher rates of return than less concentrated industries. But this result, which is consistent with some earlier studies, may be attributed to the superior performance of the larger firms and not to collusive practices. Table 4-2 reveals this pattern even more clearly. Because the rates of return of smaller firms receive a larger weight (by total assets) in Table 4-2, industry rates of return are reduced even for concentrated industries in which large firms continue to perform well.

The general pattern of these data can be seen in Table 4-3. The results of regressing differences in profit rates on concentration ratios are shown in this

Table 4-3
Differential Rates of Return by Firm Size Class Related to Concentration

$$R_4 - R_1 = -1.4 + .21{*}C_{63} \qquad r^2 = .09$$
$$(.07)$$

$$R_4 - R_2 = -2.6 + .12{**}C_{63} \qquad r^2 = .04$$
$$(.06)$$

$$R_4 - R_3 = -3.1 + .10{**}C_{63} \qquad r^2 = .04$$
$$(.05)$$

*,** significant at the 1% and 5% levels respectively.
Standard errors are shown in parenthesis.

table. These regressions reveal a significant positive relationship between concentration and differences in rates of return, especially when comparing the largest and smallest firms in an industry.[9] The three regressions taken together indicate a nonlinear, decreasing impact of concentration on relative rates of return as the size of the smaller firms is increased from R_1 to R_3.

The competitive view of industry structure suggests that rapid changes in concentration are brought about by changed cost conditions and not by alternations in the height of entry barriers. Industries experiencing rapid increases in concentration should exhibit greater disparities between large and small rates of return because of the more significant cost differences which are the root cause of rapid alternations in industry structure. The monopoly view of concentration does not imply such a relationship, for if an industry is rapidly achieving workable collusive practices there is no reason to suppose that the difference between large and small firm profit rates should increase. At the time of writing, matching data on concentration were available for both 1963 and 1967. This time span is too short to reveal much variation in concentration ratios, and so we cannot be very confident about evidence gained by regressing differences in profit rates on changes in concentration ratios. However, the persistently positive coefficient of the variable $C_{67} - C_{63}$ in Table 4-4 is consistent with the competitive viewpoint, and must increase our doubts, however slightly, about the beneficial effects of an active deconcentration or anti-merger policy.

Table 4-4
Differential Rates of Return by Firm Size Class Related to Changes in Concentration

$$R_4 - R_1 = \;\; 1.5 + .21^*C_{63} + .21(C_{67} - C_{63}) \qquad r^2 = .09$$
$$(.07) \qquad (.42)$$

$$R_4 - R_2 = -2.9 + .12^{**}C_{63} + .37(C_{67} - C_{63}) \qquad r^2 = .06$$
$$(.06) \qquad (.28)$$

$$R_4 - R_3 = -3.4 + .10^{**}C_{63} + .29(C_{67} - C_{63}) \qquad r^2 = .05$$
$$(.05) \qquad (.24)$$

*,**, respectively, 1 percent and 5 percent confidence levels.

Summary

The first part of this paper criticized the doctrine which asserts that a positive relationship exists between industry concentration and monopoly power, and then discussed problems posed by this relationship for both the theory of competition and the theory of monopoly. The concept of rivalry was shown to be implied by the horizontal demand curves of competitive theory. Rivalry, or its absence, seems to be the main conceptual difference between competition and monopoly, and this difference is not necessarily a function of industry structure. An alternative explanation of industry structure and profitability, based on competitive superiority, was then discussed. The problem faced by a deconcentration or anti-merger policy was posed on the basis of this alternative explanation of industry structure. Is there a danger that such a policy will produce more inefficiency than it eliminates? The data presented suggest that this danger should be taken seriously.

5 The Concentration-Profits Relationship*

Lee E. Preston

Any empirical investigation of the relationship between industry or market concentration and indicators of firm or industry profitability is subject to severe limitations and qualifications. We must assume that the economic groupings under analysis have been appropriately defined, and the relative importance of individual business units within each grouping appropriately measured. We must further assume that patterns of market performance arising from structural conditions on the supply side are not fully offset by conditions on the demand side, or by technological change, government intervention, or some other important aspects of the situation excluded from the empirical analysis.

Even if these basic conditions are satisfactorily met—and if accounting measures of revenues, costs, and investment can be accepted as accurate—it is quite clear that new knowledge of the relationship between industry structure and performance cannot be gained by oversimplified and monistic data manipulation. On the contrary, multi-variate and multi-equation analyses utilizing large and carefully screened collections of data permit these analytical issues to be pursued at a much higher level of sophistication. As such studies—such as the study now under way by Weston and his associates at UCLA—progress, a good deal more will be discovered about the circumstances in which measured concentration and profitability do exhibit some association. Probably other circumstances in which no association is to be found will also be identified. Discrimination between these two situations, and identification of the factors associated with each, was the goal of most of the Collins-Preston studies. It is a pleasure to see this work now being carried on on a larger scale, with greater resources, and by more sophisticated analysts.

If new and comprehensive investigations show that there is no association at all to be found between concentration and profitability in a large and appropriately categorized and analyzed collection of data, then the whole structure-performance analysis may be called into question or relegated to the category of hypothetical but untestable notions. But, frankly I doubt that the conclusions will be that surprising. At any rate, until new results are forthcoming, I shall continue to take seriously the conclusions of the very large and diverse body of studies of this topic in the literature—that is, that some association between profitability and concentration tends to be discovered in virtually all broadly selected samples of industry and firm data (even in an interesting sample of data from India that has just come to my attention!).

A different and much more important question is that of relevance. Let us suppose that there *is* a significant statistical association between measured concentration and reported indicators of profitability in some substantial group or subcategory of industries. Some people would jump immediately to the conclusion that undesirable monopoly conditions exist in all of these instances. Others would see unmistakable evidence of scale economies. Still others would proceed to a systematic analysis of the factors that might have contributed to this result. I should like to endorse the efforts of the last group, both as the appropriate research approach and as the basis for public policy formation. Efficiency may well be an important cause of monopoly, but it is certainly not the only possible cause. And even if monopoly is due to efficiency, the presence of above-normal profits indicates that the benefits of efficiency are being retained by the monopoly, rather than distributed to society at large. If a more competitive structure could achieve the same level of efficiency and pass the benefits on to customers in lower prices, then high-concentration, high-profit industries would appear "undesirable" from the viewpoint of a social policy. If, on the contrary, a more competitive structure could not achieve the same level of efficiency, then of course a case of "natural monopoly" (or oligopoly) would have been identified, and regulatory measures (or "confiscatory" tax measures) may need to be established accordingly. Whatever the facts, and whatever the policy alternatives, they are surely matters for open scrutiny and analysis, rather than for simple assertion or rejection on ideological grounds.

The contrary approach holds that nothing can be learned from this type of study because the data themselves are simply inappropriate to the questions being asked. We are all familiar enough with the deficiencies in accounting and other statistical reports. No one will argue that available reported data are accurate measures of "economic profits." The question really is whether reported data are sufficiently well correlated with "economic profit"—both as to *relative* level and as to *direction* of change—that they can be used as proxies for the desired measure for analytical purposes. While making a strong plea for the improvement and greater disclosure of appropriate data, I cannot entirely disbelieve that there is some relationship between the data reported and the data that "matter" in an analytical sense. For one thing, the goals of corporate executives and stockholders are stated and evaluated in terms of these available revenue, margin, and profit figures. Further, most of these data are made to look better by increases in economic revenues and decreases in economic (to the unit involved) costs. Hence, I shall continue to take seriously (although with some appropriate reservations) the type of results that are produced by the analysis of this data.

Combining into a single issue the problem of the facts themselves as well as their possible relevance, let me restate the question I attempted to raise with

Professors Brozen and Demsetz at the Conference: Is it *in principle* possible that situations corresponding to the price-increasing and output-reducing occurrences associated with the economic concept of "monopoly" exist anywhere in the economy? If it is *in principle* possible that such situations exist, by what indicia are they to be identified? (Or conversely, by what indicia is their absence revealed?) Clearly, if the concept of economic monopoly is dismissed as imaginary, there is no empirical or analytical matter to discuss. If the concept of economic monopoly is not imaginary, however, we shall probably continue to test for it with the same types of indicators that have proven effective in the past—that is, indicators of market share and profitability. Since these indicators so readily identify situations like automobiles, cereals, chewing gum, chocolates, cigarettes, flat glass, metal cans, matches, etc., etc., that upon closer examination do indeed reveal monopoloid characteristics of various sorts, I doubt that this traditional approach can be summarily rejected as incorrect. It is no answer to cite the "unconcentrated monopolies" (i.e., the taxi medallions and the retail pharmacies) as if they provided counter-examples. On the contrary, these license-based monopolies are distinguished from licensed competitive activities precisely by their tendency to restrict output and raise prices—the indicia of monopoly suggested by traditional theory and modern econometrics.

6 Concentration and Profits*

Stanley I. Ornstein†

The traditional hypothesis on concentration and profitability states that as concentration increases the likelihood of collusion increases, leading to higher profits in highly concentrated industries than in moderate or low concentration industries. Concentration ratios serve as a proxy for collusion since it is assumed that as concentration increases the cost of collusion decreases relative to the cost of remaining independent. The latest known count found thirty-two tests of this hypothesis with thirty-one finding a weak but statistically significant positive relationship between concentration and profits [248]. Many have accepted the evidence as confirmation of the hypothesis, regarding highly concentrated industries as monopolistic.[1] Few, however, have held that collusion is an ubiquitous feature of oligopolistic industries. Rather, most have argued that oligopolistic industries are characterized by "weak" competitive pressures.

Recently, the apparent unanimity of opinion has been challenged by articles questioning the significance of previous results [215, 38]. The purpose of this paper is to reexamine the traditional hypothesis, analyze some of the empirical problems with previous studies, and offer some new evidence on the relationship between profits and concentration in conjunction with other structural variables.

Traditional Hypothesis

The theory of pure competition and monopoly does not provide a basis for the traditional hypothesis that with few rivals a firm will earn above average profits. Unanticipated changes in demand and cost or high risk industries may lead to above average profits in competitive industries and result in differential returns both within and between high and low concentration industries. The extent of these differential returns in competitive industries depends on the lag in adjustment to initial disequilibrium and the extent of and adjustment to subsequent disequilibrium. Hence, above average returns may persist in competitive industries for long periods of time given sufficient disequilibriums, or a monopoly may experience below average profits for long periods depending on demand and cost conditions. Hence, in the long run monopoly is necessary but not sufficient for above average profits as between a competitive and monopolist industry.

With few rivals, predictions on the size of long-run profit rates are even more tenuous. There is as yet no widely accepted theory of oligopoly with the exception of dominant firm price leadership, which, at best, is applicable to a few industries, that would lead one to expect a positive relationship between concentration and profits [222]. The general expectation is that the cost of colluding decreases as the number of colluders grows smaller. This is due to lower cost of negotiations, coordination, enforcement, and the degree of interdependency increases the fewer the rivals—leading to a greater likelihood of mutual forebearance of short-run monopoly pricing. However, the instability of collusive agreements, both tacit and overt, increases with such variables as the extent of product heterogeneity, nonprice competition, differing firm cost structures, differing market shares, potential entry, and returns to cheating on agreements. Without a complete theory of oligopoly relating the cost of collusion, concentration, and the cost of competing, it is a heroic assumption to simply relate concentration and collusion.

The traditional hypothesis is also based on a somewhat restrictive view of the competitive process; viz., competition through price adjustment. As is commonly stated, but rarely given sufficient weight, competition extends well beyond changes in price. Competitive behavior does not necessarily disappear nor tend to diminish merely because fewer firms constitute the bulk of an industry's output, and in some cases, may actually be enhanced by such a development [108]. For example, technological change may lead to a change in structure without a decrease in competitive behavior. In fact, many industries such as computers, electronics, pharmaceuticals, and scientific instruments are seen to be vigorous competitors in research and development for new technologies, inventions, and innovations. Competition in more traditional non-price areas as customer service, credit, product quality, product variation, location, and advertising effort may raise average cost to the level where close to competitive profits are earned, that is, assuming a noncompetitive price, excess profits will not necessarily appear.[2] It is also generally assumed that nonprice competition within an industry is an inverse function of the number of firms, e.g., a firm can internalize more of the externalities of advertising the fewer its rivals [200]. The importance and extent of nonprice competition as a disciplinary factor is most vividly displayed in industries where price is legally fixed but firms are free to compete in other areas. For example, in transportation strong competition stems from service differences between alternative modes and has been a major factor in the secular decline of railroads [253].

Deficiencies in Methods of Prior Studies

Empirical problems that may vitiate previous results fall into two main categories: 1) errors in measurement in Census figures and accounting profit rates, and 2) misspecification of the concentration-profit relationship by ignoring variables related to both concentration and profits in the same manner.

Problems with Census data are manifold but the main difficulty for present purposes is that Census industries are classified according to supply characteristics with no regard to the demand side of the market, and thus may have little correspondence with economic markets. The merits of Census concentration ratios have also been attacked (as well as the theoretical relevancy of concentration) but attempts to provide a basis upon which to choose between alternative measures have been inconclusive [194, 125, 98]. Caution must be exercised in interpreting results based on Census measures until the significance of the distortion manifest by poor industry classifications and theoretically irrelevant concentration measures are analyzed.

In similar fashion much criticism has been leveled at accounting profit rates as being at variance with true or permanent economic profits due to distortions caused by tax laws and arbitrary accounting conventions. The importance of this problem is most apparent when attempting to account for disequilibrium conditions. Long-run profit rates are required to test the concentration-profit relationship rather than short-run accounting profits reflecting disequilibrium conditions. For example, Stigler has shown that the correlation between industry profit rates deteriorates over time [221]. It is also known that industry concentration ratios are relatively stable over time. If concentration and profits are perfectly related in one year, it is likely that profits, say ten years hence, would be unrelated to initial year concentration, but it is precisely this relationship that is hypothesized. A recent study by Brozen on the persistence of profit rate differentials identified by concentration levels has provided dramatic evidence of the tendency of above average and below average profit rates to converge to the average over time [38]. This evidence suggests that previous tests examined the wrong variable, viz., current accounting profits.

The second problem is that concentration may be masking effects of other variables which are related to both concentration and profit rates and can account for the generally weak but significant relationship usually found. Part of the relationship may be due to large firm effects. Since an industry average profit rate is the weighted average of its member firm profit rates, the largest firms will have the greatest weight. If large firms have higher profit rates than all other firms in an industry, due, for example, to economies of scale, lower costs of money capital, and a wider range of available profitable opportunities, then concentration of the four largest firms is necessarily related to average industry profit rate. Concentration measures the bias induced by large firms in average industry profit rates, or concentration acts as a proxy for the weight given profits of large firms. A potential spurious correlation is induced by this large firm effect and some empirical evidence indicates it may be substantial [51, 99, 13].

A second variable tending to obscure the concentration-profit relationship is the amount of advertising in each firm. A spurious correlation is expected between advertising and profit rates since advertising is not capitalized and thus measured profit rates may be overstated the greater advertising capital. However, even after allowing for this spurious correlation there appears to be a significant correlation between advertising and profitability, and to the extent that concentration and advertising are related, the traditional hypothesis is further weakened [247]. In addition, the largest firms are generally the absolute largest advertisers in an industry, further contributing to the possibility of concentration identifying large firm effects in average industry profit rates.

Nature of the Present Study

This study attempts to correct for two of the above criticisms by 1) adopting a stock market value measure of profitability to closer approximate permanent or long-run profits, and 2) eliminate potential spurious correlation due to large firm effects by examining individual profit rates of the largest firms in each industry.

This study follows Grunfeld and Peltzman in using stock market prices, representing the discounted value of all future earnings, as a less biased measure of long-run profits and less susceptible to transitory changes than current accounting profits [94, 184]. The stock market price is the price investors are willing to pay for claims to future earnings and as such reflects what investors expect future profits to be. The effect of transitory influences on stock prices is small relative to their effect on current profits. The dominant influences in effecting changes in the stock market value of a firm are permanent changes in current profits. Given this interpretation, an operational measure relating market value (MV), expected future earnings (R_i), and an appropriate discount rate (r) can be derived as follows:

$$MV = \sum_{i=1}^{\infty} \frac{R_i}{(1+r)^i} = \frac{R}{r} \tag{1}$$

Dividing by an appropriate capital base (K), the expected annual profit rate (π) becomes:

$$\pi = \frac{R}{K} = \frac{(MV)(r)}{K} \tag{2}$$

Adding a measure of capital introduces some of the defects inherent in accounting profit rates such as not capitalizing certain long-lived expenses. Nevertheless, this measure still avoids some of the difficulties of accounting rates since market value is a function of expectations based on permanent changes so that accounting rates may be negative while market values remain positive.

The sample selected was composed of the largest firms in each industry which have been shown elsewhere to have higher profit rates than small firms and thus tend to bias industry average profits upward. By examining inter-firm variations in profit rates this effect is eliminated.

Sample Selected

The sample tested consists of 131 non-randomly chosen U.S. manufacturing firms covering thirty-three SIC four-digit industries.[3] The firms listed by industry are shown in the appendix. To qualify for inclusion firms had to be publicly held, have assets in excess of one million dollars, and at least 50 percent of sales in the product category of their respective industry from 1947 to 1960. Increasing diversification through merger and internal expansion eliminated numerous publicly held firms from consideration, since 50 percent of sales were not maintained in the same product line over the 14-year span. For similar reasons sample size decreased rapidly after 1960, so the analysis was not carried beyond that year. The results are thus comparable to most previous studies which relied predominantly on data from the 1950s.

Variables Tested in the Present Study

The test procedure is to regress structural variables on profit rates to examine their joint and separate effects. Inter-firm variations in profit rates for three periods, 1950, 1955, and 1960, are examined as a function of: seller concentration, geographic dispersion, relative firm size, economies of scale in production, entry capital requirements, changes in firm and industry demand, changes in labor cost, capital-labor ratios, and consumer versus producer good industries.[4] Each of the variables tested will be discussed in turn. Data sources and measures of each variable are described in Appendix B on pages 253-257.

Concentration Ratios and Geographic Dispersion

In light of above comments, the theoretical significance of concentration ratios is in doubt. However, assuming that concentration ratios are an adequate surrogate measure of collusion, that is, buyers not switching between firms, entry into such an industry would most likely occur long before a joint profit maximum price-output position has been reached. Thus the basic prerequisite for long-run excess profits is strong control of entry and not concentration. Concentration, if anything, is a by-product of effective entry restrictions since large economics of scale, large capital requirements, and control of certain types of scarce resources would generally lead to a small number of large firms controlling an industry's output.

It is hypothesized that concentration ratios and firm profit rates are independent and that levels of concentration can be explained by interindustry differences in economies of scale relative to market size and absolute cost requirements for entry. Entry conditions explain the persistence of excess profit rates and also levels of concentration in industries where economies of scale and absolute capital requirements for entry are relatively large. Therefore, there should be some positive relationship between concentration and profitability due to this condition of collinearity.

This study used four-firm Census value of shipments concentration ratios and the measure of geographic dispersion developed by Collins and Preston [50]. The latter measure identifies regional markets by assuming demand is distributed in proportion to population and summing the absolute difference in the percent of value of shipments and population in each Census region. A small absolute difference indicates regional markets and vice versa. Under the traditional hypothesis a negative relationship between geographic dispersion and profit rates is expected since it is assumed that national concentration ratios understate true concentration where regional markets predominate. However, this study hypothesized no relationship between concentration and profit and thus none between geographic dispersion and profits.

Firm Size

Firm size is measured by total assets and assets relative to total industry size in value added (industry assets were not available for each year examined). The relationship of profits to firm size has been studied in numerous articles and books with investigators finding positive, negative, and no relationship between the variables.[5] Since this study is restricted to the largest firms within each industry, no significant cross-sectional relationship is expected. However, over the decade of the 1950s average size of firm in the sample tested increased while average return on equity decreased.

Barriers to Entry

Economic theory credits the persistence of long-run profit rates in excess of competitive levels to barriers to competition from new entrants and a lack of increased output from extant suppliers. Barriers to entry impose costs on entrants not incurred by extant firms such that the cost of entry and operating to a new entrant is greater than the present value of future expected returns.

Objective measures of barriers between industries and within industries are difficult to generate. To avoid the subjective indexes commonly employed, this study restricted barriers to economies of scale in production and entry capital requirements since some rough measures of these exist. Economies of scale are thought to limit entry if the size of a minimum optimal plant constitutes a large percentage of total industry output, if industry demand is relatively inelastic over a low range of outputs, and if diseconomies increase rapidly at less than optimal plant size. Entry capital requirements are thought to limit entry if a cost differential of obtaining financing through internal and external sources beyond the degree of risk involved exists between extant and entrant firms. Both measures used in this study follow from Comanor and Wilson's study where minimum optimal plant size is measured as the percentage of industry value of shipments accounted for by the average size plant of the largest 50 percent of plants. Entry capital requirements are derived from average plant size by multiplying average plant size by the ratio of industry assets to sales; that is, by assuming the average plant asset-sales ratio is in proportion to its industry asset-sales ratio [53].

Changes in Demand and Cost

Although changes in demand and supply do not unambiguously lead to increases or decreases in profit, the general expectation is a profit rise with increases in demand.[6] Naturally, concomitant changes in unit cost are crucial to profit changes. Adjustments to increasing profit due to increases in demand and less than proportionate increases in unit cost, through entry of new firms and expansion of existing firms, may lag behind changes in demand and cost and produce continuous excess profits for some firms. If entry is restricted, then changes in demand and cost may have even greater effects on long-run profits, depending on the pricing policies of firms and the rate of expansion of established firms.

In this study, increases in both industry and firm demand are expected to be positively related to firm profit rates and increases in unit cost are expected to be inversely related to profit rates.[7] Industry demand is measured by five-year percentage changes in industry output and firm demand by five-year changes in total firm assets. Changes in cost were measured by one-year percentage changes in gross average hourly earnings per unit of output for production workers.[8] In addition, differences in relative factor proportions exist within as well as between industries. This was accounted for by including the capital-labor ratio for each industry examined.

The nature of the effect of changes in labor cost on profit rate is somewhat ambiguous. Firms in industries experiencing decreases in labor cost may have higher than normal profit rates leading to a negative relationship between profit rates and labor cost. On the other hand, the most profitable firm may have the highest labor cost in the short run if it requires additional labor to sustain increasing levels of production and thereby bids up the price of labor services or more readily acquiesces to demands for wage increases. Firms may, however, be more profitable because they have superior labor resources at top wage levels but lower than industry average total average cost due to the skill of superior labor resources.

Consumer Good–Producer Good

It is often claimed that profit margins are greater in consumer good markets than in producer good markets due to the effects of advertising, information cost differentials between buyers, and greater price discretion in consumer good markets. Some studies have found a stronger relationship between structural variables and profits in consumer good industries than in producer good industries [51, 161]. To test for any significant difference between profit rates according to this categorization a dummy variable was included which took on the value of one for consumer good firms and zero for producer good firms. The determination of whether a firm manufactured consumer or producer foods was based on the destination of initial sales by class of customer for a given industry.[9] If the majority of output went to consumer outlets, it was classified as a consumer good and similarly for producer goods. Of the thirty-three industries examined, eighteen fell in the consumer good class and fifteen in producer goods.

Profit Rates

Profit rates were measured as 1) average of yearly high and low stock market value for a year divided by book value of equity, multiplied by Moody's composite long-term industrial interest rate for the appropriate year, P_1, and 2) net income after taxes to book value of equity, P_2.[10] Both measures were two-year averages 1949-50, 1954-55, and 1959-60. The expected difference in the two measures is seen in their simple correlation coefficients. The coefficients for 1950, 1955, and 1960 are +.45, +.67, and +.61, respectively, all significant at the .01 level but much lower than the usual correlations found between conventional accounting rates of return.

Findings of the Present Study

The variables were examined using a simple linear model of the following form.[11]

$$P = B_0 + B_1 C + B_2 GD + B_3 A + B_4 ESP + B_5 ERC + B_6 Q_t/Q_{t-5}$$

$$+ B_7 A_t/A_{t-5} + B_8 LC_t/LC_{t-1} + B_9 K/L + B_{10} D + e \qquad (3)$$

where:

P	=	firm profit rate
C	=	four-firm seller concentration
GD	=	geographic dispersion
A	=	firm size
ESP	=	economies of scale in production
ECR	=	entry capital requirements
Q_t/Q_{t-5}	=	five-year change in industry demand
A_t/A_{t-5}	=	five-year change in firm demand
LC_t/LC_{t-1}	=	one-year change in labor cost
K/L	=	capital-labor ratio
D	=	dummy variable
e	=	error term

The relationship between concentration and profit rates in each year are seen in the simple correlation coefficients in Table 6-1 where the sample correlation coefficient level of significance is 0.196 at the 0.05 level and 0.256 at the 0.01 level. Concentration is not significant at the 0.05 level for either measure of profit in 1950, significant at the 0.05 level for P_1 and at the 0.01 level for P_2 in 1955, and significant at the 0.05 level with P_1 and insignificant with P_2 in 1960. The measure of geographic dispersion is not significant in any year conforming to the expectation of independence between concentration and profit and has a sign contrary to the traditional hypothesis in all but one case. The highest coefficients of determination (corrected for degrees of freedom) occurred in 1955 and were 3.6 percent for P_1 and 6.4 percent for P_2. The evidence provides scant support for the traditional hypothesis. While some statistical significance between concentration and profit rates is evident in certain years, it is very weak, explains little of inter-firm variation in profit rates, and may easily be due to identification problems. Adjusting for large firm effects appears to seriously weaken the concentration-profit relationship.

Examination of the remaining variables in Table 6-1 indicates the most significant variables in relation to both measures of profit are economies of scale in production and change in industry and firm demand, for all three years. Economies of scale in production is most highly correlated with profit measured as P_1 while changes in industry and firm demand are most highly correlated with P_2. Variables displaying coefficients which are generally not significantly

Table 6-1
Matrix of Simple Correlation Coefficients—1950, 1955, and 1960

1950:

	1	2	3	4	5	6	7	8[a]	9[a]	10	11	12
1	1.000	.453	.159	.125	.019	.355	−.080	.139	.110	−.223	.005	.086
2		1.000	.169	.085	−.053	.158	.123	.405	.412	−.150	.112	−.068
3			1.000	.348	.447	.654	.187	.344	.032	−.352	.069	−.196
4				1.000	.169	.421	.007	.341	−.073	−.126	.143	−.182
5					1.000	.312	.247	.041	−.009	−.104	.347	−.156
6						1.000	.060	.138	−.030	−.341	−.034	−.051
7							1.000	.203	.098	−.002	.644	−.127
8								1.000	.100	−.084	.080	−.291
9									1.000	.067	.255	−.050
10										1.000	−.052	−.300
11											1.000	−.104
12												1.000

1955:

	1	2	3	4	5	6	7	8	9	10	11	12
1	1.000	.672	.207	.074	.190	.331	.132	.207	.220	−.223	.212	−.106
2		1.000	.276	−.034	.139	.261	.276	.492	.337	−.101	.244	−.182
3			1.000	.306	.472	.671	.159	.176	.172	−.168	.042	−.183
4				1.000	.150	.411	.007	.004	−.158	.114	−.126	−.160
5					1.000	.332	.268	.009	.112	−.103	.393	−.142
6						1.000	.060	.117	.074	.030	−.034	−.051
7							1.000	.080	.055	−.106	.644	−.127
8								1.000	.339	.027	−.054	−.325
9									1.000	−.107	.076	−.219
10										1.000	−.126	−.120
11											1.000	−.104
12												1.000

1960:

	1	2	3	4	5	6	7	8	9	10	11	12
1	1.000	.616	.215	.136	.143	.349	.077	.497	.394	.158	.075	−.051
2		1.000	.062	.065	.024	.230	.067	.327	.308	.085	.104	.175
3			1.000	.353	.452	.690	.181	.205	−.009	−.049	.063	−.208
4				1.000	.105	.421	.007	.182	−.017	.045	−.143	−.182
5					1.000	.281	.318	.093	.028	−.001	.420	−.161
6						1.000	.060	.338	.003	−.128	−.034	−.051
7							1.000	−.157	.057	−.059	.644	−.127
8								1.000	.187	−.127	−.030	.183
9									1.000	.164	.137	−.268

Table 6-1(cont.)

10					1.000	.031	−.184
11						1.000	−.104
12							1.000

[a]1950 demand figures are based on three year changes in industry production and firm growth, 1947-1950.

Variables:

$1 - P_1$	$5 - A$	$9 - A_t/A_{t-5}$
$2 - P_2$	$6 - ESP$	$10 - LC_t/LC_{t-1}$
$3 - C$	$7 - ECR$	$11 - K/L$
$4 - GD$	$8 - Q_t/Q_{t-5}$	$12 - D$

different from zero include firm size, entry capital requirements, and the dummy variable identifying producer and consumer good markets.

Regression analysis of the variables are presented in Table 6-2, which fits structural variables to P_1, and Table 6-3, which fits the variables to P_2.[12] There are some notable similarities and differences in results depending on the measure of profit rate adopted. First, I will examine the similarities. The coefficients for concentration and firm size are not significantly different from zero under both measures of profit in each year tested. Further, concentration coefficients have signs contrary to popular expectations in five out of six cases. When economies of scale in production and entry requirements are deleted concentration becomes significant in only one case, firm size remains insignificant, and the standard error increases in all cases.[13] The coefficients for entry capital requirements also proved insignificant with the exception of one case and exhibited an unexpected negative sign under P_1.

These results support the hypothesis of independence between profit rate and concentration and profit rate and firm size. In the latter case, there appears to be no systematic relationship between profit rate and firm size across the 131 firms examined.[14] Of course, this result is based on a limited sample of manufacturing firms and is further restricted by definition to firms with assets in excess of one million dollars, but more accurately to firms in excess of ten million dollars.[15] In the case of entry capital requirements, there is some reason to doubt their significance as a barrier to entry unless capital markets are hopelessly marred. The results give little support to the hypothesis that capital requirements are a significant barrier to entry.[16]

The hypothesized relationship between concentration, economies of scale in production, and entry capital requirements is tested by a regression in logarithmic form using 1958 Census data for one sample of thirty-three industries. The results with t-values in parenthesis are,

$$C = 3.5606 + 0.3106\,ESP + .0254\,ECR \qquad R^2 = 0.61 \qquad (4)$$
$$(9.82) \qquad\quad (1.11)$$

Table 6-2
Regression Results for P₁ Profit Rate and All Market Structure Variables—1950, 1955, and 1960

Year	Intercept	C	A	ESP	ECR	Q_{t-5}	A_{t-5}	LC_{t-1}	K/L	Dummy	R^2	S.E.
1950	2.045	−.0126 (−1.28)	−.1299 (−.49)	.2355** (4.05)	−.0072 (−1.63)	.0173 (1.83)	.0082 (1.26)	−.0188 (−.98)	.0001 (1.07)	.3407 (.90)	.151**	1.8489
	1.5839			.1802** (3.84)	−.0080 (−1.81)	.0146 (1.60)	.0081 (1.26)	−.0120 (−.65)	.0001 (1.03)	.4751 (1.29)	.146**	1.8538
	1.9241	.0062 (.70)	−.0337 (−.12)			.0115 (1.16)	.0092 (1.34)	−.0339 (−1.68)	−.0001 (−.38)	.3342 (.83)	.035	1.9716
	2.0242			.1869** (4.28)	−.0054 (−1.62)	.0108 (1.25)	.0094 (1.51)				.137**	1.8632
1955	3.4958	−.0208 (−1.64)	.0519 (.19)	.3235** (4.16)	−.0041 (−.72)	.0073 (1.80)	.0035 (1.34)	−.1159** (−2.95)	.0001* (2.18)	−.2990 (−.64)	.216**	2.4103
	2.7296			.2339** (4.12)	−.0052 (−.92)	.0071 (1.73)	.0031 (1.20)	−.0982** (−2.58)	.0001* (2.46)	−.1524 (−.33)	.210**	2.4191
	2.8662	.0108 (1.03)	.2045 (.42)			.0076 (1.76)	.0034 (1.22)	−.0823* (−2.01)	.0001 (1.82)	−.0408 (−.08)	.114*	2.5609
	3.1323			.2164** (3.67)	.0053 (1.19)	.0052 (1.28)	.0048 (1.79)				.144**	2.5193
1960	2.2541	−.0192 (−.82)	.2673 (.38)	.4106** (2.74)	.0196 (1.82)	.1630** (5.27)	.0471** (3.70)	.1629** (2.92)	−.0001 (−.68)	.0106 (.01)	.398**	4.4363
	1.5075			.3380** (3.01)	.0183 (1.74)	.1618** (5.27)	.0479** (3.81)	.1614** (2.91)	−.0001 (−.57)	.1458 (.17)	.405**	4.4126
	1.1746	.0276 (1.49)	.2418 (.33)			.1699** (5.61)	.0479** (3.64)	.1362* (2.39)	.0001 (.31)	.1161 (.13)	.354**	4.5975
	1.3913			.3214** (2.86)	.0122 (1.50)	.1489** (4.99)	.0534** (4.45)				.378**	4.5104

Figures in parentheses are t values

*Statistically significant at the .05 level

**Statistically significant at the .01 level

R^2 = corrected for degrees of freedom

S.E. = Standard error

Table 6-3

Regression Results for P₂ Profit Rate and All Market Structure Variables—1950, 1955, and 1960

Year	Intercept	C	A	ESP	ECR	ΔQ_{t-5}	ΔA_{t-5}	ΔLC_{t-1}	K/L	Dummy	R^2	S.E.
1950	10.8643	-.0193 (-.66)	-.8786 (-1.12)	.2683 (1.55)	.0061 (.46)	.1185** (4.23)	.0957** (4.99)	-.0856 (-1.50)	-.0001 (-.06)	-.0442 (-.04)	.197**	5.4873
	10.0378			.1396 (1.00)	.0050 (.38)	.1159** (4.29)	.0975** (5.12)	-.0745 (-1.35)	-.0001 (-.41)	.2940 (.27)	.294**	5.4995
	10.5329	.0068 (.28)	-.8193 (-1.05)			.1163** (4.20)	.0943** (4.94)	-.0945 (-1.68)	.0001 (.12)	-.0024 (-.01)	.293**	5.5017
	10.2315			.2102 (1.63)	.0010 (.10)	.1167** (4.58)	.0936** (5.12)				.296**	5.4905
1955	8,1095	.0082 (.31)	-.9459 (-.96)	.3543* (2.15)	.0104 (.87)	.0457** (5.31)	.0112* (2.03)	-.0709 (-.85)	.0001* (2.32)	.2755 (.28)	.351**	5.0961
	8.3497			.3409** (2.86)	.0111 (.84)	.0463** (5.42)	.0111* (2.02)	-.0712 (-.89)	.0001* (2.13)	.3276 (.34)	.357**	5.0739
	7.2560	.0470* (2.22)	-.8595 (-.87)			.0473* (5.46)	.1060 (1.90)	-.0361 (-.44)	.0001** (3.48)	.5287 (.53)	.334**	5.1655
	9.4028			.3150** (2.63)	.0283** (3.13)	.0422** (5.15)	.0128* (2.35)				.343**	5.1286
1960	4.8811	-.0209 (-.92)	-.3508 (-.51)	.3664* (2.50)	.0096 (.91)	.0649* (2.14)	.0439** (3.52)	.0950 (1.73)	.0001 (.59)	2.4676** (2.85)	.228**	4.3526
	3.9839			.2553* (2.31)	.0079 (.75)	.0618* (2.04)	.0458** (3.71)	.0921 (1.69)	.0001 (.45)	2.7323** (3.26)	.230**	4.3455
	3.9941	.0180 (1.00)	-.3666 (-.53)			.0763** (2.60)	.0444** (3.49)	.0765 (1.39)	.0001 (1.22)	2.5626** (2.91)	.195**	4.4432
	5.8935			.1853 (1.65)	.0082 (1.00)	.0823** (2.76)	.0376** (3.14)				.172**	4.5065

Figures in parentheses are t values

*Statistically significant at the .05 level

**Statistically significant at the .01 level

R^2 = Corrected for degrees of freedom

S.E. = Standard error

Economies of scale in production is highly significant and accounts for most of the explained variation in concentration. These results suggest that much of the weak but significant relationship found between concentration and profit rates in previous studies may have been due to economies of scale in production since it explains much of the variation in concentration and is significantly related to profit rates.[17]

The remaining variables in Tables 6-2 and 6-3 show differing relationships to P_1 and P_2. Under P_1, the most significant variable is economies of scale in production, accounting for over 50 percent of the explained variation in profit rate in 1950 and 1955. Changes in industry and firm demand have the expected sign under P_1 in all cases but are only significant in 1960 when manufacturing profits and profit margins in general were declining. Hence, firms and industries experiencing the greatest increase in demand over the 1955 to 1960 period stood out in terms of expected future earnings during 1960. It is not clear why this was not the case in 1950 and 1955 as well, if past earnings are used to estimate future earnings. However, growth as a key element in stock valuation gained increasing prominence in the latter half of the 1950s. Changes in labor cost yield conflicting results with a significant coefficient in 1955 and 1960 but of differing signs. In 1950 and 1955 the sign is negative, reflecting decreasing labor cost and high profit rates; however, a positive sign in 1960 implies the most profitable firms experience a rise in labor cost. The dummy variable is insignificant in each case indicating there is little difference in profit rates between firms operating in producer or consumer good industries.[18]

The results shown in Table 6-3 using the more conventional current net income rate of return, P_2, show a different ordering of structural relationships to profit rate. Variation in P_2 is much more sensitive to changes in industry and firm demand than is P_1. These changes in demand account for over 60 percent of the explained variation in P_2 and are generally significant at the 0.01 level. Economies of scale in production account for most of the remaining explained variation and is significant in 1955 and 1960. Change in labor cost exhibits the same pattern of signs as under P_1 but is not significant in any year. The capital-labor ratio is once again significant in 1955 only. The dummy variable is significant in 1960 only.

From these results there is relatively little basis to choose between P_1 and P_2 since they appear to offer about the same amount of information. There is a larger variance in growth under P_1 and a larger variance in economies of scale in production under P_2. One could easily expect the opposite; that is, past changes in industry and firm demand are more closely related to the discounted value of expected profits as reflected in stock market value, while economies of scale in production are more closely related to current profits measured as net income to equity. Since the former occurred in 1950 and 1955 it suggests that investors placed a lower discount rate on firms in industries where entry was relatively restricted or where there were efficiencies due to increasing plant size. The results for 1960 are more consistent with current impressions of stock investor behavior; that is, emphasis on firm and industry growth as a key element in stock market valuation. The coefficients for economies of scale in production are fairly stable between P_1 and P_2 in each year but there is great instability in growth coefficients, particularly for changes in industry growth. However, the strong results for growth relative to P_2 also indicates that P_1 is an appropriate measure since P_1 and P_2 are related and P_2 is picking up some of the effects attributable to P_1.

Clearly, the results vary somewhat from period to period. It may be argued that data for 1950 were affected by changes brought on by the Korean War and 1955 and 1960 were not normal years since one covered a period of sharp expansion of business activity and the other a period of contracting business activity. Even under these conditions it is encouraging to note the consistent significance of economies of scale in production and changes in demand from period to period. The theory of structure and profitability is however based on long-run changes in profit rates. Originally, testing three cross-sectional periods over a ten-year period using expected and current profit rates was thought to be sufficient if similar patterns were manifest in each period. Since the actual results tend to vary between periods a test of the 1950-60 decade was made pooling the cross-section data. The results with t-values in parenthesis, are,

$$P_1 = 2.9801 - 0.0107C + 0.0979A + 0.3702ESP - 0.0028ECR +$$
$$(-0.92) \quad (0.27) \quad (5.15) \quad (-0.52)$$
$$0.0088Q_t/Q_{t-5} + 0.0109A_{t-5} + 0.0451LC_t/LC_{t-1} +$$
$$(1.51) \quad (2.99) \quad (1.71)$$
$$0.0001K/L + 0.3381D \quad \bar{R}^2 = 0.115 \quad S.E. = 3.9337$$
$$(1.56) \quad (.78)$$

$$(5)$$

$$P_2 = 8.9289 - 0.0002C - 1.1998A + 0.3126ESP + 0.0058ECR +$$
$$(-0.01) \quad (-2.24) \quad (2.92) \quad (0.74)$$
$$0.0552Q_t/Q_{t-5} + 0.0167A_t/A_{t-5} - 0.0570LC_t/LC_{t-1} +$$
$$(6.36) \quad (3.07) \quad (1.45)$$
$$0.0001K/L + 0.6248D \quad \bar{R}^2 = 0.206 \quad S.E. = 5.8544$$
$$(2.50) \quad (0.96)$$

$$(6)$$

With the exception of a significant negative coefficient for firm size under P_2, the results show the same relative significance of variables as with the cross-sectional periods. Once again, concentration is not significant and most of the explained variation in profit rates comes from economies of scale in production, changes in industry demand, and changes in firm demand.

Conclusion

These tests are subject to some of the deficiencies of previous studies with similar data and time periods, yet result in findings that are contrary to previous results. By attempting to free the tests of spurious correlation due to large firm effects, the generally weak but significant concentration ratio found in other studies is seen to be even weaker and to explain little beyond mere chance (less than 4 percent for P_1 and 7 percent for P_2 at best) of the variation in interfirm profit rates. It appears that future studies correcting for additional identification problems, adjusting for differences in risk, and using improved measures of structural barriers and profit rates will find that concentration ratios act as a proxy for other variables which can explain variations in profit rates apart from collusion. In conjunction with barriers to entry measured as economies of scale in production and entry capital requirements, and accounting for long-run changes in industry and firm demand, concentration displays no independent relationships to profit rates in both producer and consumer good industries. Concentration is related to barriers to entry which, along with changes in industry and firm demand, are related to profit rates. This explanation of higher than normal profit rates is consistent with received economic theory and is not dependent on arguments of widespread conspiracies and collusive behavior. On the basis of these results, basing public policy on lowering concentration, even if concentration is a perfect signal for collusion, is misdirected. If change in structure is to be the main focus of public policy, then barriers to entry warrant investigation prior to concentration since collusion is unstable faced with low cost entry.

This study does not disprove the traditional hypothesis any more than previous studies may have laid claim to a proof. It does show, however, that prior conclusions on the degree of competitive behavior based on the concentration-profit relationship have gone far beyond those warranted by economic theory and that the evidence is, at best, very much in doubt. In short, if the foremost evidence identifying monopolistic power is the alleged concentration-profit relationship, then structural empiricists, far from having completed their work, have only begun.

Part III:
Decision Processes in Large Business Firms

Recent revisions in the theory of the firm have centered on the behavioral and managerial approaches to generating knowledge of the real world, in contrast to the singular principle of profit maximization. Since external control is generally more costly than internal control, the motives of managers become crucial and identification of their utility function imparts motivational realism into the theory of the firm. The managerial approach seeks maximization of a generalized utility function including a multiplicity of goals which may or may not explicitly contain profit maximization. The behavioral school introduces realism in the process of decision making by inducing certain behavioral characteristics to managers and groups. Hence the behavioral approach specifies explicit managerial decision rules which are not immediately maximizing.

The chapters in this section are included as both theoretical and empirical contributions to this literature. The papers by Weston and Krouse are examples of integrating the revisionist schools of thought and profit maximization, that is, with real world decision making within a firm. They serve to illuminate theoretically and descriptively the interworkings of explicit behavioral and managerial models and how they are consistent with maximization models. The chapters by Cross and McKitterick, provide in-depth case studies of management organization and the decision making

process in a large, multi-product enterprise. These chapters illustrate the new behavioral and managerial hypotheses.

Weston's paper shows how dynamic ROI planning and control of decentralized operations is not only consistent, but is necessary for the objective of wealth maximization through the use of evaluating and monitoring managerial performance. Firm targets are seen as iterative steps in the process of seeking goals and not as ends in themselves. Hence, the ROI system of planning and control as a specific decision-making process in a behavioral model can be conceptualized as a cybernetic system of dynamic information flow, feedback, review and adaptive mechanism for seeking the goal of owner wealth maximization.

The paper by Cross provides a summary of the changes in the top management organization of the General Electric Company to meet the needs of the 1970s and beyond. He begins by pointing out that a number of developments have increased the challenges to be met by the top management group in any large firm. These factors include (1) a higher rate of nominal growth; (2) increased product-market diversification; (3) shorter product life cycles; (4) greater risks in the form of larger capital outlays required in choices between alternatives involving greater uncertainty; and (5) major changes in our social value systems which effect all institutions operating in our society—business firms with particular intensity. In the effort to deal with these increased challenges effectively, the corporate executive office was expanded into a group of four to provide for overall direction of the company. The corporate executive office is assisted by two senior level staff groups. One is the corporate executive staff to provide guidance on strategic planning; the other is a corporate administrative staff responsible for current ongoing corporate level responsibilities. A corporate policy committee was formed comprising the four chief executive officers and five senior vice presidents to provide for analysis of issues of broad corporate concern. A corporate research and development staff has the responsibility for maintaining a leading edge in technology by the company.

The initial link between the activities of the corporate level and the work carried out at the operating level is provided by executive boards which head each of the ten groups to which in turn a number of the 50 divisions report. Each executive board includes as chairman one member of the corporate executive office, a senior vice president from the corporate executive staff and the group executive who continues in his role as its chief operating officer.

In summary, the paper by Mr. Cross describes how the new challenges to conducting business operations required the expansion of the top management organization of the General Electric Company. It is now structured to provide for balanced attention to the major functions to be performed in planning and operating business enterprise.

Within this framework of the expanded top management organization system in General Electric Company, the paper by Mr. McKitterick describes the initiation and development of the strategic planning process. The organization innovation is the designation of strategic business units (SBUs) superimposed on traditional groups, divisions and departments representing one or a combination of groups, divisions or departments. The SBUs are charged with strategic planning with reference to the important aspects of their changing environment: society, customers, markets, industry, government, suppliers, competitors, etc. Strategic planning involves a combination of the top-down and bottom-up approach. The corporate executive staff provides broad environmental studies which provide the broad planning premises. Within this broad framework long-range, short-range and alternative strategies are formulated by the SBU's. These are initially reviewed at the executive board level, and later by the corporate executive staff.

The continued interaction between the corporate executive staff, the executive board and the SBUs seeks to integrate individual strategies consistent with a total corporate strategy and overall objectives for the company. The system seeks to preserve initiative at the operating level at the same time providing for corporate leadership review, and effective evaluation.

The papers by Cross and McKitterick which describe the effort to *effectively combine planning capability and decision-making responsibility provide an in-depth case study of evolving corporate management processes. The view expressed by Galbraith and others that the increase of planning activities by government makes the planning and operation of business firms relatively routine is a caricature of reality. The developments evolving in our dynamic society including the expanded activities of government have increased the challenges to effective management of business firms, not mitigated them. This in-depth case study provides insights into the detailed study, analysis and continued evolution and development of corporate management systems to deal with the new and enlarged complexities of conducting effective business operations. It provides a clear and effective illustration of evolutionary developments to make the business firm a flexible and efficient organization form among the important institutions in modern society.*

Krouse's paper brings realism into a theoretical formulation of decision making within a firm. It can be viewed in part as a conceptualization of the adaptive decision-making process described by the new General Electric management system. This theoretical analysis of resource allocation and ongoing decision making has been lacking in conventional economic theories of the firm. Economists have traditionally assumed an instantaneous response to exogenous forces and attendant decisions over all components of a firm. But Krouse's paper provides a unique blend of the behavioral and managerial approaches by postulating decentralized decision making, adaptive response to targeted goals, and maximization of a generalized corporate utility function.

7

ROI Planning and Control as a Dynamic Management System

J. Fred Weston

The problem of departmentation, involving the grouping of activities and the use of specialist expertise, is a problem faced by firms of all sizes. A very small firm that has not yet grouped or specialized its activities confronts the question in seeking to optimize the efficiency of operations. A related continuing issue is the question, regardless of the firm's size, of buying specialist expertise as required, through the external market place or obtaining the flow of services through a generalized contractual relationship.

Indeed, the organization and management questions involved are applicable to all purposive organizations. The basic issue is the very general problem of seeking optimal production functions by effective grouping of activities and utilization of specialist expertise. (Cf. Coase [48, pp. 336-338] and Hirshleifer [106, pp. 11-12]). In turn, this raises a number of problems of delegating authority yet achieving effective control of decentralized operations.

One widely used method of divisional control is the return on investment (ROI) technique. ROI control has been widely criticized. Economists have regarded the use of return on investment objectives as indicative of market control. Management specialists have described defects in the ROI method for achieving effective control of decentralized operations. Behaviorists and accountants alike have questioned the motivational consequences of control by the ROI method.

Field surveys of corporated resource allocation policies developed evidence that many of the criticisms are directed against a static concept of the ROI control system with inadequate recognition of its dynamic process characteristics.[1] This proposition will be developed in three parts. One, the prevailing description of ROI and the criticisms engendered will be summarized. Two, the nature and significance of ROI as a dynamic process will be discussed. Three, the criticisms of ROI control will be evaluated in the framework of its actual characteristics.

The Static Form of ROI Control and Its Defects

Short-term business planning as reflected in the financial budgeting process has been referred to in the literature as "planning and control for profits,"[2] "management by objectives,"[3] or "the du Pont system." The du Pont Company pioneered the ROI system widely used both by divisionalized firms as well as by effectively managed small firms.[4]

The static form of the du Pont system focuses on a formula chart showing the relationship of factors affecting return on investment (ROI). The end focus of the chart is return on investment. This is shown as the product of the turnover of investment multiplied by the margin on sales, to emphasize that the return on investment can be increased either by minimizing investments per dollar of sales, or by controlling costs so that the profit margin on sales is improved. The formula chart then fans into detailing all the elements of operating investment: cash, receivables, inventories, and fixed assets (gross). The income statement provides detail for all of the factors affecting the profit margin, with emphasis on the nature and behavior of the cost elements.

Even in its static form, the ROI method of control, has a number of positive attributes. These have been summarized effectively by Professor Dearden [60, p. 125]. First, it is a single, comprehensive measure, influenced by everything that has happened which affects the financial status of the divisions. Every item in the du Pont chart is related to its effect on either turnover or profit margin, and through either of these to its effect on return on investment. If an alternative organization of the financial planning and control system is desired, the required information for doing so has been assembled.

The second advantage is that ROI measures how well the division manager has used his resource allocations, thereby providing a means for post-auditing capital investment proposals. A third advantage is that ROI is a common denominator so that comparisons can be made directly among divisions within the company, with outside companies or with alternative investment of funds generally. Fourth, it is also claimed that since the manager is evaluated on his ability to optimize ROI, he will be motivated to do so.

Criticisms of the ROI method of control have also been expressed. First are a list of technical defects that are well covered in the Dearden article [60, pp. 126-32]. These include: oversimplifying a complex decision-making process, not distinguishing the required rate of return on investments in common assets which are used in different divisions which may have different ROI targets, and difficulties arising out of accounting methods of return on investment. A review of these technical defects suggests that many of them are arbitrary procedures not inherent in the method. Many criticisms of ROI planning and control stem from the predilection of accounting systems for recording the expiration of historical costs, and hence reflect the limitations of traditional accounting methods.

A second difficulty is that of assigning responsibility. Inherently, many decision areas involve the joint participation of various divisions and various levels of authority. Consequently, assigning responsibility for results is difficult under a static method.

The third, and more fundamental criticism, is that any static control system is likely to have motivational defects. *Any* static control method will invite a wide range of practices for beating the system. In addition, there are important additional positive values not captured by the static concept. Therefore, it is important to view the du Pont system in its correct exposition: the du Pont planning and control system as a dynamic process.

It is in its dynamic process aspects that the du Pont system represents the creation of a significant addition to management technology. Detailed analysis of operations is provided in a series of individual charts on each element of investment, revenue, or cost. It is in connection with review of these individual charts that a dynamic process is generated. For each asset or investment account, historical data are provided on an annual basis for five years with the sixth or current year presented on an annual basis to date and on a forecast basis for one year [70]. In addition, data are provided on a monthly basis for the previous year and for the current year to date. Periodic forecasts are made for four quarters into the future. The forecast is repeated periodically. When the forecast and review are on a quarterly basis, the one year forecast is expressed by month for the proximate quarter and by quarter for the remainder of the year.

Thus, on a quarterly forecast and review basis, each quarter will have been projected and reviewed four times before the actual events are experienced.[5] Similar analysis is made of expenses expressed as a percentage of sales and transfers. Expenses as a percent of sales are placed in perspective by showing production as a percentage of capacity since volume influences per unit cost.

The mechanics of the du Pont planning and control system have been described. The review process makes this a dynamic system with three main elements: (1) the review process; (2) process rather than goal orientation; and (3) the adaptive learning process.

Review Process

The process begins with the periodic meetings of the firm's finance committee at which divisional proposals for funds are presented. The prospective returns on investment represent one of the criteria used to rank the alternative investment opportunities and to allocate corporate resources. Initial projections are related to the potentials for the individual areas. The subsequent analysis compares performance to projections. A periodic presentation is made by the responsible managers of divisions or departments to a review committee. The review committee is comprised of men with years of experience in diverse areas of operations in the company. The committee as a whole has experience covering a wide enough range so that the review of any department represents an *informed* review. The data are a vehicle for the significant aspect of the process—the review of the data and the adjustment of policies. Performance is related to potentials and not to any absolute standard. Thus the evaluation system provides a two-way information flow in an effective communication system. In its evaluation of an individual division or department, the review committee takes into account not only optimization for that segment, but also over-all optimization for the firm. Analysis of the data and comparisons of forecasts with actual results lead to policy modifications.

A reward and penalty system closes the loop in this process of stimulating, guiding and motivating effective managerial performance. A salary and bonus committee allocates promotions, salary adjustments and bonuses by departments. This salary and bonus committee typically includes members of the finance committee responsible for the original allocation or resources, and members of the review committee engaged in a continuing evaluation of performance.

Three aspects of the review process represent a dynamic system. One, there is a detailed information flow on key decision areas. This provides feedback in the information system loop. Two, the review process represents a monitoring of the data and other forms of information. Three, on a basis of the information, review and discussion, policies and decisions are adjusted in the attempt to improve performance. Thus, the entire process represents a method of adjusting to changes in the total economy, the industry and actions of competitors.[6]

Goals vs. Process

The ROI system must properly be seen as a *process*. Managers are not evaluated on the basis of the size of the return on investment their division earns. Performance evaluation is related to the *potential* for the division, and not to any absolute standard. A manager who is able to limit the loss in a division in a product market characterized by severe excess capacity may be rated higher than a manager who achieves a positive 20 percent return on investment in a product market area where at least temporarily the sales/capacity relations may have made possible a 30 percent return on investment.

Similarly, if the risks of a divisional operation are high, there will be a minimum screening standard or investment hurdle rate that will be higher than for a less risky division. For example, the return on investments for oil exploration will be higher than the return on the investment in the land on which a filling station is placed, because the results of the operations of the filling station are more predictable than oil exploration. A company is contemplating the establishment of a manufacturing operation in a foreign country, subject to a wide range of political as well as commercial and foreign exchange fluctuation risks. It will require a greater return on that activity than the return on expanding its capacity to produce and sell through established channels a staple consumer non-durable good.

Information and Adaptive Learning Process

The review process focuses on the difference between the actual performance of a division and the projection that the managers had made. This comparison is more important than specific goal orientation, because errors in forecasts in either direction result in misallocation of resources. In the corporate allocation of resources by the finance committee, a project may promise a ten percent return, resulting in an allocation of one million dollars for that investment. But if the expected return had been twenty percent, perhaps two million dollars investment would have been allocated. Hence, errors in either direction result in a misallocation of resources.

But it would be inaccurate to characterize the ROI system as emphasising that results conform to budgets or forecasts. The dynamic ROI system recognizes important variables external to the firm: the economy changes, competitive conditions change, elements of costs change, etc. Such changes are taken into account in evaluating managerial performance. The informed review process thus provides a basis for achieving an efficient two-way information flow.

The forecasting, information flow, review and adjustment process provides for both formal and informal multiple flows of information. The evaluations are not mechanical. The review discussions aimed at an informed evaluation of performance. This increased understanding provides a basis for a dynamic adaptive learning process. The fundamental objective of the ROI system as a dynamic process is to shorten reaction time to change or error. Its basic aim is to make the firm an effective learning and adaptive mechanism.

Evaluation of the Dynamic Management Control Process

Most of the criticisms of the ROI control method are applicable only to the static formulation. The use of any type of static control system develops incentives in the wrong direction, leads to the development of devices for "beating the system" and results in the wrong motivations. But in the dynamic management control system described, this major defect of the static ROI method does not remain. Particularly the informed review process and the two-way information flow system make for good communication and under-standing. The process then becomes a vehicle for continued improvements and provides strong motivations in the proper directions.

A major problem in the utilization of the ROI method of control is the failure of companies to adopt its dynamic elements. One reason for the failure to adopt the dynamic aspect of the ROI method of control is that so many firms came to the method relatively late. The systematic literature on the "principles of management" developed after the mid-1950s. Particularly, the literature on long-range planning did not appear until after 1955. The emergence of second-generation computers with their increased information processing and retrieval capabilities gave impetus to formal methods of planning and control. Widespread adoption of decentralized profit responsibility took place in the 1950s through the use of the concept of profit centers. Implementation of the profit center concept involves determination of the amount of profit and relating it to some base to determine a profitability rate. Thus to some degree the development of measures of performance of investment centers represents an index of the extent to which an important development in planning and control activities had taken place.

As of mid-1965, of 2,658 respondents, 60 percent indicated the use of investment centers (Mauriel and Anthony, [157]). Of those firms not using investment centers, about two-thirds indicated that they did not have two or more profit centers or that capital assets were relatively less significant in determining the performance of their business. It is difficult to assess whether the firms not employing profit centers should have done so for effective planning and control of their operations. Perhaps of greater significance is the adoption timing of investment centers in performance measures of decentralized divisions. Of 851 large American firms which responded to an inquiry with respect to how they utilized the analysis of investment center performance, 60 percent indicated that they had adopted the method after 1955 and over 37 percent had adopted the method after 1960.[7]

Hence, one reason why the ROI method of control is used in its static and pathological forms may stem from its late installation by so many other large companies. The ROI method in its static form is relatively mechanical in its installation and operation. It is thus easier to understand and easier to install. Furthermore, the review and information flow process cannot be installed as an on going dynamic system from the very beginning. There is. an important learning element involved. This may require various forms of experimentation by companies in order to superimpose a dynamic control system on the methods of management control processes then in use.

Indeed, the difficulties of applying the ROI method in a flexible and dynamic way appear to have been experienced at the du Pont Company itself. The key element has been relations with the review committee whose role is critical for the effective functioning of a dynamic planning and review process. The review committee at du Pont is the executive committee consisting of the president of the company and eight vice presidents. Some recent changes in its methods of functioning have been described.[8]

The committee meets each Wednesday. It receives monthly reports from department managers, and every quarter each manager appears to discuss what happened, why, and the outlook.
For decades, these reports were illustrated by a series of financial charts hung

from movable overhead trolleys. A man from the treasurer's office presented the data in a stylized manner while the general manager waited for questions. The crucial charts focused on the department's return-on-investment, a very rigid concept.

All this has changed. The trolleys and the chart room are gone. Instead of sitting theater-style, the executive committee now sits around an oval table. The charts are at hand in page form, but, "unless we have a question or unless the general manager wants to talk from them, we don't pick them up, . . . The old system looked backward rather than forward. Now, the thrust is to the future."

Apparently, an effective information and review process could not be achieved by the periodic presentations to the total executive (review) committee. An important organizational change was, therefore, made.[9]

Last spring, McCoy broke with another du Pont tradition by giving each executive committee member an assignment as liaison man to a department to improve the "connection between the operating groups and the policy level, and to give us better understanding of our problems."

The advantage of this new approach was expressed by one of the general managers in the following terms, "instead of worrying about keeping nine men informed . . . I can clue my man anytime. He deals with the committee and I have more time to run my business."[10]

Another important development was a more flexible approach to the application of the return on investment concept.[11]

Now, return-on-investment "is redefined every so often," says economist Charles L. Reeder, "to accept reality." Where once the minimum was fixed, today it varies—higher when the risks are greater, lower when the results are more certain (a tribute to venture analysis techniques now permeating the company) or when an investment supports an established business.

The implication that previously a rigid requirement that a return on investment of a fixed minimum rate to all types of opportunities, regardless of the degree of risk, suggests the application of the ROI method in a mechanistic way. The du Pont experience emphasizes the requirement of a dynamic, flexible continuing review process rather than a bureaucratic application. Further, strategic planning was not effectively integrated with operations planning and control at du Pont.

But the recent du Pont experience is not evidence that the failure to integrate financial planning and control with long-range or strategic planning is inherent in the ROI method system. There is nothing in the ROI method that inhibits a firm from effectively integrating it with long-range planning. Indeed, Sloan emphasized that bringing the du Pont system at General Motors in the early twenties facilitated the development of long-range strategy [217]. The installation of the du Pont system in General Motors at a time of financial crises in the early 1920s enabled Sloan and his management team to bring the General Motors' operation under control. They were then able to take the long-term view in developing a strategy for increasing their share of the market [217].

Summary

Defects in the application of ROI planning and control method have been disclosed by its originator, du Pont. Even worse errors were observed in a large number of firms which came to planning and control efforts relatively late. Direct interviews with a number of these companies provided evidence on three major types of difficulties. First, the most widespread errors involved a static approach to planning and control. A related error has been the reflection of the emphasis of the classical management theory on a strict top-down planning approach in which the standards of performance were imposed from above. The resulting arbitrariness and rigidity have resulted in continuing conflicts between the corporate office and the operating divisions. Second, these problems have been aggravated by the domination of short-term budgeting operations by traditional accounting practices. The third major defect was the closed systems approach in which budgeting was carried out without effective integration with strategic or long-range planning.

But none of the observed errors is inherent in the ROI method. The central error is in the confusion of goals and process. The goals of the firm include maximization of stockholder wealth, consumer satisfaction, expanding the capabilities of its personnel and their development as human beings and citizens, and contributions to society as a whole to which the firm bears a central responsibility. In the effort to achieve these goals, a number of operational objectives and standards are formulated. These include ROI, growth in size and in earnings per share, favorable valuation relations, growth in the firm's market share, favorable trends in the morale of its personnel as measured by low separation rates, and high ratings on social indicators. But both businessmen and theorists have committed the error of treating these objectives as ends in themselves. Without a full understanding of the dynamics of planning and control systems, business firms have installed ROI or other forms of management information systems, using the targets and standards bureaucratically.

Economists have also misinterpreted targets as goals rather than as instruments for coordination of decentralized divisions. Specific management function areas such as marketing [Kaplan, Dirlam, Lanzillotti, 121] or engineering departments [Bain, 18] are likely to place greater emphasis on the importance of targets than the general office executives. In surveying such departments an exaggerated impression of the role of targets may be obtained.

But the targets and standards by which managers seek to make the goals of the firm operational are not ends in themselves. They should be viewed rather as management instruments for engendering healthy processes in the firm. Targets and standards can be employed to contribute to an information and feedback process that is dynamic in quality, have favorable effects on the development of the firm's personnel, and can facilitate fast reaction time to change.

The ROI system of planning and control is a useful vehicle for assembling relevant information. It is not critical whether that information is focused on ROI, or other "management objectives." ROI is useful in providing information on every element of the balance sheet and income statement as a basis for further analysis. As a vehicle for a dynamic communication, feedback, and adjustment process, ROI, as well as other management information systems appropriately employed, can potentially be a useful system for developing healthy processes in successfully functioning firms.

8 General Organization Structure and Functions

Hershner Cross

My objective is to present an updating on General Electric's management structure as of late 1971. General Electric's organization retains the idea of decentralization with some evolutionary changes resulting in further development of the management concept. To many people outside the industrial world, it may sometimes appear that large organizations and enterprises undertake reorganizations for whimsical purposes or maybe to match the life style of the chief executive or something like that. Actually, most of these moves that large, medium, and small industry make result mostly from the efforts of management to adjust to changes they see taking place in the environment in which their business operates. Significant influences which affect all companies (and people) have caused us to adapt organizationally.

Obviously, first is growth. From 1963 to 1968 General Electric put in place, measured in dollars of declining real value, a second company the size of today's Westinghouse. We have been growing at the rate of over a billion dollars a year in current dollars. Another factor, of course, is diversity. In the last decade this company has grown a great many significant new businesses. Technologically, many of these have been spin-offs from some of our established businesses. From a management point of view, many of these businesses have presented big, new challenges. These include: (1) computers and automation systems; (2) time-sharing information networks in which we continue to engage heavily; (3) land-based gas turbines, one of the bright new stars in the power generation field; (4) greatly expanded chemical and medical businesses; (5) the commercial jet engine business; (6) the domestic mainline locomotive business; (7) the aerospace business; (8) the nuclear power business, and I could go on and on.

Certainly, a third factor has been the shortening life cycles of many of our products, and not consumer goods only. The rate of change in most technologies has been unbelievably rapid with a resultant great shortening of the time span over which a product can survive. Fourth, closely related to this is the magnitude of the risks involved in seeking to back the right horse to secure a payoff for the shareowners before either our competitors or we start a new horse race. This is quite a challenge.

Fifth, major changes in social values have been associated with the rise of consumerism, the urgent need to give effective attention to minority problems, and the environmental movement. These have all added external complexity to the growing complexity of internal management problems.

Several major imperatives have gradually emerged from pressures such as these. First, was the need to sharpen General Electric's strategic planning process. Second, was need to create an organizational structure for the 70's that was capable of managing growth, diversity, complexity, aggravated risk and accumulated social pressures.

I will try to compress in just a few sentences the essence of some of the thinking on strategic planning. It starts with the recognition that the new competitive facts of life increasingly have placed planning and decision making together at levels in General Electric other than the product department. This product department is the unit that has served us for many years as our basic profit center. But it is increasingly clear that instead of being in maybe some two hundred or two hundred and fifty basic businesses, each represented by the product departments as we called them, we are really in maybe forty or fifty fundamental businesses. These have been identified and designated as "strategic business units" (SBUs).

To manage growth and provide continuity, the established departmental structure has been left relatively undisturbed. But to integrate operational strategies, that is the strategies of our operating components, with corporate strategies and to optimize resource allocation, the strategic business units have been identified.

To provide increased direction and review of both planning and operating activities, the company began to make adjustments in the management structure in late 1967. First, a four-man corporate executive office was established to distribute burdens at the top. This reflects the increasing range and complexity of policies and decisions confronting the chief executive of a business firm.

Second, our five groups were reorganized into ten. The names of the groups reflect the great diversity described above:

1. Major appliances
2. Consumer products
3. Power generation
4. Power delivery
5. Industrial products

6. Components and materials
7. Construction industries
8. Aircraft engines
9. Aerospace
10. International

Each of these groups has sales averaging close to a billion dollars. The Vice President who is the Group Executive heading up each of these businesses is the chief operating officer for his business. He may be likened to the President of a very substantial company. Each of these groups has under it divisions and departments. When the five groups became ten the total number of divisions within the total structure was also increased from some twenty-five to fifty.

A corporate executive staff was established to provide planning at the top along with a corporate administrative staff to handle the ongoing daily work of the company. A comprehensive new strategic planning process was instituted throughout the company to improve the effectiveness of component planning, and to integrate it with overall corporate direction. Next, let us take a somewhat closer look at corporate level organization of General Electric to sketch the principle responsibilities of the various officers.

At the top reporting to the Board of Directors is the Corporate Executive Office made up of the Chairman of the Board and Chief Executive Officer and three Vice Chairmen and Executive Officers. The main functions of the *corporate executive office* (CEO) listed perhaps overly simply are to: (1) set overall company objectives; (2) shape strategic directions; (3) develop the company's basic management structure; (4) monitor short-term operations; (5) decide on deployment of key managers; (6) make recommendations to the Board of Directors on our big ventures and where we should be headed; (7) maintain critical external relationships and; (8) provide total company leadership.

Within this broad framework each of the three Vice Chairmen serves as an executive officer for at least three of the company's ten groups. In addition, specific areas of responsibility have been assigned to the three Vice Chairmen within the corporate executive office. These areas are: First, monitoring the overall financial condition of the company short-range. Second, insuring that strategically important external relationships are appropriately maintained. Third, monitoring the overall short-range company operating results versus plans.

The corporate executive office now has the support of a new corporate executive staff (CES) to aid in the shaping of the future direction of the company. The corporate executive staff is comprised of four Senior Vice Presidents. These gentlemen are selected on the basis of their broad business backgrounds, in some cases for their experience as group executives and others for their experience with broad corporate problems. In any case, they serve primarily as business generalists with their basic role being that of assisting the corporate executive office in the improvement of the decision-making process on matters of strategic importance to the company. The corporate executive staff is responsible for such things as appraising trends in the overall environment in which the company operates, reviewing and evaluating plans developed by the operating components to see how they fit overall corporate strategy, and, as a basis for helping the corporate executive office make resource allocations, recommending courses of action on critical issues of strategic importance to the company as a whole.

The corporate executive staff also has a responsibility for building expertise in six critical areas: (1) economic threats and opportunities, (2) human resources, (3) financial resources, (4) production resources, (5) technology and (6) legal and political constraints. These are areas expected to have crucial impact on the future thrust of the corporation, and I am sure, of many other corporations. This then is the staff which has been put in place to aid the corporate executive office in shaping the future direction of the company.

For the current ongoing staff work of the company as a whole and for certain corporate level operations, a corporate administrative staff (CAS) has been established. It encompasses work which must be done at the corporate level because the corporation is after all a single entity. This would include corporate level accounting, for example, and work which should be done at the corporate level for reasons of economy or uniformity. The corporate administrative staff is presently my responsibility. Within the CAS there are seven operations carrying out corporate level work: (1) accounting, (2) treasury, (3) trust investment, (4) legal, (5) public relations, (6) employee relations, and (7) management personnel relations. In addition, there are two components which provide services to operations on a buy-sell, self-liquidating basis. The corporate consulting services encompass the former corporate engineering, manufacturing, and marketing organizations in large part. Corporate education services incorporate many of the educational programs previously carried out by certain former corporate functional components. Lastly, there is a corporate facility services which provides certain pool services for the company, such as our company telephone network, our pooled computer installations, and the supervision and construction of our plants, factories and so on.

To provide a forum for discussion of matters of broad corporate concern, a corporate policy committee (CPC) has been established. It meets regularly on a monthly basis. The members of the corporate policy committee are the four members of the corporate executive office and the five Senior Vice Presidents. There is one additional component and a most important one reporting at the corporate level. It is corporate research and development, responsible for the generation of new technology, often beyond the scope of the operating groups. It consists of laboratories and appropriate administrative support functions, a very key point in our corporate activities.

In summary the corporate organization comprises a corporate executive office for overall direction of the company, a corporate executive staff to give guidance on the future of the company. In addition, it includes an administrative staff to carry out ongoing corporate level work, the policy committee to provide a forum for discussion by the top executives on matters of broad corporate concern, and corporate research and development to give the company a leading edge in technology.

The interface between the work being done at the corporate level and the work being done out of our operating levels is provided by a mechanism called executive boards. There is an executive board established for each of the company's ten groups. The chairman of each board is a member of the CEO with executive officer responsibility for that particular group. Serving with him is another executive officer, a senior vice president from the corporate executive staff and the group executive for the group itself.

The role of the group executive does not change. He has been and still is the chief operating officer for his group. One essential job of the executive board is to provide guidelines for the planning at the strategic business unit level and to provide evaluation and review of the strategic alternatives, strategic plans and operating plans prepared by what we now call SBUs. The strategic business units are central to the new strategic planning process. They might be departments, they might be divisions, or even groups, whichever business level logically combines the planning capability and the decision making responsibility.

Obviously, time, thought and much soul-searching went into setting up this sort of a structure and the new direction that the company is taking. The fact is that we just will not be doing business at the corporate level or in operations in ways that were possible in the 60's but which may be less applicable in the 70's. Are these changes that have been described ultimate? Are we locked in for the next decade? I doubt it very seriously. If any element of this new structure and strategy is incompatible with change, it is going to have to change too. We think, however, that the new concepts will afford us the greater flexibility required to adapt to and anticipate the new challenges ahead.

9

Resource Allocation in the General Electric Company

J.B. McKitterick*

Recent events seem to have made the problem of resource allocation the number one issue in Washington, in the average American firm, and in most families as well. From a condition of seeming unlimited power to meet its needs, our country in just five brief years has progressed to a situation in which we are all being forced to make hard choices, and conservation of resources and postponement of satisfaction are the order of the day. Politically, the whole idea of resource allocation presupposes some centralization of decision making, and this of course is anathema to most of our older generation and apparently to the very young as well.

Moreover, many of us in business were taught a brand of economics which assumed that the power to choose did not even exist. We were taught that market forces of supply and demand made the real decisions, while the creative activity of individuals merely provided the alternatives. As a result, even in the 1950s decision theory had not really affected most business school curricula, and mathematical models of the national income accounts were still unknown to a large number of economic students. Further, in the intervening years, there has been a tremendous growth in the size of our institutions. The City of New York today has a budget equivalent to that of the Federal Government when I was in college. The Federal Government now spends more than twice the entire output of the economy of thirty years ago.

Since the second World War, General Electric's sales have grown from 1.5 to approximately 9 billion dollars. The greatest part of this growth has been the result of new product development from the original electrical manufacturing technology. From our power generation, distribution equipment and electric motors we expanded into turbines, appliances, and industrial control. Later we expanded into insulation materials, chemicals, metallurgical products and most recently into electronics, aircraft engines, nuclear power and services. Building around this core of technological and managerial capabilities, General Electric has grown to become the fourth largest manufacturing enterprise in this country, participating in most of the basic industries and doing business in over 70 countries.

The conventional modern key to managing a diversified enterprise is decentralization. There are, however, some business problems for which decentralization does not furnish an automatic answer—it needs some help—and resource

123

allocation and over-all corporate planning are among those problems. Within the past year and a half General Electric has made a number of moves to strengthen its planning and resource allocation processes; and hopefully what we have done may have application to other diversified activities in business and elsewhere.

As an over-simplification, for planning purposes we made planning and decision-making assignments to the general management of selected departments, divisions and groups, using among others the test that the assigned planning function at each appropriate level—which we tentatively called a Strategic Business Unit (SBU)—ought to have the ability to accomplish integrated strategic planning on markets, products, services, facilities and organization with relatively slight concern for the actions or results of other SBUs.

In order to interface more effectively the planning decisions of each of our strategic business units with the total corporate interest, we created ten Executive Boards made up of members of the top corporate management and the Group Executive who has line responsibility for the business.

Each SBU is required to carry out a rigorous annual cycle of "bottom-up" strategic planning, forecasting and budgeting—both short and long range. At the corporate level a similar "top-down" system looks at the Company overall in terms of corporate perspectives. I would like to explain how these two planning cycles interact, and mention some of the considerations that prompted this arrangement.

Each of these cycles consists of essentially three major events: The nomination of objectives and critical problems, the preparation of responsive plans, and the decision on how to invest in and implement the plans. The Corporate planning cycle begins early in the year with a top-down long-range reassessment of the Company's position. The purpose of this review is to focus and organize the total planning effort of both operations and staff for the coming year. The review is planned by four senior vice presidents who comprise the Corporate Executive Staff. The principal concern of the Executive Staff is for the corporation's long-range plans. Hence, early each year they present to the Executive Office a two-day review of the long-range trends in world economics with particular emphasis on political, social and technical developments. From this analysis specific issues are raised bearing on the objectives, strategies and policies of the Company as a whole.

For example, looking ahead to the review early next year, we will want to look in some depth at the possible implications of the changed conditions for international trade. We will be concerned with the expanding role of government, not only with respect to its increasing control over corporate decisions, but the role of the government in controlling important customer industries such as electric power, medical care, transportation, housing, education, and so on. Then we will want to look carefully at the continuing trend toward the services sector, which is diverting consumer spending and employment away from manufacturing, to see how we can better participate in the evolution of a national market for services, and through contribution of new technology, help hold down services prices and benefit activity in the manufacturing sector.

The yield of these considerations is a series of long-range planning guidelines that go out to each staff component and operating business of the Company. The guidelines are requests that specific issues be explored, calling for studies to be made, alternate plans to be prepared so that the Company can know what its alternatives are, what the price and payoff of various courses of action are, to prepare the Company to convert future threats into business opportunities. In addition, the guidelines will request the SBUs to prepare alternate plans to accelerate or decelerate the growth of their businesses, so that we can see the investment required for future growth, and the yield of harvesting future potential.

While the Executive Staff are presenting proposed guidelines for the approval of the Corporate Executive Office, each operating component is busy analyzing its own planning situation from the "bottom-up" so to speak. Plans to diversify, to add capacity, to discontinue a line, and so on, are evaluated against a five-year forecast of the market. This market forecast is prepared by the SBU against the backdrop of the previously mentioned corporate long-range forecast of the whole economy. The corporate long-range forecast contains alternate scenarios and contingencies, for each of which a separate market forecast is prepared by the SBU.

The SBU then comes before its Executive Board. As yet, no detailed plans have been prepared. The debate is over long-range threats and opportunities, and the interface between short- and long-range profits to be contributed by the business. For example, seeing threatening market trends, the corporation may want to explore the profit profile of a fast retreat. The SBU may want to meet the same threat head on with a new plant, and after substantial outlays, achieve sizeable profits in later years.

In practice, getting good final planning guidelines for each SBU has proven to be one of the most difficult and at the same time crucial requirements of the overall planning system. After all, the SBU management would like to have the advantage of being part of the General Electric Company, but none of the disadvantages. For the most part, everyone wants to grow, no one wants to "harvest." Everyone likes to procrastinate, few like to face up to implacable problems. Everyone likes to define an easy objective, no one likes to be measured against a tough one.

Several months of the year are required to complete the selection elements of the strategic planning process in order to make sure that all good alternates are carefully considered, and that all points of view are heard.

Later in the year the resulting plans, complete with a five-year forecast of earnings, cash and investment implications, are submitted by each SBU to its Executive Board. Within the guidelined objectives, major strategic alternatives and implementation tactics are separately explored and evaluated. The Executive

Board will resolve these final decisions and recommend the plan for approval to the Executive Office.

A final corporate level planning meeting concerns itself with how to invest in these plans so as to optimize the attainment of the corporate objectives that were originally set in the initial meeting at the beginning of the year. In this final meeting the emphasis is on the short-range economic outlook. Presumably, we have our long-range goals set. We know where we want to position the Company. We have sufficient good plans in hand to reach those objectives by several alternate paths which vary in risk and cost to implement. Factoring in the short-range outlook, each plan is evaluated against several alternate possible economies, and then ranked in terms of its contribution to corporate long-range goals and short-term earnings. The Corporate Executive Staff then recommends the best set of plans and related earnings targets to the Corporate Executive Office. The approved plans provide the basis for each SBU to initiate preparation of final operating budgets, cash budgets and appropriation proposals for all major investments.

The approval of the operating plans for each SBU for the next calendar year is the subject of the final Executive Board meetings of the planning cycle.

In order to make this strategic system work, we have developed a number of very practical and interesting techniques. For instance, we have a computer model called Prom which contains a full profile of up to ten years of history for each of a number of selected businesses. The unusual thing about this model is that we can take a projected business situation and estimate how many of our businesses will do in that situation based on what the characteristics of the business have shown in the past. Thus, we can test out a wide variety of situations and decision consequences.

We use quite a few rather sophisticated modeling techniques to determine corporate trajectory, future predictions and various combinations of insight which we may wish to have in considering strategy alternatives. In one case we have a method of determining which of our businesses are suitable short-range earnings producers by evaluating the trade-off between short-range earnings potential and potential long-term damage to the business.

One thing we have learned from these modeling techniques is not to trust them implicitly. The models aren't always perfect because the modelers aren't always that perfectly smart. The models must always be confronted with judgment. Therefore, we are now using both quantitative and qualitative criteria in our evaluations. The point here is that the more criteria you have of *both* kinds, the more chance you have of being right, even if your numbers or your judgment happens to be wrong in any one criterion.

Confrontation itself is another technique we use. In the planning calendar I described and in our Executive Boards, we quite deliberately use a top-down and bottom-up confrontation of perspectives. These arenas provide a disciplined way to achieve understanding of perspectives both up and down.

As I am sure you realize, the system itself is only a tool. It happens to be a good one so far. The real task is the re-direction of General Electric to growth in earnings while moving into opportunities suggested by the shape of the future.

We launched this new effort approximately a year and a half ago and we've been through one complete cycle of the new planning system. What have we learned from it? And what remains to be solved?

The most important thing we learned was that this method gave us a more realistic picture of the Company than had surfaced before we started. We were able to establish a solid point of departure for making additional decisions on where to fix our businesses, where to grow and where to put resources for the best overall corporate balance.

What remains to be solved? Well, first of all, not all of our managers are yet accustomed to think strategically about their businesses. But the results to date have been so obviously superior to anything we have done before in planning or in making resources decisions, that only a few die-hards would like to go back to the old way of doing things.

Second, we are only beginning to get underway in sorting out the businesses that really offer the best promise and those which offer less. Notwithstanding the fact that General Electric is highly diversified, it is also highly integrated, so that any surgical process turns out to be a major operation.

Finally, we are going to have to provide some type of development activity at the corporate level for planning alternatives which go completely beyond the present organization structure. We obviously try to probe these new possibilities by organizing task forces of experts drawn from interested businesses.

We seem to be in a period when new and cogent criticism is being directed at all large institutions. Institutions themselves are working hard to upgrade the whole concept of their own function in rapidly developing a new sense of social responsibility, as well as entirely new methods of directing and controlling their own evolution. Competition in these new dimensions may in the end not only redefine what is the proper role of large and small businesses, but what is properly public and private as well.

10 Experimental Decision-Making in the Theory of the Firm

Clement G. Krouse*

In recent years motivational realism has been imaginatively added to economic theories of the firm.[1] In contrast, there has been a relative absence of theories involving propositions which focus on realism in the firm's economic decision-making process. This paper attempts such an extension without dismissing the considerable range of economic events for which existing theories have been shown valid. Central to the proposed model is the extension of the economic decision concept to mean a sequence of decisions by which the firm (1) makes a commitment to a tentative plan of resource allocation, and (2) enacts experiments to gather information as a basis for future decision-making. Specifically, the firm is considered to act by the sequential process of decision-making, operating, and then, on the basis of this experience, revising its decisions and policies rather than as implied by the single-step analysis of a set of simultaneous equations. This behavior pattern has the important decentralizing effect of reducing the firm's multi-dimensional problem to a sequence of adaptive moves in fewer dimensions.

One particular class of problems which the paper addresses are those suggested by the target rate-of-return pricing "theories." Eckstein and Fromm [73] review this literature and, using the conjectures and results of prior studies, develop perhaps the most comprehensive statement and model of full-cost, target-return oligopolistic pricing. Because of the close ties to earlier work, however, Eckstein and Fromm fail to develop a satisfactory theory for their model. Like their predecessors they neglect to give systematic consideration to the fundamental questions of why targets are formed, the determinants of target levels, or the rationale for changes to the levels. It is to these omissions of the mark-up doctrine, as well as other oligopolistic models such as Baumol [23] and Williamson [259] which use a targeted variable concept, that the current analysis is specifically directed.

The paper is organized as follows: In the first two sections a general, multiple-argument objective criterion is postulated for the firm. A "problem" decomposition technique using targeted variables to eliminate interunit externalities is next developed as a model of organizational decentralization. Key conceptual differences between the present model and conventional transfer-pricing decentralization models are noted. The last section sets forth a procedure for sequential adaption of targets, explaining the firm's target adjustment

129

mechanism as an attempt to move to maximization through "satisficing" levels of select policy variables. It is of especial interest to note that the several elements of the models are combined in a framework which explicitly decentralizes the firm's operational and decision-making tasks, and concomitantly gives a specialized structure to its internal resource allocation problem.

Decentralization and Policy Adaptation

Consider the case of a maximizing firm with a scalar-valued objective function having N arguments.

(1) $$\max_{z} g(z)$$

(2) subject to: $f(z) = 0$

Here $g(z)$ is the scalar-value utility function, and f represents M technical constraints on feasible combinations of the firm's N discretionary variables.[2]

Assume g is strictly concave, or that there exists decreasing marginal returns in each z_1. Both g and f functions are taken to be suitably continuous. All vectors are taken to be column unless transposition is indicated by a prime.

Williamson [259] and Marris [155] have amply shown that generalized preference functions with arguments explicitly stated can lead to testable economic implications. But, even though component variables of z can be specifically identified to give the complex objective empirical significance, it is not simultaneously appropriate to reason that corporate managers act to find the solution to this optimization problem as a single, integrated whole. On the contrary, the cognitive inability of corporate decision makers to efficiently solve all of the implied relations in a simultaneous model (i.e., without a convergent, iterative process to reduce complexity and problem size) has been frequently noted.[3] Thus, beginning with Adam Smith it has been observed that parts of the firm's overall management problem are efficiently detached and formed to be treated by specialized units or departments.

The process of specialization can be based on the decomposition of g and the f into components as

(3) $$g(z) = g_1(x,w) + g_2(x,y)$$

(4) $$f(z) = \begin{bmatrix} f_1(x,w) \\ f_2(x,y) \end{bmatrix}$$

The variables w, x, and y are defined such that $[\,w,x,y\,] \equiv z$ with, respectively N_w, N_x, and N_y elements ($N_w + N_x + N_y = N$). The vectors of w and y represent two subsets of the firm's discretionary variables which are fully separable from one another in g, and x represents a third subset from which neither w nor y is separable. The function g_1 given by Equation (3) is considered "large" in the sense that it involves all terms in x and w which are separable from y; conversely, g_2 is "small" in the sense that all terms separable in w are absent. From Equation (4) it is seen that such a separation of variables in general leads to a partitioning of constraints: f_1 is an M_1- vector of functions involving only x and w, and f_2 is an M_2- vector involving only x and y ($M_1 + M_2 = M$). A larger number of variable subsets more complexly separated and linking might generally be developed from the vector z; these, in turn, would lead to more detailed and, perhaps, realistic specifications of g_i and f_i functions. The simplified decomposition structure employed here is, nonetheless, sufficient for explication purposes.

Considering the g_i and f_i ($i = 1,2$) as organizational activities, decision making tasks can be assembled by kind of variable according to the formal representation

$$(5) \qquad \min_{\lambda,\eta} \quad \max_{w,x,y} \quad \left\{\, [\,g_1\,(x,w) + \lambda' f_1\,(x,w)\,] \,+ \right.$$
$$\left. [\,g_2\,(x,y) + \eta' f_2\,(x,y)\,] \,\right\}$$

The M_1-vector λ and the M_2-vector η have been introduced to accommodate the f_1 and f_2 constraints, respectively, and the saddle point of minimum cost and maximum performance is sought by the firm's management.

Unaltered, Equation (5) implies that any decentralization of decision-making activities would result in the formation of organizational units subject to extensive external effects, or externalities. Specifically, externalities can be said to exist when the firm's relevant decision variables cannot be fully separated and, subsequently, uniquely assigned to decision-making units. Thus, in Equation (5) if the activity represented by $g_1 + \lambda' f_1$ were assigned to a given unit and, similarly, activity $g_2 + \eta' f_2$ were assigned to another, then externalities to both units would exist. Neither activity would have full discretion over the x control variables; each unit would optimally need information from the other, and thus be required to engage in cooperative decision-making. Such interdependencies or externalities lead to "computational" difficulties in theoretical decentralization models and, when excessive, communication and co-ordination difficulties in actual business practice. As a consequence, in theoretical analyses of the firm economists have generally considered an absence of external effects implying complete separability, $x \equiv 0$, and assumed the problem away in their formulations, see Whinston [256, pp. 427-431] as an example.

It is precisely at this point, where external effects need to be realistically considered in a complex decentralization process, that March and Simon [149, pp. 204-205] directly place their organizational role for satisficing targets. Baldwin [2, pp. 244-246], more specifically than March and Simon, fully invokes this targeting concept to criticize the Kaplan et al [121] proposition of a corporate "target rate-of-return goal." Baldwin argues the Kaplan *et al* observations to be more correctly interpreted as the firm resolving its externalities problem by using the rate-of-return target as a "tool" in its decision-making system. This use of target variables has largely eluded further notice in the literature, and especially the target return pricing studies. Little systematic attention has been given to the firm's economic decision process, the concomitant assignment of satisficing values to selected non-price variables, and, what is equally important, with mechanisms by which target values are adjusted over time.

Targeting, Decentralization, and the Firm's Decision Process

Suppose that the firm adopts policy targets for the linking x vector of its objective variables. Denote current policy target levels as x^* and consider the firm, as suggested, to specialize its complex internal activities by the assignment of these resource variable targets.[4] Decentralizing on the basis of x^*, the firm's problem symbolically becomes

$$(6) \qquad \min_{\lambda} \ \max_{w,x} \quad [g_1(x,w) + \lambda' f_1(x,w)] \ +$$

$$\min_{\eta} \ \max_{y} \quad [g_2(x^*,y) + \eta' f_2(x^*,y)]$$

$$(7) \qquad \text{subject to:} \quad x = x^*$$

With regard to organizational structure, a consequence of the resource-directive decomposition is an internal decision precedence which is hierarchical in character. This can be clearly seen by formally rewriting the firm's problem as

$$(8) \qquad \max_{x^*} G(x^*) = \max_{x^*} \Big\{ \min_{\lambda,\mu} \ \max_{x,w} [g_1(x,w) + \lambda' f_1(x,w) + \mu'(x-x^*)] + \min_{\eta} \ \max_{y} [g_2(x^*,y) + \eta' f_2(x^*,y)] \Big\}$$

where μ is an N_x vector of Lagrange multipliers and $G(x^*)$ is defined as the function generated by the inner minimum-maximum operations. Each of the separate optimization operations of Equation (8) represents a distinct, de-coupled decision unit and their indicated order represents the organizational hierarchy of decision-making and control.

It is important to emphasize that this statement of the firm's organization and decision process is developed in a manner which eliminates externalities: the targeted x's appear in the second unit's activities, the second minimum-maxi-mum operation only as the policy assigned target parameters x^*, and the untargeted y variables do not appear in the first unit's, the firm minimum-maxi-mum operation activities. The multiplier or dual variables μ, λ, and η, which measure the worth of relaxing the several constraints, are also separated in a similar fashion. Clearly the values of these dual variables are dependent on the assigned x^*; thus, they yield important information on the bid or efficiency price the various units of the firm attach to the adaptation of x^*. This form of decomposition can be referred to as "resource directive." With this technique the (primal) problem is feasibly solved at every adaptive state. In contrast to this technique, there is price directive decomposition (corresponding to the dual problem of nonlinear programming) which has generally been the method used for transfer-pricing decentralization models, see Whinston [256]. This second technique decomposes the overall problem by setting target transfer prices by treating λ and η parametrically. The important difficulty with price-direction is that a feasible solution to the (primal) problem is not typically produced during the iterative stages of the solution, but only at the end.

Figure 10-1 indicates the manner in which the firm would be organizationally decentralized by this specific assignment of targets. Note that the second or

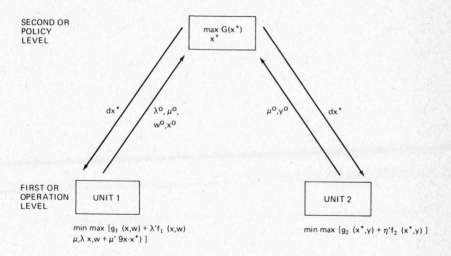

Figure 10-1. Decentralization by Targets.

policy level fully controls the firm only by iteratively assigning target values for the select resource nonprice variables. Moreover, each activity of the firm is performed separately at any point in time, and each has a "small" number of variables to manipulate.[5] As is clear from Equation (8), the goals that underlie decisions made at the operational level need not directly coincide (be identical) with the overall goals of the firm. However, they are fully consistent with that objective.

By this system of decentralization it is required that the policy level establish resource usage targets and direct the operations units to perform according to these standards. The operations units by their activity determine efficiency prices for relaxing these targets. These efficiency prices are, in turn, directed to the policy level which uses them to adjust the prevailing x^* targets. These adjustments to targets are channeled down to the operations units, while efficiency price information for adapting the targets are fed back. This is in clear distinction to the more frequently employed transfer pricing technique of decentralization, where prices are sequentially channeled down as the mode of corporate control.

Relatively simple extensions and reconstructions of the model can permit any number of specializing departments and hierarchical levels of decentralization. For example, the unit 1 (or g_1 and f_1) activity might be that of the corporate controller and the unit 2 rules those of the production, sales, etc. departments. Either or both units might be, in turn, further decentralized by additional specification of financial budget, production, sales, etc. quotas or standards (targets). The empirical studies of Heflebower [104] Kaplan *et al* [121] and Sleznick [204] and the anecdotal evidence of Chamberlain [45, pp. 84-91] and Baumol [23, pp. 36-101] suggest some of the kinds of policy targets, and hence specializing levels and units, that might in fact exist as firm's attempt to reduce their overall task complexity by decentralization.

The unit 1 and 2 interim-optimal values (y^0, x^0, w^0) and efficiency prices (λ^0, η^0, μ^0) are specific, intermediate outcomes of the operations level organizations which are aimed at and inform the firm's overall planning process at any stage, say t.[6] Using these data, new target levels for adaption state ($t + 1$) can then be designed at the policy level and fed back to units 1 and 2. The firm following such a procedure is characterized as operating in an iterative, close-looped fashion by a trial-and-error process; i.e., adapting x^* by choosing dx^* to obtain the maximum admissible $g (z)$.

Based upon the information received from its operations, a policy target adjustment rule to control the firm's entire decision-making system should, *ceteris paribus*, lead to an optimal value of the multiple argument criterion. The speed and oscillatory (or non-oscillatory) properties of convergence from initial targets to the optimal combination of arguments in the firm's utility function will follow from the particular properties of the decision rule employed.

Target Adaptation

One highly typical case is to consider the firm to adapt its policy target values such that, in moving from one iterative decision stage to the next, it always attempts an immediate improvement in the value of its overall objective criterion.[7] This requires the total differential of G to be positive, $dG > 0$, at every adaptive stage. Form this differential over the firm's discretionary variables as

$$(9) \qquad dG = \left(\frac{\partial G}{\partial \mu}\right)' d\mu + \left(\frac{\partial G}{\partial x}\right)' dx + \left(\frac{\partial G}{\partial y}\right)' dy + \left(\frac{\partial G}{\partial \lambda}\right)' d\lambda +$$

$$\left(\frac{\partial G}{\partial w}\right)' dw + \left(\frac{\partial G}{\partial \mu}\right)' d\mu + \left(\frac{\partial G}{\partial x^*}\right)^i dx^*$$

The prime represents vector transposition such that the vectors of the inner products are conformable.

In the previously outlined decentralization and specialization process, the firm has assigned specific roles to its individual operations-level units such that, given targets x^*, the following conditions obtain at their specialized optimal. By unit 1's activity

$$(10) \qquad \frac{\partial G}{\partial \mu}, \frac{\partial G}{\partial x}, \frac{\partial G}{\partial w}, \frac{\partial G}{\partial \lambda} \quad \text{all are zero; and, by unit } 2\text{'s activity}$$

$$(11) \qquad \frac{\partial G}{\partial y}, \frac{\partial G}{\partial \mu} \quad \text{all are zero.}$$

Since the actions of these first level units cause six of the seven terms of Equation (9) to be zero, the second-level policy decisions need only be concerned with choosing dx^* to affect dG.[8] Specifically,

$$(12) \qquad dG = \frac{\partial G'}{\partial x^*} dx^*$$

is all that remains, and dx^* is the adjustment required.

Consider a choice of dx^* by the simple rule

$$(13) \qquad dx^* = k \frac{\partial G}{\partial x^*}$$

where the parameter $k > 0$ is an indicator of the firm's adaptation response intensity.[9] The term $\partial G/\partial x^*$ is the gradient of G with respect to the targets, and indicates the direction of steepest increase in the overall objective when changing *only* the targeted resource variables. The adaptation rule is thus highly tractable, simply requiring the firm's upper management to adjust the small subset of target variables to attain maximal performance while merely considering *all other variables* to be constant at their prevailing levels. Further, as required

$$dG = k \frac{\partial G'}{\partial x^*} \frac{\partial G}{\partial x^*} \geqslant 0$$

so that this specific algorithm for target adjustment moves the firm continuously toward its optimal performance level.

In summary, Equations (9) - (12) again show that the adjustment of target values (i.e., specifying the dx^* policy change gradient) is the primary decision area of the second level. Aside from the current policy target values, all other variables in Equation (9) are assigned in the operations level problems as a result of the firm's decentralization. Moreover, the several units of the firm are in essence free of externalities due to the use of resource targets in the decentralization process. The policy level, however, maintains immediate direction over the lower level units since the x^0, μ^0, y^0, w^0, η^0, and λ^0 variables are functions of the x^* target values, which are adjusted at each stage of the firm's experimental process.

Summary

A variety of empirical evidence has been used to develop a model of the firm with realism in its decision-making sequence. The adaptive process set forth here: (1) provides for the treatment of a generalized corporate utility function with multiple objective variables; (2) decentralizes, on the basis of eliminating interunit externalities, the overall management problem into specializing subunits by a feasible scheme of policy target assignments; and, (3) considers the firm to move adaptively through satisficing levels toward the optimum combination of arguments in its objective function.

The traditional analysis of corporate economic behavior considers a fully centralized and non-adaptive decision-making process: the complex economic problem of the firm is, by ommission, considered to be solved in a simultaneous relations mode. Such a perspective might be appropriate when the firm's problem is "small" or when only the final state, not the internal decision-making organization or adaptive process, is of concern. In this important way the extended description of the firm offered here, i.e., the resource-directive decentralization and the associated experimental method of targeting discretionary variables, yields a model which extends the treatment of corporate events.

Appendix to Chapter 10

The Model

Consider a simplified model of the firm. Define a scalar corporate utility function with only two discretionary variables, x and y, $U = U(x,y)$. Write the technical transformation between x and y implicitly as $f(x,y) = 0$. And, suppose U can be decomposed as

$$U = U_1(x) + U_2(y) + U_3(x,y)$$

where U_3 is "small" compared to U. Refer to $\partial U_1/\partial x$ as the *specific* marginal utility of x and $\partial U_3/\partial x$ as the *conditional* marginal utility (which, of course, depends on the level of y). Similarly, specific and conditional marginal utilities of y can be given, respectively, as $\partial U_2/\partial y$ and $\partial U_3/\partial y$. Note that

$$dU = [\partial U_1/\partial x + \partial U_3/\partial x]\, dx + [\partial U_2/\partial y + \partial U_3/\partial y]\, dy$$

so that the total effect on utility of changes in both x and y are the appropriate sums of specific and conditional marginal utilities.

Consistent with the organization structure referred to in the text, divide the firm into two operational units and a policy level unit. Have the policy level assign the operations units to operate with target x^*. Subsequently, unit *1* computes the specific marginal utility of x at x^* and forwards this. Subunit *2* computes the specific marginal utility of y the conditional marginal utility of y at x, and the rate of physical transformation between x and y at x^*.

Define
$$\lambda_x = \left[\frac{\partial U_1}{\partial x}\right]_{x^*}$$

$$\lambda_y = \left[\frac{\partial U_2}{\partial y} + \frac{\partial U_3}{\partial y} \Big/ \frac{\partial f}{\partial y}\right]_{x^*}$$

λ_x may be interpreted economically as the specific marginal utility of x at x^*, and λ_y as the sum of the specific and conditional marginal utility of y at x^* divided by the technical transformation rate (also at x^*). The information on λ_x and λ_y is transmitted from the operational subunits to the policy level, where use is made of these efficiency price values to decide whether to raise or lower the target x^* *and* by what amount.

The target adjustment decision rule given in the last section requires that x^* should be increased until the specific and conditional marginal utility of x divided by the specific and conditional marginal utility of y are equal to the marginal rate of technical substitution. That is, the rule is designed to tell whether the firm is at a point like A or C in Figure 10-2 and, further, to tell which direction to move to attain optimal point B.

137

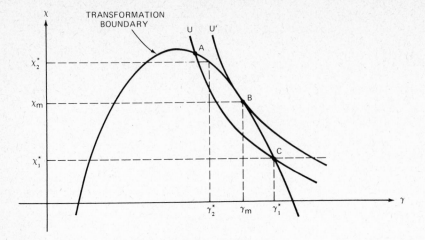

Figure 10-2. Two Choice Objects.

Part IV:
Pricing Decisions

The chapters on pricing decisions represent a specific application of the general decision-making process presented in Chapters 7 to 10. Weston's paper centers on the theoretical issues of pricing based on economic models, Schubert addresses the issue of pricing in entering a new industry and Sultan provides a case study of pricing and a marketing interpretation of a strategy for pricing turbine-generators during the decade of the 1950s.

The main controversy among economists over the last thirty years has been between full-cost or target rate of return pricing versus marginalist principles. The former are further enmeshed in the controversies over administered pricing, administered profits, collusion, organizationl slack, and, in general, a misallocation of resources in oligopolistic industries. Marginalist principles are those of the textbook-dominated profit maximization hypothesis with the atomistic case offered as the competitive ideal. Empirical studies on pricing have almost universally shown how actual pricing decisions are inconsistent with marginalist principles.

Weston's paper explains how the interpretation in previous studies stems from the use of a static partial equilibrium model under certainty rather than an appropriate dynamic general equilibrium under uncertainty model, i.e., a model consistent with the real world enrivonment of firms. He argues mark-up or target pricing heretofore lacked a theory of why and

how targets are set. The thrust of his paper offers a theory of dynamic competition in oligopoly based on a series of sequential short-run decisions within a framework of long-run planning. To economize on information and search costs, targets and goals are set and serve as managerial checkpoints in an adaptive price-searching or learning process designed to achieve the overall goal of higher levels of company performance. These targets and goals exist at various levels of the firm and serve as checkpoints in a dynamic information feedback process. Prices are only one of a number of decision variables along with capacity-investment decisions which must be considered in long-run resource allocation. Others include such variables as product quality, marketing, financing, advertising, and service organizations.

Weston offers some empirical evidence of price flexibility consistent with his model in oligopolistic industries, specifically autos, aluminum, and steel. In addition, evidence on company profits is presented which is inconsistent with the target rate of return or administered profit hypothesis. Under his model the pressures of rivalry under uncertainty stimulate the adoption of strategies designed to achieve efficiency and performance improvement. Hence, large firms are generally not sheltered from competitive pressures reflected in their pricing policies and resulting performance.

The economic and marketing literature on the pricing policy followed by *a firm when it enters a new market or produces a new product is called penetration pricing. The two extreme alternatives are to charge a relatively high price to make initial profits before other firms imitate or to charge a relatively low price in the attempt to obtain a market position. Which of these strategies is followed depends upon the environmental conditions facing the firm. One type of situation is when there has been considerable risk and expense in developing a new, unique product, so that the demand elasticity is low. The penetration pricing policy followed under these circumstances is to charge a high price at the beginning and to lower the price as other firms imitate with competing products.*

The other type of situation is illustrated in the paper by Dr. Schubert. In supplying equipment for producing electrical energy for the utilities by nuclear reactors there was nothing unique in the end product. The electricity that comes out at the end of the turbine-generator, however fueled, is the same whether the steam that goes through the turbines is heated by fossil fuels or by nuclear fuels. Hence the cost per kilowatt hour of producing electricity by nuclear energy could not be any higher than the cost of producing the electricity by fossil fuels. Yet initially the costs of producing nuclear reactors for power generation systems were higher than the ceiling set by fossil fuels.

This poses some major strategic problems for a business firm. This topic also illustrates the relation between long-range capacity, investment planning and new product planning and pricing as set forth in general terms in the Weston paper on pricing policy. The General Electric Company had to determine the proper time to come into the business, whether to run the risk of coming in too soon and incurring losses or to come in too late to find that the competition had positioned itself in a strong competitive stance. Furthermore, they had to make a decision as to whether and how long they would take this business on a turnkey basis which shifted the risk from the electric utilities to the seller of the power generation equipment.

Dr. Schubert's paper also illustrates that if after successfully entering the business, a competitive return on investment was earned, this was not because the firm controlled the market, but rather that their decisions on the timing when to come in and their ability to get their costs down would, in fact, come close to their plans and targets. It would appear from the presentation by Dr. Schubert that initial losses were incurred, that the risks were very high, that a recovery of the initial losses alone would take a number of years. Therefore, to analyze what return on investment a firm has achieved requires taking a relatively long period perspective. Thus, Dr. Schubert's paper is of value in its brief and effective summary of the fundamental facts highlighting and illustrating many topics and issues of considerable theoretical significance.

The paper by Dr. Sultan provides a case history of the turbine-generator industry for the decade of the 1950s by looking at two dimensions of competition, price and technology. He finds that large, complex equipment had a continuously lower price per kilowatt rating than smaller, less complex machines. Since the demand for generating equipment by utilities is a derived demand from final power consumers, the utilities' main concern is meeting this demand by increasing capacity and offering their services at lower prices. Hence, they were responsive to the price advantage of large, complex units. Sultan hypothesizes that the price reductions of the larger machines with the newest technology relative to smaller, less complex machines and the higher relative prices of medium size machines, improved manufacturers' profit performance, and helped finance R&D efforts, for the period of his study, 1950-61.

11 Pricing Behavior of Large Firms

J. Fred Weston

Although many studies have been made, no consensus has been reached concerning the methods by which firms make pricing decisions. A controversy continues between full-cost or target pricing and the application of marginalist principles.[1] An unsatisfactory dichotomy (frequently separated by chapters in textbooks) is also found in the treatment of the goals and behavior of atomistic firms and oligopolists. The aim of this paper is to present new evidence that helps reconcile the conflicting approaches. A three-year study, during which extensive interviews were conducted with top managements concerning their capital resource allocation decisions, yielded fresh insights into the pricing process.[2] While my experiences confirmed the well-known weaknesses of the interview technique, the discussions enable me to discern a process that: (1) explains why empirical work on the corporate pricing problem has led to conflicting views; (2) reconciles some apparent differences between decision-making in small and large firms; and (3) demonstrates that what appears to be irrational behavior in a static model is rational behavior in a dynamic world.

My plan is to begin by describing the pattern that emerged from the interviews. Next the formulation is tested by empirical studies. Finally, the analysis is used to provide a framework for explaining why other studies have often been misinterpreted. The core of the present reformulation lies in the nature of planning and control processes of firms; the key aspect of this perspective is that short-run decisions are made in the framework of longer-range planning. Thus, the underlying model for analysis is not the commonly-used static theory of the firm, but rather the theory of investment under uncertainty, with maximization of the present value of an earnings stream. Within the investment decision framework, adaptive learning by firms becomes a central feature of economic behavior, manifesting itself through the firm's use of (1) plans and standards of controls; (2) periodic review and analysis of divergences between planned and actual results; and (3) an information feedback system providing for revisions of plans, standards and policies.

In prior analysis of corporate pricing, a major source of confusion has resulted from the divergence between the time period covered in the questions posed and that of the economic model used to interpret the responses.[3] Although the Brookings [121] questionnaire began with four questions about policies over a twenty-five-year period and the Hall and Hitch [100] questions

143

asked about behavior over a number of business fluctuations, the responses were analyzed with reference to "the common analysis of short-run equilibrium in terms of marginal cost and marginal revenue" [262, p. 124]. But businessmen, being much less myopic, must have made their responses to these surveys and interviews in the context of the firm's decision processes over the extended period of time suggested by the nature of the questions posed. As a consequence, the implications of reviews, decision revisions, and other adaptive behavior of firms which constitute elements of organizational decision processes, have been confounded in the pricing policy literature. These behavioral processes are evidence that firms do in fact develop strategies for "earning while learning" [156, p. 52]. The adaptive learning processes of business firms suggest a dynamic general equilibrium model of investment under uncertainty (for brief reference, DGU) as the appropriate framework for analysis of economic consequences. In contrast, similar information elicited in other previous surveys was analyzed with reference to a static partial equilibrium model of pricing under certainty (SPC). While business investment decisions are only beginning to be guided by formal dynamic models, the adaptive processes represent a heuristic dynamics.[4] Similarly, the trial-and-error learning activities of business firms do not formally employ a general equilibrium framework, but neither are they restricted to the small number of variables of partial equilibrium analysis.

The two central themes of this paper are: first, business behavior superficially characterized as nonoptimizing by reference to an SPC model constitutes a strategic response to a DGU world and second, the DGU model suggests revision of some of the inferences derived from deterministic models. Traditional price theory has employed static partial equilibrium analysis of output decisions in "price-taking" atomistic markets and of "price-seeking" in imperfect markets. In the longer-run framework of investment decisions, additional variables with a wide range of values should enter the analysis. Forms of competition become numerous and complex. Therefore, collusion becomes more difficult and is not a simple function of the market shares of the largest firms. A related inference that atomistic market structures alone can guarantee maximal efficiency is derived from the assumptions of the SPC model. Firms in concentrated markets in a DGU model are subject to forces to achieve optimizing performance of the kind ascribed to competitive pressures.

Markup Pricing Rules

Previous surveys [100] [121] of pricing reported that instead of being guided by marginal principles, business firms used markup rules which reflected some degree of market control. The Hall and Hitch survey described full-cost pricing behavior, while the Brookings survey emphasized the predominance of target return-on-investment pricing. These two markup pricing rules are similar.[5] The full-cost pricing markup factor is applied to standard unit variable costs with overheads excluded. Target pricing is based on a fixed return on capital investment. If the ratio of investment to output is constant and if the full-cost markup base includes fixed costs, a constant relation exists between the percentage markup on total cost and the target rate of return on investment.[6] Because the two concepts are similar and "target-return on investment was perhaps the most frequently mentioned of pricing goals" [129, p. 923], its implications will be pursued.

The target-return pricing literature is a collection of observations about limited aspects of firm behavior without a systematic theory of pricing. It fails to provide an explanation of why targets are formed, how their level is determined, or why or how targets are changed. Various advantages of target-return pricing for large firms have been set forth by other writers as its rationale: (1) ". . . target-return pricing makes for price stability, since standard costs change much less frequently than actual costs or short-run demand conditions" [72, p. 269]; (2) ". . . it is particularly suitable for price leadership" [73, p. 1165]; (3) Target pricing enables a firm to manage its profits. "The foregoing data, above all, make it clear that management's approach to pricing is based upon *planned* profits" [129, p. 938]. Thus, some writers on target-return pricing tend to view it not as a form of rule-of-thumb behavior, but rather as an effective instrument for achieving market control.

A basic source of confusion in these conflicting appraisals is that the survey responses were evaluated in terms of a static short-run partial equilibrium model of pricing, while the nature of the questionnaires and views elicited business responses based on a long-run time framework. The prevailing treatment of pricing in an SPC model is well known. An alternative investment model is now briefly summarized as the frame of reference formulation in a DGU model.[7]

An Alternative Framework

Stimulated by the original work of Markowitz and Tobin, a capital-asset pricing model has been developed [136] [165] [205]. Under appropriate assumptions, a security valuation theorem is derived.

(1) $$E(R_j) = R_f + \lambda \operatorname{Cov}(R_j, R_m)$$

where:

R_j (random variable) is the rate of return on security j

R_f is the rate of return on a risk-free security

R_m (random variable) is the rate of return on the market portfolio of risky securities

λ is a positive constant equal to $[E(R_m) - R_m]/\sigma_m^2$

$\sigma_m{}^2$ is the variance of market returns which standardizes the market risk premium

Cov (R_j, R_m) is the covariance of the returns on security j with returns on the market

The intuitive logic of this theorem is that the return on a risky asset is composed of two elements. One is the risk-free return. The other is the market price of risk, λ, weighted by the asset's non-diversifiable risk measured by its covariance with fluctuations in the returns on the market.

The model can be used to indicate the influence of a firm's investment decision on its share prices [106] [166] [172]. A rule based on the security valuation theorem expressed in Equation (1) states that firm j should accept an investment project only if

$$(2) \qquad E(R_{pj}) > R_f + \text{Cov}(R_{pj}, R_m)$$

where $E(R_{pj})$ is the rate of return on the project appropriately measured.

This decision rule provides for acceptance of the project only if its expected internal rate of return exceeds the appropriate risk-adjusted discount rate for the project. Figure 11-1 presents the framework. The market line shown in Figure 11-1 represents a risk-standardized marginal cost of capital appropriate to all

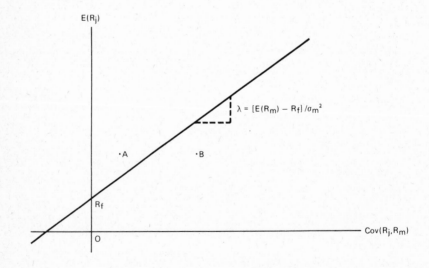

Figure 11-1. Framework for Investment Decisions.

firms and all projects. An individual investment project is described by its position in the risk-return space. For example, Project A and Project B have the same expected rate of return. However, the risk associated with Project B is greater than the risk associated with Project A. Thus Project A is an acceptable project, while Project B is not. When the firm accepts favorable projects, there will be an upward revision of the firm's share price which restores equilibrium in the financial markets by lowering $E(R_j)$. Since this theory of investment has been more fully developed elsewhere, this presentation will emphasize the more specific economic implications.

The relevant marginal analysis involves comparing the marginal efficiency of investment to the marginal cost of capital. But, more importantly, the marginal relationships are expressed in a risk-return analysis. In a DGU model the risk-return relationships, not point estimates of return are the relevant decision variables. Furthermore, the long-run nature of the investment decision brings a wider range of variables into the analysis in order to estimate the characteristics of the probability distributions of returns and to select parameters for making decisions. The investment aspect of the decisions shifts the analysis to a broader time framework. The model constitutes a conceptual framework for understanding the implications of responses by businessmen to questions involving long-run resource allocation decisions under uncertainty.

Pricing in a Resource Allocation Process

With the improvement of information processing provided by the computer, the decision to commit or recommit corporate resources involves analysis of a wide variety of variables and, because of uncertainty, a repeated assessment of the decision [56] [55]. In this broad decision process, pricing performs a role, but a wide variety of other decision variables also enter the analysis. The familiar partial equilibrium *ceteris paribus* diagrams in textbook presentations give an unnecessarily narrow view of pricing decisions in both large and small firms. In the long-run framework it is not meaningful to hold other factors constant because of their interaction with pricing decisions.[8] Other groups of variables to be considered are: (1) product characteristic vectors; (2) relative price vectors in relation to product quality; (3) the nature of the sales or dealer organization vectors involved in marketing the product; (4) advertising and other promotional effort vectors; and (5) the quality of the financing and service organizations to support product sales and use.[9]

Broad environmental influences, combined with the constraints presented by existing products and firms in the market, lead the firm to develop adaptive policies with respect to product, quality, prices, sales methods, promotion efforts, service organization and financial facilities [56] [55] [164]. These decisions, in turn, have an influence on the quantity and type of fixed investments and on the level and behavior of other costs. Even on new products, constraints are set by the market, since new products substitute in some degree for older products. The price concept itself is extremely complex on durable goods for which maintenance costs and availability of repair and service facilities are important decision variables in the purchase. In addition, the stock of used durable goods represents a multiple of any given year's flow of new output. Hence there is continuous competition between the stock of used durable goods and those newly produced.[10]

Strategies are formulated to offer either breadth or specialization in a range of combinations of product characteristics. Iterated reviews of product quality characteristics, materials characteristics, production methods, and marketing methods seek the optimal product quality, cost levels and marketing attractiveness. Since administrative discretion is exercised in selecting among alternative combinations of choices under uncertainty involving pricing decisions in relation to the other variables, atomistic firms as well as firms in concentrated industries may be said to have price policies.

The decision process involves variables each of which represents vectors of numerous dimensions. In the effort to limit the costs of compiling and processing information, goals and tasks are "factored," and operational targets are employed at several levels of the firm. In the interviews, business executives emphasized four types of financial targets: (1) return on investment; (2) growth in sales or earnings per share; (3) check points with regard to liquidity and solvency as measured by cash flows or leverage analysis; and (4) a favorable valuation relationship between the earnings of the company and the market price of its stock.

After the planning and budgeting decisions are made, managerial attention is focused on critical variables influencing the results of operations. As a consequence, statements of executives in interviews may be interpreted out of context.[11] For example, market share was said to be a goal which some firms substituted for profit maximization [129] but instead of being a goal, market share is a managerial check point in the following adaptive process. An important factor in corporate resources allocation decisions is the potential sales volume to provide a basis for capacity decisions. The size of the divergence of actual returns from expected returns will be a function of the divergence between the targeted and realized market share or total dollar value of sales. Thus, market share is likely to be regarded as an end in itself.[12] Targets or rules thus need to be distinguished from organization goals; targets are used to coordinate operating divisions in the achievement of corporate objectives.[13]

Because of change and uncertainty, emphasis was placed throughout the interview discussions on review and adjustment of decisions. The nature of satisficing behavior is also suggested by this learning process. Satisficing objectives represent check points in a firm's continuing effort to move toward higher levels of performance.[14] Thus, whether rules and targets reflect nonoptimal behavior depends upon whether they are used inflexibly or whether they are employed as instruments in a dynamic information feedback process.

Organization Processes as Viewed by the
Behavioral Theory of the Firm

An alternative interpretation of the evidence on organizational processes in the firm has been set forth in the behavioral theory of the firm [56]. Among the elements of the theory are observations on the divergence between organizational goals and individual goals. The firm is viewed as a coalition whose continuity is supported by organization slack, associated in some degree with imperfect competition. Shielded from the rigors of competition, organization slack is generated as a form of monopoly returns permitting managerial discretion.[15] Managerial discretion leads to the substitution of various forms of individual gratification at the expense of the firm's goal of profit maximization.[16]

But bureaucratic behavior is not proof of the absence of competition. Furthermore, the evidence of managerial discretion or organization slack is fragmentary at best. For example, the evidence cited by Williamson in his book devoted to the subject, is that firms laid off staff during a decline in sales [258, pp. 170-71]. But this is also consistent with maximization.[17] Bureaucracy and the divergence of organization and individual goals is found in every type of institution [4], [95], [148]. They are a characteristic of organizational behavior rather than of the economic milieu. They are associated with institutional age and encrustation rather than with size alone. They can occur under strict atomistic industry structure. With a large number of decision variables of complex dimensions and with uncertainty, an organization does not have to achieve an optimum or have maximized for survival [263]. An optimum-seeking organization need only "on-the-average" be on par with its rivals or competitors to survive in its environment.

In efficient business firms and other well-managed organizations continuous efforts are made to counter the tendency toward bureaucratization resulting from specialization and departmentation. Reviews in continuous communication, information feedback systems are one means of countering this tendency. One of the functions of corporate staff is to aid in developing an effective communication system in the firm between the headquarters and operating divisions to achieve optimum-seeking behavior toward the firm's goals.[18] For both atomistic and large firms, performance sufficient for survival is required. Within the average performance over a large number of complex decisions under uncertainty, organization slack may also develop. Organization slack may arise from lack of atomistic conditions, but this lack is not the necessary and only source. Hence the existence of organization slack is not evidence of lack of competitive behavior. *Optimum-seeking goals are consistent with satisficing or survival performance.* The gains from specialization in large organizations are offset to some degree by the increased tendencies toward bureaucratization. But there is no *a priori* basis for arguing the superiority of large vs. small firms from organization-scale considerations. Nor is there a basis for arguing superiority of atomistic conditions for achieving competitive pressures.[19]

Tests of Alternative Inferences

Previous studies, utilizing a deterministic model, have drawn a variety of inferences about the performance of large firms. The use of target-return pricing based on standard costs is held to result in inflexible prices that lag in response to changes in demand. The thrust of the argument is that standard-cost target-return pricing is used to discipline oligopolistic behavior. It is further assumed that each firm's standard costs are known to all other firms and that to maintain oligopolistic collusion large firms do not engage in price competition.[20]

The Implications of Standard Cost Systems

These inferences stem from a misconception of the role of standard cost systems in accounting control. Standard volume and cost standards are utilized along with related price estimates as the basis for improving managerial performance by seeking to separate influences on the measured results of operations. Standard costing procedures are another illustration of the use of target projections as reference points and the use of rule-of-thumb formulae for reaching tentative decisions. But these tentative formulations are followed by periodic reviews to determine required changes in strategies. The use of standard cost systems enables top management to distinguish variations from targeted performance due to departures from standard volume (volume variance), from standard cost (cost variance), and from targeted prices (price variance). Variance analysis implies adaptive processes in the firm. The frequency of reviews has been increased by managerial expertise and by the technology of handling information. With computer-assisted management control systems, frequent reviews of "actual" versus "standard" may be utilized to achieve "real time control."

The economic significance of variance analysis in managerial accounting control systems is that it represents one of the methods of achieving adaptive learning behavior. It is a misinterpretation of the nature of standard cost procedures to contrast "competitive" and "oligopolistic" pricing behavior on the basis of models distinguishing between actual unit labor cost and standard unit labor cost. (Cf. Eckstein and Fromm [73]). Standard cost systems should not be regarded as evidence of oligopolistic control, since they are used by all firms independent of size in an effort to improve managerial performance. Indeed, the concept is applicable to all types of economizing organizations. Instead of representing a procedure for institutionalizing "oligopolistic lethargy," standard cost systems are a part of financial control systems seeking to achieve adaptive behavior in a dynamic world.

The Issue of Price Flexibility

A convincing explanation has not been given for the view that the prices of monopolists or of oligopolists in collusion should be less flexible than prices in atomistic industries, given the view that each is a "profit maximizer." Each should respond promptly to demand or cost changes that move them from their "maximizing" position. The rationalization sometimes offered is that firms in concentrated industries find it easier to maintain their tenuous and imperfect collusion if price changes are not required too often. However, this rationale ignores their reaction to other dynamic variables that would be more destructive to the tenuous collusion than adjusting to price changes. Differences among industries in cost structures, frequency of cost and demand changes, and variations in income elasticity of demand for different products would also be disruptive and would make price inflexibility an unsound policy.

Stigler and Kindahl [224] provide evidence that "effective" price changes in individual products are much wider and more frequent than conventionally assumed. They also found (in a regression analysis of the standard deviation of individual price changes about the mean change as the dependent variable) that the number of price reporters was a highly significant explanatory factor. Other individual pieces of evidence provide further support for the proposition that prices are actually much more flexible than has frequently been assumed. One such bit of evidence is drawn from the automobile industry, which is widely taken as the archetype of disciplined oligopoly in which prices are highly rigid. The conventional view is based on the beginning-of-the-year dealer-recommended prices and initial manufacturing charges to the dealers. But Congressional Hearings have revealed that individual automobile manufacturers begin changing their prices to dealers in a wide variety of ways; at various times and degrees depending upon the reception of a particular model of the manufacturer's car [176]. Price changes to dealers take many forms: special bonuses for cars sold in excess of the dealer's quota, special product promotions, price variations for specified optional equipment, etc. Pricing programs are modified and adapted throughout the model year in response to changing conditions of demand and the competitive efforts of other producers.

Another illustration is the divergence between list price and actual prices in the aluminum industry [239]. The price list is a reference point for determining discounts. For example, while the list price of 29 cents a pound for aluminum ingots does not fluctuate greatly, actual prices vary widely. In early 1972 ingot prices were 22 cents a pound, a reduction of more than 30 percent from list. Prices of some aluminum products have fluctuated so frequently that they are not even included in company price lists. Furthermore, customers are sensitive to the trade-off between service and price; one of the advantages of smaller firms is their ability to vary "prices" by varying the quantity of special services provided.

Another example can be drawn from the steel industry. In connection with a change in list prices [41], Bethlehem Steel announced a change in its policy for charging for extras "giving individual customers specific gauges, width, quantities, or other special treatment. These extras have come to number in the hundreds, making it easier to shade prices." Yet steel has been generally regarded as a "homogeneous product." With product variations in the hundreds, official price data must greatly understate actual price changes. These examples and the broader evidence assembled by Stigler and Kindahl contradict the general view that there is little price competition among oligopolists. Stronger assertions, such as Galbraith's, that oligopolists do not engage in "destructive" price competition are also inconsistent with the evidence.[21]

Another variation of the administered prices thesis is that collusive behavior and market control by oligopolists is evidenced by administered profits. Profit data on twenty companies were set forth by Lanzillotti [129] to support this position. The evidence reproduced in Table 11-1 is not persuasive. First, only seven of the twenty companies could be characterized as having a target-return on investment. Second, of the seven, two were slightly below, while five firms were above the target by an average of 3.1 percentage points. Third, the return on investment is defined by business firms as the ratio of income before interest charges to total operating assets (gross or net). In the evidence presented, the profit rate measured was the return on net worth. The relevant comparison to the target specified is set forth in column 4. These average returns were in every case below the target-return on investment by substantial percentages. Fourth, average returns on net worth over any two time periods differ greatly as inspection of columns 2 and 3 readily demonstrates. This evidence does not support the conclusion that leading firms are able to "plan or administer their profits."

Industry Structure and Pressures for Efficiency

Another argument is that an atomistic industry structure is a necessary condition for continuous pressures for increased efficiency. Although this view is consistent with a deterministic model, in a dynamic world other forces may produce similar results. Repeated emphasis in the interview discussions was placed on the importance of achieving cost reduction and cost leadership. In a dynamic environment with numerous forms of rivalrous behavior, and with long lags involved in responding to actions by rivals such as changes in product quality or product differentiation, cost reduction reduces vulnerability to unfavorable events. Cost leadership reduces vulnerability to rivals' strategies. A related emphasis was on price reductions over time. The rationalization provided was "enlarging the market," which is consistent with a static model. Additionally, secular price reduction is a strategy for dealing with uncertainty. A massive type

Table 11-1

Target Rates of Return on Investment, Average Returns on Net Worth, and Average Returns on Total Assets of 20 Large Industrial Corporations, 1947-1967

	Target ROI per Lanzillotti (1)	Average Return on Net Worth		Earnings, Before Interest, on Total Assets (4)
		(2) 1947-55	(3) 1956-67	1956-67
Alcoa	10%	13.8%	8.5%	5.8%
American Can		11.6	9.4	
A & P		13.0	11.6	
du Pont		25.9	16.7	
Esso (Standard Oil N.J.)		16.0	12.1	
General Electric	20	21.4	16.6	9.7
General Foods		12.2	17.2	
General Motors	20	26.0	19.9	14.5
Goodyear		13.3	12.5	
Gulf		12.6	12.5	
International Harvester	10	8.9	7.4	6.3
Johns-Manville	15	14.9	10.2	8.5
Kennecott		16.0	11.5	
Kroger	10	12.1	12.2	6.4
National Steel		12.1	10.0	
Sears Roebuck		5.4	14.5	
Standard Oil (Indiana)		10.4	7.6	
Swift		6.9	4.4	
Union Carbide		19.2	15.3	
U.S. Steel	8	10.3	8.2	6.0
Average for the 20		14.1	11.9	

Sources: Columns 1 and 2 [129]. Columns 3 and 4 calculated from company data in Moody's *Investment Manuals, Industrials.*

of risk faced by business firms is competition from new and substitute products which threaten not only a declining total market, but also intensification of rival's efforts for increasing their share of a declining market. Since product substitution involves performance-price comparisons between existing and new products, secular price reduction is a strategy for insuring against this form of uncertainty.

In short, uncertainty induces strategies reflecting the same types of pressures for efficiency and performance improvement ascribed to atomistic industry structures in a deterministic model. Some evidence in support of this hypothesis is provided by analysis of price movements in concentrated versus atomistic industries as shown in Table 11-2. Three time periods during 1953-70 are

Table 11-2
Compound Annual Rates of Price Change in GNP, CPI, and Illustrative Concentrated and Unconcentrated Industries, U.S., 1953-1970 (based on the BLS Consumer Price Index and Components)

Time Periods	All Items CPI	Concentrated Industries		Unconcentrated Industries			Gross National Product	
		New Cars	Household Durables	Apparel Commodities	Total Services	Medical Care Services	Real	Current Dollars
1953-58	1.6	1.2	-.7	.3	3.6	4.1	1.6	4.2
1958-66	1.5	-.3	-.4	1.1	3.1	4.2	4.9	6.6
1966-70	4.8	2.0	2.9	5.2	7.4	8.6	1.9	6.8

Source: [74, pp. 250-51, Tables C-46, C-47].

covered. During the period ending in 1958, the consumer price index (CPI) rose 1.6 percent per annum. Both household durables, a concentrated industry, and apparel, an unconcentrated industry, registered price declines. During 1958-66, the CPI rose at a 1.5 percent rate and the prices of apparel increased at a 1.1 percent rate, while prices of new cars and household durables declined. In the third period, 1966-70, the rate of price increase in the concentrated industries was lower than any of the other categories in Table 11-2. Multiple regression studies of these relations between price changes and industry concentration over time, show a positive relation between concentration and the rate of price increase for the period 1953-58, but a negative relation in the other three post-war periods, 1948-53, 1958-63, and 1963-68 [139]. The evidence does not establish the proposition that large firms uniquely seek to achieve secular cost reduction and price reduction in response to uncertainty. The theory embraces atomistic firms as well. In addition, the evidence is consistent with the proposition suggested by survey responses that firms in concentrated markets in a dynamic uncertainty model are subject to pressures for optimizing performance of the kind generally attributed to competitive forces.

Conclusions

In this reformulation of the analysis of the pricing behavior of large firms within the framework of probabilistic economics, some new generalizations emerge. Behavioral characteristics regarded as irrational in the context of deterministic models are seen as dynamic strategies for dealing with uncertainty.

In a dynamic model, the forms and dimensions of competitive behavior are multiplied. The probabilities of effective collusion are reduced, and the probable gains from independent actions are increased. The price inflexibility doctrine, which lacks the support of consistent economic logic in a deterministic model, is even less supportable in an uncertainty model. Evidence is growing that large firms in concentrated industries have been responsive to changes in demand as well as to changes in cost conditions. The profit data used in the attempt to bolster the administered price doctrine is consistent with alternative hypotheses. Revision of the administered profits thesis is required. The motivations for efficiency conventionally attributed to atomistic industry structures alone are shown to be exerted also in large firms in concentrated markets through continued pressures to develop sequential strategies in response to uncertainty.

The behavioral theory of the firm was formulated on the basis of evidence on organizational processes similar to that obtained in my interviews. This theory has emphasized elements such as bureaucratic tendencies, divergence of organization and individual goals, organization slack, and managerial discretion as evidence of protection in some degree from the rigors of competition. But these organizational imperfections are common to all types of institutions, not unique to business firms. Specialization and departmentation in large firms increases efficiency, but at the cost of increased tendencies toward bureaucratization. Whether a given firm is too large or not large enough by these criteria depends on the facts of each particular case.

12 Organizing to Supply Nuclear Energy

Dr. A. Eugene Schubert

Of the many facets to the nuclear business, this presentation will limit itself to the development of central station power plant reactors based on *nuclear technology*. Popular statistics indicate that the country's need for electric power has doubled every decade and will continue to do so for some time to come. Electrical energy plays a vital role in meeting the social and economic goals of mankind. I will first trace the evolution of nuclear energy as a means of producing electric power, and then describe how the maturing of the industry has brought changes in the styles of doing business. I will also make some predictions on the future of the nuclear power industry, which involves the much-discussed breeder reactor.

Entry and Growth in Nuclear Electric Power

The world first became aware of nuclear energy in 1945 when the mission of the Manhattan Project was disclosed. It was not until the Atomic Energy Act of 1954 that the nuclear technology developed up to that time was made available for peacetime applications. One of the first major mileposts in the new industry occurred in 1955 when General Electric committed itself to build Dresden 1 for Commonwealth Edison near Chicago.

This was momentous because it represented a landmark in corporate risk-taking. The risk was two-fold: technical and financial. We were risking our future on the technical performance of a brand-new type of reactor, the Boiling Water Reactor (BRW) as opposed to the Pressurized Water Reactor. This was a reactor that was conceived and designed by General Electric on its own funds, a reactor we were willing to guarantee at 180 megawatts. Furthermore, it was comparable in size to the largest fossil plants being let at that time—and this was only 16 years ago!

The financial risk was also quite impressive. We took a turnkey contract from Commonwealth Edison at a fixed price of 45 million dollars. Dresden 1 was privately owned and financed, and the only one of the early demonstration reactors with boiling water technology. Some background suggests why General Electric chose to develop the BWR instead of the pressurized water technology.

When the government launched its nuclear submarine program, Westinghouse was assigned the pressurized water reactor and General Electric the sodium-cooled reactor. Both were successful. However, the Westinghouse commercial power program grew from the submarine program. General Electric on the other hand kept its commercial business separate, but examined all of the possible nuclear technologies sodium-cooled, gas-cooled, pressurized water, boiling water and heavy water. All of these were potentially successful reactors, and all could be made safe. We selected the BWR as having the best combination of technology and economics. Basically, we felt the BWR was a simpler system and offered more potential for improvement over a period of time than the others. Our commitment for Dresden 1 was accompanied by a major commitment in organization and facilities. We established the Atomic Power Equipment Department in San Jose and the Vallecitos Nuclear Center to support this development. The early emphasis was on engineering and technology rather than on the selling side.

Dresden went on line in 1960 and became the nation's first large-scale producer of nuclear power. Its success proved the technical soundness of the BWR design and opened the door to further acceptance. By the end of 1963 United States utilities placed orders for nine additional nuclear plants, and there were five overseas orders for U.S. manufacturers. One of the domestic plants ordered in 1963 became a significant milestone in the industry. Jersey Central Power & Light announced that it expected the General Electric boiling water reactor ordered for its proposed Oyster Creek plant would compare favorably to all available alternatives at the location in terms of cost of output. The announcement dramatically alerted the entire industry that nuclear power had "arrived" and was now economically competitive with other sources of energy.

There were seven domestic orders in 1965, twenty-one in 1966 and thirty in 1967. This brought the box score through 1967 to these totals for the four U.S. manufacturers: Domestic General Electric 18,573 MW; Westinghouse 19,498; Babcock & Wilcox 7,107; and Combustion Engineering 5,549.[1] Overseas, it was General Electric 3,203 and Westinghouse 2,167. Actually, this success brought on very difficult growing pains. The business grew too fast for us to be able to manage it properly and develop it in an orderly manner. We were happy to get the orders, but there were problems. We were really scrambling in '67 and '68 to keep abreast of the needs and requirements of customers, the AEC and the technology itself. Now we have the organization and the facilities in place to meet our commitments on schedule.

After the big rush of orders in '66 and '67, the industry's traditional cyclical buying pattern gave us a chance to catch our breath. The pace slackened to fifteen domestic orders in 1968, nine domestic and four foreign in 1969, and fourteen domestic and three overseas in 1970, before the cycle reversed itself as expected in 1971. The increase in size has been just as dramatic as the increase in the number of plants. Vallecitos in 1957 was only five MW. Oyster Creek has a rating of 640 MW, Dresden 2 is 809 MW, and we took two orders in 1971 for plants rated at 1260 MW.

Initial Cost and Prices

The nuclear power industry has matured in many ways—in technology, in manufacturing techniques, and in designs. Never before in history has a complex technology grown so fast into a major-sized industry. Not long ago, there were only two competitors, General Electric and Westinghouse, for this reactor market. Now there are five. Along the route to maturity, we've changed our style of doing business. Dresden 1 was a pioneer project that represented the real beginning of the commercial reactor business. General Electric undertook Dresden 1 as a turnkey project to get the business started. Commonwealth Edison wanted to have one company take full responsibility for this plant. Our response was to offer the turnkey. This became the preferred style of doing business world-wide, although there were notable exceptions. Speaking generally, utilities wanted to get into nuclear power and wanted turnkey commitments to off-set their own lack of experience. As a result, General Electric committed eleven turnkey plants, four of them overseas, by the middle of 1966. Tarapur in India was the first of these eleven projects and the first overseas. This two-reactor station has a total rating of 390 MW and was turned over to the Indian government in 1969. Oyster Creek, which was the first nuclear unit in the U.S. to be purchased on the basis of economic power cost alone, also was turned over as a successful operating plant in 1969. Nine Mile Point, for Niagara Mohawk, was not a turnkey plant, but was contemporaneous with Oyster Creek and used the same design reactor. Tsuruga Station for Japan Atomic Power Company has been generating at full load, 342 MW, since 1969. Dresden 2 and Dresden 3 have each operated at or near their full power of 809 MW, and Dresden 3 has been turned over to Commonwealth Edison. The 545 MW Monticello plant for Northern States Power and the 650 MW Millstone Plant for Northeast Utilities have been tested and turned over. So have the 440 MW Fukushima Plant for Tokyo Electric Power and the Nuclenor Plant of the same rating in Northern Spain. Quad Cities 1 has been licensed to load fuel, and Quad Cities 2, the last of the eleven original turnkeys, was turned over to Commonwealth Edison in 1972.

The performance of these turnkey plants has been quite good. We feel we have completely verified the large boiling water design by having run Dresden 2 and 3 up to 800 MW. If Oyster Creek was a landmark because it was the first reactor awarded on the basis of economics, Dresden 2 was a landmark because it was the first plant in a 251-inch vessel. The 251-inch vessel is the largest yet built, and is used to contain the 800 MW plants, and larger, that we are building. We had to design Oyster Creek before we had any technical feedback on large plants like it and this points up one of the fundamental problems of the nuclear business. It takes a good seven years to get the technical feedback on a nuclear plant design, which poses the question: do you innovate in 7-year cycles, or do you go ahead and quote ten or twenty plants?

Another landmark is Brown's Ferry 1 for the TVA, the first 1100-MW nuclear plant. We have complete confidence that the reactor will operate smoothly, because it's the same physical size as Dresden 2. The difference, of course, is the higher output from the fuel.

The foregoing provides a background for recounting some critical relations between costs and prices. The cost estimates of the turnkey plants were based on nuclear steam supply system designs based on Dresden 1 and subsequent development work well understood at the time. Costs of balance-of-plant equipment and plant construction were also estimated from our experience and industry sources. To these cost estimates we applied the inflation guide-lines in use during that period to arrive at firm prices. The cost estimates turned out to be low because of four factors:

(1) Many changes were made to assure performance and reliability. There were also changes required by the evolving licensing criteria coming from the AEC. Some of these changes resulted in additional equipment, with the consequent adverse effect on cost estimates. (2) The productivity of field construction labor was substantially lower than expected—a national problem not confined to the erection of nuclear power plants. (3) The inflation rate exceeded the guidelines commonly in use at the time of our estimates. (4) There were delays beyond our control. Primarily the delays were attributed to late deliveries from one pressure vessel supplier, and to evolving license criteria.

Each of our turnkeys was unprofitable, but I believe the significant point is that the General Electric willingness and ability to take these risks got the nuclear business off the ground. On the basis of our experience and the general development of the industry, the style of doing business has changed. Our current scope is the nuclear steam supply system, plus fuel. We have not taken a turnkey job since mid-1966.

By confining ourselves to supplying the steam system and the fuel, we have far greater control of our business. On the customer end, the utility now does the complete plant design—either by itself or with an architect-engineering consulting firm—procures the equipment and does the construction. The equipment involved—primarily the turbine-generator may or may not be purchased from General Electric. The utility is under no compulsion to buy a General Electric turbine-generator just because it is putting in a General Electric reactor.

This, of course, works both ways. We have supplied some turbine-generators for plants with Westinghouse reactors, and all the plants using Combustion Engineering or Babcock & Wilcox reactors have to order their turbine-generators from either General Electric or Westinghouse. This situation is very much in line with the decision we made at the outset—not to alter the classic relationship with our long-standing utility customers; namely, that we would be a supplier of equipment and the utilities would use it.

Generally speaking, the business we have booked since we stopped taking turnkey orders in 1966 has been profitable, and we expect the profit factor on each order to hold up over the years it takes to complete our commitment. This can take as long as six years. Our current contracts provide for escalation both in labor and materials, and we hope we can control our costs within these limits.

Future Developments

We see an important future for breeder reactors. A breeder reactor is one that runs with neutrons in a fast spectrum, enabling it to have enough energy to generate more neutrons than are needed. This in turn enables the fuel to be synthesized by capture of these extra neutrons. They are called breeders because they produce more fuel than they burn, and thus become a virtual unending source of supply. The significance, of course, is that breeders would extend indefinitely our uranium reserves.

Now for a look ahead to 1990. The future of the light water reactor is bright. It is clearly the way in which we can offset the diminishing reserves of coal and gas. Coal has become less desirable not only because of environmental considerations, but because of its sharply accelerating price. In this connection, there is a widespread public misconception on the thermal effects of nuclear plants versus fossil-fueled plants. By and large, fossil plants are about 40 percent thermally efficient, which means that about 60 percent of their heat has to be thrown away. Nuclear plants come out about 30 percent, with a 70 percent throwaway. When the fossil heat thrown away up the smokestack is accounted for, it turns out that nuclear plants throw away heat in about the ratio of four to three when compared with the heat rejection from fossil plants of the same electrical rating. *All* thermal power plants produce heated condenser water, and the notion that only nuclear plants do is mistaken.

By 1990 the breeder reactor will begin to make a major impact on the industry. But in order to achieve that, we have to start *today* to build demonstration breeder plants that are the analog of Dresden 1 and Indian Point 1 to prove the things we know and to find out the things we don't know. General Electric started a breeder activity as long ago as 1959 to go with its major emphasis on the light water reactor. On this pioneer program we decided the costs and the risks did not warrant an exclusive private investment. Consequently, we accepted government funding and we have been working in cooperation with the government and the utilities in developing a breeder position.

After many studies and much investigation, the technology the world has settled on to be developed is sodium-cooled fast breeders. This will permit power plant efficiences to climb back in the 40 percent range. Another factor favoring the breeder is its fuel cycle. The uranium-plutonium fuel cycle of the light water reactors and the breeder fit together perfectly. This means plutonium originally made in the light water reactors will be used to get the breeders started.

We have approximately three-hundred technical people in General Electric assigned to breeders. Our most significant accomplishment has been in design-ing, building and operating the SEFOR reactor in Arkansas. The SEFOR reactor demonstrates two important points: (1) the ability to control the fast neutron reaction, which permits us to guarantee the safety of the breeder; (2) the ability to design, build and operate a sodium system and keep it going over a long period of time with no substantial problems.

The breeder experimental facility in Arkansas is only a small part of the resources General Electric has committed to nuclear development. There are the headquarters plant at San Jose and the Vallecitos Laboratory, which account for some 3800 employees in the Bay Area of California. Our new plant in Wilmington, North Carolina, employs another 1400 people, and our fuel reprocessing plant in Morris, Illinois, another 125. All of these facilities enjoy the back-up support of General Electric's research and development people and facilities, along with other technical support.

The nuclear industry today is a young industry. It has matured to offer a needed fifth source of energy to help meet the continuing rapid increase in the demand for electricity. As an added source of energy, the nuclear alternative is a strong competitor that has proven itself on economic grounds and on environ-mental attractiveness. We who are a part of the nuclear industry believe firmly that the power generation future is a nuclear future. We can think of no reason it should not be: we see every reason it should be. Nuclear power clearly is the best way for utilities to give people the electricity they demand and in the process to do the utilities' full share in preserving the quality of the environment they, and all of us, depend on for survival.

13

Product Line Pricing and Technological Change: The Case of Sophisticated Electrical Machinery*

Ralph G.M. Sultan

With the flow of government-funded research and development at least temporarily diminished, it is appropriate to devote attention anew to classical means of funding technological change through the marketplace—the old-fashioned way technological progress used to be financed in this economy. In the electrical machinery industry, this pattern of technological financing persists, albeit with some strains. This paper will examine how technological change was (a) funded, and (b) introduced, under conditions of oligopolistic rivalry in the turbine-generator business over the 1950-61 period.

The present research is part of a larger project on the pricing of heavy electrical equipment sponsored by the Harvard Business School, and utilizing as raw ingredients the mass of data, deposition and courtroom testimony which was read into the public record during the so-called "electrical cases." One conclusion of the larger research project is that there was just more competition in the electrical equipment industry during the 1950-60 period than previous court decisions and popular impressions would indicate. Two principal dimensions of competition were price and technology. This paper relates the two.

The Industry Setting

Turbine-generators are the machines which provide electric power; they are the basic equipment of electric power stations, whether nuclear or fossil-fueled. They are massive, complex pieces of equipment, with modern machines priced at upwards of $25 million each. The United States industry represents about $1 billion in shipments annually.

Historically, General Electric has held about 60 percent market share, Westinghouse about 30 percent share, and Allis-Chalmers and foreign suppliers such as Brown Bovari of Switzerland the remainder. In recent years, Brown Bovari has increased its market share in the United States.

Needless to say, this product line is a substantial fraction of the total business of the General Electric Company, and probably an even greater portion of the annual sales of Westinghouse.[1] Its importance continues to grow, given the fact that electric power demand continues on its long-term 7 percent compound growth rate, far exceeding the rest of the economy in rate of expansion.

163

There has been a progressive increase in the size of turbine-generator units. Following World War II, a 100,000-kilowatt unit was considered "large." Today, units of 1,300,000-kilowatts are being built, and given the economic incentives which are at work, it seems likely that the trend to ever-larger units will continue.

Technological Progress in Turbine-Generators

Technological progress is unusually easy to measure in this industry. One of the best measures is the "heat rate," or the amount of coal required to generate a kilowatt-hour of electric power. From 1905 through 1965 this declined from about six pounds to less than 0.8 pounds, and progress continues, although with diminishing returns. This is an indication of the long-term reduction in *operating* costs.

On the *investment* cost side, some appreciation of progress may be gained from the fact that, according to Federal Power Commission data, a recent plant on the Commonwealth Edison System (Kindaid) carries an investment cost per kilowatt which is *lower* than the original investment cost per kilowatt of one of the *oldest* plants on the Commonwealth Edison System (Powerton), first operated in 1928. This reduction in capital cost has been achieved despite the 100 percent inflation in the dollar over the intervening years. (Cf. Federal Power Commission [79]).

This cost-reduction progress has been achieved through the combined efforts of the steam generating system manufacturers, the station designers, the electrical machinery manufacturers, and efficient utility operations. The end result has been, until recent years, steady annual reductions in electric power prices to the consumer, inflation notwithstanding, and continued growth of electric utilities' share of the energy market.

The record of technological progress is impressive. The manufacturers and their utility customers have funded this change while avoiding various bogs into which other high-technology industries have fallen. The rate of technological change has been enormous. It has been introduced with a minimum of economic disruption. It has been privately financed. Competition has been preserved. Benefits have been passed along to consumers. And this has all been sustained for approximately seventy years with only slight pause. This is a sharp contrast to the end consequence of technological strategies in other oligopolies, which have resulted in such extremes as stagnant technological change (steel?), or overly rapid technological change (aircraft?), or technological near-monopolies (computers?), or outright government subsidy combined with bankruptcy combined with technological failure (some grandiose weapons systems of the 1960s). Surely there must be something instructive about the contrasting methods of financing and introducing technological change in turbine generators.

Some issues which managers must address, in high-technology businesses, are:

1. How best may private funds be accumulated for investment in future technologies? This question is particularly germane to the technological leader firm, which in most oligopolies also happens to be the price-leader firm. It is not, for example, clear that the optimum strategy is one of leading market prices upward across-the-board, to garner extra investable funds. Other competitors will be tempted to use this extra margin to wrest market share away from the leader firm, through expanded services.
2. How may significant technological innovations be introduced to the marketplace without provoking high-risk technological competition frequently expressed through the medium of competitors' engineering promises to customers which may, or may not, be deliverable upon at some distant date?
3. How may competition be preserved, given rapid and costly technological change, and frequently an inferior cost position among follower firms in the marketplace?

Managing the Price-Technology Relationship:
Turbine-Generators

In the turbine-generator industry, such questions have manifested themselves in the issue, generally, of how to manage the "price-technology relationship." In this industry, the tool by which managers attempt to manage the price-technology relationship is the published handbook price schedule which defines the *relative* price of turbine generator units of various technologies. Through product-line pricing relationships, the pace of introduction of advanced-technology machines is managed. At the same time, through appropriate product line pricing there is a funding of yet-more advanced technologies.

Related to product-line pricing is the question of average *size* of turbine-generators being marketed; that is, how rapidly to introduce new technology. There is a distribution in unit ratings sold in any year. A few of the largest, most-advanced units are purchased by larger utilities of a pioneering bent. Some very small units are purchased by smaller power systems. The bulk of machines fall in the middle category. Over time, as system capacities and technological capabilities grow, there is a progressive shift upward in the size distribution of unit ratings (Figure 13.1).

Although "large" turbines are not necessarily tantamount to "advanced-technology" turbines, they tend to be synonymous in practice, and it is assumed they are, for working purposes in this analysis. The discussion can then be simplified to an analysis of turbine-generator price-size relationships at any point in time, and shifts in the product mix of leader versus follower firms.

In the turbine business, it appears that much thought is given to the question

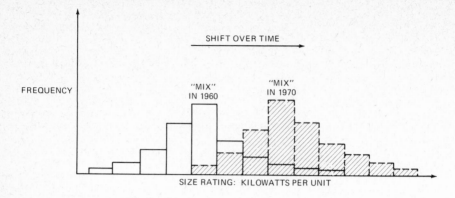

Figure 13-1. Shift in Size "Mix" of Turbine-Generators Marketed to Utility Organizations, over Time.

of how the prices of the less-advanced, 100,000 kilowatt machines should relate to the prices of highly advanced 1,000,000 kilowatt machines. The question is how to configure the "price-size" relationship, or *relative* prices, regardless of the average market level of prices which happens to prevail.[2]

Price-Size Relationships in Turbine-Generators

Turbine-generators are normally priced so that big ones cost less on a per-kilowatt basis, then do little ones. For example, according to an old General Electric price book (the one which became effective December 1951) a "tandem compound" turbine-generator of 100,000 kilowatts rating cost $2.62 million, or about $26.22 per kilowatt, while a comparable unit of 200,000 kilowatts rating cost $4.18 million, or about $23.80 per kilowatt.[3] This provides some measure of the investment cost incentive which customers had to move to the larger sized turbine-generators: by continually pressing toward the largest available units, utility organizations minimized their investment costs.

Lower initial cost was not the only benefit. The larger machines were typically the more efficient machines, in terms of fuel consumption. (And operating costs exceeded annual capital investment charges for the utilities.) Thus, lower operating costs could be achieved by the utilities through purchasing the larger machines.

If one plots the published handbook prices in dollars per kilowatt against kilowatts size of unit, at any point in time, one would normally observe (Figure 13-2) that larger units are priced lower on a per-kilowatt basis than are smaller

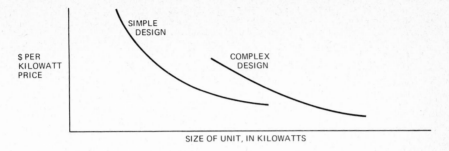

Figure 13-2. Typical Price-Size Relationship at One Point in Time.

units. However, complex designs (with lower operating costs, size for size) are priced higher than are simple designs. The complex units normally extend farther into a larger size range, where dollars per kilowatt price tends to be lowest of all.

The announcement of new products, either completely new products, more complex product lines, or the extension of an existing product line into the higher size ranges (see Figure 13-3) naturally tends to alter the competitive position of the various-sized units. The obsolescing of smaller units tends to be accelerated. Customers are induced to shift their purchases toward the larger size ranges, in order to minimize their investment costs and also their operating costs. With such product announcement, the price-size relationship may be changed.

Inflation also provides a natural opportunity to adjust the price-size relationship. Given the passage of time, and the ubiquitous forces of inflation, *all* of the

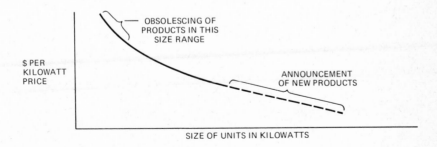

Figure 13-3. Altering the Competitive Line-up of Products Through Product Line Extension.

prices must be periodically adjusted upwards. Simultaneously, this may be a convenient occasion to alter the slope or the "tilt" of the price-size curve.

In this industry, the data of the 1950s suggest to me that historically the price curve has shifted in a *clockwise* direction, (in the manner depicted in Figure 13-4). At the extreme, the price of very large units may not be increased at all, and inflation-induced increases may be confined to the smaller sizes, maximizing the rotation of the price curve.

Note that in absolute dollar per kilowatt, prices in this typical representation (Figure 13-4) are raised *more* on the less complex design and *less* on the more complex design. Note also that *within* each series of models (within the "complex design" series of turbines itself) the price increases are progressively smaller, the larger the machine.

"Tipping the curve" therefore represents the progressive reduction of the prices of the newest, larger and more sophisticated machines (or, at least, holding the line on price increases for such models) *while the prices of the older, smaller and less sophisticated machines increase.* There is much empirical evidence, and explicit management testimony concerning this altering of the price-size curve during the decade of the 1950s.[4]

Price-size curve tilting may not be unequivocably clockwise. Medium sized units may be increased more in price than are the very smallest units. The bulk of orders consists neither of the very smallest nor of the very largest units in the price book. Short-run earnings can therefore be enhanced by increasing prices to the greatest extent in the intermediate size range, where the bulk of sales volume resides. This approach yields price changes which are smaller at the extremities of the size curve, and larger in the intermediate size range (Figure 13-5).

The very smallest and the very largest units are relatively unchanged in price. Such a maneuver will position the price increases where they are most beneficial to *current* earnings. This also provides *long-term* strategic benefit to the

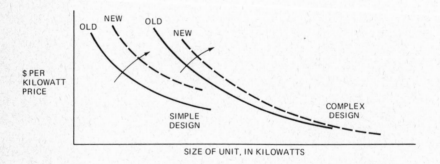

Figure 13-4. "Tipping the Curve" Clock-wise: Old versus New Price Curves.

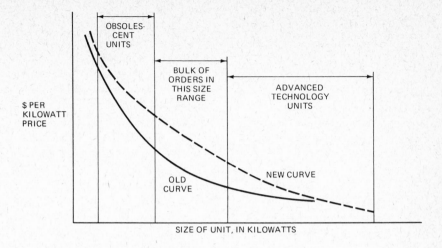

Figure 13-5. Maximizing the Price Increase for the Bulk of Current Orders; a "U-Shaped" Rotation of the Price Curve.

technological and cost leader which derives from inducing a consumer shift to the largest sizes of turbine generators.

To further complicate the story, the price curve of one product line may be tilted clockwise, and the price curve of another may be simultaneously tilted counter-clockwise (Figure 13-6). The reasons behind this complex maneuver again lie in managements' desire to foster sales of one type of machine at the expense of another.

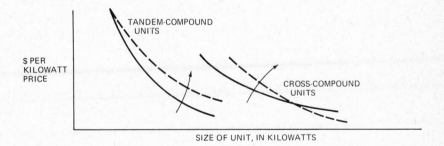

Figure 13-6. Simultaneous Clockwise Tilting of More-Sophisticated Product Line, and Counter-Clockwise Tilting of More-Sophisticated Product Line.

Economic Motivations for Curve Tipping

Significant profit payoffs accrue through the technological "leading" of the marketplace into ever larger turbine units. The author estimates that *direct* costs per kilowatt have in the past declined about 38 percent with every doubling of the average size of turbine generators produced. This does not mean that greater profits automatically accrued to the manufacturers through rapid technological innovation. While gross margins, at any point in time, may have been greater on the advanced technology units, it is also true that developing those units was a costly and risky venture for the manufacturers. One must distinguish between *direct* costs and *overhead* costs, and also the manufacturers' risks. Heavy indirect or overhead expenditures were involved, a large proportion of which were engineering development oriented.

Risks are equally burdensome: the risk of outright product failure, the hazard of producing a working, but unreliable unit, the risk of failing to meet targeted cost goals on completely new units. There is also the chance of failing to meet prescribed delivery schedules due to unanticipated manufacturing problems, and the risk of unforeseen design problems, such as rotor bursts.

Thus, the profitability of a competitor's strategy of inducing rapid change in the product mix via product-line pricing is by no means assured. If the engineering investments could be managed properly, and if technical development work proceeded step-by-step, then it could be a highly profitable strategy.

Who Shall Lead?

There is convincing statistical evidence that General Electric led the field of turbine-generator technology from 1948-62. Table 13-1 shows the market share (in units) among the three manufacturers for this, according to the size of turbine-generator ordered. General Electric had the dominant market share in units 400,000 kilowatts and larger, in this time period. These would represent the most advanced units of the time. Westinghouse was not far behind. It showed market share strength in the 300,000 to 399,000 kilowatts size range, for example. However, its market share was below average in the very largest ratings.

Allis-Chalmers had its largest market share in the very smallest ratings, those up to 100,000 kilowatts. However, it maintained a respectable share of the 300,000 to 399,000 kilowatt ratings as well. This may partly reflect a statistical quirk: the fact that Allis-Chalmers burst into its maximum market share toward the end of the period, when *all* of the ratings were higher.

The price-size curve was a major strategic tool. There is ample empirical evidence that General Electric was the leader in configuring the price-size curve. Westinghouse and Allis-Chalmers tended to follow—at least according to the

Table 13-1
Percent Share of Orders by Size of Turbine, 1948-1962

	Size of Individual Turbine-Generators, Megawatts*				
	Up to 100 mw	100 to 199 mw	200 to 299 mw	300 to 399 mw	400 mw and over
Units:					
Westinghouse	391 units	134 units	37 units	19 units	5 units
General Electric	620	253	75	29	16
Allis-Chalmers	188	26	6	5	0
Total Units	1129	413	118	53	21
% of Units:					
Westinghouse	34.6	32.4	31.4	35.8	23.8
General Electric	54.9	61.3	63.6	54.7	76.2
Allis-Chalmers	10.5	6.3	5.1	9.4	–
Total %	100.0	100.0	100.0	100.0	100.0

*Maximum rated output (not nameplate rating)

published price books of all three. Since General Electric had technological leadership, it is natural that it also had price-size curve leadership.

Factors that contribute to General Electric's leadership position, technologically, were its significantly greater sales volume base, its larger gross margin percentage, and consequently its greater capability to sustain an ambitious technical development program. It was difficult for Westinghouse and virtually impossible for Allis-Chalmers to play a leadership role in technology, given the resources of their major competitor. The direct costs savings were accessible only *after the required fund of technological know-how was in hand,* and to acquire that pool of technological know-how required overhead expenditures. Thus, it was General Electric which appeared to be in the leadership role from 1948-62.

"Tipping the Curve": Historical Book
Price Evidence

The price-size curve may be officially "tipped" either through the adjustment of book (list) prices of existing products in the line, or through the announcement of new products of greater sophistication which extend the size range. In addition, prices on the larger sizes could obviously be reduced during negotiations (via discounts) without reference to any published book price. The prevalence of historical *book* price tipping may be appraised from the announced price changes of 1946-61 as listed in Table 13-2. (The record reveals less about curve tipping through new product announcements or through discounting of list prices, even though these may be at least as important.)

Table 13-2
Summary of Announced General Electric List Price Changes, 1946-61

April 1946	+15% increase
September 1946	+15% increase
May 1947	+10% increase
December 1948	+9.2% increase
*October 1950	+10% increase, less on larger sizes
December 1951	+3.37% increase across-the-board
*March 1953	+10% average, less for larger units
*January 1955	+2% or less, average increase, U-shaped
*September 1955	+10% average, larger increase on large preferred std.
*April 1956	+10% average, mixed rotations of price curves
September 1956	+10% increase across-the-board
*April 1957	Increase small sizes (.9% to 2.5%); decrease large sizes (5.9%); U-shaped rotation of tandem compound
July 1957	+5% across-the-board
*December 1957	Adjustments (greatest increases on smaller sizes) 2% to 6%
April 1958	+3% almost across-the-board
*July 1959	Larger units: reductions $1 to $4 per kilowatt
October 1959	−5% reduction
*March 1961	Reductions −2.5% to −20.4%, larger units

*Denotes Significant Clockwise Tipping of the Price-Size Curve.

In the fifteen year period for which detailed data are available there were fifteen book price changes. Nine changes involved significant clockwise adjustments to the price curve, for at least some portion of the product line. "Tipping" of the curve in a clockwise direction occurred on the dates indicated in Table 13-2.

Curve-tilting was not invariably clockwise; nor did it always pertain to all units. In general, the record suggests that price *increases* were *maximized* for:

1. small units (as opposed to large);
2. tandem compound units, which were less complex (as opposed to cross-compound units, which were more complex);
3. units with one or two "flows," which were less sophisticated (as opposed to those which had three or four flows, and which were more sophisticated);
4. standard preferred machines (as opposed to non-ASME standard machines which were the more advanced machines).

The pattern was to keep prices low on the high-technology machines, to promote a shift in consumer demand over to these more advanced machines. Through pricing, technological change was force fed.

Customer Response to Tipping the Curve

Such price changes were of intense interest to utility customers, and their engineering consultants. One utility executive presentation by Ebasco Services Inc., suggested how utility organizations are incessantly driven toward purchasing the largest and most advanced units.[6] With even a slight clockwise tipping of the price curve, utility interest in advanced technologies was stimulated; this was the route to further economies in power generation.

Utility organizations and their engineering consultants were perenially concerned that technological opportunities were drying up; that technological barriers were appearing which could not be pierced; that there were rapidly diminishing returns from new technology. (A parallel mood prevails today, one might add.) As unit ratings climbed, diminishing returns in investment cost reductions set in with a given price-size relationship. This gave heightened impact to price changes for turbine generators in the higher ratings. Even slight modifications in the slope of the price curve would be seized upon by the most progressive utility customers in order to preserve their continually declining costs.

It may be noted that over the years, it would become increasingly difficult to achieve decreased costs without truly large leaps in the scale and sophistication of power generating plants. Under these circumstances, there is a risk that could lead to an accelerated introduction of new technology, particularly if customers' demands were nourished by wild engineering speculations and extrapolations by manufacturing firms.

Figure 13-7 shows, in exaggerated schematic, the size distribution of sales in kilowatts, sales in dollars, and contribution to profit and overhead, for both follower firm and leader firm for the 1950s. At the top of the diagram, the price curve (dollars per kilowatt versus turbine rating in kilowatts), costs, and the contribution margin per kilowatt are shown.

Prices, Direct Costs, and Margins per Kilowatt

The upper chart shows prices, direct cost, and contribution margin, in dollars per kilowatt, for each size rating of turbine-generator. The price curve follows a descending, concave path. Direct costs, it appears from glimpses of data, probably decline in an *S*-shaped curve, and it is clear that they descend faster than prices do. In the very small size range, costs per kilowatt do not decline very rapidly with an increase in unit rating, partly because the bulk of technological effort is invested elsewhere. In the intermediate size ranges, there are dramatic direct cost savings with an increase in the unit rating. Finally, when one considers the very largest sizes of turbine-generators, the rate of decline in costs slows down again partly, because maximum technological effort and learning has yet to be expended in engineering design and methods in the factory

174

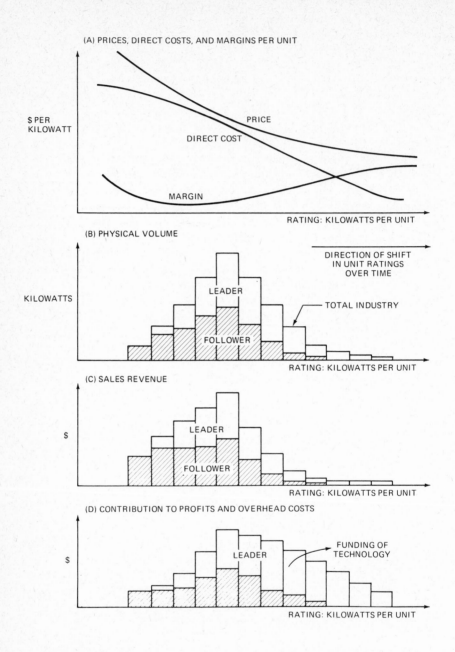

Figure 13-7. Distributions of Margins, Volume, Sales Revenue, Contribution to Profits and Overhead Cost, and Market Shares, Across the Size Range of Turbine-Generators

for the extreme-frontier units. (This progress will come later.) Thus, with an increase in turbine-generator size, direct costs decline slowly, then rapidly, then slowly again, yielding an over-all S-shaped curve.

The impact on margins, as measured in dollars per kilowatt, appear to follow an exaggerated S-shaped pattern, inasmuch as the shape of the margins curve is determined by the difference between the S-shaped direct cost curve, and a concave shaped price curve. Maximum dollars per kilowatt are earned with the most advanced, largest units, but the very smallest units are quite profitably priced as well. Margins are at their lowest in the middle size range, where the bulk of sales volume resides.

Physical Volume

The second schematic diagram in Figure 13-7 shows a histogram, the distribution of total industry physical sales volume (in kilowatts according to turbine-generator size). A skewed frequency distribution of sales volume across the product line was typical, with a long tail extending toward the largest ratings. Total industry physical volume has two components in this schematic diagram: a leader firm's sales and a follower firm's sales. The physical volume of the leader firm is skewed toward the higher unit ratings, although there is substantial overlap with the size-distribution of sales of the follower firm. The leader firm tends to produce the advanced technology units—those with the highest margins per kilowatt.

Under the inducement of lower capital costs and greater operating efficiency, customers over time, shift the entire industry product mix to the right, to the higher ratings. The leader firm funds the technology which is required, leads the shift, gets a larger share of the larger units, and is rewarded with enhanced profitability as a consequence.

Sales Revenue

Since kilowatts are priced higher at the lower ratings, sales revenue for the industry is skewed more toward the smaller ratings, compared with the distribution of physical volume over the product line. The follower firm's market share is magnified if it is measured on a dollars basis, but not magnified if measured on a kilowatts basis. The follower firm, with greater representation in its product mix of the lower ratings, has its relative stature in the industry inflated as a consequence—more than a measure of its total kilowatts would suggest.

Contribution to Profits and Overhead

Although the follower firm has its revenue buoyed through the circumstances of its product mix and the price curve, its profits tell a different story. The follower firm has the bulk of its sales in the lower profit margin units and in the middle size range. The leader firm, in contrast, has more of its sales in the highly profitable upper size range. Thus, the leader firm is relatively more profitable, whether measured on a total margin dollars basis or in percent margin dollars to sales.

Note that these are *margin* dollars (i.e., gross margins, or contribution to overhead and profit). They provide the pool of funds for spending on such activities as marketing, administration, and, in particular, advanced technology. A large portion of the enhanced gross margin of the leader firm will presumably be drained off by its hyperactive research and development activity, to insure the continued viability of the "high technology" strategy which it follows. Meanwhile, the follower firm is busy minimizing costs, since it has less margin space in which to maneuver and fewer margin dollars with which to finance.

Shifts in Prices, Costs, and Product Mix Over Time

From time to time, during the 1950s, the price curve appeared to tilt clockwise around the direct cost curve. The typical pattern of shifts in prices, costs, margins, and volume, which emerges from the study is diagrammed in Figure 13-8.

1. There is a general upward shift in price levels with inflation, and a simultaneous clockwise rotation of the price curve. The product line is extended toward less costly, higher technology units. There are long-term benefits to making this a *"U-shaped"* rotation, with minimum price increases in the very smallest as well as the very largest sizes. This will gradually quench the profitability of the very smallest sizes, and discourage growth of a too high profit niche for existing or would-be competitors. Competitors will be induced to move whole-heartedly into the more profitable middle size ranges, and beyond, following the leader.
2. Direct costs tend to shift upward with inflation, but in the very largest unit ratings, cost increases are minimized—and possibly reversed—through technological change and further extension of the product line.
3. Margins per kilowatt therefore may increase in the very largest ratings, decrease at the very smallest ratings, and be maintained at their original level in the middle size range.
4. The product mix shifts toward a higher average unit rating, with time.

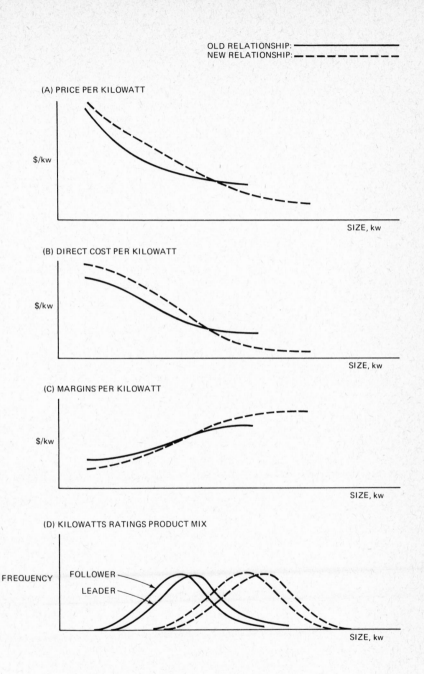

Figure 13-8. Price-Cost Margins and Product Mix Manifestations of "Tipping the Curve"

In the long run, the follower firms will creep up to the leader firms in product mix as the total market shifts. This is the time for the leader firm to tip the curve once more, to repeat the cycle. Or more likely, he takes the initiative, and tips the curve depending upon the state of his technological funding and the state of the art which is developing in the advanced ratings. Nobody can safely lapse into technological sluggishness.

Some Risks of Price-technology Progress

What are the risks resulting from this "clockwise tilting" price-technology movement? Two hazardous situations may arise:

1. The follower firms may be pressed too hard, and may, therefore, take a desperation plunge forward in technology (which *could* just succeed, in which case the leader has lost his position). Alternatively, they may resort to very aggressive pricing which could diminish the ability of the leader firm to fund his very necessary technology, but would result in severe losses to follower firms. The success of such a strategy would depend upon the extent to which the leader could continue to finance technology advances with less than normal returns compared with the ability of followers to sustain a period of massive losses.
2. A technology *ceiling* may be encountered, a barrier in design (such as the 1050°F. austenitic barrier in metallurgy, or the ability of the railways to transport ever-larger components) which blocks further progress by the leader firm, while the follower firms begin to nip at his heels. With the leader stymied in his pursuit of further advances, competitive technologies would eventually be equalized, and the competitive struggle thrown into a nontechnological (commodity) basis.

The risks of innovating too slowly are equally apparent: permitting follower firms to gather strength for an assault on the leader, diminished profitability, diminished customer goodwill and increased customer price sensitivities. Errors in management judgment are prone to fall on the side of innovating too rapidly, with an insufficient knowledge base, and therefore, too sharp a readiness to attempt technological trumps which fail. This tendency is probably innate in the system.

To play this technological pricing strategy successfully required ever larger increments of advanced technology, acclerating turbine generator complexity, mushrooming annual increments of investment and risk, and heightened exposure to losses for all parties concerned, both utilities and manufacturers. The leader manufacturer firm, setting the pace of technological change for the industry and managing the price-size relationship (and consequently the pace of new product adoption by the utilities), had a pivotal role during the 1950s. The leader ensured that the pace of change became neither too frantic nor too sluggish. The leader kept in mind the engineering possibilities, the technological condition of his competitors, the receptivity of the utility customers, and the generation of the required funds from older, established product lines which would finance the new technologies.

Conclusions

To marketers, this entire subject matter is familiar ground, more commonly discussed under the heading of "product line pricing." It is an area of strategic consideration in businesses ranging from aircraft to computers.

Many high-technology business strategies of recent decades have failed. The glamour of high technology business enterprises has temporarily faded, and with it, much of the privately financed development of new technology. One option is renewed government funding of the quest for new and advanced technologies. An alternative is private funding of technological development through the market pricing mechanism.

Part V:
The Performance of Large Firms

The emergence of the conglomerate form of mergers raised numerous economic and legal issues. Of major concern to the chapters in this section is an empirical investigation of the performance and impact on industry structure of conglomerate firms and large firms in general over the decade of the 1960s. This is an attempt to confront rhetorical suppositions with the factual evidence.

Conglomerate firms have been charged with abuse of economic power leading to such practices and phenomenon as cross-subsidization of product lines, reciprocity with suppliers and a resulting foreclosure of markets to potential suppliers, increases in aggregate and intra-industry concentration, predatory pricing, and raising barriers to entry. Little factual information beyond some government studies has been offered in support of these charges. The paper by Markham addresses itself to some of these issues.

Markham tests a number of hypotheses on public policy issues related to conglomerates. He examines their alleged practices of engaging in product cross-subsidization and reciprocal dealings with suppliers. He also looks at their impact on overall structure in the 1960s. As a basis for his tests he looks at the location of decision-making on pricing, advertising, and capital expenditures within the corporate structure to test for cross-subsidization and finds no evidence of such

practices by this method. Pricing and advertising decisions are heavily concentrated at the divisional level and investment decisions at the corporate level. This is consistent with profit maximization efforts on independent product lines. Hypothesizing that reciprocity is facilitated by the existence of a trade relation department he finds lack of empirical support for reciprocal trade dealings due to the very small percentage of companies which maintain a trade relations department.

He concludes the impact of conglomerate mergers of the 1960s on the structure of manufacturing industries has been generally overstated in terms of number and asset size of acquisitions. Major growth through acquisition has been confined to a very small percentage of the largest corporations and is inversely related to firm size. Market concentration does not appear to have increased from 1958 to 1967 due to conglomerate mergers and may have decreased due to such mergers. Finally, the charge that conglomerates eliminate potential competition that would enter through internal expansion is not supported as evidenced by his finding that in only 11 percent of 745 diversifying acquisitions did the acquiring firm consider internal expansion as a possible alternative.

The performance of conglomerate firms has also been questioned; for example, they have been charged with duping the stock market investment community, opting for short-term capital gains by excessive use of leverage and capitalizing on "unwarranted" price-earnings ratios in making acquisitions. The result of poor management would ultimately manifest itself in poor performance. The paper by Weston and Mansinghka presents tests of the efficiency performance of conglomerate firms.

Weston and Manshinghka test the efficiency performance of conglomerate firms against samples of industrial and non-industrial firms. They find that for 1958-68 and 1960-68 the growth rates of conglomerates measured in terms of total assets, sales, net income, earnings per share and market price were significantly greater than for the two non-conglomerate samples. They place greater emphasis on the economic utilization of resources or efficiency as measured by earnings performance. Examination of earnings free of leverage effects indicates that conglomerates had significantly lower earnings in the late 1950s but by 1968 there was no significant difference in earnings performance. This trend in earnings toward the average is consistent with a contribution toward economic efficiency by conglomerate firms. The charge that conglomerates played the differential price/earnings ratio game was not substantiated since these ratios for conglomerate firms were not significantly different from the other samples in 1958 or 1968. The efficiency of conglomerates, as with any firm organizational type, will ultimately be evident by their performance over a long period of time. If

the evidence through 1969 is indicative of the long run effects, conglomerates have increased the efficiency of resource allocation.

The analysis of the consequences of large firms as exemplified by concentrated industries has been approached in a segmented fashion historically. Separate tests of the relationship on concentration to profits, prices, advertising, and innovation have characterized research to date. Chapter 2, however, offered a more complete econometric approach in which the interaction of structure, performance, conduct, and regulation could be investigated. The final chapter offers a summary of many of the leading works covering the consequences of concentration in traditional performance areas as well as an assessment of the overall social gains and losses of large scale industrial operations in the United States.

Studies on concentration and innovation have produced ambiguous results. The difficult measurement problems of either inputs or outputs have not been solved. The elasticity of research and development employment with respect to firm size is less than one. But this could be because of the requirements of a threshold volume of sales for the effective utilization of a research department. It may also reflect other types of economies of scale in research and development activity. Research output is usually measured by either the number of patents or by "significant innovations." These measures are either ambiguous or subjective. The finding that, in some industry samples, the productivity of research output is higher among smaller firms is therefore subject to qualifications. The generalization that interindustry differences in inventive output are explained by differences in the technological fertility among industries is a tautology.

Recent analysis and evidence on advertising raise doubts on some earlier negative attitudes toward the role of advertising. The intellectual revisionism taking place describes advertising as an important form of competition. It has been shown how advertising provides information efficiently which results in lower prices. Even in instances where advertising costs are a high percentage of the sales dollar, it has been shown that overall distribution costs have been thereby lowered, making it possible for the prices to consumers to be lower than they would have been without advertising.

The frequently-repeated allegation that inflation has been caused by the price-raising activities of large firms is contradicted by the facts. Empirical studies for Western Europe for the period 1958-65, "shows very clearly that . . . more concentrated industries behaved exactly like less concentrated industries." See p. 231. For the same period in the United States, the results are the same. Since the 1966 inflation began, there has been an inverse relation between the degree of concentration and the extent of price changes: the more concentrated the industry, the smaller the price increases, the less concentrated the industry, the larger the price increases.

Consistent results are found for the behavior of profit performance of large firms. Over extended periods of time, large firms in concentrated industries have not earned higher rates of return than large firms in less-concentrated industries. Profit differentials at a point in time for individual firms have been narrowed by the relatively higher rate of expansion of areas with higher profitability rates in comparison with areas of lower profitability rates.

The foregoing data are consistent with the hypothesis of the operation of dynamic competitive processes in concentrated or oligopolistic industries. In addition to desirable price behavior, competition between large firms in concentrated industries has taken place in product qualities, changes in performance capabilities of products, and research and development efforts to increase market share. Industries described as oligopolies have been shown to be subject to the competitive market pressures for cost efficiency, price reduction, and product improvement of the kind that atomistic industries are supposed to produce. The factors that explain high concentration in an industry also provide the explanation for their good performance on price and profits. It is their greater capital intensity, economies of plant scale, economies of managerial systems, innovations in managerial technologies, continued pressures of large firm rivalry, efforts to attract consumer spending to their industries by relative price reductions that enable large firms to achieve relatively superior economic performance.

These factors also provide the underlying logic for quantifying the *estimates of the impact of overall performance of large firms on the U.S. economy. An earlier estimate of a net cost of sixty billion dollars lacked consistent internal economic logic. The plant and managerial scale economies, and innovations in managerial technologically are among the factors that have produced lower prices and profits determined by competitive forces. A basis was formulated for an estimate of net benefits from large firm operations in the economy in the range of forty-three to sixty-five billion dollars. These figures indicate in part some of the direct costs of carrying out proposals for breaking up large firms in the U.S. economy. Such estimates do not consider indirect effects, some of which might be favorable and others unfavorable. In most of the other developed nations, firms are encouraged to become larger by merger and other government supports. Hence of major consideration for further analysis is the impact that deconcentration would have on the relative cost levels of large firms in the United States in the increasingly competitive world economy.*

14

The Conglomerate Firm: A Factual Analysis

Jesse W. Markham*

The Conglomerate and Conventional Microtheory

The accelerated pace at which corporate enterprise has diversified through acquisition, represents a significant reordering of the means of corporate growth on the part of business management. As diversified firms have become more numerous, more conglomerate in scope, and a relatively more important subset of the economy's firm population, they have generated new management techniques, new organizational structures, and have presented a new challenge to traditional public policy. The large diversified firm has also placed an unusually heavy strain on the explanatory capabilities of the theory of the firm.

The inadequacies of microeconomic theory, even without explicitly introducing the additional complexities of diversity, in explaining the behavior of contemporary corporate enterprise have been dealt with at length in the literature, the details of which scarcely need repeating here.[1] The intensity of the debate over the relevancy of marginal analysis, the cornerstone of the theory of firm behavior, ushered in by the well-known articles of Lester, Machlup, and Hall and Hitch may have diminished, but the debate itself has not been completely resolved [100, 133, 140, 141]. Berle's inquiries into the modern large corporation led him to conclude that the institution has rendered the traditional theory of the firm obsolete [27]. Galbraith [84] has contended that the discernible disparity between the observable behavior of business firms and the behavior contemporary theory would predict has created a gap in our understanding of the operative mechanics of our industrial economy. He then attempted to close the gap with his concept of countervailing power. In a more recent assessment, Galbraith virtually eschews the conventional theory of the firm altogether, not so much on the grounds of its inadequacies but because of its irrelevancy [85].

The deficiencies and impertinencies of microeconomic theory can easily be exaggerated. Embedded in the recent rejections of the theory of the firm is the factual observation, sometimes expressed but more often implied, that the relatively simple assumptions underlying the economic models of firms and markets do not accord with the "real world." But, as Baumol [23] has reminded us, increased realism often must be purchased at a price, and this price may very well be a decrease in the insights into how the microeconomy operates.

185

Moreover, Friedman has contended that the appropriate test of theory is not whether its underlying assumptions conform with the specific details of reality, but rather whether its implications or predictions conform with observable phenomena [83].

Contemporary theory of the firm distinguishes clearly between firms having power over the market and those tightly constrained by competitive market forces. Surely few would seriously contend that the theoretical predictions that inhere in such models are not broadly in conformity with observable phenomena. The periodic dramatic announcements of new prices and newly negotiated wage contracts in highly concentrated industries confronting monopolistic labor unions make it abundantly clear that the participants are not passively responding to the relentless and impersonal forces of the market place. In contrast, the routine daily price quotations on commodities and certain manufactured products are appropriately published in the financial pages as "today's market prices," without attribution to individual companies and as pertaining to the designated hour of the day. Frequently, therefore, pronouncements to the effect that the behavior of modern large corporate enterprise bears only passing resemblance to that predicted by theoretical models of the firm is simply a matter of misapplication of models. A more accurate statement is that large and complex corporate organizations in possession of considerable discretionary power do not behave in accordance with conventional *competitive* models, but this is a different, and certainly not an entirely novel proposition.

It is still worthwhile, therefore, to distill from contemporary microeconomic models the few insights they *do* provide on the behavior of the multi-product firm. These models imply that a conglomerate producing totally independent products, under conventional profits maximizing assumptions, will set prices and rates of output identical with those that would result if each product were produced by an independent firm.[2] Moreover, even when the product demand schedules which the conglomerate firm confronts are interdependent, the price and output effects of conglomeration are attributable to the *combination* of market power *and* conglomeration, and not simply to the fact that the firm is a conglomerate. Finally the combination of market power and conglomeration is likely to lead to higher prices and lower rates of output than single-product firm market organization only when the products in question are substitutes.

The Policy Issues

Hypotheses concerning the operative mechanics and market structure effects of conglomerate firms have ranged far beyond the confines of conventional microeconomic theory. A list of those most frequently encountered in the literature is as follows:[3]

1. They engage in product cross-subsidization;
2. They are likely to engage in reciprocity dealings more than other firms;
3. They directly, through acquisition, increase overall concentration, and indirectly, through the practice of leverage and the erection of high entry barriers, increase market concentration in the entered industry's market;

and, contrariwise:

1. Conglomerates, since they are committed to no particular industry, are singularly responsive to profits objectives;
2. They are less likely to practice reciprocity because they buy from and sell to too many firms to make it practicable;
3. They are uniquely equipped, by virtue of their operations on a variety of industrial fronts, to facilitate an economical allocation of resources.

The existing factual evidence is much too incomplete to sustain or refute these conflicting hypotheses. The primary objective of the following analysis is to remedy, at least in part, this deficiency.

The Research Results

The quantitative data required for analysis of what might be broadly defined as the managerial characteristics of diversified and diversifying companies, as well as the impact of the diversification process on the structure of the American economy, were obtained mainly from the Diversified Company Survey, Compustat, and the Multinational Corporation Project data bank. Compustat data are generally familiar to financial analysts, and a description of the multinational corporation data bank is fully described elsewhere.[4] A brief description of the coverage of the Diversified Company Survey is presented in Table 14-1. It will be observed that the response rate for each size group rank of one-hundred among Fortune's largest five-hundred corporations, all of which received the data request, was fairly uniform. Results ranged from 25 percent for the corporations ranking in the 201-300 largest to 39 percent for the largest one-hundred. The approximately one-hundred data requests sent to the 501-1000 size group yielded forty-four returns. By visual inspection the responding corporations were spread fairly evenly throughout each size group. Responses from corporations making individual acquisitions of one-hundred million dollars or more in assets are shown separately; these companies were asked to supply more detailed data on acquisitions of this size so that they could be subjected to more detailed analysis.

Table 14-1
Corporate Survey Returns by Size Range of Company

Rank Range	No. of Corporations Reporting No Acquisitions of $100 million or more	No. of Corporations Reporting Acquisitions of $100 million or more	Total	Percentage
1–100	31	10	41	19
101–200	32	2	34	16
201–300	23	2	25	12
301–400	31	1	32	15
401–500	34	1	35	17
501–1000 and Anonymous	44	–	44	21
Totals	191	16	211	100

Managerial Aspects of Diversified Corporations and their Policy Implications

A reasonable assumption is that, subject to several important qualifications, meaningful conclusions on certain managerial aspects of large corporations may be adduced from where, in the corporate managerial structure, the decision is made. Specifically, the more decisions concerning such matters as pricing, advertising, research and development, and capital investment are centered in divisions or production units the more likely they are to be made independently of those made in other divisions and production units. It was further hypothesized that rational pursuit of profits objectives would require independent pricing of products and services in cases where their production costs and market demands were independent. However, decisions on capital outlays among products within the firm would necessarily reflect interdependence. Hence, within the multi-product firm it would be expected that pricing and advertising decisions would be more heavily concentrated at the division or operating unit level than capital investment decisions, and to a lesser extent R & D decisions.

In general, the survey results confirm these hypotheses. The managerial level at which pricing, advertising, R & D and capital expenditures decisions were made, expressed as percentages of all reporting corporations, are shown in Table 14-2. The reporting companies, except in cases where it was impossible to do so, were subdivided into producer-goods and consumer-goods companies. For 202 of the 211 responding corporations, 29 percent reported that pricing decisions, 35 percent that advertising decisions, 45 percent that R & D decisions, and 80 percent that capital investment decisions, were made at the corporate management level. For the same set of decisions involving only acquired firms (Table 14-2a) the respective percentages were significantly lower, suggesting that acquired firms were accorded greater autonomy than divisions resulting from

Table 14-2

Location of Managerial Decisions Expressed as a Percentage of All Reporting Companies

Type of Decision	Level of Managerial Decisions	Percentages		
	No. of Co's.:	57 Consumer	114 Producer	202 All
Pricing	Other	3	1	2
	Profit Center or Operating Unit	48	52	51
	*Mixed	19	19	18
	Corporate	30	28	29
		100	100	100
Advertising	Other	2	–	1
	Profit Center or Operating Unit	42	44	44
	*Mixed	16	22	20
	Corporate	40	34	35
		100	100	100
R & D Expenditures	Other	2	–	1
	Profit Center or Operating Unit	15	31	26
	*Mixed	23	29	28
	Corporate	60	40	45
		100	100	100
Capital Expenditures	Other	1	–	1
	Profit Center or Operating Unit	–	3	4
	*Mixed	18	16	15
	Corporate	81	81	80
		100	100	100

*Generally Mixed means that the decision is initially made at the lower unit and reviewed by the next highest organizational unit; e.g., a "mixed" decision on price between operating unit and corporate management means that the pricing decision is initially made at the operating unit and reviewed by corporate management.

internal expansion. Only 10 percent of the responding corporations shifted the price-making function from the acquired firm to corporate management; the corresponding figures for advertising, R & D and capital expenditures were respectively 16 percent, 24 percent, and 50 percent. Such current operating decisions as those concerning price and advertising tend to be exercised by corporate management slightly more often in consumer-goods than producer-goods firms.

In interpreting these data it must be born in mind that they were compiled from the returns of *all* reporting corporations. Some of the largest one-thousand industrial corporations are obviously not diversified, a larger number are only

Table 14-2a

Location of Management Decisions for Acquired Companies Expressed as a Percentage of All Reporting Companies Making Acquisitions

Type of Decision	Location of Managerial Decisions	No. of Co's.:	Percentages 49 Consumer	96 Producer	173 All
Pricing	Left with Acquired Firm		27	33	30
	*Mixed		63	55	58
	Moved to Corporate		10	12	12
			100	100	100
Advertising	Left with Acquired Firm		37	26	28
	*Mixed		43	56	52
	Moved to Corporate		20	18	20
			100	100	100
R & D Expenditures	Left with Acquired Firm		22	12	14
	*Mixed		41	64	59
	Moved to Corporate		37	24	27
			100	100	100
Capital Expenditures	Left with Acquired Firm		4	2	2
	*Mixed		41	34	37
	Moved to Corporate		55	64	61
			100	100	100

*Mixed generally means that the decision is initially made at the lower unit and reviewed by the next highest organizational unit; e.g., a "mixed" decision on price between operating unit and corporate management means that the pricing decision is initially made at the operating unit and reviewed by corporate management.

slightly diversified, and an undetermined number are not organized along divisional or operating unit lines. In corporations falling in these categories, all important decisions are very likely made at the corporate level, in some instances because the company is engaged in a single or several closely related products or product lines where the issue of interdependent decision-making, or "cross-subsidization," is not especially applicable.

While there are no readily available means for eliminating corporations falling in essentially single-product line categories, a substitute technique could be employed. Professor Charles Berry has calculated diversification indexes at the two-digit and the four-digit level for a large number of companies appearing on *Fortune*'s list of the largest five-hundred for the years 1960 and 1965.[5] One hundred and fourteen, over one half of the survey reporting companies answering the decision-making location questions, could be matched with Berry's indexes for 1965. It was hoped that a cross-tabulation of the decision-making location for reporting corporations with various ranges of diversification indexes would more clearly establish the relationship between the location of decision-making with respect to the four types of decisions and the degree of diversification. The diversification ranges used were zero, 0.01-0.20, 0.21-0.40, 0.41-0.60, 0.61-0.80, and 0.81-1.00. If the 114 companies on which the relevant data were calculated were divided into producer and consumer industry companies, they would have been so thinly spread over sixty possible cells that the results would not have been very meaningful. Even when the producer-goods/consumer-goods firms are combined the spread is still quite thin, but for what they are worth they are shown in Table 14-3 and 14-4.

The cross-tabulations yielded a few modestly surprising results. In the highly diversified reporting corporations having two-digit Berry indexes greater than 0.80, neither the pricing nor advertising decision is ever made at the corporation management level, whereas capital expenditure decisions nearly always are. R & D decisions, while mostly left to divisions, are sometimes made at the corporate level. This result is not surprising. It will be noted, however, that scarcely any discernible systematic differences can be detected among the completely undiversified and the intermediate diversification ranges—the pricing and adver-tising decision does not appear to be relegated more to operating units or divisions in any continuous linear pattern as diversification increases.

A similar analysis employing Berry's four-digit SIC diversification indexes yields a more continuous relationship between diversification and decision location. In general, the higher the diversification index the more likely are pricing, advertising and R & D decisions to be made at the division rather than at the corporate management level. For example, reporting corporations falling into the two relatively undiversified classifications having Berry four-digit diversification indexes of zero and 0.01-0.20 each account for 2.7 percent of all reporting companies. They both account for 5.9 percent of the responses stating that the pricing decision was made by corporate management. In contrast, highly diversified companies having indexes falling in the 0.81-1.00 class account for 34.1 percent of all reporting companies and for only 0.43 percent of the responses stating that the pricing decision was made at the corporate manage-ment level. This positive relationship between degree of diversification and apparent divisional autonomy also holds for advertising and R & D decisions. Again, the capital expenditures decision is predominantly centered in corporate management irrespective of the degree of diversification.

It has been urged in the literature that the existence of a trade relations department in a company may at least be suggestive of the practice of reciprocity. The rationale for inferring a rough association between the two appears to be that it would be highly improbable that a corporation, especially one that is large and highly diversified, would practice reciprocity without creating a unit within the organization responsible for communicating informa-tion on suppliers to those who manage the company's sales. The Harvard

Table 14-3

Cross Tabulation of Decision Location and Degree of Diversification (2-digit level) for 114 Reporting Companies

| Type of Decision | Berry 2-digit Index, 1965 | | | | | | | % of |
	0.0	.01−.20	.21−.40	.41−.60	.61−.80	.81−.100	Total	114 Firms
All 114 firms	13.1%	14.9%	21.0%	25.6%	21.0%	4.4%	100%	100%
Pricing								
Other	.0%	.0%	.0%	.0%	100.0%	.0%	100%	0.9%
*% Total	.00	.00	.00	.00	4.76	.00		
Division	12.7	9.5	19.1	23.8	28.6	6.3	100	55.3
% Total	.97	.63	.91	.93	1.36	1.57		
Mixed	.0	12.5	31.3	37.4	12.5	6.3	100	14.0
% Total	.00	.84	1.51	1.46	.59	1.57		
Corporate	20.6	26.5	11.8	26.5	14.7	.0	100	29.8
% Total	1.57	1.75	.56	1.04	.70	.00		
								100.0%
Advertising								
Other	.0%	.0%	.0%	.0%	100.0%	.0%	100%	0.9%
% Total	.00		.00	.00	4.76	.00		
Division	8.3	10.4	22.9	22.9	29.2	6.3	100	42.1
% Total	.63	.70	1.09	.93	1.39	1.57		
Mixed	4.5	9.1	13.6	40.9	22.7	9.1	100	19.3
% Total	.34	.61	.65	1.59	1.08	2.28		
Corporate	23.3	23.3	16.3	23.3	14.0	.0	100	37.7
% Total	1.78	1.56	.78	.91	.67	.00		
								100.0%
R & D								
Other	.0%	.0%	.0%	.0%	100.0%	.0%	100%	.9%
% Total	.00		.00	.00	4.70	.00		
Division	3.2	12.9	25.8	25.8	22.6	9.7	100	27.2
% Total	.24	.86	1.23	1.01	1.08	2.45		
Mixed	3.2	9.3	21.9	28.1	34.4	3.1	100	28.1
% Total	.24	.62	1.04	1.10	1.64	.70		
Corporate	26.0	20.0	12.0	26.0	14.0	2.0	100	43.8
% Total	1.98	1.34	.57	1.02	.66	.46		
								100.0%
Corp. Exp.								
Other	.0%	.0%	.0%	.0%	100.0%	.0%	100%	.9%
% Total	.00	.00	.00	.00	4.71	.00		
Division	.0	.0	.0	60.0	40.0	.0	100	4.4
% Total	.00	.00	.00	2.34	1.90	.00		

Table 14-3 (cont.)

Type of Decision	Berry 2-digit Index, 1965							% of 114 Firms
	0.0	.01–.20	.21–.40	.41–.60	.61–.80	.81–.100	Total	
Mixed	15.0	10.0	20.0	30.0	20.0	5.0	100	17.5
% Total	1.15	.67	.95	1.17	.95	1.25		
Corporate	13.6	17.0	19.3	23.9	21.6	4.5	100	77.2
% Total	1.04	1.14	.92	.97	1.03	1.12		
								100.0%

*% total of reported companies having diversification indexes in the indicated class.

Business School Survey was designed to ascertain the extent to which responding corporations had such trade relations departments, and to ascertain whether they served as a conduit for information on sales and purchases.

It is obvious that the test is at best crude and suggestive rather than conclusive. Trade relations departments may certainly exist for a host of purposes other than that of enabling the practice of reciprocity dealings, a conclusion borne out by the field study that preceded the final formulation and dissemination of the data request. On the other hand, it is equally plausible that some form of sporadic and informal reciprocity may occur without benefit of the services of an organizational unit designed to facilitate its practice.

The request for data on trade relations departments and their activities generated more inquiries from responding companies concerning the meaning of the question than any other data request. While the question was phrased in straightforward factual terms, it was evidently interpreted by some respondents—presumably those familiar with the literature on the subject—as equivalent to "Does your firm practice reciprocity?", a question that had been considered and rejected for obvious reasons. In the case of all requests for clarification the respondent was urged simply to respond to the question as factually stated. A check of the returns in instances where it was possible confirmed that they did so. Whether the responses as a whole reflect a bias, and how much, is impossible to determine.

Of the 211 responding corporations, 195 answered the trade relations question, of which thirty-one or about 16 percent, maintained trade relations departments, 164, or about 84 percent, did not. The conclusions to be drawn from these data clearly depend upon the extent of the association between the maintenance of trade relations departments and the likelihood that reciprocity is practiced. If the relationship is strong, it can be concluded that a relatively small percentage of the corporate populations have established an organizational unit concerned with reciprocity dealings.

The data were analyzed further to ascertain whether maintenance of trade relations departments could be associated with any of the other important

Table 14-4

Cross Tabulations of Decision Location and Degree of Diversification (4-digit level) for 114 Reporting Companies

Type of Decision	Berry 4-digit Index, 1965						Total	% of 114 Firms
	0.0	.01–.20	.21–.40	.41–.60	.61–.80	.81–.100		
All 114 firms	2.7%	2.7%	3.6%	19.3%	37.2%	34.1%	100%	100%
Pricing								
Other	.0%	.0%	.0%	.0%	.0%	100.0%	100%	.9%
*% Total	.00	.00	.00	.00	.00	2.94		
Division	1.6	1.6	1.6	12.7	38.1	44.4	100	55.3
% Total	.59	.59	.45	.66	1.05	1.30		
Mixed	.0	.0	6.3	18.7	43.7	31.3	100	14.0
% Total	.00	.00	1.75	.96	1.17	.92		
Corporate	5.9	5.9	5.9	32.4	35.2	14.7	100	29.8
% Total	2.18	2.18	1.64	1.70	.95	.43		
								100.0%
Advertising								
Other	.0%	.0%	.0%	.0%	.0%	100.0%	100%	.9%
% Total	.00	.00	.00	.00	.00	2.94		
Division	.0	.0	.0	16.7	35.4	47.9	100	42.1
% Total	.00	.00	.00	.86	.95	1.40		
Mixed	4.5	4.5	4.5	13.6	27.3	45.6	100	19.3
% Total	1.67	1.67	1.25	.70	.73	1.34		
Corporate	4.7	4.7	7.0	25.6	46.4	11.6	100	37.7
% Total	1.67	1.67	1.94	1.32	1.25	.34		
								100.0%
R & D								
Other	.0%	.0%	.0%	.0%	.0%	.0%	100%	.9%
% Total	.00	.00	.00	.00	.00	.00		
Division	.0	3.2	3.2	12.9	29.1	51.6	100	27.2
% Total	.00	1.18	.89	.67	.78	1.50		
Mixed	.0	.0	3.1	18.8	31.3	46.8	100	28.1
% Total	.00	.00	.86	.97	.84	1.37		
Corporate	6.0	4.0	4.0	24.0	48.0	14.0	100	43.8
% Total	2.22	1.48	1.11	1.25	1.29	.41		
								100.0%
Cap. Expend.								
Other	.0%	.0%	.0%	.0%	.0%	100.0%	100%	.9%
% Total	.00	.00	.00	.00	.00	2.94		
Division	.0	.0	.0	20.0	40.0	40.0	100	4.4
% Total	.00	.00	.00	1.03	1.08	1.17		

Table 14-4 (cont.)

Type of Decision	Berry 4-digit Index, 1965							% of 114 Firms
	0.0	.01 – .20	.21 – .40	.41 – .60	.61 – .80	.81 – .100	Total	
Mixed	5.0	5.0	.0	15.0	45.0	30.0	100	17.5
% Total	1.85	1.85	.00	.78	1.21	.88		
Corporate	2.3	2.3	4.5	20.5	36.3	34.1	100	77.2
% Total	.85	.85	1.25	1.06	.97	1.00		
								100.0%

*% total of reported companies having diversification indexes in the indicated class.

characteristics of the reporting corporations. For both producer- and consumer-goods companies the Berry diversification indexes were considerably higher for those corporations reporting no trade relations departments than for those who did. This suggests but only suggests, that "reciprocity" (having a trade relations department) is less likely to be practiced by highly diversified companies than by other corporations. The differences between consumer-goods and producer-goods firms were not statistically significant. On the other hand, the ratio of diversifying acquisitions to total acquisitions made in the period 1961-70 was slightly higher for producer-goods companies and significantly higher for consumer-goods companies having trade relations departments than for those that did not. It is therefore tempting to draw the conclusions that trade relations departments may be more a concomitant of the diversification process than of the actual or potential practice of reciprocity dealings. However, the data also show that the average number of diversifying acquisitions between 1961 and 1970 was substantially higher for companies having no trade relations departments than for those who did, thus suggesting that the relationship is simply a result of the smaller number of non-diversifying acquisitions made by companies having no trade relations departments.

The Effect of Diversifying and other Acquisitions on the Size Distribution of Firms

By employing regression analysis, it was possible to ascertain the possible effects all acquisitions, and diversifying acquisitions, have had on the rank change and size distribution of manufacturing corporations. The results of the analysis are presented in Table 14-5. The variable "number of diversifying acquisitions" was obtained from survey responses, where companies reported acquisitions having the principal effect of obtaining entry into a new four-digit industry. The ratio of such acquisitions to total acquisitions turned out to be considerably smaller than that calculated from FTC data for the same time period—slightly less than 50 percent as compared with nearly 80 percent.

Table 14-5
Regressions of Size and Rank Change Variables on Acquisition Activities

		R	Significant Level
(1) Fortune Rank 1969–Fortune Rank 1964:	Sales growth from Acquisitions (1)	−.3674	.001
(2)	Sales growth from Acquisitions (2)	−.4300	.001
(3)	Asset growth from Acquisition (1)	−.3924	.001
(4)	Asset growth from Acquisition (2)	−.3023	.001
(5) Assets 1970 attributable to 1961-1970 acquisitions (1)	1961 total assets	−.1892	.031
(6) (2)	1961 total assets	−.1918	.028
(7) Sales 1970 attributable to 1961-1970 acquisitions (1)	1961 sales	−.2067	.019
(8) Sales 1970 attributable to 1961-1970 acquisitions (1)	Average market share, 1964	−.1800	.036
(9) (2)	share, 1964	−.1400	.076
(10) Assets 1970 attributable to 1961-1970 acquisitions (1)	share, 1964	−.1300	.093
(11) (2)	share, 1964	−.1200	.102
(12) Berry diversification index 2-digit level	share, 1964	−.1900	.016
(13) 4-digit level	share, 1964	−.2100	.011
(14) Number diversifying acquisitions 1961-1970 (C)	share, 1964	−.1400	.217
(15) (P)	share, 1964	−.1100	.163
(1) Excluding post-acquisition growth			
(2) Including post-acquisition growth			
(C) Consumer-Goods Firms			
(P) Producer-Goods Firms			

From the first set of regressions relating change in *Fortune* rank between 1964 and 1969, it is clear that a rise in rank is significantly related to all four of the asset and sales measures of 1961-70 growth attributable to acquisition. In the computations a negative result when subtracting an earlier year from a later year rank means that company rose in rank, hence the negative regression coefficients mean that a rise in rank was associated with growth through acquisition. For all four regressions the coefficients are negative, fairly large, and significant at the 1 percent level.

The results of regressions (5), (6) and (7), however, strongly suggest that growth through acquisition over the period 1961-70 was inversely related to the size of firm in 1961. In all cases the regression coefficients relating growth through acquisition to the size of firms in 1961 are negative in sign; only in one regression are the results not significant at the 5 percent level. While the coefficients are not large, they indicate that larger firms owed relatively smaller percentages of their 1970 size to acquisitions made in 1961-70 than smaller firms within the one-thousand largest corporations.

It was also possible, by making use of an average market share index computed for corporations in the Harvard Multinational Corporation project, to explore the relationship between the average market shares of corporations and their number of diversifying mergers, and their 1961-70 growth attributable to all acquisitions. The average market share index used was computed by averaging the market shares of individual corporations in five-digit industries for the year 1964. All regressions of this index on growth-through-acquisition variables and on the number of diversifying acquisitions yielded negative coefficients, although none was significant at the 5 percent level. However, when regressed on both the Berry two-digit and four-digit diversification indexes for 1965, the coefficients were negative and, in both cases, significant at the 5 percent level. The results suggest, although the relationship is not especially strong, that (1) firms having relatively smaller shares of their respective markets grew more through acquisition in 1961-70 than those having larger shares of their respective markets and; (2) the more highly diversified the company the smaller its average market share.

Diversifying Acquisitions and Market Concentration

Strictly conglomerate mergers, by definition, have no direct effect on the level of market concentration. The market shares of the acquired firm are not additive to any of those of the acquiring firm. It has been argued, however, that such conglomerate acquisitions may very well affect the level of market concentration indirectly. The financial and managerial resources of the acquiring firm may eventually enable the acquired firm to increase its market shares. However, the effect of conglomerate acquisitions on market concentration would depend on a number of factors. If the acquired firm was already one of the largest firms, and if its subsequent increase in market share was at least in part at the expense of firms not among the top four, such acquisitions may have the indirect effect of increasing the level of market concentration. If the acquired firm was relatively small, and if the post-acquisition growth in market share was partially at the expense of the largest four, such acquisitions might be expected to lead to a decrease in market concentration.

The only data available for measuring these indirect effects are the concentration ratios at the three-digit SIC level. In computing these ratios, the three-digit SIC industry to which the FTC assigned acquired companies in conglomerate acquisitions were first arranged in a frequency distribution. The three-digit industries in which acquisitions numbered less than three were eliminated. Wherever possible a weighted concentration index for each of the eighteen remaining three-digit industries was computed from the four-digit concentration ratios available for the census years 1947, 1958, and 1967. The eighteen three-digit industries for which these calculations could be made are shown in Table 14-6.

While the deficiences in these data for the purpose at hand may be obvious they merit a brief comment. First, concentration ratios for all the four-digit industries that comprise each three-digit industry group are not available from census data; the three-digit concentration ratios are therefore calculated from incomplete data. Second, the true indirect effect of conglomerate acquisitions may be registered at the four-digit level, and this effect may be obscured by offsetting movements in the concentration ratios of other four-digit industries comprising the three-digit industry group. Third, one can only speculate on the time span in which such indirect effects may reasonably be expected to manifest themselves in the form of changing concentration levels. And finally, in view of the host of factors that produce changes over time in concentration ratios, it

Table 14-6

Changes in Concentration in 3-digit SIC Industries Most Frequently Acquired into in Diversifying Acquisitions in the Period 1961-1970

SIC	1947	1958	1967	Directional Change 1958 to 1967
203	56	31	30	Decrease
221	–	25	30	Increase
231	9	11	17	Increase
261	–	46	45	Decrease
262	–	–	26	Increase
281	74	54	42	Decrease
291	37	32	33	Increase
331	52	53	49	Decrease
333	–	70	64	Decrease
349	25	19	18	Decrease
354	20	21	17	Decrease
355	26	34	27	Decrease
356	56	49	29	Decrease
358	49	51	33	Decrease
361	61	55	48	Decrease
366	–	92	92	No Change
371	53	68	81	Increase
372	72	57	53	Decrease

would be naive to attribute such changes to any single factor such as conglomerate acquisitions.

These qualifications aside, if conglomerate acquisitions had a decisive effect on the level of concentration in acquired industries, this effect should have revealed itself in the years 1958 to 1967 when most such acquisitions occurred. While the pattern is far from consistent, there is no evidence that conglomerate acquisitions have produced an increase in the level of market concentration, or at least they had not had this effect by 1967. In fact, if one were forced to render a judgment, it would be somewhat safer to conclude that such acquisitions may possibly have reduced the level of market concentration over this period. Of the eighteen three-digit industry groups, twelve registered decreases. and one registered no change. However, in view of the uncertainties attending causal relationships and the deficiencies in the data, the safest conclusion is that conglomerate acquisitions appear to have had no pronounced effect on the level of market concentration over the period 1958-67.

Diversifying Acquisitions and Potential Competition

One of the frequently voiced antitrust concerns over diversifying acquisitions is that they may eliminate *potential* competition by eliminating potential entrants. The premise underlying this argument is that if diversification through acquisition were foreclosed, acquiring firms might very well enter the same industries through internal expansion. Hence, diversifying acquistions reduce potential competition, and, ultimately actual competition in the markets of acquired firms.

The Harvard Business School survey data shed modest light on this issue. Each company included in the survey was asked, in the case of each diversifying acquisition, whether expansion into the acquired firm's industry by internal expansion had been analyzed and considered as an alternative means of gaining entry. For seventy-nine of the 745 diversifying acquisitions reported by 193 companies for the 1961-70 period, the acquiring companies stated that internal expansion had been analyzed, and considered as a possible alternative to acquisition. Internal expansion was therefore given sufficiently serious consideration to be analyzed in 11 percent of all entries into new four-digit SIC industries eventually entered by the acquisition route. While there are no means for determining the number of instances in which the acquired firm would have in fact entered through internal expansion had the acquisition route been foreclosed, it very likely would have occurred in fewer than 11 percent of the acquisitions. It would seem reasonable to conclude from these data that for the vast majority of diversifying acquisitions internal expansion is not considered as a feasible alternative to acquisition.

Summary and Conclusions

The objective of this analysis has been to subject current hypotheses concerning conglomerate enterprise to factual tests. Perhaps the most accurate assessment of the results could be summarized, with appropriate adaption to the subject at hand, in Professor Mason's often repeated caveate: "No one familiar with the statistical . . . material pertaining to the business performance of firms and industries would deny the extreme difficulty of constructing from this material a watertight case for or against the performance of particular firms in particular industries. Few, on the other hand, would deny that . . . an informal judgment is possible."[8] Obviously, the results of the analysis fall far short of establishing a water-tight confirmation or refutation of the various and conflicting hypotheses tested. However, they do provide a basis for several judgmental conclusions:

First, the "conglomerate" merger wave of the 1960s almost certainly had less impact on the overall structure of the American economy than is commonly believed: (1) The number and asset-volume of "conglomerate" acquisitions, by most reasonable definitions of "conglomerate," appear generally to have been overstated; (2) acquisitions have been partly offset by selloffs by the same companies; and (3) growth through acquisition over this time period is negatively correlated with 1961 firm size.

Second, market concentration in industries most frequently acquired into, as measured at the three-digit SIC level, registered more decreases than increases over the period 1958-67. Since a significant percentage of the acquisitions classified as conglomerate by the FTC become horizontal at the three-digit level, this result is somewhat surprising, suggesting that whatever effects mergers may have had on concentration were overshadowed by other factors. One such factor that may possibly have contributed to this result is the fairly weak but statistically significant negative correlation between the average market concentration index of individual firms at the five-digit SIC level and their 1961-70 growth attributable to acquisition.

Third, analysis of such conglomerate firm practices as "cross-subsidization" and "reciprocity dealings" yield results that can best be described as failing conclusively to support any of the conflicting hypotheses. The test used to ascertain the improbability of cross-subsidization (product interdependence) was the extent of divisional or operating unit independence in making pricing and advertising decisions. In all reporting companies having very high indexes of product diversification, such decisions were made at the operating or division level rather than by corporate management. However, in over one-quarter of all reporting companies, including some fairly diversified companies, pricing and advertising decisions were made at the corporate level. In contrast, decisions on new capital outlays are generally made at the corporate management level. These results may refute any hypotheses that highly diversified corporations are generally organized to engage in cross-product subsidization. Except for the very highly diversified firms, neither do they confirm the counter-hypothesis that diversified firms are rarely organized to engage in cross-product subsidization.

The test for the prevalence of reciprocity dealings leads to a similar qualified conclusion. Of the 207 reporting corporations, 14 percent maintain trade relations departments, 80 percent do not, and 6 percent did not supply the requested information. The policy implications of these data hang heavily on the reliability one places on the test itself. About all that can be said on this issue is that the presence of trade relations departments has sometimes been offered as evidence of the practice of reciprocity; by employing the same test, it can be concluded that 80 percent of the reporting corporations are not visibly organized to practice reciprocity.

Fourth, companies that have diversified through acquisition generally have not considered internal expansion as an alternative means of entering the acquired firms' industries. In only seventy-nine, or 11 percent, of the 745 reported diversifying acquisitions did the acquiring firm analyze internal expansion to the point of considering it as an alternative to acquisition. It is highly probable that internal expansion would have actually occurred in less than 11 percent of these cases had the acquisition route been foreclosed. On the other hand, it is virtually certain that in some cases the perceived low probability of the acquisition being challenged under Clayton Act, Section 7 was a reason for *not* analyzing internal growth as an alternative. Nevertheless, it would seem reasonable to conclude that: (1) in a large majority of diversifying acquisitions the acquisition does not eliminate a potential competitor in *those* acquired firms' industries; (2) a severe constraint on diversifying acquisitions would possibly stimulate some internal expansion in, and into, *other* industries; and (3) the average growth of those firms that did grow through diversifying acquisitions in 1961-70 would have been less had such a severe constraint existed.

15

Tests of the Efficiency Performance of Conglomerate Firms

J. Fred Weston and
Surendra K. Mansinghka*

Many aspects of conglomerate firms have now been studied. The literature on portfolio theory is relevant for appraising diversification aspects of conglomerate firm performance.[1] Other aspects of the economic theory of conglomerates have been treated in various papers.[2] A comprehensive analysis of legal aspects has been made.[3] Business motivations for conglomerate diversifications have been described.[4] The conglomerate merger movement has also received considerable scrutiny with regard to its public policy effects.[5]

However, empirical tests of conglomerate performance remain limited.[6] Most of the studies to date test aspects of the effects of mergers generally. Professor Eamon Kelly compared a sample of twenty-one firms growing 20 percent or more by acquisitions from 1946 to various terminal dates through 1963 with similar firms growing internally. He found no significant differences in profitability between the two groups.

Professor Thomas F. Hogarty analyzed the success of forty-three mergers by the criteria of post-merger investment performance (capital gains plus dividend returns) adjusted by an investment performance index (IPI) for the industry of the acquiring company.[8] Using measurements including reinvestment of dividends, he classified fourteen failures (F), nineteen ambiguous (A), and five successes (S). For an IPI of 10 percent, a failure was defined as a return of 9 percent or less, a success was a return of 11 percent or more, and the ambiguous category represented returns between 9 and 11 percent. Not assuming reinvestment of dividends, the distribution was 3 S, 19 A and 21 F.

On the hypothesis of a probability of success of 0.5, Professor Hogarty found his results significant. But the returns for "ambiguous" groups was not statistically significantly different from their industry IPI's. Hence, for applying his statistical test, it would have been as plausible to test for a 0.5 (or 0.333) probability of failure. By this test, the merging firms' failure performance would have been significantly lower than hypothesized on measurements assuming reinvestment of dividends and not significantly different on the measurements not assuming reinvestment of dividends.[9] Professor Hogarty's study suggests at worst no significant difference between the postmerger performance of the merging firms and the IPI of their respective pre-merger industries. The implications of such a finding are analyzed in connection with the results of our study.

Edward J. Heiden analyzed fifty-seven firms with large acquisitions during the period 1951-61. He related profits to a number of variables, finding all to be positively associated with profits except merger activity, which had a small negative association.[10]

Gort and Hogarty examine a number of aspects of mergers generally. Their statistical analysis indicates that the stockholders of acquired firms gain on the average, while the owners of acquiring firms lose on the average. They found that mergers have an approximately neutral effect on the aggregate worth of firms that participate in them.[11]

Professor Samuel R. Reid's studies include data evaluating a sample of conglomerate firms for the decade ending in 1961. He utilized three measures he characterized as reflecting the interests of managers, three reflecting the interests of stockholders. Professor Reid concluded that more actively merging firms and firms that diversified to a greater extent in their merging activity scored higher on the criteria related to managers' interests and lower on criteria related to stockholders' interests.

Lorie and Halpern studied the performance of 117 mergers taken from the Federal Trade Commission listing for 1954-67 of all mergers in manufacturing and mining in which the acquired firm had ten million dollars or more of assets.[12] In the Lorie and Halpern study the focus is particularly on the possibility of "deception of investors." The mergers which they studied were therefore ones in which the shareholders of the acquired company received for their shares relatively complicated instruments such as convertibles or warrants rather than cash, common stock, ordinary preferred stock or bonds.[13]

The investment return to stockholders of the acquired firms was analyzed on various bases comprehended in the period six months prior to the merger to two years after the merger. In general, the investment return performance to stockholders of the acquired firms was superior to the market performance of broad market indexes for comparable periods of time. For example, the mean rates of return for the periods twelve and fourteen months subsequent to the mergers were 9.34 percent and 9.52 percent, respectively, while corresponding rates for the market index were 7.73 percent and 7.38 percent.

Smith and Schreiner compared the efficiency of portfolio selection by conglomerates with that by investment companies.[14] Their findings indicated superior portfolio performance for investment companies. Their data on the investment companies was based on actual performance. However, portfolio results of the conglomerates was a simulation based upon the industries in which the conglomerate firms appeared to be operating. Further, the distinctive economic functions of conglomerates are not primarily diversification. Indeed, it has been demonstrated that "homemade diversification" is an effective substitute for corporate or other institutional diversification under the assumptions of perfect capital markets.[15]

Since the data of the previous empirical studies ended predominantly in the early or mid-1960s, an updating is clearly required.[16] Also, most of the studies dealt with mergers generally. Of the three empirical studies dealing with conglomerate mergers, the Lorie and Halpern study is specialized to the point of view of stockholders in acquired companies. The Smith and Schreiner study focuses on aspects of conglomerate diversification under a form of simulation for conglomerates. Only the Reid studies are directly comparable to this paper.

To evaluate the findings of the previous studies and related issues, the present study begins with a comprehensive empirical analysis of the performance of conglomerate firms. We employ a number of measures paralleling the performance measures presuming to reflect the interests of managers and individual stockholders as well as institutional investors. However, our greatest emphasis is on criteria related to economic efficiency. After the results of our own study are presented, an evaluation is made of the most comparable previously published study of the performance of conglomerate firms. Next, some supplementary data sources for evaluating conglomerate performance are presented. Finally, some comments on the significance of the findings are made.

Identification and Selection of Conglomerate Firms

The term "conglomerate" is ambiguous and the meaning of the term itself has undergone a substantial transformation.[17] The confusion is aggravated by the classification system employed by the Federal Trade Commission in reporting on merger activities in three categories. *Horizontal mergers* involve firms in the same industry. *Vertical mergers* represent firms at different levels of the production process in the same industry. *Conglomerate mergers* are "all other" mergers. Conglomerate mergers are further divided into "product extension and geographic extension" and "other" mergers.

Much of the ambiguity stems from the emphasis in the Census Standard Industrial Classification (SIC) system on characteristics of products for defining "industries". The more relevant consideration from the standpoint of the economic effects of mergers is the extent to which research, manufacturing, marketing and other managerial capabilities are extended or complemented in a merger.[18] From this standpoint it would be more informative to label product and market extension mergers as "concentric" or "congeneric." These terms suggest that the merging firms possess related characteristics.

The "other" category of conglomerate firms could further be subdivided between management conglomerates and financial conglomerates. In management conglomerates the avowed objective was to provide general management services in the form of planning, organizing, directing, and controlling or specific management staff expertise in the areas of research, production, manufacturing, marketing, finance, etc. Financial conglomerates were limited to taking ultimate financial responsibility and providing the financial planning and control functions. As a practical matter, many of the firms termed "conglomerates" reflected a mixture of the characteristics.

Since the word "conglomerate" carries some ambiguity, we attempt to give some explicit content to the term.[19] We are focusing on firms that have entered into a broad program of diversification achieved to a substantial degree by external mergers and acquisitions rather than by internal development. In selecting the companies to be included in the study, two criteria are therefore relevant. The first is the extent to which growth was achieved from external sources and the second is the degree of diversification represented by the external mergers and acquisitions.

To implement these criteria, we first compiled a list of firms. We began with all firms involved in three or more mergers during the period 1960 through 1968.[20] In making our compilation we sought to adjust for underreporting. If a firm's assets grew at a rate greater than 10 percent per year, the possibility of growth by merger was further investigated. In addition, if acquisitions, adjusted for post-merger growth, aggregated more than five-hundred million dollars, or if the firm appeared to have been involved in at least two major acquisitions or a number of smaller acquisitions (as indicated by the increase in the number of subsidiaries listed in Moody's in the period between 1960 and 1968), we judged it to be a candidate for application of our two screening rules.

Screening Rule #1 sought to determine the firms for which 20 percent or more of the increase in total assets during the period 1960-68 was accounted for by external acquisitions. In view of the fact that the acquired or merged firms would have continued to grow separately, if the merger had not taken place, we attempted to adjust for this factor. The total assets of the acquired or merged firms for the years subsequent to acquisition were adjusted by the subsequent growth in their total assets calculated at the growth rate of their industries.[21] *Screening Rule #2*, the diversification criterion, was that in 1968 the firm was involved in ten or more three-digit SIC industry categories or in five or more two-digit SIC categories.[22] Application of these criteria led to the selection of sixty-three firms as conglomerates on which data were computed.[23]

Two control samples were selected, one of industrial companies only and one combining both industrial and nonindustrial companies. Since most of our companies were included in the *Fortune* 500 Industrial Companies list, our control sample of industrial companies was selected by applying a table of random numbers to the Fortune lists of 500 largest industrial companies excluding, of course, the companies already included in our conglomerate study. To provide a further check, we selected a second control group from the combined directory of large corporations from *Fortune* which in 1968 constituted five-hundred industrial companies and two-hundred and fifty non-industrial companies.[24] The two random sample groups were chosen as control groups for the comparisons of performance next presented.

The Comparative Performance of Conglomerate Firms

Since previous studies measured growth, we have done so also. Our main reason for doing so is to test our hypothesis that the findings of some of the previous studies of lower growth in the earnings per share or market price of conglomerate firms were due to the relatively early terminal dates of the studies.[25]

Data on Comparative Growth Rates

Four averages of growth rates are set forth in Table 15-1.[26] The data in Table 15-1 presents the results of calculations of both the unweighted and weighted mean values, the median values, and the geometric means.[27]

The growth rates for the conglomerate firms were higher on all seven items measured and for both time periods. The magnitude of the differentially higher growth rates for the conglomerate firms was greatest for the unweighted means, and smallest for the weighted means. The geometric means were somewhat lower than the unweighted arithmetic means, while the median values were moderately higher than the results from the calculations of the weighted arithmetic averages.

The magnitudes of the growth rates for the aggregate items were larger than growth rates measured on a per share basis. This is to be expected, of course, since the per share data reduces the growth rates of the aggregates in proportion to the increase in the number of shares issued as a result of the mergers. For the conglomerate firms, growth rates for total assets, sales and net income were in the range of 17 to 20 percent. The growth rates on a per share basis were in the range of from 12 to 15 percent. In contrast, for the two random samples, utilizing the median values, the growth rates for total assets, sales and net income were approximately 9 to 10 percent. The growth rates of earnings and market price per share were only slightly less.

A meaningul comparison of the results requires analysis of the statistical significance of the differences between the measures of central tendency. For the unweighted arithmetic means presented in Table 15-1, F-statistics were calculated, comparing the conglomerate firms successively with *Sample 1*, with *Sample 2*, and with *Samples 1* and *2* individually but simultaneously.

Table 15-2 shows a consistent pattern between both time periods. The arithmetic means of growth rates were significantly higher for the conglomerates as compared with *Sample 1* or *Sample 2* separately or simultaneously. The differences in the growth rates between the two random samples were generally not significant.

No great importance is attached to these measurements of the differential growth rates. For any of the measures calculated the difference in growth rate is primarily a function of the extent of merger activity of the conglomerate firms.

Table 15-1

Growth Measures for 63 Conglomerate Firms Compared with Two Other Samples of Firms, 1958-1968 and 1960-1968

| 1958-1968 | Arithmetic Mean Values | | | | | | Median Values | | | Geometric Mean | | |
| | Unweighted | | | Weighted | | | | | | | | |
	C[1]	M	N	C	M	N	C	M	N	C	M	N
1. Total Assets	22.8%	12.6%	10.2%	15.8%	8.5%	7.9%	18.0%	9.7%	9.6%	21.7%	12.2%	9.9%
2. Sales	24.0	11.6	10.1	16.3	8.5	6.2	17.1	9.2	8.8	22.8	11.3	9.8
3. Net Income	20.7	10.4	11.6	17.7	8.4	7.8	20.6	10.0	9.6	22.7	10.9	11.4
4. Earnings Per Share	12.6	8.7	8.9	11.5	7.5	6.5	12.1	8.1	7.3	13.4	9.0	8.7
5. Mkt. Price-High	15.6	11.9	9.8	13.0	10.0	8.2	13.9	8.7	8.9	15.1	11.5	9.5
6. Mkt. Price-Low	16.8	12.0	10.5	13.7	9.7	8.3	15.2	8.6	8.8	16.2	11.5	10.1
7. Mkt. Price-Average*	15.9	11.8	10.0	13.3	9.9	8.2	14.3	8.4	9.2	15.5	11.4	9.7
1960-1968	C	M	N	C	M	N	C	M	N	C	M	N
1. Total Assets	26.0%	12.8%	11.1%	17.2%	8.9%	8.9%	20.1%	9.9%	10.0%	24.2%	12.4%	10.7%
2. Sales	28.7	12.0	10.9	17.7	8.4	6.5	20.7	9.8	9.6	25.9	11.0	10.5
3. Net Income	26.1	12.8	11.4	18.8	9.0	7.4	22.4	10.9	9.6	26.9	13.0	11.2
4. Earnings Per Share	18.7	10.8	8.5	12.0	8.6	6.9	13.6	8.5	7.7	18.3	10.6	8.7
5. Mkt. Price-High	16.9	10.3	9.1	13.9	8.8	7.5	16.4	9.6	7.7	16.0	9.9	8.7
6. Mkt. Price-Low	16.3	10.4	8.6	13.6	9.2	6.7	14.3	7.8	8.0	15.5	9.9	8.3
7. Mkt. Price-Average*	16.6	10.4	8.9	13.8	8.9	7.2	14.9	9.5	8.4	15.8	9.9	8.6

*Arithmetic mean of annual high and low prices.

[1]The notation used in the table:

C represents the conglomerate sample: 61 firms in 1958, 63 in 1968.

M represents the random sample of industrial firms: 61 in 1958, 63 in 1968.

N represents the random sample of industrial and non-manufacturing firms: 58 in 1958 and 63 in 1968.

Source: Moody's *Industrial Manual*; Moody's *Handbook of Common Stocks*; Standard & Poor's *Stock Market Encyclopedia*; Individual Company *Annual Reports*.

Table 15-2
Means of Growth Rates in Key Financial Items, 1958-68 and 1960-68

| | 1958-1968 | | | | | | |
| | Sample Means of Growth Rates | | | F-Statistics[1] | | | |
	C	M	N	C,M	C,N	M,N	C,M,N
Total Assets	22.8%	12.6%	10.2%	16.25S	26.56S	2.53	18.28S
Sales	24.0	11.6	10.1	22.13S	27.60S	1.01	21.72S
Net Income	20.7	10.4	11.6	19.50S	15.74S	.413	13.57S
Earnings per share	12.6	8.7	8.9	4.86S	4.59S	.008	3.33S
Market Price-High	15.6	11.9	9.8	4.52S	13.28S	1.77	6.40S
Market Price-Low	16.8	12.0	10.5	2.98S	12.96S	.760	6.52S
Market Price-Average	15.9	11.8	10.0	5.16S	13.25S	1.30S	6.47S

| | 1960-1968 | | | | | | |
| | Sample Means of Growth Rates | | | F-Statistics[1] | | | |
	C	M	N	C,M	C,N	M,N	C,M,N
Total Assets	26.0%	12.8%	11.1%	23.06S	30.27S	1.09	23.07S
Sales	28.7	12.0	10.9	22.36S	26.38S	.471	22.12S
Net Income	26.1	12.8	11.4	11.83S	15.80S	.555	12.26S
Earnings per share	18.7	10.8	8.5	7.48S	14.42S	2.02	9.46S
Market Price-High	16.9	10.3	9.1	11.44S	17.98S	.564	10.77S
Market Price-Low	16.3	10.4	8.6	8.61S	17.85S	1.11	9.55S
Market Price-Average	16.6	10.4	8.9	10.55S	18.20S	.790	10.53S

[1]S following the F-Statistic indicates that the relationship is significant at the 10% level.
Source: Same as Table 15-1.

This applies to the growth rates of the earnings per share as well as the growth rates in market price per share. The more critical measurements reflect the effectiveness of the economic utilization of resources by the three groups.

Comparative Performance Measures

Earnings performance measures for sixty-three conglomerate firms compared with the two other samples of firms for the years 1958 and 1968 were computed. Multiple measures are provided, representing alternative methods of measuring earnings performance. To measure earning power before the influence of financial leverage, the earnings are related to total assets. Since this represents all forms of assets financed by debt or equity, the costs of sources of funds utilized to finance total assets must be included in the numerator.[28] Our first measure is earnings before interest and preferred stock dividends to total assets. Whether the numerator should be before or after taxes is a matter of dispute in the financial literature, so we made the calculations both before and after taxes.[29] We also calculated the returns on net worth. Since net worth may be defined to include preferred stock or to exclude it, we made the calculations for 1968 both ways.[30]

The comparative earnings performance of the conglomerate firms and the two random samples are set forth in Table 15-3. Four methods of averaging were again employed.[31] There is no great difference between the four measures of central tendency. The unweighted means tend to be the highest and the geometric means the lowest, with the weighted averages somewhat below the unweighted averages and the median values somewhat higher than the geometric means. The profitability of the conglomerates appeared to be somewhat lower in 1958 than for the random samples, but approximately the same in 1968. Since the differences are relatively moderate, their implications can be determined only by examination of the statistical tests of significance.

In Table 15-4, statistical tests of the significance between the means of the earnings ratios are set forth. For the year 1958, in most instances, the earnings of the samples of firms were significantly higher than the earnings of the conglomerate firms. By 1968, there was no significant difference in any of the earnings measures employed, nor between the three groups.[32]

Two possible explanatory influences on earning power performance are examined in Table 15-5. Price/earnings ratios are calculated, along with their significance measures on two bases. The first set of price/earnings ratios included all firms. In the second set of calculations, unusual price/earnings ratios were excluded.[33] There were no significant differences between either of the two sets of price/earnings ratios.[34] In 1968, at the height of the popularity of conglomerate firms, their price/earnings ratios, unadjusted, were the highest of the three. However, the difference between the price/earnings ratios of the conglomerate firms and *random sample #1* was non-significant in 1968. The difference between the price/earnings ratios of the conglomerate firms and *random sample #2* for the unadjusted ratios was significant with the conglomerate firms' price/earnings ratios being somewhat higher. After adjustment, the difference remained significant, but the price/earnings ratios of the *random sample #2* firms was higher than for the conglomerates.

These data are contrary to the general impression that one of the reasons for the high growth in earnings per share of the conglomerate firms was that they were able to play the differential price/earnings ratio game. On the contrary, their price/earnings ratios as a group average were not significantly different from the price/earnings ratios of other firms. On this point, however, averages may be misleading. There was wide dispersion in the price/earnings ratios of conglomerate firms, suggesting great differences in their characteristics and prospects.

Table 15-3

Earnings Performance Measures for 63 Conglomerate Firms Compared with Two Other Samples of Firms, 1958, 1968

| | Arithmetic Mean Values | | | | | | Median Values | | | Geometric Mean | | |
| | Unweighted | | | Weighted | | | | | | | | |
1958	C	M	N	C	M	N	C	M	N	C	M	N
1. EBIAT/Total Assets	5.8%	9.2%	6.8%	5.6%	7.6%	4.9%	5.2%	8.2%	6.2%	5.1%	8.1%	5.2%
2. EBIT/Total Assets	8.7	16.7	12.6	8.5	13.2	8.9	8.0	14.4	11.6	7.1	14.1	9.2
3. Net Income/Net Worth	7.6	12.6	10.7	8.0	10.1	9.0	7.7	10.5	9.8	7.5	11.2	8.7
1968	C	M	N	C	M	N	C	M	N	C	M	N
1. EBIAT/Total Assets	10.4%	8.5%	7.6%	8.3%	8.1%	5.4%	7.5%	7.8%	7.0%	7.5%	8.0%	6.2%
2. EBIT/Total Assets	15.1	15.6	13.3	12.2	14.3	8.7	11.7	13.5	12.0	11.9	13.1	10.1
3. Net Income/Net Worth	13.3	12.4	12.0	12.4	12.2	10.9	13.0	12.7	11.5	12.6	11.7	10.9

Explanation of abbreviations and terms:

The abbreviation EBIAT refers to earnings before interest and preferred stock dividends, but after taxes. EBIT refers to earnings before interest, preferred stock dividends and taxes. Net income refers to net income plus preferred stock. Net worth includes preferred stock.

Source: Same as Table 15-1.

Table 15-4

Significance Tests for Earnings Performance Measures, 1958, 1968

	1958 Sample Means			F-Statistics			
	C	M	N	C,M	C,N	M,N	C,M,N
1. EBIAT/Total Assets	5.8	9.2	6.8	8.83S	1.10	6.12S	6.21S
2. EBIT/Total Assets	8.7	16.7	12.6	17.13S	5.47S	4.52S	9.54S
3. Net Inc/Net Worth	7.6	12.6	10.7	10.52S	4.30S	2.08S	6.05S

	1968 Sample Means			F-Statistics			
	C	M	N	C,M	C,N	M,N	C,M.N
1. EBIAT/Total Assets	10.4	8.5	7.6	0.44	0.93	1.37	0.70
1a. EBIAT/Total Assets*	9.4	8.2	7.5	0.21	0.50	0.80	0.37
2. EBIT/Total Assets	15.1	15.6	13.3	0.02	0.38	2.33	0.44
3. Net Inc/Net Worth	13.3	12.4	12.0	0.81	1.98	0.12	0.85
4. Net Profit/Equity	14.2	12.4	12.2	0.99	1.44	0.06	0.98

Abbreviations have the same meaning as in Tables 15-2 and 15-3. New measures introduced: Net profit to equity represents net income less preferred dividends to net worth excluding preferred stock.

Total Assets* represents total assets plus the difference between the balance sheet values of preferred stock and estimated book value of preferred stock. The additions to total assets were respectively $5.7, $0.5, and $1.7 billions for the conglomerates, random sample #1 and random sample #2.

Source: Same as Table 15-1.

A dilemma confronted the conglomerate firms with depressed price/earnings ratios. If they merged with firms with higher price earnings, the conglomerates would suffer initial dilution in earnings per share which would at least initially depress growth rates in earnings per share. The disadvantage of a differentially lower price/earnings ratio in merger activity can be offset by offering non-equity forms of securities in exchange or utilizing delayed equity forms such as convertibles and warrants.

Table 15-5 provides information on this point also. Debt to net worth ratios were measured on two bases. On the first basis, preferred stock was included in net worth but not in debt. With net worth including preferred stock, the predominant portion of which for conglomerates was convertible, the ratio of debt to net worth was 169 percent. This compared with 87 percent for *Random Sample #1* and 201 percent for *Random Sample #2*. The debt ratios of the conglomerate firms were significantly higher than those of *Random Sample #1* firms in both 1958 and 1968. In 1958 the debt ratios of the conglomerate firms were significantly lower than the *Random Sample #2*, including non-industrial firms, but nonsignificantly different in 1968. As compared with industrial firms,

Table 15-5
Significance Tests of Factors Influencing Earnings Performance, 1958, 1968

	1958 Sample Means			F-Statistics			
	C	M	N	C,M	C,N	M,N	C,M,N
1. Price/Earnings Ratios	15.2X	14.6X	18.3X	0.02	0.37	0.96	0.36
2. (Price/Earnings) Adjusted*	17.2X	14.9X	15.8X	0.83	0.34	0.22	0.51
3. Debt/ Net Worth Incl. P/S**	95%	56%	155%	8.19S	2.13S	6.24S	4.33S

	1968 Sample Means			F-Statistics			
	C	M	N	C,M	C,N	M,N	C,M,N
1. Price/Earnings Ratios	19.4X	18.7X	16.7X	0.10	4.60S	0.74	0.97
2. (Price/Earnings) Adjusted	19.4X	20.2X	16.7X	0.26	4.61S	4.22S	2.82S
3. Debt/Net Worth Incl P/S	169%	87%	201%	10.25S	0.33	5.45S	3.46S
4. Debt + P/S / Equity	233%	94%	210%	5.95S	0.09	5.67S	3.00S

*The adjustment for the price earnings ratios was to exclude ratios exceeding 100 times and those with negative values exceeding 50 times.
**P/S refers to preferred stock. Other abbreviations have the same meanings as in Tables 15-2, 15-3 and 15-4.
Source: Same as Table 15-1.

therefore, the conglomerate firms employed higher debt ratios, both in 1958 and in 1968. In addition, as compared with both samples, the debt ratios of the conglomerate firms grew more rapidly during the decade.

Implications of Defensive Diversification

Some preliminary implications of the data in the foregoing tables may be indicated. The conglomerate firms had lower profitability rates in the late 1950s. On the average, their price/earnings ratios were not significantly different from the price/earnings ratios of other firms. Utilizing leverage, however, they were able to raise the return on their net worth. But measurement of returns on total assets, which is free of the effects of financial leverage, is a more meaningful figure. The returns on total assets for the conglomerates in 1958 were generally significantly lower than for the other samples. However, by 1968 the returns on total assets were not significantly different.

Thus one of the motives for conglomerate mergers was defensive diversification.[35] Defensive diversification may be defined as diversification to avoid adverse effects on profitability from developments taking place in the firm's traditional product market areas.[36] Hence the foregoing data are consistent with the proposition that the conglomerate firms perform the economic function of preserving the values of ongoing organizations as well as restoring the earning power of the entities.[37] In addition, the conglomerate firms avoid the costs of bankruptcy.[38]

Analysis of the backgrounds and acquisition histories of the conglomerate firms suggests that they were diversifying defensively to avoid (1) sales and profit instability; (2) adverse growth developments; (3) adverse competitive shifts; (4) technological obsolescence; and (5) increased uncertainties associated with their industries. These five types of undesirable future states are set forth in greater detail in Table 15-6, summarizing the forms of defensive diversification motives among the sixty-three conglomerate firms in the study.

The largest single number of the firms came from the aerospace industry. This industry is subject to wide fluctuations in the total market demand, abrupt and major shifts in product mixes, and a tendency toward excess capacity by entry from firms in other industries in bidding on individual major systems and

Table 15-6
Forms of Defensive Diversification Motives Among Conglomerate Firms

Defensive Diversification Stimulus	Conglomerate Firm Identification Numbers (See Table 15-10)
A. Aerospace (instability, uncertain growth, shifts in product mix)	5, 6, 11, 35, 36, 37, 38, 40, 43, 47, 55, 63
B. Industrial machinery (instability)	3, 16, 21, 22, 32, 60, 62
C. Auto parts (instability, change in mix)	17, 18, 29, 30, 39, 59
D. Secular decline in market (low growth)	4, 7, 27, 31, 42, 44, 50, 51, 57
E. Slow growth in sales or profits (low growth in sales, depressed profits)	1, 10, 12, 14, 20, 33, 34, 41, 58
F. Adverse competitive shifts in international market (low growth, depressed profits)	28, 53, 54
G. Changes in environment requiring multi-unit operations (profit pressures)	25, 48
H. Natural resources and tax considerations (instability in profit margins, low future growth)	2, 8, 9, 13, 15, 26, 45, 52, 56, 61
I. Need for new technology (slow growth, depressed profits)	19, 24, 49
J. Miscellaneous special circumstances	23, 46

Source: Moody's *Industrial Manual*; Moody's *Handbook of Common Stocks*; Standard & Poor's *Stock Market Encyclopedia*; Individual Company *Annual Reports*.

programs. The industrial machinery and auto parts companies were also subject to considerable instability in sales. In addition, another important change affected the auto parts industry. As the automobile became increasingly complex, the manufacturers shifted their mix of make or buy products, although the percentage of their purchases stayed about constant. However the relatively more complex automobile parts, most significant for the final performance of the automobile, came to be increasingly produced by the manufacturers of the final product. For example, up to the middle 1950s, Ford bought most of its transmissions from Borg-Warner. At that time, Ford began building its own transmissions, and Borg-Warner sought to diversify out of auto parts.

Low growth prospects were associated with a major secular decline in some markets. This was characteristic of the railway equipment industry, textiles, movie distribution (at an earlier period), and the tobacco industry. A related problem was slow growth in sales or declining profit margins due to persistently unfavorable excess capacity conditions in the industry.

The next two categories are related to changes in the nature of the market. Adverse competitive shifts in the international sewing machine market stimulated Singer to a diversification program. Similarly, fundamental changes in the retailing business were brought about by the shift from public to private automobile transportation within the city and the suburbanization of the population.

Another large category of conglomerates are firms originally based in the natural resources industries. These industries are characterized by instability in demand and supply relationships resulting in substantial fluctuations in product prices and in profit margins. In addition, a number of the natural resource firms were stimulated to diversification by rising corporate tax rates in order to utilize more effectively the tax shelter provided in natural resource operations.

Finally, a number of firms sought to diversify in the attempt to acquire access to the new technologies that had developed after World War II. Illustrative was the need of firms in the electrical industry to develop an electronics capability.

The classification of these diverse firms into a small number of forms of defensive diversification involves some overgeneralization. Some of the conglomerates pursued positive programs such as applying advanced technology in industries and firms where technology had lagged (e.g., Litton Industries). Others were attempting to utilize effectively special capabilities in financial planning and control (e.g., IT&T and Transamerica).

But defensive diversification was a strong motivation among the conglomerate firms. Consistent with the important role of defensive diversification are our findings that profitability of the conglomerate firms was below average in the late 1950s and had improved to average levels by 1968. In this connection, Professor Samuel R. Reid found that on measurements similar to those employed in the present study the conglomerate firms had less favorable performance on profitability measures. In the following section, therefore, the Reid study will be examined.

Managerial vs. Stockholder Benefits of Conglomerate Mergers

The most comprehensive of the previous tests of the economic performance of conglomerate firms was by Professor S. R. Reid.[39] Professor Reid's analysis distinguished between tests that represented the interests of the managers of the firms and those that represented the interests of the owners of the firms.

The three measures Professor Reid used to reflect managers' interests are (1) growth in sales, (2) growth in assets, and (3) growth in employment. The three measures he uses to reflect the stockholders' interests are (1) growth in the market value of shares, (2) growth in the ratio of net income to total assets, and (3) growth in the ratio of net income to sales. Professor Reid found that the growth rates in the three measures reflecting managers' interests were favorable for conglomerates compared with other companies, while the conglomerates performed less effectively on measures reflecting the stockholders' interests.

But Professor Reid's conclusions are at variance with his own data. In his detailed industry analysis of his six measures of performance, the results were either not significant or significant in the wrong direction. The results of his six Tables, 9-3 through 9-8, are summarized in our Table 15-7.[40] The nonsignificant—or significant in the wrong direction—number of industries comprised ten or more of the fourteen industries for each of his six measures. His industry analysis shows no significant difference in the performance of the conglomerate firms as compared with nonmerging firms or firms engaging in different types of mergers. Furthermore, the results did not differ for his measures purporting to distinguish between the interests of managers and the interests of stockholders.

When Reid does not group his firms by industry, his data on the conglomerates compared to non-merging firms is consistent with his generalization. However, the performance of the conglomerate firms, by his own data, was more favorable for all six ratios than for firms engaging in other forms of merger activity.[41] Furthermore, the fact that the data grouped by industry shows no significant difference between the conglomerate firms and all other firms suggests that it is the greater weighting of a small number of industries that produced the results for his total sample.

Conceptual difficulties mar two of his three measures intending to reflect stockholder interests. Professor Reid measured profitability by the ratio of net income available to common stockholders divided by total assets. If profits are to be related to total assets, financial charges should be added back to reflect other sources of funds utilized to finance total assets.[42] Otherwise the measure of net income divided by total assets penalizes firms with greater leverage and particularly firms that are increasing leverage over the time period measured. Since the conglomerate firms were utilizing more debt and they were increasing their debt at a faster rate over time than other firms, dividing net income available to common stockholders by total assets biases the performance of the conglomerate firms downward.

Table 15-7

Tabulation of Significance Tests Results for Professor Reid's Six Measures for 14 Industries, Comparing the Performance of Conglomerate Firms and Firms with no Merger Activity

Managers' Interest Variables	(1) Signi- ficant	(2) Not Signi- ficant	(3) Signifi- cant in Wrong Direction	(4) Total of Not Significant or Significant in Wrong Direction
1. Growth in Sales	3	11	0	11
2. Growth in Assets	2	10	2	12
3. Growth in Number of employees	2	12	0	12
Subtotals	7	33	2	35
Stockholders' Interest Variables				
4. Growth in Market Price	4	9	1	10
5. Net Income to Total Assets	3	9	2	11
6. Net Income to Total Sales	3	8	3	11
Subtotals	10	26	6	32

Source: Reid [192]. Tables 9-3 — 9-8, pp. 186–188.

Professor Reid's other measure of profitability was the time trend in the ratio of profits to sales. This ratio has little economic significance in the context of the present analysis. The ratio of profit to sales varies greatly among industries, depending primarily upon the characteristic turnover of assets into sales. On the average, industries with high ratios of profits to sales are capital intensive with a low turnover of assets and conversely for industries with high turnovers.[43] Trends in the ratio of profits to sales, therefore, reflect primarily the industry mix of the firms rather than any measure of inherent profitability or managerial performance. Since the conglomerate firms were by definition changing their product mix, Reid's measure of the ratio of profits to sales simply reflects the fact that conglomerate firms were moving into product areas with higher turnovers of assets into sales. Characteristically, these are associated with lower profit margins on sales than industries with lower total asset turnovers.

Thus, two of the three measures purporting to reflect stockholder interests contained conceptual defects. The third test Reid employed was growth in market price of common shares—a measure which suffers from the defect of its early terminal year, 1961. Professor Reid's conclusion, therefore, that the conglomerates operated effectively for the managers, but not for the stockholders has no valid empirical basis. Nor is his implication that conglomerate firms were not efficient supported by the data. The data from our own studies support the conclusion that the performance of the conglomerate firms, on the average to date, satisfies the criterion of efficient economic performance. However, the question may be raised whether the terminal year of 1968 is too early to reflect the critical impacts on conglomerates during 1969. Data were not available for 1969 while our study was in progress. However, from a number of other sources, data through 1969 for segments of the analysis performed in our broader study are available as a check on our results.

Other Empirical Evidence on Conglomerate Performance

Forbes, Fortune and *News Front* magazines compile annual performance results for up to one-thousand firms. These data provide a basis for further analysis of conglomerate performance.

The Forbes Data

Forbes compiles data which permit calculation of median values of six performance measures for five-hundred or more firms as well as for two categories termed by *Forbes* "conglomerates" and "agglomerates."[44] *Forbes* defines conglomerate companies as those which have found a central focus for their operations, while the agglomerate companies have diversified without finding a central thread. The two categories are combined for analysis of "multi-industry" firms.

The *Forbes* measures summarized in Table 15-8 permit comparisons with each of the major categories of analysis employed in our study. *Forbes* calculates a five-year annual increase in sales.[45] The median values of the growth rates in sales of the multi-industry companies were at least double the growth rate in sales for the broader sample of firms. The growth rate in earnings per share for the multi-industry companies ranged from 12.2 percent to 12.7 percent for the two five-year periods, ending in 1968 and 1969, respectively, about 50 percent better than the performance by the total of the *Forbes* firms. *Forbes* measured the gain in market price in terms of a total percentage increase for a five-year period. The multi-industry companies performed more than twice as well as the broad sample; growth for both declined when 1969 is taken as the terminal year.[46]

Forbes calculates three profitability measures. The first profitability measure is a five-year average combined return on debt and equity. This is comparable to our measure of earnings before interest plus preferred stock dividends, (but after taxes) to total assets, except that the *Forbes* denominator does not include current liabilities. The results confirm the findings of our analysis. The five-year average combined return on debt and equity for the multi-industry companies for the period ending in 1968 was slightly higher than the *Forbes* broader group.

Table 15-8

Performance Comparisons Between Multi-Industry Companies and *Forbes* Total Large Firms, 1963-1969*

| | Forbes' Firms | | Multi-Industry Companies | |
	1963-68	1964-69	1963-68	1964-69
Number of Companies	500	578	38	47
1. Five-year annual increase in sales	9.0%	9.9%	20.0%	19.05%
2. Five-year annual increase in per-share earnings	8.6	7.05	12.7	12.2
3. Price gain for five-year periods	70.5	17.15	140.0	60.2
4. Five-year average combined return on debt and equity	9.7	9.6	10.0	9.6
5. Five-year average return on equity	12.4	12.5	12.6	13.4
6. Last year's return on equity	12.0 (67-68)	11.65 (68-69)	12.2 (67-68)	11.85 (68-69)

*Median values compared on all items.
Sources: *Forbes*, Vol. 103 (January 1, 1969), pp. 37-41, 53-66, 78, 80, 91.
Forbes, Vol. 104 (January 1, 1970), pp. 44-81, 96-99, 227-231.

For the period ending in 1969 there was no difference in the median values of the five-year average returns for the two groups.

The results of the *Forbes* data on the other two measures of earning performance were also the same as for our study. Both the five-year average return on equity and the 1969 return on equity for the multi-industry companies was slightly higher than the earnings performance of the *Forbes* total number of large companies. The *Forbes* data, therefore, provide confirmation of the results of our study.

The Fortune Data

Fortune magazine each year calculates the ten-year compound annual growth rates of earnings per share for its sample of five-hundred industrial firms and the ratio of net income to net worth. These results are summarized for our sample of conglomerate firms compared with the total *Fortune* five-hundred firms for the most recent five years through 1969. The results are tabulated in Table 15-9. For the ten-year periods ending in 1965 and 1966, the compound annual growth

Table 15-9

Comparisons of the Performance of Conglomerates with the *Fortune* 500 Firms, 1965-1969*

	Ten-Year Compound Annual Growth Rates of EPS			Net Profit to Stockholders' Equity		
Years Ended	Fortune 500**	Conglom- erates	Conglom- erates less Fortune 500	Fortune 500**	Conglom- erates	Conglom- erates less Fortune 500
1969	7.10	9.91	+2.71	11.3	11.8	+0.5
1968	8.71	11.98	+3.26	11.7	12.9	+1.2
1967	6.59	8.57	+1.98	11.3	12.4	+1.1
1966	6.09	5.99	−0.10	12.7	13.2	+0.5
1965	6.04	5.74	−0.30	11.8	12.4	+0.6

*Medians of the growth rates of percentage returns for each group of companies are reported.

**Comparisons with our two random samples does not change the direction of the differences, but the magnitudes are sometimes larger, sometimes smaller.

Source: Fortune Magazine, *Directories of Largest Corporations*, 1966-1970.

rates of the *Fortune* five-hundred companies were higher than for the conglomerate firms. Beginning in 1967, the conglomerate firms began to outperform the *Fortune* five-hundred firms by relatively larger differentials. For the ratios of net income to net worth, the conglomerates outperformed the *Fortune* five-hundred in every year.[47]

The News Front Data

News Front compiles data on the one-thousand largest manufacturing companies in the United States.[48] The firms are grouped by SIC categories. In its 1969 presentation *News Front* presented a category, SIC 3999, "diversified/ conglomerate companies," in which are listed 47 firms. Presenting data for 1968, the diversified/conglomerates averaged a return on stockholders' equity of 12.1 percent, compared to 12.2 percent for "average manufacturing."[49] The difference between the performance of the multiindustry companies and "average manufacturing" described by *News Front* is negligible.

Conclusions

Most of the earlier studies of mergers covered periods ending in the early or mid-1960s. The present study, supplemented by compilations from *Forbes*,

Fortune and *News Front* magazines, extends the analysis through 1969. Our empirical findings suggest three generalizations.

First, the conglomerate firms outperformed samples of other firms or broader groups of firms on all of the growth measures. Contrary findings of some other studies resulted from their early terminal dates before the mid-1960s. However, we do not attach great significance to these measures, since they reflect primarily the extent of past merger activity by the conglomerate firms. More important, will be the growth in market price per share over a period of years in the future, after the ability of the conglomerate firms to sustain a growth rate in earnings per share over an extended period has been tested.

Second, the earnings performance measured by the ratio of net income to net worth is somewhat higher for conglomerate firms, but the difference is not statistically significant. This somewhat higher return on net worth did not result from the differentially higher price/earnings ratios of conglomerate firms in mergers because on the average the price/earnings ratios of conglomerate firms were not significantly different from the price/earnings ratios of other samples of firms. The higher returns on net worth of the conglomerate firms resulted from the larger and increasing percentage of leverage employed by them during the decade of the '60s. The effects of the higher leverage of conglomerate firms on their longer-run success has not been fully tested.

Third, we attached greatest significance as a measure of the economic performance of conglomerate firms to the ratio of earnings-plus-financial charges to total assets or to net worth-plus-debt. Unless the acquired firms have substantially higher returns on total assets than the conglomerate firms, or higher rates of return on total assets than firms on the average, the ratio of earnings to total assets of the conglomerate firms are relatively little influenced by accounting distortions. The data indicate that the earnings of conglomerate firms on total assets or debt-plus-equity were not significantly different from other firms in 1968. The data indicate that the earnings rates of the conglomerate firms in the late 1950s or the early 1960s, however, were significantly lower than the earnings on total assets or net worth-plus-debt for other groups of firms.

It appears, therefore, that an important economic function of conglomerate firms has been bringing the profitability of firms with depressed earnings up to the average for industry generally. This function was particularly important in connection with defensive diversification. A large proportion of the conglomerate firms developed out of industries in which adverse developments in their economic environments had either taken place or were in prospect. Therefore, the most appropriate test of the earnings performance of conglomerate firms is not superior earnings performance, but whether they were able to achieve at least average earnings performance.[50]

In many respects the conglomerate movement may be regarded as the development of a new industry. Economic principles predict, therefore, that the

Table 15-10
List of Conglomerate Companies

Company Name	
1. AMK	33. Kidde (Walter)
2. American Metal Climax	34. Kinney National Service, Inc.
3. American Standard	35. Ling-Temco-Vought
4. American Tobacco (Brands)	36. Lear Siegler
5. Avco	37. Litton Industries
6. Avnet	38. Martin Marietta
7. Bangor Punta	39. Midland-Ross
8. Boise Cascade	40. Monogram Industries, Inc.
9. Cities Service	41. National Distillers & Chemical
10. City Investing	42. National General Corporation
11. Colt Industries	43. North American Rockwell
12. Consolidated Foods	44. Northwest Industries
13. Continental Oil	45. Occidental Petroleum
14. Dart Industries (Rexall Drug & Chemical)	46. Ogden
15. Diamond Shamrock	47. Olin Mathieson Chemical
16. Dresser Industries	48. Rapid-American
17. Eaton Yale & Towne	49. Reliance Electric
18. Eltra	50. Republic Corporation
19. Emerson Electric	51. SCM
20. Emhart (Amer. Hardware Co.)	52. Signal Companies
21. FMC	53. Singer
22. Fuqua Industries	54. Studebaker-Worthington
23. GAF	55. Teledyne
24. General Telephone & Electronics	56. Tenneco
25. Genesco	57. Textron
26. Georgia-Pacific	58. Transamerica Corporation
27. Glen Alden	59. TRW
28. Grace (W.R.)	60. U.S. Industries
29. Gulf & Western Industries	61. U.S. Plywood-Chempion Papers
30. Houdaille Industries	62. White Consolidated Industries
31. Indian Head	63. Whittaker
32. International Tel. & Tel.	

earning power of this group of firms would tend to equality with the earning power of firms on the average. Theory also predicts great variations in earnings performance among individual conglomerate firms.

The superior performance of individual firms in new industries has characteristically attracted an excess number of firms and firms without the requisite managerial or product characteristics for survival. Hence, as a new industry, one

Table 15-11
List of Industrial Companies Included in Random Sample No. 1, Drawn From 1968 *Fortune* **500**

Company Name

1. Addressograph Multigraph
2. Allied Products
3. American Biltrite Rubber
4. American Home Products
5. Anheuser-Busch
6. Bath Industries
7. Bemis
8. Bendix
9. Bristol-Myers
10. Castle and Cooke
11. Celanese
12. Central Soya
13. Cessna Aircraft
14. Chrysler
15. Coca-Cola
16. Continental Can
17. Corn Products (CPC International)
18. Crown Zellerbach
19. Dana
20. Deere
21. DuPont (E.I.) de Nemours
22. Eagle-Picher Industries
23. Ethyl
24. Factor (Max)
25. Falstaff Brewing
26. Federal Pacific Electric
27. Fibreboard
28. Gardner-Denver
29. General Dynamics
30. Gerber Products
31. Gillette
32. Goodrich (B.F.)
33. Hershey Foods

34. Hormel (Geo. A.)
35. International Paper
36. Keebler
37. Mayer (Oscar)
38. McGraw-Hill
39. McLouth Steel
40. Miles Laboratories
41. Mobil Oil
42. National Dairy Products (Kraft Co.)
43. National Union Electric
44. Pennwalt
45. Polaroid
46. Pullmann
47. Rex Chainbelt
48. Reynolds (R.J.) Tobacco (Industries)
49. Riegel Textile
50. Rockwell Manufacturing
51. Sanders Associates
52. Scovill Manufacturing
53. Sharon Steel
54. Sinclair Oil
55. Smith (A.O.)
56. Smith Kline & French Laboratories
57. Standard Brands
58. Sterling Drug
59. Times Mirror
60. Triangle Industries
61. Warnaco
62. Western Publishing
63. Xerox

would expect the failure rate among conglomerates in the near future to be somewhat higher than among industry generally. But there will be individual conglomerate firms that will achieve higher-than-average profitability over

Table 15-12

List of Companies Included in Random Sample No. 2, Drawn From 1968 *Fortune* 500, 250

Company Name	
1. Albertson's	32. Goodyear Tire & Rubber
2. Allied Stores	33. Great Atlantic & Pacific Tea
3. Amerada Petroleum	34. Great Northern Paper
4. American Sugar	35. Harris Trust & Savings Bank
5. Anaconda	36. Hershey Foods
6. Arlan's Department Stores	37. Inland Container
7. Armco Steel	38. Kellogg
8. Atlantic Richfield	39. Libbey-Owens-Ford
9. Bemis	40. Magnavox
10. Black and Decker Manufacturing	41. Mellon National Bank & Trust
11. Blue Bell	42. Michigan National Bank
12. Brockway Glass	43. National Biscuit
13. Burroughs	44. North Carolina National Bank
14. Carpenter Technology	45. Northeast Utilities
15. Caterpillar Tractor	46. Northern Pacific Ry.
16. Certain-teed Products	47. Northrop
17. Chesebrough-Pond's	48. Otis Elevator
18. Chicago, Milwaukee, St. Paul & Pacific Railroad	49. PepsiCo
	50. Potlach Forests
19. City Stores	51. Rath Packing
20. Coca-Cola	52. Sterling Drug
21. Collins Radio	53. Tecumseh Products
22. Commonwealth Edison	54. Union Tank Car Co.
23. Continental Illinois National Bank & Trust	55. Uniroyal
	56. U.S. Steel
24. Cook Coffee	57. United Utilities
25. Crown Cork & Seal	58. Universal Oil Products
26. Cudahy	59. Virginia Electric & Power
27. Cummins Engine	60. Vulcan Materials
28. Dow Chemical	61. Walter (Jim)
29. Endicott Johnson	62. Western Publishing
30. Florida Power & Light	63. Wrigley (Wm.) Jr.
31. Gimbel Brothers	

periods of time. The success of individual conglomerates, as is true of firms generally, will depend upon the relative abilities of their managements for achieving operating efficiency and for making the shifts in their product-markets required by the changing economic environment.

16

J. Fred Weston

Concentration and Discretionary Market Power

The main basis for the attack on concentration has been the structural approach to industrial economics. The structural theory states that high concentration or oligopoly can be equated with collusion and shared monopoly. It is argued that while there may be rivalry between oligopolists, awareness of the interdependence of their actions leads to either overt or spontaneous collusion. Since these views were introduced into the economic literature in 1933, they have come to be the standard textbook point of view. [46]

The structural approach to oligopoly holds that when concentration, variously measured, exceeds some number, the effects on competition will be adverse. (Blair [30], Mueller [170]). This view stems from the economic theory of the idealized atomistic market model in which there are so many sellers and buyers in an industry that each one is too small for its individual behavior to have a perceptible effect on industry price or output. Much empirical research beginning during the 1950s and continuing through the 1960s yielded results that appeared to be consistent with this theoretical model (Weiss [248]).

The structural theory was embraced in a stream of Supreme Court decisions from the Philadelphia Bank Case (1963) through Von's Shopping Bag (1966). The acme of the structural approach was expressed in the Department of Justice guidelines announced on May 30, 1968 which made a 10 percent market share, when the four-firm concentration ratio exceeds 40 percent, a danger signal, and in the FTC's complaint in the Cereal Case initiated in 1972 that oligopoly can be equated to shared monopoly. As the structural theory became dominant in public policy applications, some defects in that body of doctrine have become increasingly evident. As empirical research has continued, new findings and new insights require a reassessment of the economic consequences of concentration and large firms. The analysis will cover the relation between concentration and prices, profits, advertising and product innovation in the succeeding sections.

Price Performance in Concentrated
Versus Unconcentrated Industries

Two propositions have been formulated with regard to prices. One formulation is that firms with discretionary power have power over the market place and the

225

consumer. They are not constrained by the forces of supply and demand. They set inappropriately high prices to exact persistently high profits. This leads to inflation. A second formulation is based on a wage-price spiral. Unions seeing the large profits of oligopolistic firms demand wage increases beyond the size of productivity increases. In order to maintain high profits, firms raise prices as these labor costs increase and the wage-price spiral is set in motion. Advertising is said to aggravate this process because advertising is used to stimulate demand for the product. These advertising costs must be added to and recovered in the price of the product. Hence, prices must therefore necessarily be higher than they otherwise would be in the absence of advertising.

The main factual evidence relied on to support these assertions are cited in Study Paper Number Two of the Cabinet Committee on Price Stability. It was stated that between 1953 and 1957, prices in the steel industry rose in the face of declining output [170]. The context of the discussion of Study Paper Number Two is that it was the persistently high profit that led to the high wage demands and that the price increases took place in order to maintain the high profit. This simply does not accord with the facts. Table 16-1 sets forth the profit rates of the steel industry compared with the profit rates on equity of all manufacturing since the beginning of 1950. Abstracting from the abnormal conditions of the Korean War, the profits of the steel industry were declining and, on the average, were below the profit levels for all manufacturing.

While a full discussion of the wage-profit-price relation is beyond the scope of this paper, some salient points may be noted. The doctrine of countervailing power that unions developed to counter giant firms is not supported by the evidence of strong unions in the building trades with thousands of small employers. Guild union strength in the services industries generally also contradicts the thesis. While not a complete theory, Henry Simon's analysis that capital intensive industries provide labor leaders with "the valuable hostages of large sunk investment," and hence opportunities for fostering effective unionization, carries strong economic logic and has greater consistency with empirical data.[1]

Let us also look at the evidence in broader terms. In Table 16-2 data on the

Table 16-1
Comparative Rates of Return on Stockholders' Equity, All Manufacturing vs. the Iron and Steel Industry, 1950-1969.

Time Period	All Manufacturing	Iron and Steel Industry
1950	11.3%	10.6%
1954-1959	12.9%	12.2%
1960-1969	11.1%	7.7%

Source: Federal Trade Commission—Securities and Exchange Commission, *Quarterly Financial Report for Manufacturing Corporations*, 1950-1969.

Table 16-2

Changes in Industry Sector Prices of the Wholesale Price Index, Weighted and Unweighted Averages Grouped by Industry Concentration Ratios, 1967-1971

4-Firm Concentration Ratio Value of Shipments–1967 Ratios	Number of Industries	Average % Unweighted Price Change	Average % Weighted Price Change
Less than 25	19	17.8	16.2
26-50	35	14.6	16.5
51-75	28	16.8	14.8
76 and over	12	10.7	8.5
Total	94		
Less than 50	54	15.7	16.4
Greater than 50	40	15.0	12.9
Total	94		

Source: *4-Firm Concentration Ratio*, U.S. Bureau of the Census, Census of Manufactures, 1967, Special Report Series: Concentration Ratios in Manufacturing, MC67(S)-2.1, U.S. Government Printing Office, D.C., 1970, Table 5. *Industry-Sector Price Indexes*, U.S. Department of Labor, Bureau of Labor Statistics, *Monthly Labor Review*, March, 1972, pp. 107-108.

wholesale price index are presented, summarizing price changes from 1967 to the end of 1971 by four groups of industries. The industries are grouped by concentration ratios quartiles with the group with lowest concentration represented by concentration ratios of less than 25 percent and the highest quartile representing industries with concentration ratios exceeding 75 percent.

A simple average of price change for each concentration group is calculated. The group of industries with the lowest concentration, below 25 percent, experienced the highest average percentage of price change of 17.8 percent. In contrast the group with the highest concentration, over 75 percent, experienced the lowest average percentage of price change of 10.7 percent. When the four groups are further summarized into two groups, the less than 50 percent group experienced a slightly greater degree of price change than the greater than 50 percent concentration groups.

A weighted average of price changes was also calculated to reflect the relative size of the industries by their value of shipments, the same basis upon which the concentration ratios were calculated. Again, the weighted averages demonstrate that the highest percentage price changes have taken place in the industries of lowest concentration. Indeed, the percentage price increase for industries of less than 25 percent concentration for the largest four firms was almost double the average weighted price change for the industries in which the four largest firms accounted for 76 percent or more of industry value of shipments.

Thus, the evidence from the recent inflationary period in the United States does not support the assertion frequently made that the cause of inflation or large price increases has been large firms in concentrated industries. The facts are the reverse. The overall pressures for price increases have been blunted in the most concentrated industries.

It has also been argued that the basic cause of price inflation in the United States is the existence of the monopoly power of unions and the willingness of large firms in concentrated industries to agree to large wage increases that are then passed on in the form of price increases. It has been further argued that because of these structural problems, monetary and fiscal policy no longer can be effective in bringing inflationary pressures under control. Relevant data for testing these arguments is set forth in Table 16-3 which analyzes price changes during the period 1958 through 1966 before the escalation of hostilities in Southeast Asia. The average of unweighted price changes for the sample of industries covered by Table 16-3 was about 7 percent. An average of the weighted price changes was about 4 percent. The change in the overall wholesale price index for this same period of time was 5.5 percent. Thus, overall price changes were slightly over .5 percent per year, much below the 4 to 5 percent price increases experienced after 1966.

The contrast between the magnitude of price changes among the less concentrated industries as compared with the more concentrated industries is again striking. For the unweighted price changes in industries with less than 25 percent concentration, the average price changes during the 1958-66 period was 10.4 percent. In contrast for the industries with concentration of 76 percent and over the average price range was 1.8 percent for the total period. This represents an average price change per annum of virtually zero. For the weighted price

Table 16-3
Changes in Industry Sector Prices of the Wholesale Price Index, Weighted and Unweighted Averages Grouped by Industry Concentration Ratios, 1958-1966

4-Firm Concentration Ratio Value of Shipments–1963 Ratios	Number of Industries	Average % Unweighted Price Change	Average % Weighted Price Change
Less than 25	10	10.4	7.9
26-50	16	7.7	2.9
51-75	11	7.2	3.5
76 and over	5	1.8	4.6
Total	42		
Less than 50	26	8.7	3.9
Greater than 50	16	5.5	4.1
Total	42		

Source: *4-Firm Concentration Ratio*, same as Table 16-2. *Industry-Sector Price Indexes*, U.S. Department of Labor, Bureau of Labor Statistics, *Handbook of Labor Statistics*, 1971, Table 123, pp. 287-288.

changes the average increase in the industries of less than 25 percent of concentration was about 8 percent for the period or about 1 percent per annum. For the industries with concentration of 76 percent or over, the average weighted price changes was 4.6 percent for the period or slightly over 1/2 of 1 percent per annum.

These data in fact do not support the frequently made argument that the cause of price inflation in the United States has been either labor and/or business monopoly. Contrasting the magnitude of price changes during the two periods of time compared has strong evidential value. It has been argued by some that even if monetary and fiscal policy had been different and even if war in Vietnam had not escalated after 1966, that the United States would still have experienced an inflation problem because of the monopoly power of strong unions and/or large business firms. The facts simply do not support that assertion. In the 8 years' period between 1958 and 1966 the average price increases measured by the wholesale price index was about 5.5 percent per annum representing about 1/2 of 1 percent price increase per annum. During the four year period, 1967-71, average price change for the wholesale price index was approximately 14 percent. This represents an annual rate of price increase during the period of 3 1/2 percent per annum. This is an annual average rate of increase of about six times the rate of the annual average increase in the wholesale price index during the 1958-66 period.

Furthermore, the extent of price increase was much smaller in concentrated industries than in less concentrated industries. To attribute to union monopoly a role as the major causal factor in the price inflation after 1966 is not supported by the facts. Furthermore, the relatively greater increase in prices in the less concentrated industries as compared with the most concentrated industries is evidence that business concentration is not responsible for the price inflation after 1966. Indeed the effect of high concentration has been to blunt the degree of price inflation. The underlying cause of the price inflation after 1966 has been the lack of adequate monetary and fiscal policies to offset the escalation of expenditures connected with heightening of war activity in Southeast Asia.

More sophisticated techniques have also been applied in the analysis of the relationship between concentration and the degree of price inflation. The correlation analysis between price change and the degree of concentration has been made for four postwar periods.

The relationship between concentration and price change has been studied by regression analyses for several time periods as shown in Table 16-4. In the simple regression analyses the relationship between concentration and price change was either not significant or negative, that is, the greater the concentration in an industry, the lower price changes were likely to be.

L. Weiss [245] extended the previous simple regression analysis into a multiple regression analysis. He adjusted for output change by introducing a

Table 16-4
Regression Results with $\frac{P_1}{P_0}$ as Dependent Variable

Equation	Period	Constant	Concentration C	Output Q_1/Q_0	Unit Materials $\dfrac{S_1-VA_1}{S_0-VA_0} \big/ \dfrac{Q_1}{Q_0}$	Unit Wage $\dfrac{W_1}{W_0} \big/ \dfrac{Q_1}{Q_0}$	Hourly Earnings $\dfrac{W_1}{W_0} \big/ \dfrac{MH_1}{MH_0}$	Productivity $\dfrac{Q_1}{Q_0} \big/ \dfrac{MH_1}{MH_0}$	R^2
(1)	1953-59	105.2 (3.6)	.1126 (.0848)						.020
(2)	1953-59	23.65 (10.16)	.0849 (.0342)	−.0224 (.0298)	.4995 (.0483)	.3325 (.0691)			.695
(3)	1953-59	32.9 (13.9)	.051 (.041)	−.043 (.033)	.5058 (.0479)		.418 (.117)	−.198 (.049)	.720
(4)	1959-63	102.4 (1.4)	−.043 (.027)						.039
(5)	1959-63	38.5 (11.4)	−.013 (.021)	−.023 (.035)	.393 (.067)	.265 (.071)			.540
(6)	1959-53	23.4 (15.4)	−.025 (.021)	−.025 (.034)	.424 (.034)		+.542 (.121)	−.195 (.056)	.590
(7)	1953-63	23.8 (8.4)	+.0779 (.0360)	−.014 (.021)	.311 (.044)	.321 (.058)			.73
(8)	1963-68	1.1510	−.00113 (.00065)						.067
(9)	1963-68	.6508	−.00052 (.00046)	−.02553 (.00639)	.51950 (.07735)	−.05023 (.07713)			.624
(10)	1963-68	.5639	−.00042 (.00047)	−.02535 (.00731)	.51459 (.07985)		.02922 (.06201)	−.00062 (.13983)	.624
(11)	1967-68	.8282	−.00041 (.00016)	−.00087 (.00363)	.11440 (.03227)	.09670 (.05509)			.26

(12)	1967-69	1.1428	−.00128 (.00040)	.116
(13)	1963-69	1.2602	−.00205 (.00109)	.068

Standard errors in parentheses

Source: S. Lustgarten, "Industrial Market Structure and Administered Price Inflation," Ph.D. Dissertation (UCLA, Graduate School of Business) 1971.

Industry Variables—4-digit SIC Industries

S_t = Value of Industry Shipments in year t
P_t = Price Index in t
Q_t = S_t/P_t
VA_t = Value Added in t
MH_t = Production Worker Manhours Employed in t
W_t = Production Worker Payroll
C = Four-firm Concentration Ratio

Similar results were found for Western Europe. See Louis Phlips, *Effects of Industrial Concentration: A Cross-Section Analysis for the Common Market*, Amsterdam, North-Holland Publishing Company, 1971.

variable for output change and for selected cost increases. The cost increases analyzed were for unit material costs and unit wage costs. Professor Weiss still found a negative but non-significant relationships between concentration in the multiple regression analysis in all of the time periods except the period 1953-59. The statistical findings of Professor Weiss have been summarized and updated in a doctoral dissertation by Steven H. Lustgarten and presented in Table 16-4.

A multiple regression analysis which seeks to adjust for demand changes, for changes in cost and other influences on price changes is desirable. Professor Weiss's methodology is open to question. No direct measure of quantity was available from the Census data that he employed. To obtain quantity change he divided value of shipments by prices, but prices are the dependent variable. To obtain changes in unit materials and in unit-wage costs, Weiss divided by the quantity change, thus he divided his independent variables by his dependent variables. The statistical consequences of this procedure are at best uncertain. Furthermore, the years 1953-59 were a period in which large increases in capital costs took place for the concentrated industries which are generally capital intensive. The capital equipment boom which took place in 1955 was likely to have been greater in the concentrated industries than in the less-concentrated industries. But in his analysis Professor Weiss did not adjust for changes in capital costs. Hence, his finding of a slight positive correlation between concentration and price change for the 1953-59 period in some of his multiple regression analyses may be due simply to the failure to adjust for the increase in capital cost that took place in the concentrated industries to a greater degree than in the less concentrated industries during that period.

By every level of analysis therefore, the weight of evidence supports the conclusion that the higher the level of concentration of an industry the smaller price changes are likely to be. Indeed, our data are consistent with the hypothesis that large firms in concentrated industries generally have followed the policy of seeking to reduce their prices in competition with products that are close substitutes for their products. Both the simple and direct comparisons as well as more sophistical statistical techniques demonstrate that the more concentrated industries are likely to achieve lower prices over time than less concentrated industries.

Large Firms and Target Return Profits

Another argument sometimes made is that for various reasons large firms are able to manage or plan their profits [129]. It has been argued by J.K. Galbraith that the widespread practice of planning by business firms is evidence of market control [85]. This is a misconception of the nature of planning in business firms. Since the end of World War II, firms both small and large have been attempting to improve their planning and control efforts. Nor is the use of a target rate of return on investment in planning and control processes a basis for controlling either profits or prices. The target return concept is used in two ways by business firms. Most generally, it is used as an investment hurdle rate in allocating corporate funds to different divisions or departments in the budgeting process. Funds are not allocated unless the plans indicate that the minimum required return on investment requirement will be earned. In this sense, the target return is a minimum rate. The firm hopes that overall it will achieve more.

The other way in which the target rate of return is used is a hoped-for goal of overall profitability in relationship to the firm's cost of capital. This is another concept derived from the business finance literature. Unless a firm over the long run can earn at a rate that will cover its cost of acquiring funds, the firm cannot remain in existence.

Thus the main use of target returns is as a device for screening and evaluating alternative investment opportunities. It by no means ensures that the targets will be achieved. The main significance of the use of targets by business firms is their role as a part of a process in the attempt to improve the efficiency and effectiveness of management.

The foregoing propositions can be tested by empirical data. In Chapter 11, I analyzed the hypothesis that large firms price with a reference to a target return on investment. While there was a close correspondence between the ROI specified by Lanzillotti and the average return on net worth for the period 1947 through 1955, extending the data a subsequent decade showed that in six of the seven examples of companies for which he set forth targets, even measured by return on net worth, there was a relatively sharp decline in the realized average return on net worth. This suggests that if the returns on net worth had been high relative to some average, that competitive forces were pushing these returns down toward the average during the subsequent decade.

Table 16-5 updates these materials through 1970, focused on two time periods, 1968-70 and 1965-70. For the inflationary period 1968-70, out of the seven cases for which Lanzillotti has specified a target ROI, the average return on net worth was lower than the target (return on total assets) reported by Lanzillotti. For both the time period 1968-70 and from 1965-70, the return on total assets was again substantially below the target return on investments. The average return on net worth for Lanzillotti's sample of twenty companies declined from 14.1 percent for the period 1947-55, to 11.9 for the period 1956-67, and declined further to 10.7 for the period 1968-70. Earnings on total assets was even lower in the period 1968-70—it was 7.2 percent.

In Table 16-6 another approach to analysis of the profit data was developed. The sample was increased from twenty companies to thirty companies. In addition to calculating average returns on net worth, measures of dispersion of returns on net worth was also calculated. The findings for the period 1957-66 were that the returns on net worth among the sample of thirty large companies (including the Lanzillotti twenty) were highly variable ranging from 4.3 percent

Table 16-5
Target Rates of Return on Investment, Average Returns on Net Worth, and Average Returns on Total Assets of 20 Large Industrial Corporations, 1965-1970

Company	Target ROI (1)	Average Return on Net Worth		Earnings Before, Interest, on Total Assets	
		(2) 1968-70	(3) 1965-70	(4) 1968-70	(5) 1965-70
Alcoa		10.0%	10.0%	6.3%	6.3%
American Can	10%	9.7	10.5	6.4	6.8
A & P		7.5	8.2	5.2	5.7
du Pont		14.4	16.1	10.6	11.6
Esso (Std. Oil N.J.)		12.4	12.3	8.3	8.4
General Electric	20	12.5	14.4	6.7	7.5
General Foods		16.7	16.9	9.5	10.2
General Motors	20	13.8	18.1	9.7	12.2
Goodyear		11.6	11.8	7.4	7.4
Gulf		11.9	12.0	8.5	8.6
International Harvester	10	5.5	7.3	4.9	5.8
Johns-Manville	15	10.0	10.2	7.8	8.0
Kennecott		13.8	12.5	10.5	10.1
Kroger	10	12.5	12.6	6.3	6.2
National Steel		8.4	9.4	5.5	6.4
Sears Roebuck		12.8	13.3	8.2	8.1
Standard Oil (Ind.)		9.8	9.3	7.4	7.3
Swift		6.3	5.7	4.4	4.2
Union Carbide		9.5	11.8	6.4	7.8
U.S. Steel	8	5.9	6.3	4.3	4.6
Average		10.7	11.4	7.2	7.9

Source: Standard and Poor's *Compustat Tape.*

for one company up to 30.2 percent for the highest. Incremental returns for the period 1957-66 were also calculated. Here the range was even greater. It was a negative 94.4 percent for one firm ranging up to a positive 30.8 percent for the highest.

In addition, the range of both average and incremental returns over the period was studied. These were so variable that no formal statistical test would be required to establish the wide disparity in the range of both average and incremental returns. These data were also developed to cover the inflationary period 1967-70. Even greater dispersion was observed in all of the profitability measures of average returns, incremental returns and the range of returns.

The return on net worth data carried through the period 1970 demonstrate that if large firms have target rates of return, they have not been successful in

Table 16-6

Dispersion of Realized Average and Incremental Returns on Net Worth, 29 Companies, 1967-1970

Company	Return on Net Worth (1967-70)		Range of Average Returns on Net Worth		Range of Incremental Returns on Net Worth	
	Average	Incremental	Low	High	Low	High
1. IBM	17.7%	17.3%	17.0%	19.1%	8.8%	29.8%
2. Ford	9.1	49.0	1.9	13.4	−28.2	280.2
3. Xerox	23.7	18.6	21.9	26.4	13.7	19.5
4. U.S. Steel	5.7	−10.9	4.2	7.4	−396.	41.1
5. General Electric	13.4	−8.2	10.9	16.0	−169.	40.3
6. General Motors	14.9	−161.6	6.2	18.3	−25.5	222.6
7. Goodyear	11.7	.8	9.6	12.7	−38.8	20.8
8. Litton	15.8	3.0	12.1	22.0	−11.1	49.4
9. Sears Roebuck	12.9	10.5	12.5	13.2	8.6	14.8
10. International Harvester	6.2	−390.1	4.5	8.2	−70.	184.
11. Beckman Instruments	8.1	−10.4	6.9	10.7	−65.9	30.7
12. Lockheed	4.8	122.3	−36.7	15.5	−47.3	155.3
13. Alcoa	10.1	3.5	9.4	10.7	−12.9	23.8
14. Purex	16.8	5.4	13.8	20.6	5.3	49.6
15. Northrup	13.7	15.9	13.8	14.2	10.3	21.7
16. Standard Oil, N.J.	12.5	7.7	12.0	13.0	−14.0	24.5
17. Reynolds Metal	7.4	−2.0	4.7	9.4	−156.	368.
18. Swift	6.4	−.76	4.3	8.4	14.9	1485.
19. American Can	10.1	−12.9	8.9	11.6	−52.4	9.5
20. A & P	7.8	−10.9	7.1	8.9	−81.1	36.9
21. du Pont	14.3	4.0	12.7	15.9	−82.	43.
22. General Foods	16.9	14.2	17.5	15.9	−88.	97.
23. Johns-Manville	9.8	1.5	8.2	10.8	−38.7	40.1
24. Kennecott	12.4	55.2	7.8	15.8	−110.	76.1
25. Kroger	12.1	−12.6	10.7	12.6	−36.9	23.5
26. National Steel	8.6	−9.9	6.8	9.3	−91.	12.9
27. Gulf	12.1	−2.1	10.4	13.2	−25.	19.6
28. Boeing	6.3	−106.9	1.3	11.2	−1.6	507.1
29. Union Carbide	9.7	−9.1	8.7	10.5	−128.	40.4

Source: Standard and Poor's *Compustat Tapes*

achieving rates of return equal to the aspirations represented by these targets. Furthermore, over time the realized returns by large firms have been trending downward from the levels measured by Lanzillotti at the earlier period. Finally during the recent inflationary period of 1968 through 1970, large firms on the average in terms of their profitability on net worth have performed less favorably than was achieved during the prior periods. Thus, inflationary periods have not represented a favorable period for the profitability of the largest corporations.

These results on the profitability trends of large firms are also consistent with the findings that price changes have been inversely related to the degree of concentration. The higher the degree of concentration in an industry, the smaller the percentage increase in price changes is likely to be. The factual evidence has demolished the theory that large firms have been the cause of the recent inflation. The converse is true. The evidence is also inconsistent with the theory that large firms are able to manage or control their profits. These findings further underscore and emphasize that the planning and control activities of large firms have not freed them from market forces as Galbraith has asserted. Rather the planning and control activities of the large firm have represented attempts to adjust to the dynamic changes that occur in the markets in which they operate.

Advertising and Concentration

When we turn to concentration and advertising, it is difficult to separate analysis from emotionalism. All of us have been terribly irritated by advertising in its ubiquitous and incessant manifestations. There is hardly anyone who at one time or another has not wished that advertising could somehow or another be eliminated, reduced, improved or made more aesthetically satisfying and inform-ative. This is another highly complex issue and space simply does not permit a full treatment of the impact of advertising on all aspects of modern society.

Once again the economic evidence on the role of advertising is conflicting and the research story is yet incomplete. One set of studies holds that advertising, particularly in consumer goods industries, is a major cause of high concentration. These studies also found that advertising and high concentration are associated with profit rates higher than in industries where there is less advertising and less concentration [53, 54, 146].

Other studies show little or no relationship between the intensity of advertising and concentration [228]. The Federal Reserve Bank of Philadelphia in its study of the subject came to the conclusion that there was "no significant correlation."[2] A study by Backman concluded that "there has been no relationship between the intensity of advertising and either the level of concentration or the trend of concentration"[15]. Backman also points to substantial shifts in market shares over time in high advertising industries such as drugs, beer, cigarettes, soft drinks, razor blades, small appliances, hair preparations, dentifrices and others [15, p. 63-79, 102-112]. The Backman study also concluded that the intensity of advertising was not associated with the levels of profits [15, p. 146-154].

Whether prices are higher because they must cover the cost of advertising is also moot. Advertising is one among a number of manifestations of competition. In that advertising stimulates large volume purchases, economies of scale are made possible. Professor Scherer has set forth the competitive aspects of advertising effectively.

In duopolistic price rivalry . . . there is reason to expect, at least as a first approximation, that the sellers will cooperate on joint profit-maximizing strategies. But advertising rivalry appears to be different in several respects. First, price cuts can be matched almost instantaneously unless concessions can be kept secret, whereas it takes weeks or even months to set a retaliatory nationwide advertising campaign in motion. During this interim, the initiator enjoys market share and profit gains at the laggard's expense. The longer the lag between initiation and matching, the stronger the incentive to spend on image differentiation will be. Fear of being left behind by its rivals spurs each oligopolist to anticipate the worst and to initiate campaigns, even if it means provoking an advertising race (not unlike an arms race) which carries expenditures beyond the level maximizing collective profits. Second, success at image differentiation depends at least as much upon the way the appeal is presented as on the amount of money spent. The outcome of an advertising campaign is therefore uncertain. Moreover, any fool can match a price cut, but counteracting a clever advertising gambit is far from easy [200, p. 335].

This quotation from Scherer illustrates the general principle that recognition of interdependence does not necessarily lead to collusion when the potential gains from not colluding are greater than the gains from colluding. There is no effective way of disciplining or controlling rivals with regard to the potential gains from advertising, product innovation and the wide range of other competitive varibles discussed above. This was the basis for the conclusion by Backman that high advertising provided no assurance of favorable profitability. He stated that "intensive advertising assures no permanent advantages to the advertiser . . . Competitive pressures are constantly eroding the position of leading brands despite continued largescale expenditures for advertising" [15, p. 153-154].

But what of the argument that advertising does in fact give business power over the consumer? The argument goes that products are increasingly complex and that advertising is used to make exaggerated claims rather than to inform the consumer about the characteristics of products. It is further alleged that through the use of psychological techniques in advertising, the consumer becomes a puppet of business utilizing advertising and that the consumer is without real freedom of choice. I lay no claim to expertise in the psychological aspects of advertising. My reading of this literature indicates that there are indeed some very powerful techniques that can be used to sway the consumer.

On the other hand we are all aware of examples in which no amount of advertising could have obtained product acceptance. From the varied advertising messages employed by different firms in the same industry, it appears that appeals are being made to different types of tastes and requirements and that the ultimate market share is determined by a complex of economic, cultural, sociological and psychological factors in relationship to which advertising performs an uncertain role. What impresses one in reading the literature on advertising is that despite highly sophisticated statistical procedures it is difficult to demonstrate how effective or ineffective a particular advertising campaign has been. We are left with the general conclusion that a major factor in advertising decisions by business firms is the fear that the rival *may* mount a campaign that turns out to be highly successful.

Professor Yale Brozen has taken a fresh look at advertising. He cites evidence to support the proposition that advertising performs an information function of benefit to consumers. For example, the costs of advertising of breakfast cereals is greater than for cookies, but the total distribution costs are less. He refers to studies which establish that in states where the advertising of services in connection with eye glass examinations and prescription eye glasses is permitted the prices are substantially lower than in states where such advertising is not permitted.[3]

A final comment with respect to advertising is that in our general disaffection with the institution of advertising we have to consider the alternatives. While one could hope that consumers would respond to a higher level of appeals, or that despite the base appeals which appear to make advertising most effective, that business firms (as well as politicians) would appeal only to the higher motives in man. I join in the general aspiration that people could somehow better achieve the ideal of human perfectability. In the real world, however, the ultimate evaluation of advertising must be in terms of the general consequences of practical alternatives and their realistic economic effects. To achieve the goals implicit in abolishing all advertising would require constraints on consumer freedom of choice. Government control of the quality of advertising would involve problems which would make the court cases involved with defining pornography, games in the exercise of sweet reason. Even the more moderate policy of restricting the amount of dollars that could be spent on advertising would transform the temporary success that may have been achieved by firms through advertising into a more permanent market position. Such a freeze or ceiling on advertising would have potentially undesirable anticompetitive effects. This is another unsettled area, but it provides no basis for an assured conclusion that advertising increases concentration or that it provides market power or high profits.[4]

Concentration and Innovation

One of the areas of research that has been subject to considerable empirical study in recent years has been sources of innovation and the relation between size and inventiveness or innovation. One of the important stimuli to investigation in this area was the view of Professor Schumpeter that there must be a promise of some monopoly position for at least a temporary period required to stimulate innovation [202]. This implies some kind of patent system to protect the returns of the inventor. In this connection Schumpeter emphasized the process of creative destruction of a firm's market position as a consequence of rapid imitation of successful innovation. He held that the investments required to achieve innovation may be substantial. Without a period of some protection against erosion of market position and sufficient returns to reward the risk, research and development activities would be discouraged.

In response to these theories by Schumpeter a large number of empirical studies have been undertaken. While there has been considerable research in the area, the research that has been performed has been subject to two major limitations. First, the number of industries that have been covered is relatively limited. A second limitation of the empirical studies of innovation is represented by very serious measurement problems. The subject of analysis to which size of firm and concentration are related has been difficult to define. Some studies focus on the *output* of research and development measured by "significant inventions" or the number of patents. Obviously, the judgment of what represents a "significant invention" may be quite different from the standpoint of its general, social, and economic impact on either profitability or incentives to further research and development activity from the standpoint of the individual business firm. The dangers of equating the numbers of patents regardless of dollar magnitudes involved or any other measurements of impact or significance are too obvious to require elaboration.

Other studies have used research and development input with employment as an index of inventive activity. The significance of research and development employment varies from industry to industry, within firms, and between firms in a given industry. Also, since the Internal Revenue Code of 1954 permitted expensing of research and development outlays, an increase has taken place in the amount of expenditures that have been labeled research and development expenditures. An additional problem is that the significance of basic research versus applied research and between applied research and prototype production activity represent boundary lines difficult to draw. But empirical research always poses difficulties in measurement and it is not intended by these criticisms to imply that the studies have no value. Nevertheless, the measurement problems involved are much greater than ordinarily observed.

Three results appear to follow from the empirical studies. One is that the elasticity of research and development employment with respect to firm size is less than one [216]. The lower ratio of research and development employment to firm sales for large firms as compared with small firms may have alternative explanations. A minimum threshold of research and development employment may raise the ratio for small firms. Another possibility is that large firms may encounter diminishing returns from the employment of research and development personnel either on the demand side or in their production functions.

The second empirical finding is that the productivity of research and development expenditures appears to be higher for smaller firms than for large firms. Mansfield states the point and provides a rationale [147]:

Second, holding research and development expenditures constant, the effects of firm size on the average productivity of such expenditures turn out to be negative in each industry and statistically significant in two of the three industries. Thus, contrary to popular belief, the inventive output per dollar of research and development expenditure in most of these cases seems to be lower in the largest firms than in large and medium-sized firms. In part, this may be due to looser controls and greater problems of supervision and co-ordination in a very large organization.

It will be observed from this quotation that this study by Mansfield was limited to three industries. Also crucial is that the dependent variable that is being predicted is the number of significant inventions "weighted roughly by a measure of their importance [147, p. 335].

The final conclusions have been well stated by Professor Scherer [198]:

Differences in technological opportunity—e.g., differences in technical investment possibilities unrelated to the mere volume of sales and typically opened up by the broad advance of knowledge—are a major factor responsible for interindustry differences in inventive output. Inventive output does not appear to be systematically related to variations in market power, prior profitability, liquidity, or (when participation in fields with high technological opportunity is accounted for) degree of product line diversification.

The major determinant of the productivity of research and development outlays is the nature of the industry in which research and development outlays take place. The empirical studies support the conclusion that the characteristics of uneven technological fertility of industry provide a major explanation for variations in research and development activity between industries. One of the strong competitive stimuli to product innovation by smaller firms may be efforts to erode the position of larger firms with economies of scale by new product development that will enlarge the market position of the smaller firm within the broader industry boundaries. Thus if there is greater incentive to innovate by smaller firms in an industry, it would provide corroborative evidence of significant scale advantages in established product lines by the larger firms.

241

Evaluation of Overall Performance

This brings us to a consideration of overall performance characteristics or accomplishments. One's general assessment will reflect the philosophical point of view with regard to the implications of concentration. Professor Scherer presents a summary table of the social losses attributable to the exercise of monopoly power in the United States. His estimates are presented in Table 16-7. Professor Scherer qualified the precision of these estimates. He stated, "This is an inherently 'iffy' and subjective task, so it must be received with the appropriate grain of salt"[200, p. 408]. Nevertheless his estimates have been widely quoted and used as a basis for seeking to dramatize the heavy cost of concentration in the United States.[5]

Professor Scherer's estimates are anomalous in terms of the prior analyses he himself had performed. After recognition and a clear discussion of the processes of competition inherent in advertising, product quality improvement and product development, Professor Scherer compartmentalizes this discussion and sets it aside. In drawing conclusions about the overall effect of concentration in the U.S. economy, he ignores his prior sections in which he analyzed competitive processes.

Table 16-7
Scherer's Estimates of the Costs of Monopoly Power in the United States, 1966

	Percentage of GNP, Circa 1966
Dead-weight welfare losses due to monopolistic resource misallocation: unregulated sectors	0.9
Dead-weight losses due to pricing distortions in the regulated sectors	0.6
Inefficiencies due to deficient cost control by market sector enterprises insulated from competition	2.0
Inefficiencies due to deficient cost control by defense and space contractors	0.6
Wasteful promotional efforts	1.0
Operation at less than optimal scale for reasons other than differentiation serving special demands	0.3
Cross-hauling costs and transportation costs associated with distorted locational decisions	0.2
Excess and inefficient capacity due to industrial cartelization and the stimulus of collusive profits	0.6
Total Losses Due to Market Power	6.2

Source: F.M. Scherer [200, p. 408]

I have made an alternative set of estimates consistent with Professor Scherer's book in total, related to the evidence developed in the essays in this volume. They are set forth in Table 16-8. My results differ greatly from those of Scherer. Unlike Scherer's single-valued estimate, I have provided a range of values since present research knowledge does not provide a basis for a precise number. The basis for my estimates are indicated.

I have assigned a net contribution from the utility industry after recognition of the costs of regulation. In part, stimulated by the greater predictability of demand (until the impact of the inflationary period beginning in 1966) associated with the increased government spending programs stimulated by the war in Southeast Asia and the pressures of the regulatory process, management planning and control systems have been effectively developed in the Utilities before their adoption in nonregulated industry. This has been a factor in the superior productivity achievement of the Utilities.[6] For the period 1948-66,

Table 16-8

Estimates of the Benefits of the Economic Gains from Large Scale Industrial Operations in the United States, 1970

	Percentage of GNP		
	Gains		Losses
1. Superior productivity record of electric utilities and telephone utilities	.5 to .7		
Less: Costs of regulation			−.2 to −.3
2. Lower costs and prices resulting from economies of plant scale	.4 to .6		
3. Lower costs and prices resulting from multi-divisional operations	1.5 to 2.0		
4. Lower costs and prices resulting from economies of vertical integration	.4 to .5		
5. Improvements in managerial technology and cost control in defense industries	.3 to .7		
6. Avoidance of subsidies to small-scale industries	1.5 to 3.0		
7. Contribution to large-scale operations from advertising	.7 to .9		
Less: Net economic wastes of advertising			−.3 to −.5
8. Losses resulting from large-scale union operations			−.7 to −1.4
Totals	5.3 to 8.4		−1.0 to −1.9
Net Gains from Large Scale Operations in the U.S. Economy	4.3 to 3.4	or	7.4 to 6.5

total factor productivity for the private domestic business economy in the U.S. increased at an annual percentage rate of 2.5 percent.[7] For communications and public utilities, the percentage gain per year was 4 percent. The productivity record of communications and public utilities was therefore 60 percent better than that of the economy as a whole.[8]

My estimate of the benefits from economies of scale are based in part on Chapter 16 of Edward F. Denison's monograph, *The Sources of Economic Growth in the United States* [62]. Denison summarizes the lengthy discussion of the role of economies of scale and increased specialization in the following statement. "I therefore ascribe to economies of scale associated with the growth of the national market 0.27 percentage point of 2.93 percent growth rate of national product in that period. (1929-57)" [62, p. 175].

Again, contrary to some views, evidence on performance in the defense industries impresses me with the managerial improvements achieved attempting to deal with advanced technology, high risks, increasing entry leading to excess capacity, arbitrary behavior by the powerful monopsonistic buyer—the Federal government, frequent contract changes, and a wide range of problems dealing with advancing the state of the art. Many important advances in managerial technology in considerable measure due to developments in the defense industry include: long-range planning, project planning techniques including PERT, CPM, etc.

The industry that most closely approximates the competitive ideal of atomistic numbers is agriculture. Yet agriculture has achieved continued government subsidies of substantial magnitudes, for many years running over five billion dollars per year in direct benefits and substantially more in indirect effects. Small business, in general, in the United States has received a wide variety of subsidies.

The foregoing items indicate the basis for the estimates set forth in Table 16-8. Combining low positive with the negative estimates, the range is 3.4 percent to 4.3 percent. Subtracting the negative figures against the high positive estimate, the range of contributions of concentration is 6.5 percent to 7.4 percent. Translated into dollars for our present trillion dollar economy, the most probable range of net contributions of concentration to economic performance is from forty-three billion to sixty-five billion dollars. These are minimal estimates of the direct benefits of large scale operations and industry concentration in the United States; they also indicate the order of magnitude of the direct costs of breaking up large, efficient firms in the effort to atomize the U.S. economy.

Conclusions

The data on concentration and prices presented earlier in this chapter have demonstrated that price increases have been lower during the inflationary period from 1966-to-1971 the higher the degree of concentration in an industry. The weighted price changes for the industries with concentration over 50 percent was 3.5 percent lower than for the industries with concentration less than 50 percent. Total corporate sales in 1971 were one trillion, 615 billion; industries with concentration of over 50 percent account for one-third of the total value of shipments. If the 3.5 percent factor is applied to one-third of total corporate sales, the benefit in lower selling prices is roughly nineteen billion dollars. If the same degree of lower prices were applied to the less concentrated two-thirds of the economy as well, the total benefits from concentration would rise to approximately fifty-seven billion dollars. Any estimates of these kinds are subject to a myriad of qualifications, but these numbers provide a check demonstrating internal consistency with the analysis set forth above. The fifty-seven billion estimate falls within the boundaries of the forty-three to sixty-five dollar estimates range of benefits to the U.S. economy from large scale business operations.

The preceding analysis has not purported to demonstrate that all aspects of concentration are good and that no aspects are bad. It does, however, emphasize that the mechanical applications of concentration tests fail to reflect a basic understanding of modern industrial competitive processes. I see no basis for being apologetic about the structure and performance of the American economy. In what country is economic performance superior? Possibly Japan and West Germany have excelled in recent years, but by the criteria of the structural theory, both have more sins of concentration than the U.S.

Ralph Nader has stated:

But the rebuttal: Isn't this the most productive economy the world has witnessed and the highest standard of living? Certainly it is among them and certainly the largest among them. But does this mean that economic crime, armaments, poverty, waste, pollution, disease, bureaucracy's invisible chains and a deteriorating quality of life have to be the price of progress? Why compare our Gross National Product to other nations when we should be comparing it to our unrealized potential? [173, pp. i-ii]

However this statement assigns guilt to "the enterprise system" for a wide range of problems of an advanced industrialized, urban society, without proof in the over 1,150 pages which follow. These criticisms are applicable in an equal or greater degree to the USSR. There are predictable differences between the ideal and reality. But careful analysis is required to provide responsible guidance on how to narrow the difference over time.

The elements that have been retarding progress in the U.S. economy have come mainly from sources external to the operations of business firms. Many obviously have derived from national policies related to maintaining an effective posture in the international political and military environment. On these and related areas considerable additional research needs to be performed.

There is a vast difference between the assumptions of the atomistic market model and actual behavior. In the real world, adjustments to change are not automatic or instantaneous and these adjustment processes are of the greatest theoretical and practical interest. The atomistic theory assumes that all firms are equally able in choosing methods of production, selection among inputs and achieving what is referred to as the best "production function." In the real world these decisions make the difference between efficient and inefficient firms. In the real world discretionary behavior takes place in business firms with regard to important elements that are assumed away in the atomistic theory. Thus, analyses which are supposed to be absent in atomistic firms are, in fact, the heart of decision-making and discretionary choices in small firms as well as large. The small farmer exercises discretion in the selection of crops and the appropriate mixes of capital equipment, labor and fertilizer. The small retailer must choose among different locations, different groups of products and different strategies between price, volume, advertising, personal service, etc. I refer to the small farmer and small retailer because these are presumed to be the archetype of atomistic firms in the textbook theory of pure and perfect competition.

The thrust of the accumulating evidence is that the development of concentrated industries or oligopolies is a result of competition and an expression of competitive processes. We see the competitive forces operating from both directions. In some industries a dominant firm with more than 50 percent market share, and in some instances close to 100 percent market share, had resulted mainly from mergers at the turn of the century, underlying competitive forces (with the help of divestiture decrees in two industries and a salutary antitrust climate as well) moved the industries to a larger number of firms with changing market shares over a period of years. The decline in the market share of the dominant firm took place without divestiture in other industries, e.g., agricultural implements, cans, meat packing, steel, leather, sugar refining, etc.

From the other direction, industries which formally were characterized by a large number of firms have been replaced by oligopolies. This, again, was a result of competitive processes which weeded out a large number of firms either through the bankruptcy or merger route. Indeed, in a long-term perspective it is clear that the reduction from hundreds of firms in an industry over a period of decades is a result of the operation of competitive forces. In the operation of these competitive forces in this long perspective, merger activity may be seen as a superior alternative to bankruptcy. It is a superior alternative to bankruptcy in preserving some organization values and the use of executive workers, plants and equipment in more productive use than would have been achieved if the firm had been broken up and sold off at auctions through the bankruptcy courts with executive talent and workers dispersed to other firms and perhaps other industries.

As a consequence of these processes, assumptions of the atomistic model upon which the structural theory depends, are not appropriate for some industries or markets. For such industries it would not be possible for a large number of sellers and buyers as required by the atomistic model to exist in competitive and efficient markets. For many important industries or markets, technological, managerial and economic realities make the existence of large numbers of sellers or buyers impossible and irrelevant as a standard in any sense and provide no basis for *presumptions* about the conduct and performance of such industries. With the many dimensions of products and decision-making, it is not possible *a priori* to predict whether a market with five, ten or one-hundred sellers or buyers would be more competitive than a market with two sellers or buyers [186].

All of this shows that the structural approach to oligopoly which equates it with shared monopoly is without foundation in fact or in the reality of market behavior. Empirical evidence is consistent with the theory of dynamic competition by large firms in concentrated markets [159, 255]. Price increases have been smaller in concentrated industries. It is precisely the factors that explain concentration that explain their moderation in price increases. It is the greater capital intensity; it is the greater research and development activities; it is the continued pressures of large firm rivalry; it is efforts to attract consumer spending to their products by price reductions, that explain why firms in concentrated industries succeed in offsetting the general inflation to some degree. Instead of the general myth that some people are seeking to perpetrate that the present inflation is due to oligopoly which is equated to shared monopoly, the facts are the opposite. Concentration reflects and creates economic efficiency, which moderates the inflationary pressures rather than causing them.

Industries described as oligopolies are subject to the same competitive market pressures for cost reduction, price reduction, product improvement of the kind that atomistic industries were supposed to have produced. The atomistic model upon which the structural theory is based is a useful abstract for some purposes. However, it is misleading as a guide for industrial economic theory and policy.

Appendixes

Appendix A:
Participants

Conference on
Industrial
Economics

November 21-22-23, 1971
General Electric Company
Crotonville, Ossining, New York

Academic Participants

Professor Armen A. Alchian
Economics Department
University of California-Los Angeles

Professor William F. Baxter
Law School
Stanford University

Professor Charles H. Berry
Woodrow Wilson School
Princeton University

Miss Betty Bock
The Conference Board

Professor Robert S. Bork
Law School
Yale University

Professor Ward S. Bowman, Jr.
Law School Yale University

Professor Yale Brozen
Graduate School of Business
University of Chicago

Professor Robert D. Buzzell
Graduate School of
Business Administration
Harvard University

Professor Ronald H. Coase
Law School
University of Chicago

Professor William S. Comanor
Graduate School of Business
Stanford University

Professor Roger Cramton
Law School
University of Michigan

Professor Harold Demsetz
Department of Economics
University of California-Los Angeles

Professor James M. Ferguson
College of Business Administration
University of Rochester

Professor Michael Gort
Department of Economics
State University of New York at
Buffalo

Professor Michael Granfield
Graduate School of Management
University of California-Los Angeles

Professor Bob R. Holdren
Economics Department
Iowa State University

Professor Michael Intriligator
Economics Department
University of California-Los Angeles

Professor Neil H. Jacoby
Graduate School of
Business Administration
University of California-Los Angeles

Professor David R. Kamerschen
Economics Department
University of Missouri

Professor Clement G. Krouse
Graduate School of
Business Administration
University of California-Los Angeles

Dean Robert F. Lanzillotti
College of Business Administration
University of Florida

Professor Jesse Markham
Graduate School of
Business Administration
Harvard University

Professor John S. McGee
Economics Department
University of Washington

Professor John Narver
Graduate School of
Business Administration
University of Washington

Dean Phil C. Neal
Law School
University of Chicago

Professor Douglas Needham
Economics Department
State University College at Brockport

Professor Ralph L. Nelson
Economics Department
Queens College of the City University
of New York

Professor Stanley Ornstein
Graduate School of
Business Administration
University of California-Los Angeles

Professor B. Peter Pashigian
Graduate School of Business
University of Chicago

Professor Sam Peltzman
Department of Economics
University of California-Los Angeles

Professor John Peterman
Law School
University of Chicago

Professor Lee E. Preston, Jr.
School of Management
State University of New York at
Buffalo

Professor H. Paul Root
School of Business Administration
University of Michigan

Mr. Ronald Shrieves
Graduate School of
Business Administration
University of California-Los Angeles

Professor Ralph G. Sultan
Graduate School of
Business Administration
Harvard University

Professor Lester Telser
Economics Department
University of Chicago

Professor John M. Vernon
Economics Department
Duke University

Professor Alex Vicas
Department of Economics
McGill University

Professor John T. Wenders
Economics Department
University of Arizona

Professor J. Fred Weston
Graduate School of
Business Administration
University of California-Los Angeles

Professor Oliver E. Williamson
Economics Department
University of Pennsylvania

General Electric
Company Participants

Joseph M. Bertotti
Manager-Educational Relations

L. Earle Birdzell, Jr.
Counsel-Special Legal Assignments

J. Moreau Brown
Administrator
Educational Support Programs

James Bruce
Litigation and Antitrust Counsel

David W. Burke
Manager-Corporate
Public Relations Programs

Hershner Cross
Senior Vice President
Corporate Administrative Staff

Robert M. Estes
Senior Vice President
Corporate Exeuctive Staff,
General Counsel and Secretary

Robert L. Fegley
Manager-Public Relations Planning
and Research Operation

Stephen K. Galpin
Manager-Community and
Government Relations

William C. Gaygan
Consultant-Acquisitions/Dispositions
Analysis-Corporate Accounting
Operation

Walter K. Joelson
Manager-Economic Studies,
Planning Development Staff

William F. Kennedy
Staff Executive-Corporate Executive
Staff

John B. McKitterick
Vice President-Planning
Development Staff

Douglas S. Moore
Vice President-Corporate Public
Relations

Robert W. Newman
Manager-Data Management
Planning Development Staff

Winston H. Pickett
Staff Executive
Corporate Executive Staff

Charles S. Reed
Senior Vice President
Corporate Executive Staff

William K. Reed
Manager-Business Environment
Studies, Business Environment Staff

Lindon E. Saline
Manager-Corporate Education
Services

Walter A. Schlotterbeck
Vice President and
Corporate Counsel

251

Roland W. Schmidt
Manager-Physical Science
and Engineering R&D Center

Sidney Schoeffler
Manager-Plans Evaluation, Planning
Development Staff

A. Eugene Schubert
Vice President-Strategic Planning
and Review Operation,
Power Generation Group

Saadia M. Schorr
Manager-International Planning
Operation, International Business
Support Division

Clifford H. Springer
Consultant Corporate Systems
Development

Edmund B. Tucker
Consultant-Educational Relations
Educational Relations Operation

Donald J. Watson
Manager-Educational Support
Operation

Ian H. Wilson
Consultant-Business Environment
Research and Planning,
Business Environment Staff

Appendix B: (To Chapter 6) Sources of the Data and Adjustments for Data Deficiencies

1. Concentration Ratios—All concentration ratios are measures of the four-firm percentage of industry value of shipments. They were taken from Census data except for the motor vehicle industry whose ratios were calculated from production figures published in *Ward's Automotive Yearbook*, XXIII (May 15, 1961), pp. 56-57
   Source: U.S. Congress, Senate, Subcommittee on Antitrust and Monopoly, *Concentration Ratios in Manufacturing Industries*: 1958, Washington, D.C., 1962

2. Index of Geographic Dispersion—The index was calculated from regional Census data on value of shipments for each four-digit industry covered. In some instances only two or three Census regions were reported which necessitated combining population percentages in a similar manner. Population figures for each region were taken from Census data covering yearly population estimates. When value of shipments was not available value added figures were used. Value added figures were used for meat packing, steel, and primary copper.
   Source: U.S. Bureau of the Census, *U.S. Census of Manufactures: 1954*, Vol. II, Industry Statistics, 1957; U.S. Bureau of the Census, *U.S. Census of Manufactures, 1958*, Vol. II, Industry Statistics, 1962: U.S. Bureau of the Census, *Statistical Abstract of the United States: 1960*, Washington, D.C., 1960.

3. Firm Size—Asset figures were used unadjusted total firm assets as reported in Moody's Industrial Manual in the years studied. These figures were normalized by the use of industry valued added figures taken from Census data.

4. Economies of Scale in Production—All figures were derived from Census data except for motor vehicles since Census data covers both motor vehicles and parts. Bain's estimate of 5 percent was used for the measure of economies of scale in motor vehicles. Value of shipments were used to calculate average plant size in most cases, however, when shipments were not available due to large-scale integration, value added figures were used. This occurred only in the cases of steel and primary copper.
   Source: U.S. Bureau of the Census, *U.S. Census of Manufactures: 1958*, Vol. II, Industry Statistics, 1962.

5. Entry Capital Requirements—Gross book value of assets were measured as of December 31, 1957, and were taken from Census figures. These figures are applied to economies of scale figures for 1958. Estimates from three-digit totals were used when four-digit figures were not available. This was necessary for paper and pulp and man-made fibers.

Source: U.S. Bureau of the Census, *U.S. Census of Manufactures: 1958,* Col. II, Industry Statistics, 1962.

6. Industry and Firm Demand—Percentage changes in industry production were seasonally adjusted December to December figures for marketing groups as compiled by the Federal Reserve. These figures are comparable to SIC three and four-digit industry groupings. Changes in firm demand were measured as changes in firm assets.

Source: U.S. Board of Governors of the Federal Reserve System, *Industrial Production, 1957-59* Base, Washington, D.C., 1962; *Moody's Industrial Manual,* annually.

7. Labor Cost—Cost was measured as annual percentage change in average gross hourly earnings of production workers relative to output per man-hour in each four-digit industry.

Source: U.S. Department of Labor, Bureau of Labor Statistics, *Employment and Earnings,* Washington, D.C., monthly; U.S. Bureau of the Census, *Annual Survey of Manufacturers,* 1950, 1955, and 1960.

8. Profit Rates—The ratio of stock market value to stockholder's equity was calculated by taking the average of high and low market values in a given year and dividing by the average book value of equity at the beginning and end of each year. Two-year averages were used for each cross-section studied, for example, the average of 1959-60 for 1960. Net income after taxes was adjusted for extraordinary gains or losses but not for interest payments or officers' salaries. In the case of Ford Motor Company there is no stock price quoted prior to 1954, however, earning per share are available so historic and industry price-earnings ratios were used to estimate market value for 1949 and 1950.

Source: *Moody's Industrial Manual,* New York, annually; *Standard and Poor's Industry Surveys,* annually; Federal Trade Commission, *Rates of Return for Identical Companies in Selected Manufacturing Industries, 1955-1960,* Washington, D.C., 1961.

The Sample, 4-Digit SIC Industries and Individual Firms

SIC No.

2011 — *Meat Packing*
    Armour
    Cudahy
    Morrell
    Swift
    Wilson

2033 — *Canned Fruits & Vegetables*
    California Packing
    H.J. Heinz
    Libby, McNeill and Libby
    Stokely-Van Camp

2051 — *Bread & Related Products*
American Bakeries
Continental Baking
General Baking
Interstate Bakeries
Ward Baking

2052 — *Biscuits & Crackers*
National Biscuit
Sunshine Biscuit
United Biscuit

2071 — *Confectionary Products*
E.J. Brach
Hershey Chocolate
Peter Paul

2073 — *Chewing Gum*
American Chicle
Wrigley (Wm., Jr.)

2082 — *Malt Liquors*
Anheuser Busch
Falstaff
Olympia
Pabst

2085 — *Distilled Liquors*
American Distilling
Distillers Corp. (Seagrams)
National Distillers
Schenley
Walker (Hiram)

2111 — *Cigarettes*
American Tobacco
Liggett and Myers
Phillip Morris
R. J. Reynolds

2211 — *Weaving Mills, Cotton*
Bates
Cone Mills

2211 — *Weaving Mills, Cotton* (cont.)
Dan River
Reeves Bros.
Stevens, J.P.
West Point

2511 — *Wood Furniture*
American Furniture
Basset Furniture
Drexel Furniture
Kroehler

2611 — *Paper & Pulp Mills*
Crown Zellerbach
Hammermill
International Paper
Kimberly-Clark
Mead
West Virginia

2823 — *Cellulostic & Man-Made
Fibers*
American Enka
American Viscose
Celanese

2834 — *Pharmaceutical Preparations*
Abbott Laboratories
Parke Davis
Searle, G.D.
Warner Lambert

2841 — *Soap & Other Detergents*
Colgate-Palmolive
Proctor and Gamble

2871 — *Fertilizers*
American Agri. & Chem.
International Minerals
Smith-Douglas

2911 — *Petroleum Refining*
Continental Oil

2911 — *Petroleum Refining* (cont.)
Gulf Oil
Phillips Petroleum
Shell
Standard Oil (Calif.)
Standard Oil (N.J.)
Texaco

3011 — *Tires & Inner Tubes*
Firestone
Goodrich
Goodyear
U.S. Rubber

3141 — *Footwear*
Brown Shoe
Craddock-Terry Shoe
Endicott-Johnson
Genesco
International Shoe
Weyenberg Shoe

3211 — *Flat Glass*
Libby-Owens-Ford
Pittsburgh Plate Glass

3221 — *Glass Containers*
Anchor-Hocking
Owens-Illinois
Thatcher Glass

3241 — *Cement, Hydraulic*
Alpha Portland
General Portland
Ideal
Lehigh Portland
Lone Star
Penn-Dixie Cement

3275 — *Gypsum Products*
National Gypsum
U.S. Gypsum

3312 — *Blast Furnaces & Steel Mills*
Bethlehem
Inland
Jones and Laughlin
National
Republic
U.S. Steel
Youngstown

3331 — *Primary Copper*
Anaconda
Cerro
Phelps Dodge

3334 — *Primary Aluminum*
Alcoa
Kaiser
Reynolds

3411 — *Metal Cans*
American Can
Continental Can

3520 — *Farm Machinery*
J.I. Case
Deere and Co.
International Harvester

3571 — *Computing & Related Machines*
Addressograph
Burroughs
IBM
National Cash Register

3691 — *Storage Batteries*
Electric Storage Battery
Gould-National Batteries
Globe-Union

3711 — *Motor Vehicles*
Chrysler

3711 — *Motor Vehicles* (cont.)
    Ford
    General Motors

3721 — *Aircraft*
    Boeing
    Douglas
    Lockheed

3721 — *Aircraft* (cont.)
    McDonnell
    North American

3871 — *Watches & Clocks*
    Benrus
    Bulova
    Elgin-National
    Hamilton
    Longine-Wittnauer

Notes

Notes

Chapter 1
Trends and Causes of Concentration—A Survey

*The presentation in this Chapter has benefitted from the studies conducted in the Research Program in Competition and Business Policy and discussions with Harold Demsetz, Michael Intriligator, Steven Lustgarten, and Ronald Shrieves. The assistance of Nanci Grottke and Patrick Smith is also acknowledged with appreciation. An earlier version of this paper was included in the Proceedings of a Conference on "Contemporary Challenges to American Business-Society Relationships," Graduate School of Management, UCLA, 1972.

1. Joe S. Bain, INDUSTRIAL ORGANIZATION, John Wiley & Sons, Inc., (1968) 2nd. Ed., also his BARRIERS TO NEW COMPETITION, Harvard University Press, (1956); Richard Caves, AMERICAN INDUSTRY: STRUCTURE, CONDUCT, PERFORMANCE, Prentice-Hall, Inc., (1964); John Kenneth Galbraith, THE NEW INDUSTRIAL STATE, Houghton Mifflin Company, (1967); Willard F. Mueller, A PRIMER ON MONOPOLY AND COMPETITION, Random House, Inc., (1970), and "Industrial Structure and Competition Policy," Study Paper No. Two, Cabinet Committee on Price Stability, U.S. Government Printing Office, January 1969; Ralph Nader, Speeches and THE CLOSED ENTERPRISE SYSTEM, The Nadar Study Group Report on Antitrust Enforcement, Mark J. Green, Project Director and Editor, with introduction by Ralph Nader; F.A. Scherer, INDUSTRIAL MARKET STRUCTURE AND ECONOMIC PERFORMANCE, Rand McNally & Company, (1970); William G. Shepherd, MARKET POWER & ECONOMIC WELFARE: AN INTRODUCTION, Random House, Inc., (1970); Leonard W. Weiss, CASE STUDIES IN AMERICAN INDUSTRY, John Wiley & Sons, Inc., (1967) and views summarized in "Quantitative Studies of Industrial Organization," FRONTIERS OF QUANTITATIVE ECONOMICS, M.D. Intriligator, Ed., North-Holland Publishing Co., (1971); Morton Mintz and Jerry S. Cohen, AMERICA, INC., Dial Press, (1971) and John M. Blair, ECONOMIC CONCENTRATION, Harcourt, Brace, and Jovanovich, (1972).

2. Jules Backman, ADVERTISING AND COMPETITION, New York University Press, (1967); Donald Dewey, THE THEORY OF IMPERFECT COMPETITION: A RADICAL RECONSTRUCTION, Columbia University Press, (1969); John S. McGee, IN DEFENSE OF INDUSTRIAL CONCENTRATION, Praeger Publishers, (1971); Murray N. Rothbard, POWER AND MARKET: GOVERNMENT AND THE ECONOMY, Institute for Humane Studies, Inc., (1970).

3. Neil H. Jacoby, "Antitrust Policy Reexamined," JOURNAL OF POLITICAL ECONOMY, 58 (February 1950) pp. 61-69; "Perspectives on Monopoly,"

JOURNAL OF POLITICAL ECONOMY, 59 (December 1951) pp. 514-27; "The Relative Stability of Market Shares," JOURNAL OF INDUSTRIAL ECONOMICS, (March 1964) pp. 83-107; "The Conglomerate Corporation," THE CENTER MAGAZINE, II, 4 (July 1969) pp. 1-13; "The Role of Giant Corporations in the American and World Economies," HEARINGS BEFORE THE SUBCOMMITTEE ON MONOPOLY OF THE SELECT COMMITTEE ON SMALL BUSINESS UNITED STATES SENATE, NINETY-FIRST CONGRESS, July 9, 10 and 11, 1969, pp. 502-513.

4. Eugene M. Singer, ANTITRUST ECONOMICS: SELECTED LEGAL CASES AND ECONOMIC MODELS, Prentice-Hall, Inc., (1968); George J. Stigler, THE ORGANIZATION OF INDUSTRY, Richard D. Irwin, Inc., (1968); J. Fred Weston and Sam Peltzman, PUBLIC POLICY TOWARD MERGERS, Goodyear Publishing Company, Inc., (1969); Oliver E. Williamson, CORPORATE CONTROL AND BUSINESS BEHAVIOR, Prentice-Hall, 1970.

5. Cf. Walter Adams, "The Case for Structural Tests," in Weston and Peltzman, op. cit., Chapter 2. See also Mark Green's statement of initial postulates: "Second, although both will be discussed, it is anticompetitive *structure* more than *conduct* which cripples industrial performance and which should be the emphasis of rational antitrust policy." THE CLOSED ENTERPRISE SYSTEM, Preface, p. x (Underlining in the original). Note that concentration is equated to "anticompetitive"; what is a major issue of industrial economics is taken as a first premise in "The Nader Study Group Report on Antitrust Enforcement."

6. The use of employment forces average concentration downward due to differing labor intensity across concentration levels, however, value added was not available for the earlier Census. The distribution of value added in 1963 and 1967 is less skewed to the lower concentration deciles and average concentration weighted by value added for our sample, in contrast to employment, shows a decline in concentration from 38.0 to 37.4 percent, respectively.

7. All percentages were calculated from the Federal Trade Commission, ECONOMIC REPORT ON CORPORATE MERGERS, Washington, D.C., U.S. Government Printing Office, 1969, pp. 668 and 673.

8. The merger data is based on the period 1948 to 1968, but the lack of correspondence between periods does not bias the results since most of the large mergers took place in the later years. Specifically, the 1954 to 1967 period covered 80 percent of larger mergers from 1948. Federal Trade Commission, ECONOMIC REPORT ON CORPORATE MERGERS, Washington, D.C., U.S. Government Printing Office, 1969, pp. 43 and 64.

9. See e.g., William G. Shepherd, "Trends of Concentration in American Manufacturing Industries, 1947-58," REVIEW OF ECONOMICS AND STATISTICS, (May 1964) pp. 200-212. The FTC attributes the rise to mergers and differential growth rates, however, conglomerate mergers accounted for 73 percent of all large mergers from 1948 to 1968 by their classification. Federal

Trade Commission, ECONOMIC REPORT ON CORPORATE MERGERS, Washington, D.C., U.S. Government Printing Office, 1969, p. 673.

Chapter 2
Conceptual Framework of an Econometric
Model of Industrial Organization

*We are grateful for the comments and suggestions of our colleagues H. Demsetz, M. Granfield, N.H. Jacoby, and S. Peltzman. Research assistance was provided by D. Leach, N. Grottke, N. Hasson, S. Dittrich. This study was supported by the Research Program in Competition and Business Policy at UCLA.

1. Useful recent reviews of previous approaches to industrial organizations are Scherer [200] and Weiss [248]; Phillips and Williamson [185].

2. Examples of traditional case studies include the Adelman [2] study of A&P and the Kaysen [122] study of United Shoe Machinery. More recent case studies using some quantitative or econometric techniques include the Meyer *et al.* [160] study of transportation, the Caves [43] study of air transport and its regulators, and the MacAvoy [142] study of natural gas, the Fisher [82] study of petroleum exploratory drilling, the Horowitz and Horowitz [108] study of the brewing industry, the Wallace *et al.* [238] study of the textile industry, and the Vernon *et al.* [236] study of the tobacco industry.

3. Examples of the applications of the basic paradigms of price theory to industrial organization include the Lerner [131] measure of monopoly power, the Harberger [102] study of the costs of monopoly, the Dorfman and Steiner [68] study of advertising and quality, the Bain [18] study of barriers to entry, and the Leibenstein [132] study of "x-efficiency."

4. Examples of studies comparing data on derived statistics, such as concentration ratios, include Nelson [177] and Weiss [243].

5. Studies seeking to explain observed differences in concentration among industries include the Rosenbluth [195] study of Canadian industries and for U.S. industries, Pashigian [181, 182], Mann *et al.* [146], Guth [97] and Greer [93].

6. Studies seeking to explain changes in concentration over time include Nelson [177], Weiss [242], Shepherd [206], and Kamerschen [120].

7. Studies relating concentration and profits include Bain [17, 18] Stigler [221, 222], Mann [145], Asch [11], Hall and Weiss [99], George [86], Collins and Preston [51] and Telser [229], and Ornstein [179].

8. Studies relating concentration and prices include de Podwin and Selden [67], and Weiss [245].

9. Studies relating concentration and wages include Weiss [244] and Allen [5].

10. Studies relating concentration and advertising include Telser [228], Comanor and Wilson [53, 54], and Weiss [247].

11. Studies relating concentration and research and development measures include Horowitz [109], Markham [151], Hamberg [101], Schmookler [201], Scherer [198, 199], and Comanor [52].

12. Studies relating concentration and productivity include Terleckyj [230], Kendrick [124], Bock [33], Bock and Farkas [34] and Mueller [169]. For fundamental analysis of investment behavior and derived productivity analysis see Jorgenson [118], Eisner and Nadiri [75], and Jorgenson and Griliches [119].

13. In this summary treatment some details are, of course, omitted.

14. This point is developed further in the discussion of our own empirical findings.

15. Cf. Williamson [260], also Weston [254].

16. Some basic references on econometrics include Christ [47], Malinvaud [144], Wonnacott and Wonnacott [265], Dhrymes [65], and Theil [231].

17. Econometric models of the U.S. economy include the Brookings Model, discussed in Duesenberry et. al., Eds. [69]; the Wharton-EFU model discussed in Klein and Evans [126] and in Evans [77] and the FRB-MIT—Penn Model discussed in Rasche and Shapiro [189], and de Leeuw and Gramlich [66]. For a survey of macroeconometric models including models of the U.S. and other countries see Nerlove [178].

18. In the Brookings model of the U.S. economy, the overall model is composed of certain "blocks" and the entire structure is "block recursive." The method of estimation is to separately estimate individual blocks and then reestimate the complete model to obtain consistent estimators. See Duesenberry, Klein, Fromm, and Kuh [69]. Thus present quantitative studies of industrial organization, to the extent that they are not reestimated in the larger framework, give *inconsistent* estimators. The estimation of a single equation from a simultaneous equation system in general results in biased and inconsistent estimators, e.g., estimates of the marginal propensity to consume from a single equation consumption function. See the references cited in footnote 16.

19. By no means is the approach presented here the *only* econometric approach to industrial organization. For other econometric approaches see Mueller [168] and Grabowski and Mueller [92].

20. For econometric studies of production functions see Walters [240] and Brown, ed. [36].

21. For econometric studies of cost functions see Johnston [117] and Walters [240].

22. For econometric studies of demand functions see Wold and Jureen [264] and Houthakker and Taylor [110].

23. Some of the previous studies of these decisions are cited above in Footnotes 3-12. Some of the macroeconometric models used in Footnote 17

present comparable decisions at a more aggregative level. Thus, the Brookings model includes price formation equations and labor requirement equations for six sectors.

24. These relationships were formulated with clarity by Pashigian [181].

Chapter 3
Concentration and Profits: Does Concentration Matter?

1. Eliot Jones, for example, remarks that, "In 1904 there were some seventy-five independent refiners all told . . . . Had the total independent output been concentrated in a few large refineries, competition with the Standard Oil Company would have been much more vigorous and successful." THE TRUST PROBLEM IN THE UNITED STATES [59] (1929). George Stigler has pointed out that, "When the Sherman Act . . . was passed in 1890, most economists and most non-economists believed that an industry with a modest number of firms could be tolerably competitive." "The Changing Problem of Oligopoly," Proceedings of the Mont Pelerin Society Three (1966).

2. "The key to the situation is the position of the consumers, rather than that of the producers. Has every consumer a choice of efficient and independent producers to buy from? If so, there is no monopoly, even if one combination should control three quarters of the output." J.B. Clark and J.M. Clark, THE CONTROL OF TRUSTS 184-5 (1912).

3. H.R. Seager, INTRODUCTION TO ECONOMICS 150 (1905); C.J. Bullock, INTRODUCTION TO THE STUDY OF ECONOMICS 178 (1908); F.W. Taussig, PRINCIPLES OF ECONOMICS i, 53-55 (1915); E.R.A. Seligman, PRINCIPLES OF ECONOMICS 345 (1921).

4. J.B. Clark, THE CONTROL OF TRUSTS 13 (1901).

5. Eliot Jones, op. cit. 538-540.

6. Inasmuch as no failures were included in the thirty-five consolidations examined since only those with ten years history of earnings were included in the sample, the decline in earnings is underestimated.

7. Simons spoke out strongly against concentration largely to offset the drive in government and the press at that time to force independent firms into cartels (as under NRA) and combinations [213. p. 72].

8. Horizontal mergers of large groups of firms may overconcentrate an industry for efficient operation, as appears to have been the case in the turn of the century merger wave. However, such overconcentration appears to be a *temporary* phenomenon, judging by the experience of these amalgamations. Of those merging a majority of the capacity in their industries, 40.4 percent failed and 6.4 percent went through voluntary financial reorganization. Shaw Livermore "The Success of Industrial Mergers," 50 QUARTERLY JOURNAL OF ECONOMICS at 75 (1935-36).

Of those which escaped this fate, most appear to have lost market share rather quickly. Of the few who lost market share slowly, some were broken up by dissolution decrees. However, even these were dropping in share before they were dissolved. American Tobacco, formed in 1890 with 91 percent of the cigarette market, declined to 83.6 percent in 1893. It acquired additional companies in 1894 and 1895 which brought it back to 85.6 percent of the market, but then dropped to 80.9 percent in 1896. Continued acquisitions brought it back to 93 percent in 1899. This position faded rather quickly to 75.9 percent in 1903. [U.S. Bureau of Corporations. REPORT OF THE COMMISSIONER ON THE TOBACCO INDUSTRIES 329 (1909)]. Similarly, Standard Oil's share of market declined from 88.15 percent in 1899 to 83.38 percent in 1904 to 67.10 percent in 1909 despite acquisitions during this period; Ralph W. & Muriel E. Hidy, PIONEERING IN BIG BUSINESS (1955) for data on Standard's crude runs to stills.

9. Richard Posner indicates that limits on market share above which mandatory deconcentration would be applied would result in *less* competitive behavior. "The threat of dissolution may . . . have a serious discentive effect. Firms may hold back from expanding sales to the point at which they would become subject to dissolution under the statute, even if they are more efficient than their competitors" [186].

Chapter 4
Industry Structure, Market Rivalry
and Public Policy

*We acknowledge with appreciation the inclusion of this paper by permission of R.H. Coase, Editor of the *Journal of Law and Economics* in which the Demsetz paper will be forthcoming.
**The author wishes to thank the Research Program in Competition and Public Policy at U.C.L.A. for financial and professional assistance in the preparation of this manuscript.

1. This difference in profitability was called to my attention by Professor R.H. Coase.

2. Let $D(P)$ represent market demand and let there be n firms that initially share this output equally, each firm's share being Q/n. Assume that one of these firms increases its output by q units, each of the other firms continuing to produce Q/n. The output of the one firm which expands can be written

$$Q/n + q = D(P) - \frac{n-1}{n} Q$$
$$q = D(P) - Q.$$

The derivative with respect to price yields

$$\frac{dq}{dp} = D'(P) - \frac{dQ}{dp}.$$

In the absence of rivalry, however, $\frac{dQ}{dp} = 0$. The slope of the demand curve facing a single firm always is identical to the slope of the market demand curve if other firms do not respond to the price change. The elasticity of the firm's demand curve is

$$\frac{dq}{dp} \frac{pn}{Q} = D'(P) \frac{pn}{q}$$

$$= n \text{ times the market elasticity of demand.}$$

3. The best rationale, in terms of information cost, for using concentration as an index of collusion is given by Stigler [204]. But even in this treatment, very high concentration, so high that it is rarely observed, is required before significant improvements in the ability to collude are achieved, and the Stigler paper does not analyze the effect of entry on collusion.

4. A detailed discussion of the implicit notion of team production that underlies these arguments can be found in A.A. Alchian and H. Demsetz, "Production, Information Costs, and Economic Organization," AER (forthcoming).

5. For a discussion of the social costs that might be incurred by deconcentration, especially in the context of scale economies, see McGee [159].

6. This statement is incorrect if a deconcentration or anti-merger policy causes firms to adopt socially less efficient methods of colluding than would be adopted in the absence of such a policy.

7. Since firms are segregated by absolute size, for some industries the R_3 firms will be relatively large. A better test could be secured by contrasting the rates of return for the 10 percent largest and 10 percent smallest firms in each industry. But the data do not allow such a comparison.

8. On the margin of output, however, these large firms need not have an advantage over small firms, just as fertile land has no advantage over poor land for producing marginal units. The failure of the large firms to become more dominant in these industries suggests the absence of such advantage.

9. Three adjustments in procedure and invariables were undertaken to analyze certain problems in the data and the theory.

(1) It is believed by some that the profits of firms, and especially of small firms, is hidden in administrative wages. To check on the possibility that this phenomenon might have accounted for the data relationships shown above, the data were recalculated after adding back to profits all administrative salaries of

firms in the R_1 asset size class. Although this increased very slightly the rates of return for this asset size class, as, of course, must be the case, no correlation between concentration and rate of return was produced. In fact, rates of return so calculated were virtually perfectly correlated with the rates of return shown above for this asset size.

(2) The asset size categories used to calculate the above data are uniform over all industries. Some industries, however, had no firms in the largest asset size category, and these were dropped from the sample. An alternative method was used to check on the impact of this procedure. For each industry, the largest asset size class was redefined so as to include some firms in every industry. The mechanics of the procedure was to categorize asset sizes more finely and choose the largest three size categories containing some observations for each industry. These were then counted as the larger firms in each industry, and the rate of return for these firms was then compared to those firms contained in the three smaller asset size categories containing some observations. The unweighted average difference between large firm rate of return, R_L, and small firm rate of return, R_S, compared with industry concentration is shown below. The table is consistent with the text tables.

C_{63}	$R_L - R_S$
0–20%	6.4%
20–30	9.4
30–40	7.0
40–50	7.0
50–60	12.8
over 60	14.0

(3) The efficiency argument suggests that for a given degree of industry concentration, measured by the four firm concentration ratio, the greater the difference between the sizes of the largest firms and the sizes of the smallest firms, the larger will be the disparity between R_4 and R_1. A linear regression of $R_4 - R_1$ on C_{63} and the average size of firms in the R_4 class yields a positive but not highly significant coefficient for the variable "average asset size of firms in the R_4 class." Also, there was a small reduction in the significance of the coefficient of C_{63}.

Chapter 5
The Concentration Profit Relationship

*For a more complete statement of the position summarized by Professor Preston in the brief comment he kindly permitted us to include in this volume see references [49, 50, 51, 188].

Chapter 6
Concentration and Profits

*The comments of J. Fred Weston, Sam Peltzman and Harold Demsetz are gratefully acknowledged. This study was supported by the Research Program in Competition and Business Policy, UCLA.

1. This position is widely held. See, e.g., [257]. As one leading proponent has stated: "I think that practically all observers are now convinced that there is something to the traditional hypothesis . . . I doubt that we need many more general concentration-profit studies." Leonard Weiss, [248, p. 193].

2. Some evidence of this is seen in William A. Jordon, AIRLINE REGULATION IN AMERICA, (Baltimore: Johns Hopkins Press, 1970).

3. Firms were matched with SIC industries by consulting Annual Editions of: MOODY'S INDUSTRIAL MANUAL, (New York: Moody's Investors Services); MILLION DOLLAR DIRECTORY, (New York: Dun & Bradstreet); and STANDARD AND POOR'S INDUSTRY SURVEYS.

4. Certain variables are included because of significance in other studies, rather than on strong theoretical grounds. Since there is controversy over which set of variables is more appropriate, the reader can choose his subset from the correlation matrix for purposes of analysis. However, for the most likely subsets of variables, the conclusions remain the same.

5. In recent studies Hall and Weiss find a positive relation while a negative relation is found in J.M. Samuels and D.J. Smyth, "Profits, Variability of Profits, and Firm Size," ECONOMICA, 35 (May 1968), pp. 127-139.

6. Clearly, it is unanticipated changes in demand and cost that change profit. Only percentage changes in both variables are examined in this study. Variations about the trend are being examined in a forthcoming study.

7. This is the conventional expectation of unanticipated changes in demand on profit. Clearly costs can rise to offset increased demand or new entrants can reduce profit rates.

8. Changes in material cost is only available in census years and is not included.

9. This information is available in U.S. Bureau of the Census, CENSUS OF MANUFACTURERS, 1958, Washington, Government Printing Office, (1962).

10. Since the same interest rate is applied to all profit rates only the ratio of market to book value is required for cross-section analysis. However, the three periods were subsequently pooled, requiring use of interest rates.

11. Logarithmic forms were also tested yielding similar results and therefore are not presented.

12. Geographic dispersion is not included due to its insignificance.

13. The simple correlation coefficients between concentration and economies of scale in production for the three years are +0.654, +0.671, and +0.690,

all highly significant at the 0.01 level. Hence, the concentration coefficient may be insignificant due to this condition of collinearity, so economies of scale in production as well as entry capital requirements were removed to discover the effect on concentration.

14. The relationship was also tested using absolute size of firm and no significant relationship appeared.

15. Some previous studies have indicated that profit rates and size rise monotomically up to a certain size level, then profit rates decline slightly and level off as size increases. H.O. Stekler, PROFITABILITY AND SIZE OF FIRM (Berkeley: University of California Press, 1963).

16. This observation clearly holds for 1950 and 1960 results, but the 1955 results are somewhat obscured by the high correlation between entry capital requirements and the capital-labor ratio. When the capital-labor ratio is removed from the regression in 1955, entry capital requirements become significant at the 0.01 level under P_2 and shift from a negative to a positive but insignificant coefficient under P_1. However, in general, it appears to have little influence on profit rates.

17. The immediate question is whether this regression is spurious or reflects the expected relationship noted above; that is, large economies of scale and high capital requirements lead to a small number of firms controlling output. Comanor and Wilson [53] find an even stronger relationship (approximately 80 percent of variation in concentration is explained by economies of scale in production and entry capital requirements) in their study but are skeptical of the high correlation since (1) merger activity may be higher in high barrier industries and (2) the measure of scale economies used is related to plant concentration, which may be expected to be correlated with firm concentration and thus conclude the relationship is probably spurious. They expect that industries where average plant size for leading firms is large relative to the total market have high four-firm concentration ratios. The former basis lacks empirical support and there is some evidence contradicting the latter. Ralph Nelson [177] found that the level of plant concentration bears little relation to the level of firm concentration. Furthermore, he found that the average plant size of leading firms was not positively related to firm concentration, but, in fact, large leading firm plant size was more commonly associated with low than with high concentration industries. However, there is a more serious problem with this measure of economies of scale. It is strongly related to the number of firms in an industry which, in turn, is highly related to concentration for purely tautological reasons.

18. Using a subsample of 48 firms covering 13 consumer good industries for which advertising data was available, for 1954-1955 and 1959-1960, produced the following regressions with t-values in parentheses

1955:
$$P_1 = 3.1496 + .1582ESP + .0331\,Ad/S \qquad R^2 = .20$$
$$ (2.89) \qquad\quad (0.28)$$

$$P_2 = 10.9333 + .3188\,ESP - .1662\,Ad/S \qquad R^2 = .08$$
$$(1.87) \qquad\qquad (-0.45)$$

1960:
$$P_1 = 4.2381 + 0.2475\,ESP + 0.3147\,Ad/S \qquad R^2 = 0.26$$
$$(2.26) \qquad\qquad (1.23)$$

$$P_2 = 7.7812 + 0.2958\,ESP + 0.1961\,Ad/S \qquad R^2 = 0.15$$
$$(1.88) \qquad\qquad (0.53)$$

The advertising to sales ratio Ad/S, is not significant in any case while economies of scale in production is significant at the 0.05 level using P_1 and at the 0.10 level using P_2. It should be noted these results are opposite those of Comanor and Wilson who found economies of scale to be insignificant and advertising-sales significant. For further results see, [179].

Chapter 7
ROI Planning and Control as a Dynamic Management System

1. The companies interviewed include the following: A&P, Alcoa, American Can, Beckman Industries, Boeing, Borg-Warner, Douglas Aircraft, du Pont, Everest and Jennings, Fluor, Ford, General Foods, General Electric, General Motors, General Precision, Goodyear, Gulf, Hughes Aircraft, IBM, International Harvester, Johns Manville, Kennecott Copper, Kroger, Lear-Siegler, Litton, Lockheed, Mattel, National Cash Register, National Steel, North American Aviation, Northrup, Pabst Brewing, Purex, Reynolds Metal, Radio Corporation of America, Revell, Reynolds Metals, Robertshaw Controls, Sears Roebuck, Standard Oil (Indiana) Standard Oil (N.J.), Statham Instruments, Swift, Tridair Industries, U.S. Steel, Union Carbide, Whittaker, Xerox.

2. This has caused a confusion by writers such as Galbraith [85] in associating planning with control. The present exposition will seek to clarify the relationship.

3. Management by objectives (MBO) involves processes similar to return on investment (ROI) planning and control.

4. Surprisingly, although du Pont began to develop and utilize the system before 1910, there was no description in the literature of the du Pont system's details until after the late 1940s, Kline and Hessler [127]. Even the early presentations covered only the mechanical aspects of the system. The concepts were not really brought alive until Alfred Sloan's book in 1964. My own understanding was not developed until after a number of direct interviews, including a presentation in the Chart Room of the du Pont Company in Wilmington, Delaware, and a rereading of Sloan's book after a number of my field studies were completed. In addition, to confusion about its implications,

there is also misunderstanding about the system itself. This is reflected in Dearden [60] where the "case against ROI control" is directed against its static, not its dynamic, elements.

5. In highly dynamic departments the forecast review may be monthly and even weekly.

6. In their research on implementation of the management by objectives approach, Carroll and Tosi found that frequency of review is highly related to goal clarity and indices of organizational effectiveness. Their attempts to quantify the quality of the review process yielded less conclusive results. S.J. Carroll, Jr., and Henry L. Tosi, "The Relationship of Characteristics of the Review Process to the Success of the 'Management by Objectives' Approach," JOURNAL OF BUSINESS 44 (July 1971) pp. 299-305.

7. When the learning aspects of the dynamic control system are taken into account, it is sobering to reflect upon persistent differentials in organization effectiveness that may have been caused by the considerable lag in the adoption of modern management control methods in a large number of large American corporations.

8. "Lighting a Fire Under the Sleeping Giant," BUSINESS WEEK, September 12, 1970, p. 41. The foregoing quotation suggests that the process orientation of the effective utilization of ROI planning and control has become bureaucratized and mechanized in du Pont itself.

9. Ibid, p. 40.

10. Ibid.

11. Ibid.

Chapter 9
Resource Allocation in the
General Electric Company

*The developing planning process described in this paper will be seen in different perspectives by different General Electric executives who will not necessarily concur with all the views expressed by the author. The planning process is described at the interface between headquarters and operations and no effort is made to describe the planning interface between executive management and the board of directors.

Chapter 10
Experimental Decision Making in the
Theory of the Firm

*This study was supported by the Research Program in Competition and Business Policy, UCLA.

1. See, especially, Baumol [23], Marris [155] and Williamson [259].

2. Constraint equation (2) is formed as an equality since the vector is taken to include "organizational or resource slack" variables in the sense of the Cyert and March [55, pp. 36-38] definition, see also Williamson [259, Chapter 3]. Specifically, let the original form of the constraint be $h(\hat{z}) < 0$ where h is an M-vector of functions and $\hat{z}$ is an (N-M)-vector. Define the M-vector of organizational slack variables $s = [z_1^2, z_2^2, \ldots, z_M^2]^T$. Make s a variable of the problem to be determined such that $h(\hat{z}) + s = 0$. The $z_i - i = 1, 2, \ldots, M$—are squared in s and that it is consequently not necessary to consider additional sign constraints. Simply rewrite this constraint by an appropriate change of notation as $f(z) = 0$ and suitably redefine the objective function g. Such slack is a rent paid organizational units to facilitate decentralization and subsequent control.

3. Dearborn and Simon [58] clearly set forth particular evidence of this "bounded rationality." It should be emphasized that uncertainties in the firm's economic processes can also lead to decentralization, but only (deterministic) problem size and complexity are explicitly considered to be causal here.

4. The firm does not establish target (transfer) prices for its internal activities as is more conventional in decentralization schemes. Rather, the targets are assigned to such quantities as profits, return-on-investment or sales, which are herein referred to as resource variables.

5. The firm's original problem require $N + M$ variables (x, y, w, λ) be solved for simultaneously. After decentralization the policy level controller is concerned only with N_x variables (x^*), subunit 2 at the operations level simply with $N_y + M_1$ variables ($y, \hat{\lambda}$) and subunit 2 at the operations level with $2N_x + N_w + M_2$ variables (μ, x, w, η). Clearly each subunit's activity might be further reduced in size by a reiteration of the above scheme.

6. The "o" superscript attached to these variables indicates that they are intermediate "optimal" values premised on current target level assignments, x^*. The $\mu^0, \lambda^0, w^0, n^0$, and y^0 will change as the second-level control adaptively adjusts x^*. As will be clear later, it is this functional dependence on assigned targets which allows the firm's second-level to fully manage the firm by the use of a relatively small set of variables.

7. It should be emphasized that this is only one possible behavioral mode for such adaptation. It, however, is a widely observed form, see Cyert and March [55, p. 34]. Other strategies could easily be devised; for example, to minimize the stages required to achieve a particular level of convergence in the values of policy target variables.

8. Note that if organizational or resource slack variables had not been introduced, then $\partial G/\partial \lambda = f_1(x, w)$ would not necessarily be set to zero by the unit 1 operation nor would $\partial G/\partial \mu = f_2(x, y)$ be necessarily zero by unit 2's activities. Subsequently, the firm's policy target adaptation procedures would need to be more complex. This simplification of the overall management process is the same role Cyert and March give to slack. As must be clear, in using the organization slack concept the assumption is made that the rent paid to the

operational units, measured by the sum of values taken on by the slack variables, is less than the increased cost of the policy-level control and, further, less than the cost of using the market price mechanism for negotiating such services, see Coase [48].

9. It should be noted that the larger the value of k, the larger will be the adjustment jumps in the targets, dx^*. Concomitantly, a large k will also increase the chance of over-reaction errors, as is clear in the simple example in the appendix.

Chapter 11
Pricing Behavior of Large Firms

1. In a comprehensive survey of some sixty British and U.S. studies of price determination [210], Professor Silberston finds the evidence inconclusive with respect to full-cost or target pricing policy versus the application of marginal principles. Silberston appears to favor an emphasis on a full-cost approach in the initial procedures for assembling the cost information for pricing. In the processes of pricing over time, however, he recognizes important qualifications reflecting marginalist and behavioral qualifications (See also Andrew [6], Langholm [128], and Robinson [193]). A recent economic study by Eckstein and Fromm [14] also yielded mixed results. In summarizing the relative importance of cost and demand elements they state:

... While the different forms of the equations yield varying results on the relative importance of the competitive mechanism vis-a-vis oligopolistic pricing, there is pretty strong evidence that equations combining both mechanisms are superior to equations using either approach in isolation [73, p. 1171].

2. The companies interviewed include the following: A&P, Alcoa, American Can, Beckman Industries, Boeing, Borg-Warner, Douglas Aircraft, du Pont, Everest and Jennings, Fluor, Ford, General Electric, General Foods, General Motors, General Precision, Goodyear, Gulf Oil, Hughes Aircraft, IBM, International Harvester, Johns-Manville, Kennecott Copper, Kroger, Lear-Siegler, Litton, Lockheed, Mattel, National Cash Register, National Steel, North American Aviation, Northrup, Pabst Brewing, Purex, Radio Corporation of America, Revell, Reynolds Metals, Robertshaw Controls, Sears Roebuck, Standard Oil, Indiana, Standard Oil, N.J., Swift, Statham Instruments, Tridair Industries, U.S. Steel, Union Carbide, Whittaker, Xerox.

These include the twenty firms listed in [22] and twenty additional with similar characteristics (large firms in concentrated industries). Ten were small firms. Interviews with some firms were arranged by McKinsey & Co.; discussions with the others were facilitated by their participation in executive educational programs at UCLA.

3. One fundamental difference between the surveys in the Brookings Study and my own survey has important substantive implications and affected the nature of the responses. The Brookings Study surveyed sales departments and sales executives. My own survey began as a study of corporate resource allocation policy and so involved discussions with executives at corporate levels not responsible for specific management functions. From the standpoint of a specific functional area such as the sales department, operating standards or objectives become targets. From the standpoint of the corporate level, there is a continuous trade-off analysis between a wide range of variables. Pricing is only one and probably of relatively second-order importance in the hierarchy of operational standards and objectives employed by the firm.

4. The increasing importance of probabilistic economics has been empha-sized by McCall [158].

5. The two pricing rules can be expressed in the equation form used as a basis for econometric studies [73].

$$P_f = (1 + m)(ULC + UMC)$$
$$P_r = ULC + UMC + F/X + \pi K/X$$

where:

P_f	=	price per unit based on full-cost pricing formula
P_r	=	price per unit based on return-on-investment target pricing
ULC	=	unit labor cost
UMC	=	unit material cost
F	=	total fixed costs
X	=	quantity of units produced for the relevant planning horizon
K	=	investment (usually defined as total operating assets with depreciation added back)
m	=	profit markup when full-cost pricing is used
k	=	profit rate on investment, appropriately defined as earnings before interest and depreciation, when total assets are defined as above

6. Then $m = b\pi$ where b is some constant. The equivalence of the two methods can be illustrated by a numerical example. With the turnover of investment into total costs of two times and a markup on total cost of 10 percent before taxes, the return on investment before taxes would be 20 percent.

7. McCall [158] has emphasized how probabilistic economics leads to formal models of increased diversity and richness as illustrated by his references

to the work of Dhrymes, Mills, Tisdell, and Zabel. The present paper develops the implications of such uncertainty models for the behavior of firms. A dynamic general equilibrium model of investment under uncertainty is summarized to emphasize the framework within which adaptive decisions processes of firms are stimulated to optimum-seeking behavior.

8. The theory of monopolistic competition in the Chamberlinian style is also subject to this criticism of treating inherently long-run adjustment processes within a partial equilibrium framework.

9. These variables are demand-increasing costs. Demsetz [61] has shown that the interaction of pricing with demand-increasing costs leads to competitive results.

10. An example is the strategy of Alfred Sloan in the early 1920s to aim to increase General Motor's share of the market of the expense of the Model T Ford, both to sell at roughly the same price [217].

11. Another illustration of misinterpretation of the statements of businessmen is represented by the 1924 article by Donaldson Brown, who had been Vice President of Finance at both du Pont and General Motors. This article has been widely quoted by economists as evidence of the use of target rate-of-return pricing by General Motors since the early 1920s. A key quotation from Brown [37] is the following:

Thus it is apparent that the object of management is not necessarily the highest attainable rate of return on capital but rather the highest return consistent with attainable volume, care being exercised to assure profit with each increment of volume that will at least equal the economic cost of additional capital required. Therefore, the fundamental consideration is the economic cost of capital to the individual business.

This formulation cannot correctly be characterized as target return-on-investment pricing. Particularly inappropriate is its characterization as a kind of "noblesse oblige" approach to pricing in that a firm is satisfied with a just price and a just return, since providence enabled the firm to achieve a dominant position in the market (Lanzillotti [129]). Effective business strategy, efficient management organization development, and continued high level of efficiency are required to maintain a market position. Brown's statement represents a decision rule that an investment should not be undertaken unless its expected return exceeds the firm's relevant incremental cost of capital, taking the appropriate degree of risk into account [163].

12. It is in this framework that the sales maximization hypothesis of Baumol [23] should appropriately be viewed. The objective of sales maximization was expressed by businessmen on the assumption that investments had been committed and, therefore, sales maximization would result in favorable capacity utilization. Without special assumptions, sales maximization will not maximize share price.

13. In less effective management organizations, rules begin to take on a life of their own, and the formal processes begin to reflect some rigidities associated with the rules. These rigidities represent a pathological condition, not characteristic of companies with good performance records.

14. A formal development of the role of adaptive behavior in moving from various satisfying levels to wealth maximization has been made by Clement G. Krouse, "Multiple Objectives and Adaptive Decision-Making in the Theory of the Firm" (MS).

15. "For purposes of studying behavior in the monopoly sector where conditions of discretion frequently prevail, the discretion models may often be the most appropriate: they provide a fruitful and orderly way with which to structure a broad range of monopoly practices" [258, pp. 170-171].

16. The theory postulates maximization with respect to nondiscretionary expenditures; individual goals are substituted for organization goals with respect to discretionary expenditures—managerial staff and "other perquisites" [258].

17. Williamson's regression analysis [258, pp. 132-3] of executive compensation with general and administrative expenses, concentration, entry barrier level, and percentage of managers to the total board membership is not conclusive. The direction of causality of the omitted profit variable is not "obvious."

18. This has been recognized in more recent writing in the behavioral tradition as an important function of the headquarters staff in contributing to the superior efficiencies of the multidivisional form of firm organization [260].

19. The discretionary behavior theory also implicitly assumes separation of owner and managerial control. In a multiple regression analysis Lewellen and Huntsman [134] have found a significant net relation between executive compensation and profits, but no significant net relation between executive compensation and sales. This suggests that the traditional view of divergence of owner and managerial interests is not supported by the evidence.

20. Ironically, it is extremely difficult to obtain information on cost accounting procedures and standard cost systems from individual firms because such information is regarded as highly proprietary and as being of great potential value to competitors.

21. "And, to repeat, rivalry continues in advertising, product improvement, gadgetry and the like where it is not destructive. The automboile industry with three large and strong firms and one weaker one is cited more often than any other as the classical manifestation of oligopoly" [85, p. 911]. In the statement in which Galbraith argues that there is absence of "destructive" rivalry, he also refers to the few survivors of an industry in which hundreds of firms had existed in earlier years and which since 1950 has witnessed the disappearance of Nash and Hudson (into American Motors) and the "destruction" of the Studebaker and Packard motor car companies. Galbraith's assertions are internally inconsistent.

Chapter 12
Organizing to Supply Nuclear Energy

1. MW signifies megawatts, a standard measure of generating capacity.

Chapter 13
Product Line Pricing and Technological Change:
The Case of Sophisticated Electrical Machinery

*This study was supported solely by the Division of Research of the Harvard Graduate School of Business Administration.

1. See "The Third Step for Westinghouse" BUSINESS WEEK, October 2, 1971.

2. The determination of the average price level in the marketplace is another issue, not addressed in this present paper.

3. These prices applied to tandem-compound turbine-generators operating at 2400 pounds steam pressure, and $1000°$ to $1050°$ Fahrenheit steam temperatures.

4. The terminology "tipping the curve" originates with managers in this industry.

5. Over the 1925-63 period.

6. December, 1958, Ebasco Services Inc., Utility Executive Conference, Electrical cases litigation, national exhibit 2NX-411.

Chapter 14
The Conglomerate and Conventional Microtheory

*This paper sets forth some of the research results soon to appear in Jesse W. Markham, CONGLOMERATE ENTERPRISE AND PUBLIC POLICY Division of Research, Harvard Graduate School of Business Administration, Harvard University Press.

1. The several pages that follow were adapted from an earlier article. (Markham [152]).

2. A more detailed treatment of the models supporting this proposition may be found in Palda [180].

3. For a detailed discussion of these hypotheses Cf. Markham [152].

4. See Vaupel and Curhan [235].

5. Berry's index is defined as $D = 1 - \sum_{i=1}^{n} (P_i)^2$ where P is the percentage of the firm's employment in each two-digit, or four-digit industry. The values of D vary from nearly one for the very highly diversified firm to zero for the single

two-digit, or four-digit firm. *Cf.* Charles H. Berry, "Corporate Growth and Diversification," JOURNAL OF LAW AND ECONOMICS 14 (October 1971) 371-384.

6. Since these data were analyzed it has been possible to ascertain the four-digit SIC industry for acquired firms, 1961-70, thus permitting an analysis of changes in concentration using the Census of Manufactures' familiar concentration ratios. The preliminary results lead to essentially the same conclusions as those set forth here.

7. However, as explained in fn. 6, Supra., the conclusions derivable from four-digit and three-digit concentration data are essentially the same.

8. ECONOMIC CONCENTRATION AND THE MONOPOLY PROBLEM (Cambridge: Harvard University Press, 1957) p. 368.

Chapter 15
Tests of the Efficiency Performance
of Conglomerate Firms

*Research support was provided by the Research Program in Competition and Business Policy, UCLA. Helpful comments were received from A.A. Alchian, M. Goudzwaard, N.H. Jacoby, R.H. Mason and K. Smith. Research assistants participating in data compilation included: Kent Alves, Scott Dittrich, Jorge Ramos, Whitt Jones and Nanci Grottke. Ronald Shrieves carried a major responsibility in the computer calculations. A somewhat different version of this chapter appeared in the JOURNAL OF FINANCE of September 1971 with a reply by Samuel R. Reid. Comments by other writers as well as by Professor Reid, along with our rejoinders, appeared in later issues of the JOURNAL OF FINANCE.

1. See Fama [78], Lintner [137], Markowitz [154], Sharpe [208], and Tobin [232].

2. A useful sample would include Girt [88, 89], Mueller [167], Narver [173, 174], Reid [192], Stone [226], Udell [234], Weston [250, 252], Weston & Peltzman [249] and 32 papers in the Spring 1970 Edition of the ST. JOHN'S LAW REVIEW [227].

3. Some of the relevant papers are Asch [12], Bicks [28], Blair [29], Bock [31, 32], Day [57], Patterson [183], Turner [215] and 18 items in [227].

4. Various aspects are treated in Ansoff [7, 8], Berg [26], Weston [251] and in a number of management journal articles.

5. See especially the discussion in STUDIES BY THE STAFF OF THE CABINET COMMITTEE ON PRICE STABILITY [42], pp. 69-81; see also [88] with the introductory statements by Senator Philip A. Hart of Michigan and by members of the Federal Trade Commission.

6. The 1171-page special edition of the ST. JOHN'S LAW REVIEW on conglomerate mergers contains no article with empirical data on the comparative performance of conglomerate firms [227]. Two empirical articles in the volume deal with other aspects of performance. The S.E. Boyle paper analyzes the pre-merger growth and profitability characteristic of acquired companies. The paper by T.F. Hogarty reviews earlier historical studies of the success of mergers generally.

7. Kelley [123].

8. Hogarty [107].

9. The sample is relatively small and subject to some other questions. Twenty-eight of forty-two firms had pre-merger sales growth at least as large as their respective industries, but fourteen (one-third) therefore did not. The median difference was 13 percent and the mean difference was 31 percent—the same magnitude of difference in investment performance was classified as "failure." Finally, some of the mergers were "marriages of necessity" because one or both partners before the merger had been experiencing substantial pre-merger managerial or competitive difficulties. Well-known examples include American Motors and Hudson Motor Car, Smith Corona and Marchant Calculators involved in the formation of SCM, and Carpenter Steel and Northeastern Steel (in reorganization at the time of acquisition).

10. Heiden [105].

11. Gort and Hogarty [90].

12. Lorie and Halpern [138].

13. Since this kind of "funny money" (Lorie and Halpern's term) was alleged to be characteristic of conglomerate mergers, their sample of firms is presumed to be of "conglomerates." However, no formal criteria for selection were employed.

14. Smith and Schreiner [218].

15. Myers [172].

16. The Heiden and Reid studies ended in 1961, the Kelly and Hogarty studies ended in 1963 and 1964, respectively. The conglomerate merger movement did not really get underway until the mid-1960s, and peaked in 1967 and 1968. In fact, a fair test of the conglomerate merger movement is possible not even today since a number of additional years would be required for implementation of the strategies associated with these corporate development programs.

17. For a more complete discussion, see Weston [250, 252].

18. For further development of these criteria see Weston [250, pp. 52-54].

19. Previous studies have not employed analytical criteria for identification of conglomerate firms. Hence this paper sets forth the selection criteria explicitly.

20. We relied on a number of sources to provide candidates for potential inclusion in our study including the Federal Trade Commission reports and a number of lists compiled by financial magazines and brokerage firms.

21. These were computed from the growth in total assets between the year of acquisition and the terminal 1968 date from the Federal Trade Commission Securities and Exchange Commission QUARTERLY FINANCIAL REPORT ON INDUSTRIAL CORPORATIONS or national income generated in the industrial category from the national income statistics of the United States Department of Commerce as reported in various issues of the SURVEY OF CURRENT BUSINESS. We sought to employ the three-digit standard industrial classification category where available.

22. The FORTUNE PRODUCT DIRECTORY was the main source of data. Where information was not otherwise available, we sought on a judgment basis to determine the degree of diversification through review of the product descriptions and descriptions of the nature of subsidiaries provided in the annual investment manual, MOODY'S INDUSTRIALS. In contrast to the procedure in the FTC's report on mergers, we did not include a company where the firm was involved in only one major merger *and* where at the end of the period the firm did not meet our *Screening Rule #2* with regard to the degree of diversification.

23. Some firms which passed our *Screening Rule #2* were not utilized in the final study because of unavailability of required data.

24. The companies that had already been included in the conglomerate group were excluded. We did not, however, in order to avoid bias, exclude the companies that had already been picked in our *Random Sample #1*. Five companies appeared in both samples. The firms in the three samples are listed in Tables 15-10, 15-11, and 15-12 at the end of this chapter.

25. Since we did not attach great importance to the findings of our growth measures, the selection of the period 1958-68 was determined by the ready availability of data from standard financial information sources. We also used the period 1960-68 since 1960 was the initial year in some studies reported in the Federal Trade Commission Report on Mergers [81]. Both initial years are years of depressed business activity, while 1968 was a year of inflationary growth. However, data for our control samples covered the same period.

26. The growth figures utilized in the averages were obtained by calculating a compound annual rate of increase between the initial years and the terminal years. Such a measure of growth may give undue weight to either the initial or terminal year. There are three considerations justifying this method of calculating growth rates: (1) Since all the growth measures are averaged over some sixty companies, random influences on growth measures will tend to be averaged out; (2) the same procedures were utilized for the conglomerate firms as for the two random samples of firms; (3) comparative measures of average growth rates were not the central emphasis of the study.

27. For the weighted averages, the sums of the individual items for each company were calculated for the initial and terminal years. The ratios of the terminal to initial year sums were used to calculate the growth rates expressed in compound annual percentages. For the other three measures of central tendency, the compound annual growth rates were computed for each company.

These were then used to calculate by standard statistical procedures, the median, the "unweighted arithmetic mean," and the geometric mean. All averages are, of course, "weighted" implicitly. We judged the median to be the measure of central tendency least subject to haphazard weighting for these data.

28. For a precise measure, we would deduct non-interest-bearing liabilities from total assets and then calculate the ratio of earnings before interest and taxes or earnings before interest alone to total assets minus non-interest bearing liabilities. However, since the non-interest-bearing liabilities do not ordinarily represent a large percentage of total assets, for comparing groups of companies it is more convenient to take the ratios to total assets.

29. See, for example, AMERICAN ECONOMIC REVIEW, LVI (June 1968), pp. 333-391.

30. Preferred stock is a hybrid security. In that the return on preferred stock is typically limited, it gives the common shareholders of the company an opportunity for leverage in addition to that achieved by the use of debt. On the other hand, since the dividends on the preferred stock do not represent a fixed obligation, the nonpayment of which constitutes a technical default leading to bankruptcy, it does not involve the degree of risk in a leverage measure that debt represents. In addition, the existence of preferred stock as a security junior to all forms of debt represents an additional cushion reducing the risk of common stockholders. Hence from the standpoint of creditors, preferred stock represents net worth. From the standpoint of the common stockholders of the company, however, preferred stock represents an additional element by which the income to common stock may be leveraged. Therefore definitions of net worth including and excluding preferred stock were employed.

31. In Table 15-3, for the weighted averages, the numerators and the denominators are summed separately; the totals are used to calculate the ratios. For all of the other measures of central tendency, the ratios are first calculated, then used in the standard statistical procedures for determining the three other measures of central tendency.

32. In analyzing the data on preferred stock, we noted a substantial disparity between the stated balance sheet values of preferred stock for the conglomerate firms and estimates of more realistic values of the preferred stocks based on prevailing dividend yields, call prices or liquidating values. For 1968 we calculated adjusted earnings rates on total assets, adding to the total assets of each of the three sets of companies, the difference between our estimate of an appropriate balance sheet value of preferred stock and the stated value. As shown in Table 15-4, the differences in the earning power among the three groups of companies remained nonsignificant.

33. If the price/earnings ratio was greater than one-hundred times, or a negative multiple of fifty or more, we excluded it in the second set of calculations.

34. The second set of price/earnings ratios, including the large negative ratios

for some of the conglomerate firms, raised the average for the remaining conglomerates somewhat above the average price/earnings ratios of the other two samples. However, the differences in the means remained nonsignificant.

35. Other aspects of a theory of the timing of the conglomerate mergers movement are discussed in Weston [250, pp. 50-52].

36. This could also be expressed as changing the product market mix of the firm's portfolio of capital budgets. Again, from the standpoint of the economy as a whole, it would make no difference whether investors provided their own diversification or whether the individual firms achieved diversification, under the assumptions of no bankruptcy costs and no costs of rebuilding an effective organization.

37. An elaboration of how the conglomerate firms achieve these functions is set forth in Weston [250, 251].

38. It is probable that some individual conglomerate firms will go through reorganization or bankruptcy. This would not be inconsistent with the above proposition. The point is that more of these entities would have been forced into reorganization and bankruptcy if they had not achieved successful defensive diversification.

39. There are a number of justifications for examining the Reid [191, 192] studies in somewhat more detail. Most of the other studies dealt with the success of mergers or merging firms generally. These studies are at least indirectly relevant since if merging generally is unsuccessful for firms, by implication, the probability is that conglomerate merging would also be unsuccessful. However, the possibility also exists that the diversification and other characteristics of conglomerate mergers could also increase the probability of their success. These possibilities provide a rationale for studies focused on conglomerate merger activity.

In addition, the Reid study received considerable attention and has important public policy implications. His presentation to a subcommittee of the Senate Judiciary Committee was written up in some detail in the financial press. For example, see, "Growing from Within May Pay Off Faster," BUSINESS WEEK, (September 17, 1966), pp. 44-45. In addition, Senator Philip A. Hart, Chairman of the Subcommittee on Antitrust and Monopoly of the Committee on the Judiciary of the United States Senate, in calling for a Federal Trade Commission study of the conglomerate mergers and in his statement opening the hearings on conglomerate mergers, leaned heavily on the findings of Professor Reid's study. Senatory Hart expressed the position, as did a number of other members of government regulatory agencies, that conglomerate firms had demonstrated no economic efficiency, that in fact the contrary was true. An important public policy implication that followed was that conglomerate mergers could therefore be prohibited because there were no economic efficiency considerations against which such a policy would have to be balanced.

40. Reid [192, pp. 186-188].

41. See Reid [192, Table 9-1, p. 185].

42. See any standard textbook on business finance.

43. For details see Gupta [96].

44. FORBES, Vol. 103 (January 1, 1969), Vol. 104 (January 1, 1970).

45. The five-year growth percentages are measured by Forbes by averaging the three initial years and calculating the growth to the values for the terminal years. For example, in the January 1, 1970 issue of FORBES, the three initial years averaged were 1963, 1964 and 1965; the terminal year was 1969. The five-year growth rates for sales and earnings per share are medians of the compound annual growth rates calculated for individual companies. For market prices, the total percentage changes for the five-year periods are calculated.

46. The decline in market prices for the conglomerates was greater in 1969 than for the broader sample of firms. This was due to a number of influences, including the development of adverse government attitudes, reflected in tax law changes along with a number of antitrust suits and threats. Also, declines in earnings for individual conglomerates raised uncertainties about the others. However, for both of the five-year periods analyzed, ending in 1968 and in 1969, the five-year market performance of the multi-industry firms was more than double the growth in the market price of shares for the broader FORBES sample.

47. These differences would not be statistically significant. We did not employ statistical tests of significance to the data from FORBES, FORTUNE and NEWS FRONT because our analysis of the four types of averages indicated to us that the measure of central tendency the median *probably* was most free of distortions. The use of the median precludes the utilization of the usual statistical tests of significance. However, the pattern of behavior analyzed in detail on our own data provided us with a judgmental basis for evaluating the significance of the differences. The 50 percent or more superiority of the conglomerate firms on the five-year increase in sales, the increases in earnings per share growth for the later years, and the gains in market price through 1969 leaves no doubt that these differences were significant. The small differences in the return on total assets or the combined return on debt and equity or the average or individual returns on equity were not significant.

48. NEWS FRONT, June-July, 1969, p. 70.

49. NEWS FRONT, June-July, 1969, p. 56. The averages computed by NEWS FRONT are the weighted arithmetic means.

50. On the one hand, if the earnings performance of the conglomerate firms had been markedly superior to industry generally, they would be subject to charges that they possessed monopoly power, as have other large firms which have achieved high profitability rates over a period of time. On the other hand, because their earnings as a group have not been significantly higher than industry generally, the conglomerate firms have been charged by their critics as not contributing to improvements in economic efficiency. Yet to improve earnings

up to the average, or to avoid falling below the average, represents a contribution to economic efficiency.

Chapter 16
Large Firms and Economic Performance

1. Henry C. Simons, "Some Reflections on Syndicalism," ECONOMIC POLICY FOR FREE SOCIETY, University of Chicago Press, 1948, p. 132: originally appeared in JOURNAL OF POLITICAL ECONOMY, March 1944, pp. 1-25. The following discussion by Simons written in 1944 constitutes a forecast of events in the steel industry during the decades of the fifties and sixties.

"Frankly, I can see no reason why strongly organized workers, in an industry where huge investment is already sunk in highly durable assets, should ever permit a return on investment sufficient to attract new capital or even to induce full maintenance of existing capital. If I were running a union and were managing it faithfully in the interest of the majority of its members, I should consistently demand wage rates which offered to existing firms no real net earnings but only the chance of getting back part of their sunk investment at the cost of the replacement outlays necessary to provide employment for most of my constituents during their own lifetimes as workers. In other words, I should plan gradually to exterminate the industry by excessive labor costs, taking care only to prevent employment from contracting more rapidly than my original constituents disappeared by death and voluntary retirement."

2. "Advertising and Charlie Brown," BUSINESS REVIEW, Federal Reserve Bank of Philadelphia, June 1962 p. 11.

3. Brozen, Yale, "An Ivory Tower (Chicago) View of Advertising," MS of presentation before the AAA Eastern Annual Conference, New York, June 5, 1972.

4. John M. Vernon, MARKET STRUCTURE AND INDUSTRIAL PERFORMANCE: A REVIEW OF STATISTICAL FINDINGS. Boston: Allyn and Bacon, 1972.

5. This sixty billion dollar figure was also used in the June 1971 draft of Report on Antitrust by the Nader Study Group headed by Mark J. Green, published under the title, THE CLOSED ENTERPRISE SYSTEM. One can do no better in appraising this study and its relationship to the subject at hand than by quoting from a review of it by Richard A. Posner (Professor of Law, University of Chicago), "Nader on Antitrust" in THE NEW REPUBLIC of June 26, 1971. Posner states:

". . . Although the authors are plainly aware of the existence of a substantial body of professional opinion opposed to many of their pet ideas the range of their references indicates that they carefully conceal the existence of alternative views. They refer extensively to my own articles on antitrust, for example, where the articles support their conclusions but one would never know from reading their study that those articles, and much other theoretical and empirical work, refute many of the Study Group's fondest notions, such as that reciprocal buying is a major menace to competitive markets . . . The weaknesses of the study are considerable, but so are the strengths. As a review of the literature on the failures of antitrust policy, the study is impressively thorough. . . . Worse than the contradictions, the tendentiousness, and the tone of the study is its superficiality. . . . Contrary to the impression that the authors sedulously cultivate, the economics profession is deeply divided on the antitrust significance of concentration and oligopoly, advertising, and product differentiation, reciprocal buying, vertical integration, diversification, and other key phenomena. If we turn our attention to the social and political consequences of monopoly, our bearings become still more uncertain." pp. 22-24.

6. The productivity performance of the utilities belies the disparaging criticisms by some economists on the effectiveness of regulation of the public utilities.

7. From unpublished, preliminary estimates by John W. Kendrick.

8. I have also indicated some costs of regulation. My own view of the regulatory process is the following: Inherently any attempt administratively to substitute for the market place involves some losses. On the other hand, it appears that regulatory policy on the average is taking advantage of the very heavy fixed costs and therefore the generally decreasing-costs characteristics of public utility operations. Utility rates are set on the basis of expectations of further growth and efficiency. Regulation has permitted economies from efficiency and growth to be retained partially by the firms, but the larger portions have been passed-on to consumers of utility services.

References

References

[1] Adelman, M., "The Measurement of Industrial Concentration, 1940-47," REVIEW OF ECONOMICS AND STATISTICS, 33 (November 1951), pp. 269-96.

[2] _____, A&P: A STUDY IN PRICE-COST BEHAVIOR AND PUBLIC POLICY, Cambridge, Mass.: Harvard University Press, 1959.

[3] Alchian, A.A., "Uncertainty, Evolution, and Economic Theory," JOURNAL OF POLITICAL ECONOMY, 58 (June 1950), pp. 211-21.

[4] Alexis, M. and Wilson, C.Z., ORGANIZATIONAL DECISION MAKING, Englewood Cliffs, N.J.: Prentice-Hall, 1967.

[5] Allen, B.T., "Market Concentration and Wage Increases: U.S. Manufacturing, 1947-64," INDUSTRIAL AND LABOR RELATIONS REVIEW, 21 (April 1968), pp. 353-66.

[6] Andrews, P.W.S., ON COMPETITION IN ECONOMIC THEORY, London: Macmillan & Co., 1964.

[7] Ansoff, H., "Strategies for Diversification," HARVARD BUSINESS REVIEW, 35 (September-October 1957), pp. 113-24.

[8] _____, "A Model for Diversification," MANAGEMENT SCIENCE, 4 (July 1958), pp. 392-414.

[9] _____ and Weston, J. Fred, "Merger Objectives and Organization Structure," QUARTERLY REVIEW OF ECONOMICS AND BUSINESS, 2 (August 1962), pp. 49-58.

[10] _____, CORPORATE STRATEGY, New York: McGraw-Hill, 1965.

[11] Asch, P., "Industry Structure and Performance: Some Empirical Evidence," REVIEW OF SOCIAL ECONOMY, 25 (March 1967), pp. 167-82.

[12] _____, "Conglomerate Mergers and Public Policy," MSU Business Topics, 15 (Winter 1967), pp. 61-7.

[13] _____ and Marcus, Matityahu, "Returns to Scale in Advertising," THE ANTITRUST BULLETIN, 15 (Spring 1970), pp. 33-42.

[14] Averch, H. and Johnson, L., "Behavior of the Firm Under Regulatory Constraint," AMERICAN ECONOMIC REVIEW, 52 (December 1962), pp. 1052-69.

[15] Backman, J., ADVERTISING AND COMPETITION, New York: New York University Press, 1967.

[16] _____, "An Analysis of the Economic Report on Corporate Mergers," Presentation to the Senate Subcommittee on Antitrust and Monopoly, January 20, 1970.

[17] Bain, J.S., "Relation of Profit Rate to Industrial Concentration: American Manufacturing 1936-40," QUARTERLY JOURNAL OF ECONOMICS, 65 (August 1951), pp. 293-324.

[18] _____, BARRIERS TO NEW COMPETITION, Cambridge, Mass.: Harvard University Press, 1956.

[19] Bain, J.S., INDUSTRIAL ORGANIZATION, New York: John Wiley & Sons, Inc., 1968, 2nd. Ed.

[20] _____, "Changes in Concentration in Manufacturing Industries in the United States, 1947-66: Trends and Relationships to the Level of 1954 Concentration," REVIEW OF ECONOMICS AND STATISTICS, 152 (November 1970), pp. 411-16.

[21] Baldwin, W., "The Motives of Managers, Environmental Restraints, and the Theory of Managerial Enterprise," QUARTERLY JOURNAL OF ECONOMICS, 78 (May, 1964), pp. 238-56.

[22] Baumol, W.J. and Quandt, R.E., "Rules of Thumb and Optimally Imperfect Decisions," AMERICAN ECONOMIC REVIEW, 54 (March 1964), pp. 23-46.

[23] _____, BUSINESS BEHAVIOR, VALUE, AND GROWTH, New York: Macmillan, 1959.

[24] _____, BUSINESS BEHAVIOR, VALUE, AND GROWTH, New York: Macmillan, 2nd Edition, 1966.

[25] Baxter, W.T. and Oxenfeldt, A.R., "Costing and Pricing: The Cost Accountant versus the Economist," in STUDIES IN COST ANALYSIS, ed., David Solomons, Homewood, Ill.: Irwin, 1968.

[26] Berg, Norman, "Strategic Planning in Conglomerate Companies," HARVARD BUSINESS REVIEW, 43 (May-June 1965), pp. 79-92.

[27] Berle, A.A., THE TWENTIETH CENTURY CAPITALIST REVOLUTION, New York: Harcourt, Brace and World, 1954.

[28] Bicks, R.A., "Conglomerates and Diversification Under Section 7 of the Clayton Act," ANTITRUST BULLETIN, 2 (November-December 1956), pp. 175-86.

[29] Blair, J.M., "The Conglomerate Merger in Economics and Law," GEORGETOWN LAW JOURNAL, 46 (Summer 1958), p. 672.

[30] _____, ECONOMIC CONCENTRATION, New York: Harcourt, Brace, and Jovanovich, 1972.

[31] Bock, B., ANTITRUST ISSUES IN CONGLOMERATE ACQUISITIONS, Studies in Business Economics, Number 110, New York: National Industrial Conference Board, 1969.

[32] _____, "Conglomerate Mergers, Joint Ventures, and Potential Competition," THE CONFERENCE BOARD RECORD, 5 (February 1968), pp. 2-6.

[33] _____, "The Concentration-Productivity Quandary," National Industrial Conference Board, THE CONFERENCE BOARD RECORD, 4 (1967), pp. 2-7.

[34] _____, and Farkas, J., CONCENTRATION AND PRODUCTIVITY, SBE No. 103, New York: The Conference Board, 1969.

[35] Bower, J., "Planning within the Firm," AMERICAN ECONOMIC REVIEW, 60 (May 1970), pp. 186-94.

[36] Brown, M., Ed., THE THEORY AND EMPIRICAL ANALYSIS OF PRODUCTION, NBER, Studies in Income and Wealth, Princeton: Princeton University Press, 1967.

[37] Brown, D., "Pricing Policy in Relation to Financial Control," MANAGEMENT AND ADMINISTRATION, 7 (February, March, April 1924), pp. 3-15.

[38] Brozen, Y., "The Antitrust Task Force Deconcentration Recommendation," THE JOURNAL OF LAW AND ECONOMICS, 13 (October 1970), pp. 279-92.

[39] _____, "Concentration and Structural and Market Disequilibrium," ANTITRUST BULLETIN, 16 (Summer 1971), pp. 241-56.

[40] _____, "The Persistence of 'High Rates of Return' in High Stable Concentration Industries," JOURNAL OF LAW AND ECONOMICS, 14 (October 1971), pp. 501-12.

[41] BUSINESS WEEK, "Bethlehem Steel's New Price Gambit," (May 9, 1970), p. 21.

[42] Cabinet Committee on Price Stability, Studies by the Staff of the Cabinet Committee on Price Stability, Washington, D.C.: U.S. Government Printing Office, 1969.

[43] Caves, R., AIR TRANSPORT AND ITS REGULATORS, Cambridge, Mass.: Harvard University Press, 1962.

[44] _____, AMERICAN INDUSTRY: STRUCTURE, CONDUCT, PERFORMANCE, Englewood Cliffs, N.J.: Prentice Hall, 1964.

[45] Chamberlain, N., THE FIRM: MICROECONOMIC PLANNING AND ACTION, New York: McGraw-Hill, 1962.

[46] Chamberlin, E., THE THEORY OF MONOPOLISTIC COMPETITION, Cambridge, Mass.: Harvard University Press, 1933.

[47] Christ, C., ECONOMETRIC MODELS AND METHODS, New York: John Wiley and Sons, 1964.

[48] Coase, R.H., "The Nature of the Firm," ECONOMICA 4 (1937), pp. 386-405.

[49] Collins, N.R. and Preston, L.E., "Concentration and Price-Cost Margins in Food Manufacturing Industries," THE JOURNAL OF INDUSTRIAL ECONOMICS, 14 (July, 1966), pp. 226-42.

[50] _____, CONCENTRATION AND PRICE-COST MARGINS IN MANUFACTURING INDUSTRIES Berkeley: University of California Press, 1968.

[51] _____, "Price-Cost Margins and Industry Structure," REVIEW OF ECONOMICS AND STATISTICS, 51 (August 1969), pp. 271-86.

[52] Comanor, W.S., "Market Structure, Product Differentiation, and Industrial Research," QUARTERLY JOURNAL OF ECONOMICS, 81 (November 1967), pp. 639-57.

[53] _____ and Wilson, T.A., "Advertising, Market Structure and Perform-

ance," REVIEW OF ECONOMICS AND STATISTICS, 49 (November 1967), pp. 423-40.

[54] _____, "Advertising and the Economics of Scale," AMERICAN ECONOMIC REVIEW, 59 (May 1969), pp. 87-98.

[55] Cyert, R.M., and March, J.G., A BEHAVIORAL THEORY OF THE FIRM, Englewood Cliffs, N.J.: Prentice-Hall, 1963.

[56] _____ and Kamien, M.I., "Behavioral Rules and the Theory of the Firm," in Phillips, A. and Williamson, O.E., Eds., PRICES: ISSUES IN THEORY, PRACTICE AND PUBLIC POLICY, Philadelphia, University of Pennsylvania Press, 1968.

[57] Day, R.E., "Conglomerate Mergers and the Curse of Bigness," NORTH CAROLINA LAW REVIEW, 42 (1964), p. 539.

[58] Dearborn, D. and Simon, H. "Selective Perception: A Note on the Departmental Identification of Executives," SOCIOMETRY, 21 (June 1958), pp. 140-44.

[59] Dearden, J. and Edgerly, W.S., "Bonus Formula for Division Heads," HARVARD BUSINESS REVIEW, 43 (September-October 1965), pp. 83-90.

[60] _____, "The Case Against ROI Control," HARVARD BUSINESS REVIEW, 47 (May-June 1969), pp. 124-35.

[61] Demsetz, H., "The Welfare and Empirical Implications of Monopolistic Competition," ECONOMIC JOURNAL, 74 (September 1964), pp. 623-641.

[62] Denison, E.F., THE SOURCES OF ECONOMIC GROWTH IN THE UNITED STATES, Supplementary Paper No. 13, published by Committee for Economic Development, January, 1962.

[63] Dewing, A.S., "A Statistical Test of the Success of Consolidations," QUARTERLY JOURNAL OF ECONOMICS, 36 (November 1971), pp. 84-101.

[64] Dewey, D., THE THEORY OF IMPERFECT COMPETITION: A RADICAL RECONSTRUCTION, New York: Columbia University Press, 1969.

[65] Dhrymes, P., ECONOMETRICS, New York: Harper and Row, 1971.

[66] deLeeuw, F. and Gramlich, E.M., "The Federal Reserve-MIT Econometric Model," FEDERAL RESERVE BULLETIN, 54 (January 1968), pp. 11-29.

[67] de Podwin, H.J. and Selden, R.T., "Business Pricing Policies and Inflation," JOURNAL OF POLITICAL ECONOMY, 71 (April 1963), pp. 110-27.

[68] Dorfman, R. and Steiner, P.O., "Optimal Advertising and Optimal Quality," AMERICAN ECONOMIC REVIEW, 54 (December 1954), pp. 826-36.

[69] Duesenberry, J., Klein, L.R., Fromm, G., and Kuh, E., Eds., THE BROOKINGS ECONOMETRIC MODEL OF THE UNITED STATES ECONOMY, Chicago: Rand-McNally, 1965.

[70] E.I. du Pont de Nemours & Co., EXECUTIVE COMMITTEE CONTROL CHARTS, Wilmington, Delaware: du Pont, 1959.

[71] Earley, J.S., "Recent Developments in Cost Accounting and the 'Marginal Analysis,' " JOURNAL OF POLITICAL ECONOMY, 63 (June 1955), pp. 227-42.

[72] Eckstein, O., "A Theory of the Wage-Price Process in Modern Industry," REVIEW OF ECONOMIC STUDIES, 31 (October 1964), pp. 267-86.

[73] _____ and Fromm, G., "The Price Equation," AMERICAN ECONOMIC REVIEW, 58 (December 1968), pp. 1159-83.

[74] ECONOMIC REPORT OF THE PRESIDENT, Washington, 1971, Tables C-46 and C-47, pp. 250-51.

[75] Eisner, R. and Nadiri, M., "Investment Behavior and Neo-Classical Theory," REVIEW OF ECONOMICS AND STATISTICS, 51 (August 1968), pp. 369-82.

[76] Ellert, J., "Industrial Concentration, Market Disequilibrium and the Convergence Pattern in Industry Rates of Return." Unpublished paper presented before the Industrial Organization Workshop, University of Chicago, January 27, 1972.

[77] Evans, M., MACROECONOMIC ACTIVITY: THEORY, FORECASTING, AND CONTROL: An Econometric Approach, New York: Harper, 1969.

[78] Fama, E., "Risk, Return, and Equilibrium: Some Clarifying Comments," JOURNAL OF FINANCE, 23 (January 1968), pp. 29-40.

[79] Federal Power Commission, STEAM-ELECTRIC PLANT CONSTRUCTION COST AND ANNUAL PRODUCTION EXPENSES, 22nd Annual Supplement, 1969, Washington, D.C.

[80] Federal Trade Commission, STATISTICAL REPORT NO. 5, LARGE MERGERS IN MANUFACTURING AND MINING, 1948-69, February 1970.

[81] Federal Trade Commission Staff, ECONOMIC REPORT ON CORPORATE MERGERS, Washington, D.C.: U.S. Govt. Printing Office, 1969.

[82] Fisher, F.M., SUPPLY AND COSTS IN THE U.S. PETROLEUM INDUSTRY, Baltimore: Resources for the Future, 1964.

[83] Friedman, M., "The Methodology of Positive Economics," ESSAYS IN POSITIVE ECONOMICS, Chicago: University of Chicago Press, 1953, p. 32.

[84] Galbraith, J.K., AMERICAN CAPITALISM, THE CONCEPT OF COUNTERVAILING POWER, Cambridge, Mass.: Riverside Press, 1952.

[85] _____, THE NEW INDUSTRIAL STATE, Boston: Houghton Mifflin Company, 1967.

[86] George, K.D., "Concentration, Barriers to Entry, and Rates of Return," REVIEW OF ECONOMICS AND STATISTICS, 50 (May 1969), pp. 273-75.

[87] Gordon, R.A., BUSINESS LEADERSHIP IN THE LARGE CORPORATIONS, Berkeley: University of California Press, 1961.

[88] Gort, M., DIVERSIFICATION AND INTEGRATION IN AMERICAN INDUSTRY, Princteon, N.J.: National Bureau of Economic Research, 1962.

[89] _____, "An Economic Disturbance Theory of Mergers," QUARTERLY JOURNAL OF BUSINESS, 83 (November 1969), pp. 624-642.

[90] _____ and Hogarty, T.F., "New Evidence on Mergers," JOURNAL OF LAW AND ECONOMICS, 13 (April 1970), pp. 167-84.

[91] Goudzwaard, M.B., "Conglomerate Mergers, Convertibles and Cash Dividends," QUARTERLY REVIEW OF ECONOMICS AND BUSINESS, 9 (Spring 1969), pp. 53-62.

[92] Grabowski, H. and Mueller, D.C., "Industrial Organization: The Role and Contribution of Econometrics," AMERICAN ECONOMIC REVIEW, 60 (May 1970), pp. 100-05.

[93] Greer, D.F., "Advertising and Market Concentration," SOUTHERN ECONOMIC JOURNAL, 38 (July 1971), pp. 19-32.

[94] Grunfeld, "The Determinants of Corporate Investment," in the DEMAND FOR DURABLE GOODS, ed. Arnold Harberger, Chicago Press, 1960.

[95] Grusky, O. and Miller, G.A., THE SOCIOLOGY OF ORGANIZATIONS: BASIC STUDIES, New York: Free Press, 1970.

[96] Gupta, M.C., "The Effect of Size, Growth, and Industry on the Financial Structure of Manufacturing Companies," JOURNAL OF FINANCE 24 (June 1969), pp. 517-29.

[97] Guth, L., "Advertising and Market Structure Revisited," JOURNAL OF INDUSTRIAL ECONOMICS, 19 (April 1971), pp. 179-98.

[98] Hall, M. and Tideman, T., "Measures of Concentration," JOURNAL OF AMERICAN STATISTICAL ASSOCIATION, 62 (March 1967), pp. 162-68.

[99] _____ and Weiss, L., "Firm Size and Profitability," REVIEW OF ECONOMICS AND STATISTICS, 49 (August 1967), pp. 319-31.

[100] Hall, R.L. and Hitch, C.J., "Price Theory and Business Behavior," OXFORD ECONOMIC PAPERS, 2 (May 1939), pp. 12-45.

[101] Hamberg, D., R AND D: ESSAYS ON THE ECONOMICS OF RESEARCH AND DEVELOPMENT, New York: Random House, 1966.

[102] Harberger, A.C., "Monopoly and Resource Allocation," AMERICAN ECONOMIC REVIEW, 44 (May 1954), pp. 77-97.

[103] Hart, P. and Prais, S., "The Analysis of Business Concentration," JOURNAL OF THE ROYAL STATISTICAL SOCIETY, Part 2 (1956), pp. 150-91.

[104] Heflebower, R., "Observations on Decentralization in Large Enterprises," JOURNAL OF INDUSTRIAL ECONOMICS, 9 (November 1960), pp. 7-22.

[105] Heiden, E.J., "Mergers and Profitability," Unpublished manuscript, University of Wisconsin, 1969.

[106] Hirshleifer, J., INVESTMENT, INTEREST, AND CAPITAL, Englewood Cliffs, N.J.: Prentice-Hall, 1970.

[107] Hogarty, T.F., "The Profitability of Corporate Mergers," JOURNAL OF BUSINESS, 43 (July 1970), pp. 317-27.

[108] Horowitz, A. and Horowitz, I., "Firms in a Declining Market: The Brewing Case," JOURNAL OF INDUSTRIAL ECONOMICS, 13 (March 1965), pp. 129-53.

[109] Horowitz, I., "Firm Size and Research Activity," SOUTHERN ECONOMIC JOURNAL, 28 (January 1962), pp. 298-301.

[110] Houthakker, H. and Taylor, L., CONSUMER DEMAND IN THE UNITED STATES, 1929-1970: ANALYSES AND PROJECTIONS, Cambridge, Mass.: Harvard University Press, 1966.

[111] Hymer, S. and Pashigian, P., "Firm Size and Rate of Growth," JOURNAL OF POLITICAL ECONOMY, 70 (December 1962), pp. 556-69.

[112] INDUSTRIAL PRICES AND THEIR RELATIVE INFLEXIBILITY, Senate Document No. 13 (January 1935).

[113] Jacoby, N.H., "Perspectives on Monopoly," JOURNAL OF POLITICAL ECONOMY, 59 (December 1951), pp. 514-27.

[114] _____, "The Relative Stability of Market Shares," JOURNAL OF INDUSTRIAL ECONOMICS, 12 (March 1964), pp. 83-107.

[115] _____, "The Role of Giant Corporation in the American and World Economies," Hearings before the Subcommittee on Monopoly of the Select Committee on Small Business, United States Senate Ninety-First Congress July 9, 10, and 11, 1969.

[116] _____, "The Conglomerate Corporation," THE CENTER MAGAZINE, 2 (July 1969), Reprint.

[117] Johnston, J., STATISTICAL COST ANALYSIS, New York: McGraw-Hill, 1963.

[118] Jorgenson, D., "Capital Theory and Investment Behavior," AMERICAN ECONOMIC REVIEW, 53 (May 1963), pp. 247-59.

[119] _____ and Griliches, Z., "The Explanation of Productivity Change," REVIEW OF ECONOMIC STUDIES, 34 (July 1967), pp. 249-83.

[120] Kamerschen, D.R., "Market Growth and Industrial Concentration," JOURNAL OF THE AMERICAN STATISTICAL ASSOCIATION, 63 (March 1968), pp. 228-41.

[121] Kaplan, A.D.H., Dirlam, J.B. and Lanzillotti, R.F., PRICING IN BIG BUSINESS Washington, D.C.: Brookings Institution, 1958.

[122] Kaysen, K., UNITED STATES VS. UNITED SHOE MACHINERY CORPORATION, Cambridge, Mass.: Harvard University Press, 1956.

[123] Kelly, E.M., THE PROFITABILITY OF GROWTH THROUGH MERGERS, University Park, Pa.: The Pennsylvania State University, 1967.

[124] Kendrick, J.W., PRODUCTIVITY TRENDS IN THE UNITED STATES, Princeton: Princeton University Press, 1961.

[125] Kilpatrick, R., "The Choice Among Alternative Measures of Industrial Concentration," THE REVIEW OF ECONOMICS AND STATISTICS, 49 (May 1967), pp. 258-60.

[126] Klein, L.R. and Evans, M., THE WHARTON ECONOMETRIC FORE-CASTING MODEL, Philadelphia: University of Pennsylvania, 1967.

[127] Kline, C.A., Jr. and Hessler, H.L., "The du Pont Chart System for Appraising Operating Performance," NATIONAL ASSOCIATION OF COST ACCOUNTANTS BULLETIN, Supplement, 33 (August 1952), pp. 1595-1619.

[128] Langholm, O., FULL COST AND OPTIMAL PRICE: A STUDY IN THE DYNAMICS OF MULTIPLE PRODUCTION, Oslo, Norway: Universitets-forlaget, 1969.

[129] Lanzillotti, R.F., "Pricing Objectives in Large Companies," AMERICAN ECONOMIC REVIEW, 48 (December 1958), pp. 921-40.

[130] Latane, H.A., "Portfolio Balance—The Demand for Money, Bonds, and Stocks," SOUTHERN ECONOMIC JOURNAL, 29 (October 1962), pp. 71-76.

[131] Lerner, A., "The Concept of Monopoly and the Measurement of Monopoly Power," REVIEW OF ECONOMIC STUDIES, 1 (1933), pp. 157-75.

[132] Leibenstein, H., "Allocative Efficiency vs. X-Efficiency," AMERICAN ECONOMIC REVIEW, 56 (June 1966), pp. 392-415.

[133] Lester, R.H., "Shortcomings of Marginal Analysis for Wage-Employment Problems," AMERICAN ECONOMIC REVIEW, 36 (March 1946), pp. 63-82.

[134] Lewellen, W.G. and Huntsman, B., "Managerial Pay and Corporate Performance," AMERICAN ECONOMIC REVIEW, 60 (September 1970), pp. 710-20.

[135] Lintner, J., "Optimal Dividends and Corporate Growth Under Uncertainty," QUARTERLY JOURNAL OF ECONOMICS, 78 (February 1964), pp. 49-95.

[136] _____, "The Valuation of Risk Assets and the Selection of Risky Investments in Stock Portfolios and Capital Budgets," REVIEW OF ECONOMICS AND STATISTICS, 67 (February 1965), pp. 13-37.

[137] _____, "Security Prices, Risk, and Maximal Gains from Diversification," JOURNAL OF FINANCE, 20 (December 1965), pp. 586-91.

[138] Lorie, J.H. and Halpern, P., "Conglomerates: The Rhetoric and the Evidence," JOURNAL OF LAW AND ECONOMICS, 13 (April 1970), pp. 149-66.

[139] Lustgarten, S.H., INDUSTRIAL MARKET STRUCTURE AND ADMIN-ISTERED PRICE INFLATION, Unpublished Ph.D. Dissertation, UCLA, 1971.

[140] Machlup, F., "Marginal Analysis and Empirical Research," AMERICAN ECONOMIC REVIEW, 36 (September 1946), pp. 519-54.

[141] _____, "Theories of the Firm: Marginalist, Behavioral, Managerial," AMERICAN ECONOMIC REVIEW, 52 (March 1967), pp. 1-33.

[142] MacAvoy, P.W., PRICE FORMATION IN NATURAL GAS FIELDS, New Haven: Yale University Press, 1962.

[143] _____, McKie, J.W., and Preston L., "High and Stable Concentration Levels, Profitability, and Public Policy: A Response," JOURNAL OF LAW AND ECONOMICS, 14 (October 1971), pp. 493-500.

[144] Malinvaud, E., STATISTICAL METHODS OF ECONOMETRICS, Second Edition, translated from the French, Chicago: Rand McNally, 1970.

[145] Mann, H.M., "Seller Concentration, Barriers to Entry, and Rates of Return in Thirty Industries, 1950-60," REVIEW OF ECONOMICS AND STATISTICS, 48 (August 1966), pp. 296-307.

[146] _____, et. al., "Advertising and Concentration: An Empirical Investigation," JOURNAL OF INDUSTRIAL ECONOMICS, 16 (November 1967), pp. 34-45.

[147] Mansfield, E., "Industrial Research and Development Expenditures: Determinants, Prospects and Relation to Size of Firm and Inventive Output," JOURNAL OF POLITICAL ECONOMY, 72 (August 1964), pp. 319-40.

[148] March, J.G., HANDBOOK OF ORGANIZATIONS, Chicago: Rand McNally, 1965.

[149] _____, and Simon, H., ORGANIZATIONS, New York: John Wiley, 1958.

[150] Markham, J., "Survey of the Evidence and Findings on Mergers," in BUSINESS CONCENTRATION AND PRICE POLICY, National Bureau of Economic Research, Princeton: Princeton University Press, 1955.

[151] _____, "Market Structure, Business Conduct, and Innovation," AMERICAN ECONOMIC REVIEW, 55 (May 1965), pp. 325-26.

[152] _____, "Antitrust and the Conglomerate: A Policy in Search of a Theory," Conglomerate Mergers and Acquisitions: Opinion and Analysis, ST. JOHN'S LAW REVIEW, Special Edition, 44 (Spring 1970), pp. 282-91.

[153] _____, CONGLOMERATE ENTERPRISE AND PUBLIC POLICY, Harvard Graduate School of Business Administration, Division of Research, Harvard University Press, forthcoming.

[154] Markowitz, H., PORTFOLIO SELECTION, New York: Wiley, 1959.

[155] Marris, R., THE ECONOMIC THEORY OF 'MANAGERIAL' CAPITALISM, New York: Free Press of Glencoe, 1964.

[156] Marschak, J., "Decision Making: Economic Aspects," INTERNATIONAL ENCYCLOPEDIA OF THE SOCIAL SCIENCES, New York: Crowell Collier and Macmillan, 1968, Volume 4, pp. 42-55.

[157] Mauriel, J.J. and Anthony, R.N., "Misevaluation of Investment Center Performance," HARVARD BUSINESS REVIEW, 44 (March-April 1966), pp. 98-105.

[158] McCall, J.J. "Probabilistic Microeconomics," BELL JOURNAL OF ECO-NOMICS AND MANAGEMENT, (Autumn 1971), pp. 403-33.

[159] McGee, J.S., IN DEFENSE OF INDUSTRIAL CONCENTRATION, New York: Praeger, 1971.

[160] Meyer, J.R., Peck, M.J., Stenason, J., and Zwick, C., THE ECONOMIES OF COMPETITION IN THE TRANSPORTATION INDUSTRIES, Cambridge, Mass.: Harvard University Press, 1959.

[161] Miller, R.A., "Market Structure and Industrial Performance: Relation of Profit Rates to Concentration, Advertising Intensity, and Diversity," THE JOURNAL OF INDUSTRIAL ECONOMICS, 17 (April 1969), pp. 100-15.

[162] Mintz, M., and Cohen, J.S., AMERICA, INC., New York: Dial Press, 1971.

[163] Modigliani, F. and Miller, M.H., "The Cost of Capital, Corporation Finance and the Theory of Investment, AMERICAN ECONOMIC RE-VIEW 48 (June 1958), pp. 261-97.

[164] Monsen, J., Jr. and Downs, A., "A Theory of Large Managerial Firms," JOURNAL OF POLITICAL ECONOMY, 73 (June 1965), pp. 228-29.

[165] Mossin, J., "Equilibrium in a Capital Asset Market," ECONOMETRICA, 34 (October 1966), pp. 768-83.

[166] _____, "Security Pricing and Investment Criteria in Competitive Markets," AMERICAN ECONOMIC REVIEW, 59 (December 1969), pp. 749-55.

[167] Mueller, D.C., "A Theory of Conglomerate Mergers," QUARTERLY JOURNAL OF ECONOMICS, 83 (November 1969), pp. 643-59.

[168] _____, "The Firm's Decision Process: An Econometric Investigation," QUARTERLY JOURNAL OF ECONOMICS, 81 (February 1967), pp. 58-87.

[169] Mueller, W.F., "Competition, Efficiency and Antitrust: A Policy Maker's View," in EIGHTH CONFERENCE ON ANTITRUST ISSUES IN TO-DAY'S ECONOMY, New York: National Industrial Conference Board, 1969, pp. 17-23.

[170] _____, "Industrial Structure and Competition Policy, Study Paper Number 2," STUDIES BY THE STAFF OF THE CABINET COMMIT-TEE ON PRICE STABILITY, Washington, D.C.: U.S. Government Printing Office, 1969.

[171] _____, A PRIMER ON MONOPOLY AND COMPETITION, New York: Random House, 1970.

[172] Myers, S.C., "Procedures for Capital Budgeting under Uncertainty," INDUSTRIAL MANAGEMENT REVIEW, 9 (Spring 1968), pp. 1-19.

[173] Nader, R., "Introduction," THE CLOSED ENTERPRISE SYSTEM, The Nader Study Group Report on Antitrust Enforcement, Mark J. Green, Editor.

[174] Narver, J.C., CONGLOMERATE MERGERS AND MARKET COMPETITION, Berkeley: University of California Press, 1967.

[175] _____, "Some Observations on the Impact of Antitrust Merger Policy on Marketing," JOURNAL OF MARKETING, 33 (January 1969), pp. 24-31.

[176] Nelson, G., Chairman, Subcommittee on Monopoly, Senate Select Committee on Small Business, Planning, Regulation, and Competition: AUTOMOBILE INDUSTRY-1968, HEARINGS BEFORE SUBCOMMITTEES OF THE SELECT COMMITTEE ON SMALL BUSINESS, UNITED STATES SENATE, JULY 10 & 23, 1968, Washington, D.C.: U.S. Government Printing Office, 1968.

[177] Nelson, R.L., CONCENTRATION IN THE MANUFACTURING INDUSTRIES OF THE UNITED STATES, New Haven, Conn.: Yale University Press, 1963.

[178] Nerlove, M., "A Tabular Survey of Macro-Econometric Models," INTERNATIONAL ECONOMIC REVIEW, 7 (May 1966), pp. 127-75.

[179] Ornstein, S., THE RELATIONSHIP OF MARKET STRUCTURE TO THE PROFITABILITY OF LEADING FIRMS IN SELECT U.S. MANUFACTURING INDUSTRIES, 1950-1960, Unpublished Doctoral Dissertation, UCLA, 1970.

[180] Palda, K., ECONOMIC ANALYSIS FOR MARKETING DECISIONS, Englewood Cliffs, New Jersey: Prentice-Hall, 1969, pp. 137-39.

[181] Pashigian, P., "Market Concentration in the United States and Great Britain," JOURNAL OF LAW AND ECONOMICS, 11 (October 1968), pp. 299-319.

[182] _____, "The Effect of Market Size on Concentration," INTERNATIONAL ECONOMIC REVIEW, 10 (October 1969), pp. 291-314.

[183] Patterson, J.M. and Patterson, J., "Conglomerates: The Legal Issues," BUSINESS HORIZONS, 11 (February 1968), pp. 39-48.

[184] Peltzman, S., "Entry in Commercial Banking," THE JOURNAL OF LAW AND ECONOMICS, 8 (October 1965), pp. 11-50.

[185] Phillips, A. and Williamson, O.E., eds., PRICES: ISSUES IN THEORY, PRACTICE, AND PUBLIC POLICY, Philadelphia: University of Pennsylvania Press, 1967.

[186] Posner, R., "Oligopoly and the Antitrust Laws: A Suggested Approach," 21 STANFORD LAW REVIEW, 21 (June 1969), pp. 1562-1606.

[187] Prais, S.J., "The Statistical Conditions for a Change in Business Concentration," REVIEW OF ECONOMICS AND STATISTICS, 40 (May 1958), pp. 268-72.

[188] Preston, L.E., THE INDUSTRY AND ENTERPRISE STRUCTURE OF THE U.S. ECONOMY, New York: General Learning Press, 1971.

[189] Rasche, R.H. and Shapiro, H.T., "The FRB-MIT Econometric Model," AMERICAN ECONOMIC REVIEW, 58 (May 1967), pp. 123-49.

[190] Renshaw, E.F., "The Theory of Financial Leverage and Conglomerate Mergers," CALIFORNIA MANAGEMENT REVIEW, 11 (Fall 1968), pp. 79-84.

[191] Reid, S.R., "Mergers for Whom: Managers or Stockholders?", HEARINGS BEFORE THE SUBCOMMITTEE ON ANTITRUST AND MONOPOLY OF THE COMMITTEE ON THE JUDICIARY, United States Senate, 89th Congress, Second Session, pp. 1914-1931.

[192] _____, MERGERS, MANAGERS, AND THE ECONOMY, New York: McGraw-Hill, 1968.

[193] Robinson, A., "The Pricing of Manufactured Products," ECONOMIC JOURNAL, 60 (December 1950), pp. 771-80.

[194] Rosenbluth, G., "Measures of Concentration," BUSINESS CONCENTRATION AND PRICE POLICY, Princeton: Princeton University Press, 1955.

[195] _____, CONCENTRATION IN CANADIAN MANUFACTURING INDUSTRIES, Princeton: Princeton University, 1957.

[196] Rothbard, M.N., POWER AND MARKET: GOVERNMENT AND THE ECONOMY, Institute for Humane Studies, Inc., 1970.

[197] Rubinstein, M.E., "A Synthesis of Corporate Financial Theory," JOURNAL OF FINANCE, forthcoming.

[198] Scherer, F.M., "Firm Size, Market Structure, Opportunity and the Output of Patented Inventions," AMERICAN ECONOMIC REVIEW, 55 (December 1965), pp. 1097-1125.

[199] _____, "Market Structure and the Employment of Scientists and Engineers," AMERICAN ECONOMIC REVIEW, 57 (June 1967), pp. 524-31.

[200] _____, INDUSTRIAL MARKET STRUCTURE AND ECONOMIC PERFORMANCE, New York: Rand McNally, 1970.

[201] Schmookler, J., INVENTION AND ECONOMIC GROWTH, Cambridge, Mass.: Harvard University Press, 1966.

[202] Schumpeter, J.A., CAPITALISM, SOCIALISM, AND DEMOCRACY, New York: Harper and Row, 1950.

[203] Securities and Exchange Commission, SURVEY OF AMERICAN LISTED CORPORATIONS, DATA ON PROFITS AND OPERATIONS, 1936-1942, (1944).

[204] Selznick, P. TVA AND THE GRASS ROOTS, Berkeley: University of California Press, 1949.

[205] Sharpe, W.F., "Capital Asset Prices: A Theory of Market Equilibrium under Conditions of Risk," JOURNAL OF FINANCE, 19 (September 1964), pp. 425-42.

[206] Shepherd, W.G., "Trends of Concentration in American Manufacturing Industries, 1947-58," REVIEW OF ECONOMICS AND STATISTICS, 46 (May 1964), pp. 200-12.

[207] _____, MARKET POWER AND ECONOMIC WELFARE: AN INTRO-
DUCTION, New York: Random House, 1970.

[208] Sharpe, W.F., PORTFOLIO THEORY AND CAPITAL MARKETS, New
York: McGraw-Hill, 1970.

[209] Shubik, M., "Objective Functions and Models of Corporate Maximization," QUARTERLY JOURNAL OF ECONOMICS, 75 (August, 1961),
pp. 345-75.

[210] Silberston, A., "Price Behavior of Firms," ECONOMIC JOURNAL, 80
(September 1970), pp. 511-82.

[211] Simon, H.A. and Bonini, C.P., "The Size Distribution of Business Firms,"
AMERICAN ECONOMIC REVIEW, 48 (September 1958), pp. 607-17.

[212] _____, "On the Concept of Organizational Goal," ADMINISTRATIVE
SCIENCE QUARTERLY, 9 (June 1964), pp. 1-22.

[213] Simons, H.C., "The Requisites of Free Competition," AMERICAN
ECONOMIC REVIEW, 26 (March 1936, Supplement), pp. 68-76.

[214] Singer, E.M., ANTITRUST ECONOMICS: SELECTED LEGAL CASES
AND ECONOMIC MODELS, Englewood Cliffs, N.J.: Prentice-Hall, 1968.

[215] _____, "Industrial Organization: Price Models and Public Policy,"
AMERICAN ECONOMIC REVIEW, 60 (May 1970), pp. 90-99.

[216] Shrieves, R.E., INNOVATION AND MARKET STRUCTURE: FUR-
THER EVIDENCE, Unpublished Ph.D. Dissertation, UCLA, 1972.

[217] Sloan, A.P., Jr., MY YEARS WITH GENERAL MOTORS, Garden City,
N.Y.: Doubleday & Company, 1964.

[218] Smith, K.V. and Schreiner, J.C., "A Portfolio Analysis of Conglomerate
Diversification," JOURNAL OF FINANCE, 24 (June 1969), pp.
413-428.

[219] Steiner, G.A., MANAGERIAL LONG-RANGE PLANNING, New York:
McGraw-Hill, 1963.

[220] _____, TOP MANAGEMENT PLANNING, New York: Macmillan,
1969.

[221] Stigler, G., CAPITAL AND RATES OF RETURN IN MANUFACTUR-
ING INDUSTRIES, Princeton, N.J.: Princeton University Press, 1963.

[222] _____, "A Theory of Oligopoly," JOURNAL OF POLITICAL ECON-
OMY, 72 (February 1964), pp. 44-61.

[223] _____, THE ORGANIZATION OF INDUSTRY, Homewood, Ill.:
Richard D. Irwin, Inc., 1968.

[224] _____ and Kindahl, J.K., THE BEHAVIOR OF INDUSTRIAL
PRICES, New York: National Bureau of Economic Research, 1970.

[225] Stiglitz, J.E., "A Re-Examination of the Modigliani-Miller Theorem,"
AMERICAN ECONOMIC REVIEW, 59 (December 1969), pp. 784-93.

[226] Stone, J.M., CONGLOMERATE MERGERS: THEIR IMPLICATIONS
FOR THE EFFICIENCY OF CAPITAL AND THE THEORY OF THE
FIRM, Unpublished Thesis, Harvard University, 1969.

[227] ST. JOHN'S LAW REVIEW, CONGLOMERATE MERGERS AND ACQUISITIONS, 44 (Spring 1970), Special Issue.

[228] Telser, L., "Advertising and Competition," JOURNAL OF POLITICAL ECONOMY, 72 (December 1964), pp. 537-62.

[229] _____, "Some Determinants of the Returns to Manufacturing Industries," Report No. 6935, Center for Mathematical Studies in Business and Economics, University of Chicago, 1969.

[230] Terleckyj, N.E., SOURCES OF PRODUCTIVITY CHANGE: A PILOT STUDY BASED ON THE EXPERIENCE OF AMERICAN MANUFACTURING INDUSTRIES, 1899-1953, Unpublished Ph.D. Dissertation, Columbia University, 1958.

[231] Theil, H., PRINCIPLES OF ECONOMETRICS, New York: Wiley, 1971.

[232] Tobin, J., "Liquidity Preference as Behavior Toward Risk," REVIEW OF ECONOMIC STUDIES, 67 (February 1959), pp. 65-86.

[233] Turner, D., "Conglomerate Mergers and Section 7 of the Clayton Act," HARVARD BUSINESS REVIEW, 78 (May 1965), pp. 1313-95.

[234] Udell, J.G., "Social and Economic Consequences of the Merger Movement in Wisconsin," WISCONSIN ECONOMY STUDIES, 3 (May 1969).

[235] Vaupel, J.W. and Curhan, J.P., THE MAKING OF MULTINATIONAL ENTERPRISE, Boston: Division of Research, Harvard University, 1969.

[236] Vernon, J.M., et. al., "An Econometric Model of the Tobacco Industry," REVIEW OF ECONOMICS AND STATISTICS, 51 (May 1969), pp. 149-58.

[237] Vickers, D., THE THEORY OF THE FIRM: PRODUCTION, CAPITAL, AND FINANCE, New York: McGraw-Hill, 1968.

[238] Wallace, W.H., et. al., "An Economic Model of the Textile Industry in the United States," REVIEW OF ECONOMICS AND STATISTICS, 45 (February 1968), pp. 13-22.

[239] WALL STREET JOURNAL, "Aluminum Book Prices Have Been Boosted, but Competition Keeps Actual Quotes Down," February 1, 1972, p. 28.

[240] Walters, A.A., "An Econometric Survey of Production and Cost Functions," ECONOMETRICA, 31 (January-April 1963), pp. 1-66.

[241] Walton, T.F., CORPORATE FINANCE ACCUMULATION, Unpublished Ph.D. Dissertation, UCLA, 1971.

[242] Weiss, L.W., "Factors in Changing Concentration," REVIEW OF ECONOMICS AND STATISTICS, 45 (February 1963), pp. 70-77.

[243] _____, "Average Concentration Ratios and Industrial Performance," JOURNAL OF INDUSTRIAL ECONOMICS, 11 (July 1963), pp. 247-52.

[244] _____, "Concentration and Labor Earnings," AMERICAN ECONOMIC REVIEW, 56 (March 1966), pp. 95-117.

[245] _____, "Business Pricing Policies and Inflation Reconsidered," JOURNAL OF POLITICAL ECONOMY, 74 (April 1966), pp. 177-87.

[246] _____, CASE STUDIES IN AMERICAN INDUSTRY, New York: John Wiley & Sons, Inc., 1967.

[247] _____, "Advertising, Profits, and Corporate Taxes," REVIEW OF ECONOMICS AND STATISTICS, 51 (November 1969), pp. 421-30.

[248] _____ "Quantitative Studies of Industrial Organizations," in FRONTIERS OF QUANTITATIVE ECONOMICS, edited by Michael D. Intriligator, Amsterdam: North-Holland Publishing Co., 1971.

[249] Weston, J.F. and Peltzman, S., Eds., PUBLIC POLICY TOWARD MERGERS, Pacific Palisades, California: Goodyear Publishing Company, 1969, Part V on Conglomerate Mergers.

[250] _____, "Diversification and Merger Trends," BUSINESS ECONOMICS, 5 (January 1970), pp. 50-57.

[251] _____, "Mergers and Acquisitions in Business Planning," RIVISTA INTERNAZIONALE DI SCIENZE ECONOMICHE E COMMERCIALI, 17 (April 1970), pp. 309-320.

[252] _____, "The Nature and Significance of Conglomerate Firms," ST. JOHN'S LAW REVIEW, 44 (Spring 1970), pp. 66-80.

[253] _____, "The Industrial Economics Background of the Penn Central Bankruptcy," JOURNAL OF FINANCE, 26 (May 1971), pp. 311-26.

[254] _____, "ROI Planning and Control," BUSINESS HORIZONS, 15 (August 1972), pp. 35-42.

[255] _____, "Pricing Behavior of Large Firms," WESTERN ECONOMIC JOURNAL, 10 (March 1972), pp. 1-18.

[256] Whinston, A., "Price Guidelines in Decentralized Organizations," in (eds.) W. Cooper, H. Leavitt, and M. Shelly, NEW PERSPECTIVES IN ORGANIZATION RESEARCH, New York: John Wiley, 1964.

[257] White House Task Force on Antitrust Policy, Report 1 (in Trade Regulation Reports, supplement to no. 415, May 26, 1969) at 1-8.

[258] Williamson, O.E., THE ECONOMICS OF DISCRETIONARY BEHAVIOR: MANAGERIAL OBJECTIVES IN A THEORY OF THE FIRM, Englewood Cliffs, N.J.: Prentice-Hall, 1964 pp. 170-71.

[259] _____, THE ECONOMICS OF DISCRETIONARY BEHAVIOR: MANAGERIAL OBJECTIVES IN A THEORY OF THE FIRM, Chicago: Markham Publishing Co., 1967.

[260] _____, CORPORATE CONTROL AND BUSINESS BEHAVIOR, Englewood Cliffs, N.J.: Prentice-Hall, 1970.

[261] _____, "The Vertical Integration of Production: Market Failure Considerations," THE AMERICAN ECONOMIC REVIEW, 61 (May 1971), pp. 112-23.

[262] Wilson, T. and Andrews, P.W.S., OXFORD STUDIES ON THE PRICE MECHANISM, Oxford: Clarendon Press, 1951.

[263] Winter, S., Jr., "Economic 'Natural Selection' and the Theory of the Firm," YALE ECONOMIC ESSAYS, 4 (Spring 1964), pp. 225-72.

[264] Wold, H. and Juréen, L., DEMAND ANALYSIS, New York: John Wiley and Sons, 1954.
[265] Wonnacott, R. and Wonnacott, T., ECONOMETRICS, New York: John Wiley and Sons, 1970.

Index

About the Contributors

The contributors to this volume are listed below in alphabetical order:

Yale Brozen, Professor of Business Economics, Graduate School of Business, University of Chicago.

Ronald H. Coase, Professor, The University of Chicago Law School and Editor of *The Journal of Law & Economics.*

Hershner Cross, Senior Vice President, Corporate Administrative Staff, General Electric Company.

Harold Demsetz, Professor of Economics, University of California, Los Angeles, California.

Michael D. Intriligator, Professor of Economics, University of California, Los Angeles, California.

Clement G. Krouse, Assistant Professor of Business Economics and Finance, University of California, Los Angeles, California.

John B. McKitterick, Vice President-Planning Development, General Electric Company.

Surendra K. Mansinghka, Assistant Professor of Administration, School of Administration, University of California, Riverside, California.

Jesse W. Markham, Professor of Business Administration, Graduate School of Business Administration, Harvard University, Boston, Massachusetts.

Stanley I. Ornstein, Assistant Research Professor of Business Economics, Graduate School of Management, University of California, Los Angeles, California.

Lee E. Preston, Melvin H. Baker Professor of American Enterprise, School of Management, State University of New York at Buffalo, New York, New York.

A. Eugene Schubert, Vice President, Strategic Planning and Review Operation, Power Generation Group, General Electric Company.

Ronald E. Shrieves, Assistant Professor of Business Economics and Finance, University of Tennessee, Knoxville, Tennessee.

Ralph G.M. Sultan, Associate Professor of Business Administration, Graduate School of Business Administration, Harvard University, Boston, Massachusetts.

J. Fred Weston, Professor of Business Economics and Finance, University of California, Los Angeles, California.